PETE FRAME'S
ROCKIN' AROUND BRITAIN
ROCK 'N' ROLL LANDMARKS OF THE UK AND IRELAND

OMNIBUS PRESS

"I'm sitting on a railway station got a ticket for my destination…" (see page 21)

Published by Omnibus Press
(A Division of Book Sales Limited)
Copyright © 1999 Pete Frame

ISBN: 0.7119.6973.6
Order No: OP 48090

A catalogue record for this book is available from the
British Library.

Printed in Great Britain by Redwood Books Limited,
Trowbridge, Wiltshire.

Exclusive Distributors
Book Sales Limited,
8/9 Frith Street,
London W1V 5TZ, UK.

Music Sales Corporation,
257 Park Avenue South,
New York, NY 10010, USA.

Music Sales Pty Limited,
120 Rothschild Avenue, Rosebery,
NSW 2018, Australia.

To the Music Trade only:
Music Sales Limited,
8/9, Frith Street,
London W1V 5TZ, UK.

Visit Omnibus Press at http://www.omnibuspress.com

Black Lion Lane (London W6) The now demolished Island Records warehouse, former home to Bob Marley, lying low after an assassination attempt.

Marc Munroe

Heddon Street (London W1) Site of the front cover for *Ziggy Stardust* by David Bowie

Nikki Russell

As an ancient rock historian with leftie leanings and a head full of arcane rubbish, I am always happy to help anyone who asks. But when someone pilfers from my work without consultation or credit, I get a little miffed. Since this was happening more and more, I took to introducing occasional deliberate mistakes into my etchings and scratchings – so that I would be amusued rather than vexed when I saw them repeated. I'd like to tell you about a classic example, one of my favourites.

The book you are now holding was first published ten years ago, in a much shorter, less comprehensive version titled *The Rock Gazetteer of Great Britain*… and, of course, I dropped in a few fabrications as usual. Some found their way into other publications.

One national newspaper (which I am too honourable to name, of course) surprisingly ran one of my howlers without checking its factual basis. While I can't accuse this title of plagiarism, I am still rather surprised that their research wasn't a little more thorough. With great ballyhoo, they printed photographs of six 'Scenes from Rock History', one of which was a magnificent half-page shot of a bridge over the turbulent River Exe near Tiverton in Devon. This, according to the caption, was "where New York folkie Paul Simon wrote 'Bridge Over Troubled Water'".

I think not. The story was a figment of my imagination, popped into *The Rock Gazetteer* to ensnare pirates.

I interviewed Paul Simon for some eight hours, and anyone who heard the resulting BBC Radio series *The Paul Simon Songbook* will know that his epic hit was inspired not by a babbling brook in the west country, but by the classic recording of 'Oh Mary Don't You Weep' by gospel quartet The Swan Silvertones. Towards the end, the Reverend Claude Jeter pledges "I'll be your bridge over deep water". We played Simon's sketchy demo of the song, which was pieced together a good 3,000 miles from Tiverton.

In the ten years since the publication of *The Rock Gazetteer*, the story has apparently infiltrated the consciousness of some Devonians, who now firmly believe it – even though no photograph or other documented evidence exists to support it. It's a pretty picture: Paul Simon sitting on the bank, chewing on the end of his Biro, watching the river flow... "When you're weary, feeling, er..."

As Ken Kesey wrote in *One Flew Over The Cuckoo's Nest*: "It's the truth, even if it didn't happen."

When I told the national newspaper that they had big egg on their face, one of their legal wheels came on the phone – to explain the error, but also to tell me that litigation could be very expensive.

Oh well, it's all good fun!

I am pleased to tell you that this revised edition contains no deliberate mistakes... and if you believe that, you'll believe anything.

If any readers have snippets of information for future editions – like "Sporty Spice used to live next door to me in Railways Cuttings" or "Van Morrison used to buy his newspaper in the shop where I worked" – I would be delighted to hear from you. You can write to me c/o the publisher or e-mail me on pframe@primex.co.uk

And you'll get a credit, of course.

I cannot go without thanking the elusive Cally, who designed the original *Rock Gazetteer* and propitiously re-appeared just in time to design this new edition. Also all the folks at Omnibus Press – especially Andrew King, whose brainwave it was to republish the book, and my indefatigable editor Chris Charlesworth, whom I first met in November 1973 when we both interviewed Linda Ronstadt at her house somewhere in that maze of streets under the Hollywood sign. It was just after Gram Parsons' death, and Emmylou Harris was sitting in the corner, quietly working on some embroidery. I had to go on to some other pressing appointment, while Chris went out drinking with them at the Sundance Saloon in Calabassas. Story of my life.

Pete Frame, February 1999

Every effort has been made to trace the copyright holders of the photographs in this book but one or two were unreachable. We would be grateful if the photographers concerned would contact us.

Cover map courtesy of G. I. Barnett & Sons Ltd, with thanks to Michael Barnett.

Picture research by Nikki Lloyd & Lisa Quas Grateful thanks to all the record companies that gave permission for the reproduction of the various record sleeves.

Other Omnibus Press books by Pete Frame:
Rock Family Trees
More Rock Family Trees
The Beatles & Some Other Guys Rock Family Trees of the Early Sixties

Rock Around Britain is a thorough modification of *The Rock Gazetteer*, published by Banyan Books in 1989.

Cover & Book designed by Cally at Antar (Suffolk)

Respectfully dedicated to anyone who ever climbed into a van to go and play a gig.

The author would like to thank Kingsley Abbott, Jackie Adams, Steve Adams, Chloe Alexander, Charley Anderson, Clive Anderson, Dave Anderson, Sharon Anderson, Hugh Ashley, Robin Askew, Gordon Astley, Mike Badger, David Bailey, Barry Ballard, Jan Ballard, Paul Barber, Ian Barclay, Stephanie Barnes, Frank Barrett, Duncan Bartlett, Roger Batchelor, Graham Battye, Dawn Bebe, Eugen Beer, David Belcher, James Belsey, Don Berrow, Danny Betesh, Bryan Biggs, Chris Biggs, Will Birch, Johnny Black, Karl Blanch, Simon Blaxland, Eddie Blower, Steve Bonnett, Richard Boon, Stuart Booth, Billy Bragg, David Bragg, John Braley, David Brown, Mick Brown, Tony Brown, Paul Burnell, Alan Cackett, Peter Cadle, Cally, Melissa Cambridge, Allan Campbell, Angela Carless, Roy Carr, Alan Carruthers, Tim Carson, Pete Chambers, Jane Chapman, Paul Charles, Chris Charlesworth, Andy Cheeseman, Pam Cheshire, Andy Childs, Roger Childs, Dan Chisholm, Sue Clarke, Alan Clayson, Pete Clements, Jeff Cloves, Andy Coker, Paul Cole, Ray Coleman, Ian Collington, Glen Colson, Luke Crampton, Jamie Crick, Nigel Cross, Sophie Culmer, John

Culshaw, Francis Curry, Mike D'Abo, Terence Dale, Graham Dancer, Brian Dann, Trevor Dann, Mike Darkside, Gareth Davies, Geoff Davies, Geraint Davies, Jez Davies, Mike Davies, Fred Dellar, Campbell Devine, Jeff Dexter, Martin Disney, Peter Doggett, Roger Dopson, Ed Douglas, Bill Drummond, Billy Duchart, Chris Duke, Mark Dutton, Tim Earnshaw, John Ellis, Royston Ellis, Angela Evans, Julian Evans, Roan Fair, Tim Finlay, Rob Finnis, Roy Fisher, M J Fitzgibbon, John Fleet, Tony Fletcher, John Florance, David Ford, Richard Ford, Ashley Franklin, David Freeman, Mariella Frostrup, Trevor Fry, Paul Gambaccini, Craig Gerrard, John Gibson, Victoria Gibson, Robert Gillatt, Marcus Gray, Dominic Green, Vanessa Green, Marc Jones, Mark Glyn Jones, Kevin Golding, Martin Goldman, Simon Goodwin, Jonathan Green, Sid Griffin, Dai Griffiths, Tim Grundy, Robert Gurney, Jon Hammond, Frank Hanly, Diana Hare, Keith Haynes, Colin Hill, Dave Hill, Judy Hill, R S Hill, Colin Harper, Paul Harris, Nicola Haywood-Thomas, Michael Heatley, Chris Hewitt, Richard Hoare, Brian Hogg, Howard Holmes, ZaZa Horne, Guy Hornsby, Mick Houghton, Terry Hounsome, Kevin Howlett, Patrick Humphries, Tricia Ingrams, Andy Ivy, Jerry James, David Jennings, David Johnson, Gary Jones, Mark Jones, Tim Jones, Robert Jones, Tom Kennedy, Andy Kershaw, Andrew King, Steve King, Vic King, Steve Kingston, Jane Kutlay, Eileen Kyte, Bob Lamb, Bob Langley, Nick Langley, Colin Larkin, Peter Latham, Alastair Law, Phil Lawton, Barry Lazell, Graham Ledger, Spencer Leigh, Martin Lever, Peter Levy, Jon Lewin, Dave Lewis, Jeremy Lewis, Mark Lewisohn, Polly Lloyd, Brian Long, Richard Lowe, Ray Lowry, Jeff Lynne, Bill McCue, Tony McGartland, Carl McLean, Ian McLean, Gary McLean, Colin Macleod, Mac Macleod, Phil McMullen, Steve Manthorp, Howard Marks, Pat Marsh, Andrew Martin, Dave Martin, Nick Martin, Steve Massam, Glen Matlock, Tony Maycock, Rob Maynard, I Mercer, Pete Moody, Sally Moon, John Morgan, Willie Morgan, Jonathan Morrish, Sarah Mortimer, John Moulson,

Judith Mullarky, Andy Murray, Neil Murray, Richard Myers, Paul Mysak, Gaye Napier, Fraser Nash, Richard Nash, Deborah Neal, Anne Nightingale, Suzanne North, Chrissie Oakes, Peter O'Brien, Johnny Ogden, Baz Oldfield, John Oley, Eamonn O'Neill, Annie Othen, Jeff Owen, Michael Park, John Peel, Ian Penman, Bob Petherick, Simon Phillips, Robin Pike, John Platt, Pauline Poole, Julie Porter, Cozy Powell, Mark Pendergast, Phil Philo, Kevin Piper, Mike Plumbley, Rob Pomeroy, Hilary Power, Gary Price, Mark Price, Matthew Price, Rocky Prior, Harry Prytherch, Andy Pyle, John Quinn, Patrick Raftery, Mike Read, Janet Reeder, Dafydd Rees, Jim Reeve, Bill Reeves, John Repsch, David Revill, Tim Rice, Louise Riddiough, Martin Roach, John Robb, Ira Robbins, Louie Robinson, Neil Robinson, Nick Robinson, Johnny Rogan, Robin Ross, Richard Rudin, John Russell, Nikki Russell, Barry Rutter, Mark Saggers, Alison Saunders, James Scanlon, Piet Schreuders, Steve Scott, Captain Sensible, Cathy Shea, Tom Sheehan, Elaine Shepherd, Pete Silverton, Paul Simmons, Jim Simpson, Dave Sims, Carol Singleton, Steve Singleton, Clive Skelhon, Ken Slater, Jo Small, Phil Smee, Adam Smith, Giles Smith, Keith Smith, Nigel Smith, Steve Smith, Stewart Smith, Jan Sneum, Rob Southwood, Jeff Speed, Anne Spencer, Colleen Staplehurst, Neville Staples, Hilda Stark, Martin Stephenson, Mark Stewart, Ed Stobart, Jon Storey, Neil Storey, John Sugar, Phil Sutcliffe, Mike Sweeney, Derm Tanner, Ian Tatlock, Brian Tawn, John Taynton, Kevin Thomas, Paul Thompson, Alan Timms, Eric Tingley, John Tobler, Tim Treadwell, Pete Trewavas, Phil Trow, Justin Tunstall, Chris Turley, Pete Turner, Steve Turner, Robin Valk, Johnnie Walker, Ron Watts, Chris Welch, Matthew Wells, Paul Welsh, Charles White, Richard Williams, Jim Wiltshire, Paul Wood, Tony Worgan, Mel Wright, Annabel Yonge, Susan Young and – most of all – the other Steve Turner, the Lincolnshire-based walking rock encyclopaedia, for their assistance in the compilation of this book.

CONTENTS

Flagship HMV record store at 363 Oxford Street, London W1. The trouser fashion dates this as some time in the Seventies.

The same place, different era, before the days of shoplifting & shopfitting.

BEDFORDSHIRE

BEDFORD

In December '62, The Beatles played at the Corn Exchange in St. Paul's Square. In '63, they returned to the town twice – to appear at the Granada in St. Peter's Street. Other stars to grace that cinema's stage include Little Richard, Sam Cooke, Jimi Hendrix, the Stones, The Ronettes – but not Gene Vincent, who was under a Musicians Union ban, and had to sing from the stairs leading up to it!

The Corn Exchange

Tony Poole and Ross McGeeney, the instigators of Seventies band Starry Eyed And Laughing, met at Bedford Modern School, where rock author John Tobler was also a reluctant pupil.

The Kursaal Flyers played their final gig at the Nite Spot in '77. Roadie Glen Churchman was moved to disrobe on stage... resulting in local paper headline "Punk Rock Group Simulates Homosexual Acts On Stage"!

Local Nineties indie gigs include the Angel in Elstow Road and Esquire's in Bromham Road.

A local Our Price record shop is managed by Dave Lewis, editor and publisher of the excellent Led Zep fanzine *Tight But Loose*.

The Pecadiloes (sic) emerged as '97 indie frontrunners.

BIGGLESWADE

Home of Stevie V, who reached number two with Dirty Cash in '90.

DUNSTABLE

Birthplace of singer Duke D'Mond, 25.2.45 (Barron Knights).

In December '56, Jimmy Young wrote off his Jaguar near Dunstable, returning home from a variety engagement in Edinburgh. He was severely bruised and suffered slight concussion.

The California Ballroom at the foot of Dunstable Downs was the county's hottest venue during the 'Sixties/Seventies, when everyone from The Rolling Stones (four times, starting in July '63) to Cream (November '66), Jimi Hendrix (October '67) to Ike & Tina Turner played there. First headliners were Russ Sainty & The Nu Notes in March '60; Jimmy Page played there with Carter Lewis & The Southerners in December '63. The bar overlooked the back of the stage, allowing dumb-ass punters to pour beer on Pink Floyd (February '67), whose innovations were beyond their understanding. It survived until punk – presenting the last gig on the Clash/Buzzcocks White Riot tour in May '77 and a seminal performance by The Damned (when Rat Scabies was refused service at the nearby Windsock pub) – but was then bulldozed to make way for a housing estate.

The town's other venue was the much posher Queensway Hall. Almost every big group has visited, including Fairport Convention, who played a glorious *Zigzag* benefit in October '69, Wishbone Ash who made their world début there in November '69 and R.E.M. who played there in November '84. Steve Marriott & The Moments even played there!

The first issue of *Zigzag* with Sandy Denny

(Pete Frame Collection)

GOLDINGTON
Sometime home of Ricky Valance, who topped '60 charts with 'Tell Laura I Love Her' (his one and only hit) – the foundation for a 40-year career and celebrity golf status.

GREAT BRICKHILL
Sometime home of Wishbone Ash mainman Andy Powell.

LEIGHTON BUZZARD
Home of The Barron Knights, pop funsters for nigh on 40 years. P'nut Langford was educated at Linslade Secondary Modern; Butch Baker at Cedars Grammar.

Also home to Kajagoogoo, whose five minute career peaked on their début hit, 'Too Shy'. The latter evolved from Art Nouveau, who also made a couple of indie records. Ellis, Beggs & Howard was a latterday Kajagoogoo spin-off.

Both The Clash (in October '76, supporting Shepherds Bush band The Rockets) and The Damned played very early provincial gigs at the Tiddenfoot Leisure Centre, just a kiss away from the scene of the Great Train Robbery starring Pistols collaborator Ronnie Biggs.

LUTON
Birthplace of Mick Abrahams, 7.4.43 (Jethro Tull, Blodwyn Pig); Clive Bunker, 12.12.46 (Jethro Tull); Paul Young, 17.1.56 (Q Tips, solo); Nick Hawkins, 3.2.65 (Big Audio Dynamite).

A grim place... but during the Sixties, it was jumping! The Majestic Ballroom in Mill Street (later a bingo hall) presented everyone of note, including The Beatles in April '63 (the week 'From Me To You' was released) and the Stones in November '63. They both returned to play the Odeon in Dunstable Road – in September '63 and April '64, respectively – gigs which sparked off a local beat-group boom. Within weeks, support spots at the Majestic were being taken by The Avengers, The Raving Cannibals, Yenson's Trolls, The Hustlers, Les Fauves and various other contenders.

Another hot venue was the TUC Hall in Church Street, where Russ Sainty & The Nu Notes were supplanted by groups like Zoot Money's Big Roll Band and The Moody Blues.

The Cresta Ballroom in Alma Street was a variety venue, which attempted the transition to teenage music but failed. Now replaced by an office block which houses the headquarters of Friends of the Earth.

First local group to release a record were Terry Judge & The Barristers, who entered a talent contest and won an Oriole contract. A fiver would have been a more useful prize. Next up were Bryan & The Hangmen, who cut a single for EMI after an enforced name change to Bryan & The Brunelles.

In November '64, The Beatles visited Luton for the third and last time to play at the Ritz in Gordon Street, which was a favourite venue on the package show circuit. Everyone from Cilla Black to Stevie Wonder appeared there. In April '65, The Supremes walked around town between shows, and dropped down to the Dolphin coffee bar in Waller Street (now crushed under the Arndale Centre) to see where the action was! To their glee, they found disc jockey Hairy Mick Robson playing Tamla Motown records.

When not a disco/local group venue, the Dolphin was a folk club presenting singers like Alex Campbell, Bert Jansch, Julie Felix, Tom Paxton and Donovan – playing his first paid gigs. The club later moved to the Tudor Café in Upper George Street.

In January '65, PJ Proby's troubles started when he split his velvet trousers onstage at the Ritz in Gordon Street. The curtain was lowered, his microphone switched off, and the cinema management, who declared his act obscene, refunded punters' money and called the police. Reduced from a sex god to a figure of fun, he was dropped from the package tour and he watched his career go down the tubes.

Pink Floyd played Caesar's Palace in October '67.

After playing at the local Beachcomber Club (part of the Caesar's Palace complex), two Blackpool bods moved down to join two Lutonians as Jethro Tull. To support himself, singer Ian Anderson (who lived in Studley Road) worked as a cleaner at the ABC cinema in George Street and earned a local reputation as the nutter who walked around town with a lampshade on his head.

Tull guitarist Mick Abrahams later started Blodwyn Pig with various mates from local bands like McGregor's Engine – including bassist Andy Pyle (who'd worked as a mechanic at Shaw & Kilburn's in Dunstable Road). Pyle was later in The Kinks with another Luton lad, John Gosling – graduate of the Grammar School, now the Sixth Form College.

In January '69, local MP Gwilym Roberts tried to muster support to ban the continuous pop music on BBC Radio 1. He claimed it could damage the health, silly fellow.

Starting in April '69, the first twelve issues of the wonderful pioneering rock magazine *Zigzag* were published from 7 Five Oaks in the nearby village of Caddington.

Punk group UK Decay created a bit of excitement, but the town's most celebrated Eighties export was Paul Young who used to live up Wigmore Lane and worked for a while at Vauxhall Motors... as did Luton's very first pop act The Mudlarks, who reached the '58 top three with 'Lollipop'! Their first gigs were at the Wesleyan Church in Chapel Street and they used to live round the corner from the Three Horseshoes public house in Leagrave.

In January '70, Yes elbowed guitarist Pete Banks after a dubious gig at the College of Technology (now the University!) in Park Square – and the same venue saw the conclusion of Mott The Hoople's variety tour (April '72), where they shared the bill with Max Wall and a knife thrower who used the group for target practice against the dressing room door! Ian Dury was an art teacher there.

Elton John's straw boaters were made at Olney's hat factory and stars like U2, Eurythmics and Phil Collins had their natty leather trousers made at Peter Kay's place in Dudley Street.

Shirley Bassey made her first public appearance in Luton – in a touring revue, *Memories Of Al Jolson* (singing 'Stormy Weather') – and Duke D'Mond & The Barron Knights made

their world début at the Electrolux Social Club. They also played many of their early gigs at Beechwood Road School Youth Club – when they were still called Dickie Demon & The Barron Knights.

That splendid poet John Hegley grew up here and put the town on the literary map with such gems as *I Remember Luton As I'm Swallowing My Crouton*.

Driving home up the M1 in December '78, after playing the Hope & Anchor in Islington, Joy Division first discovered that singer Ian Curtis suffered from epilepsy. He had a fit in the car and was taken to the Luton & Dunstable Hospital, just off junction 11.

Thrilled Skinny were late Eighties hopefuls/Peel faves who disguised their identities with such witty pseudonyms as Simon Goalpost and Utensil Realname.

In the Nineties came DJ/recording artiste Crucial Robbie and techno act Cyclob (aka Chris Jeffs).

STANBRIDGE

Every rock encyclopaedia ever written has Stanbridge as the birthplace of Ten Years After bass player Leo Lyons, 30.11.44 – but he was in fact born in Nottinghamshire, as you would expect. However, his mate, former Jethro Tull drummer Clive Bunker runs a drumming school at his home/studio here... not to mention boarding kennels.

Woburn Abbey   *(Woburn Abbey)*

WOBURN

Hordes of hippies converged on the Duke of Bedford's stately gaff for England's first Flower Power festival in summer '67. The likes of Jeff Beck and Arthur Brown provided the entertainment. Some saw it as the first instance of the exploitation and commercialisation of the previously organic, self-contained underground scene. A second festival in July '68 featured the Jimi Hendrix Experience, T Rex, Family, Pentangle and Geno Washington.

BERKSHIRE

ALDERMASTON
Among the Campaign for Nuclear Disarmament marchers of the early Sixties were Rod Stewart, Chris Dreja (Yardbirds) and Paul Jones (Manfred Mann).

ALDWORTH
During the early Seventies, Marianne Faithfull and her son Nicholas lived with her mother at a cottage in this village.

ASCOT
In May '69, John Lennon laid out £145,000 for Tittenhurst Park, a Georgian mansion set in 72 acres off the road between Ascot and Sunningdale. The Beatles were filmed on a lake in the grounds and the album *Imagine* was recorded in his home studio. Video footage of John and Yoko in an all white room was shot here. When John moved to America in September '73, Ringo bought it and rented out the studio. Whitesnake recorded *Come And Get It* there, allowing David Coverdale to relax in a master bedroom with a mirrored ceiling.

David Bowie was an extra in *The Virgin Soldiers*, filmed on location at Ascot in summer '68.

In '70, Leapy Lee and his mate Alan Lake (husband of Diana Dors) became involved in a pub fracas at the Red Lion in Sunningdale. The relief manager was knifed and Leapy was sent to prison for three years (to see a superabundance of 'Little Arrows'), Lake for eighteen months. At the time, Lee was living at Cedar Wood in Larch Avenue; Lake and Dors at Orchard Manor, Shrubs Hill.

In '87, the ultra-successful Five Star moved from Romford to a larger residence in Sunningdale – but moved on again in '90.

BURNHAM
Birthplace of Tracey Ullman, 30.12.59 (three Top Ten hits in '83).

BRACKNELL
The Headliners released a couple of singles in the Sixties, and Them Howlin' Horrors were tipped for stardom in '84... but nothing happened!

Two of Yardbird Keith Relf's sons (April, his widow, lives here) have a band; they made their début at South Hill Park Community Centre.

The 2,000 capacity Bracknell Sports Centre in Bagshot Road was a hot venue in the Seventies.

Home town of bass player Steve Rippon (Lush) and teenage Blur-wannabes Snug.

BRAY
Home of Howard Jones.

CAVERSHAM
In April '60, John Lennon and Paul McCartney spent a week's holiday here, staying at the Fox And Hounds on the junction of Westfield and Gosbrook Roads. (The landlady was Paul's cousin.) It was here that they played an Everly Brothers-style acoustic set under the name of The Nerk Twins.

HUNGERFORD
Military Surplus was a local band. Singer Chris Bowsher later formed Radical Dance Faction.

LAMBOURN
Charisma boss Tony Stratton Smith (RIP) lived here in the early Eighties, when his interest in horse racing eclipsed his enthusiasm for the record biz.

MAIDENHEAD

Skindles Hotel in Bath Road was a popular venue in the Seventies.

NEWBURY

In October 67, Mick Jagger purchased a country estate, Stargroves. The Who recorded 'Won't Get Fooled Again' in the home studio there.

Producer Jimmy Miller also lived in Newbury.

The Plaza Ballroom was never the same after Jimi Hendrix played there in February '67.

PANGBOURNE

Jimmy Page lived here in the late Sixties/early Seventies, at 4 Shooters Hill.

PURLEY

Deep Purple's Ian Gillan lived here during the early Eighties and played for the local police football team.

READING

Birthplace of Vincent Crane, 21.5.43 (Atomic Rooster); Mike Oldfield, 15.5.53.

Students passing through the University included Arthur Brown (Crazy World Of), Andy Mackay (Roxy Music), Richard Boon (Buzzcocks manager), Malcolm Garrett (Buzzcocks sleeve designer) and Jane Collings (Buzzcocks shirts designer). Geoff Goddard, who was living at 5 Ormsby Street when he composed hits for John Leyton and other Joe Meek acts, quit the music biz and took a job in the University's catering dept. The neo-mod group Secret Affair made their début at the Uni in January '79, supporting The Jam.

During the Fifties, Marianne Faithfull lived at 41 Milman Road and briefly attended Christ Church School,

Rare Sally & Mike Oldfield offering

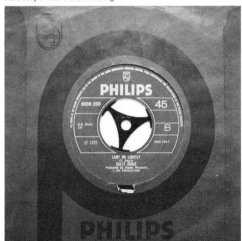

before moving on to St. Joseph's Convent in Upper Redlands Road. Also educated there was Sally Oldfield, who would later form the duo Sallyangie with her brother Mike.

The first local musician to find national acclaim was blues singer/guitarist Mike Cooper in the late Sixties, and R&B combo Jive Alive have been going for almost 20 years.

In June '71, after ten years in different locations, the National Jazz Blues & Rock Festival moved to Reading where it has since remained. In its first year, there were 112 drug arrests in what the *News Of The World* called "a jamboree of pop and pot". Among the billions of acts who've played there are Blur ('93), Bjork ('95), Page & Plant ('98). New Order went out on a high note in '93; The Stone Roses went out on a bum note in '96.

(GM Records)

1973 Reading Festival live album

Hatched in a semi-derelict Cemetery Junction squat, next door to the Sikh Temple, Clayson & The Argonauts were *Melody Maker*'s pick-to-click in '76, but global fame proved elusive. So disturbing was an early performance at the Target pub in Hosier Street, that the landlord produced a revolver and hustled the group from the premises.

In '78, before The Buggles hit, Trevor Horn was making ends meet by playing bass in the resident band at the Top Rank.

In March '79, Roy Orbison visited 45 Fawley Road to see Michelle Booth, who had been hospitalised in a coma after being attacked and hurled from a speeding train. His specially taped message had helped her recovery.

Tudor Lodge (named after a local pub) were Seventies folk rockers; Twelfth Night were early Eighties heavy metal hopefuls; The Lemon Kittens were imaginative early Eighties arty types led by Danielle Dax.

Robyn Hitchcock mentions Reading in his song 'I Often Dream Of Trains'.

Tudor Lodge single, after the Tudor Lodge Pub!

Ian Gillan was once a director of Reading Football Club.

Van Morrison recorded some demos at Audiogenic Studios in Crown Street. Locals say that while he was ensconced there, the place was as impregnable as Fort Knox!

The press proclaimed the arrival of "the Thames Valley Sound" when Chapterhouse and Slowdive made ripples in the early Nineties. Radical Dance Faction, Coloursound and Chuck were also around; in the mid-Nineties came Bennet and Cuckooland.

Girl group The Period Pains and Brat-poppers Gel seemed set for late Nineties success.

The Alleycat Complex in Katesgrove Lane is a breeding ground for local talent.

The Alleycat Complex

(Reading Evening Post)

SLOUGH

Birthplace of Cliff Bennett, 4.6.40 ('Got To Get You Into My Life'); drummer Dave Ballinger, 17.1.41 (Barron Knights); singer Rod Evans, 19.1.47 (Deep Purple); drummer Mark Brzezicki, 21.6.57 (Big Country).

The Beatles/Roy Orbison tour opened at Slough Adelphi in May '63.

The Maze were late Sixties locals; Ian Paice and Rod Evans left them to join Deep Purple. Robert & The Remoulds played the late Seventies London circuit. Sledgehammer were Seventies heavy metal grinders. 1000 Yard Stare and Foam were early Nineties indie hopefuls. The Wax Doctor (Paul Saunders) won mid-Nineties acclaim as a dj/remixer.

Police shot their video of 'Roxanne' at the Fulcrum Centre; Kate Bush filmed 'Army Dreamers' in Black Park – also the location for the video promoting Bob Marley's 'Buffalo Soldier'.

In December '76, after years of grinding round the world, the great Welsh band Man played their final gig at the Fulcrum Theatre in Queensmere.

Sweet singer Brian Connolly died at Wexham Park Hospital in February '97.

STOKE POGES

The video for The Human League hit 'Don't You Want Me' was shot in the grounds of the Stoke Palace Hotel in Stoke Green.

STREATLEY

The late Martin Rushent's Genetic Studio (Stranglers, Human League, etc) was located at Wood Cott on Streatley Hill, near Goring.

WARGRAVE

Once home for record producer Tony Visconti and his wife Mary Hopkin.

WINDSOR

Birthplace of singer Stephen Patman, 8.11.68 (Chapterhouse).

The Ricky Tick Club, housed in the Star & Garter pub, was a prime mid-Sixties Rhythm & Blues venue. As resident group, The Rolling Stones played there 16 times between January and July '63 – at which point the Ricky Tick relocated to the Thames Hotel, where they played six times. It was here that Brian Jones met Linda Lawrence, later to be mother of his child. For a while they lived with her parents in Windsor. Other groups to play the Ricky Tick included the local Hogsnort Rupert & his Good Good Band (featuring soon-to-be famous producer John Anthony on vocals), Zoot Money & his Big Roll Band, John Mayall's Bluesbreakers, The Graham Bond Organisation, The Jimi Hendrix Experience and even Pink Floyd. For the famous Yardbirds scene in the movie *Blow Up*, the club was meticulously reconstructed at Elstree Studios.

Late Seventies group Fischer Z promised much but achieved little – as did frontman John Watt in his subsequent solo career.

Slough's mighty Sledgehammer

(Reflection)

Windsor residents have included Elton John, Jimmy Page and Rod Stewart. In '98, Elton's 18th century mansion, Woodside in Crimps Hill (actually in New Windsor), had its Grade II Listed status removed after its owner made modifications which included the removal of a Doric porch and the addition of a swimming pool.

In May '80, Jimmy Page purchased Michael Caine's Thames-side residence, The Old Mill House in Clewer Village, for a reported £900,000. It was there, nine months later, that John Bonham died after an intense vodka binge. In July '89, Page sold it for £1.2 million.

Rod Stewart lived here with Deirdre Harrington during the early Seventies, at Cranbourne Court – a mansion he purchased from Lord Bethell for around £89,000. You'd pay that much for a chicken coop in Windsor these days. Rod occasionally popped into the Fox and Hounds pub in nearby Englefield Green for drop of brandy.

For its 6th and 7th years (July '66 and August '67), the National Jazz Blues & Rock Festival was held at Balloon Meadow on Windsor Racecourse. In '66, Cream unveiled themselves and The Who smashed up their equipment; '67 was dominated by flower power and marked the débuts of Fleetwood Mac and Chicken Shack.

The Psykick Dancehall (named after the' 79 Fall track) in the Old Trout public house became a well known indie gig in the early Nineties. Love Cut and Airstream (whose album celebrated the Ricky Tick) were the top local Nineties indie bands; hot producer/remixer Andy Weatherall is a local lad.

WOKINGHAM

Birthplace of guitarist Martin Stone,11.12.46 (Chilli Willi); guitarist Andrew Sherriff, 5.5.69 (Chapterhouse).

Woodcray Studios at Manor Farm in Finch Hampstead Road started small but later attracted the likes of Then Jerico and All About Eve.

Sixties popsters Marmalade, still big on the cabaret circuit, are now based here.

Operational base of late Nineties country rockers Montrose Avenue.

WOODLANDS St. MARY

Drummer Cozy Powell was living here, until his death on the M4 near Bristol in April '98.

WRAYSBURY

Birthplace of Louise Cordet, 8.2.46, who reached the '62 Top Twenty with 'I'm Just a Baby'.

Original UK poster for the film

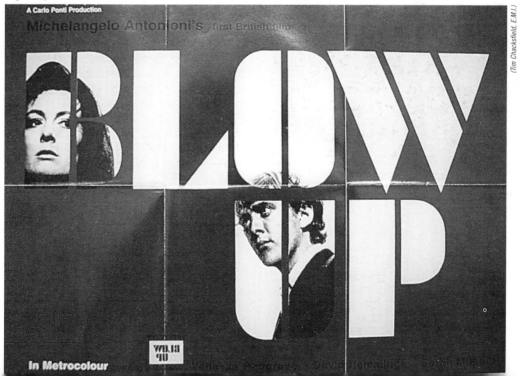

(Tim Chacksfield, E.M.I.)

BRISTOL

Birthplace of pianist Russ Conway, 2.9.27; Roger Cook, 19.8.40 (Blue Mink, etc); Roger Greenaway, 23.8.42 (David and Jonathan, etc); drummer/singer Robert Wyatt, 1945 (Soft Machine); drummer Timmie Donald, 1946 (White Trash); singer James Warren, 25.8.51 (Stackridge, Corgis); singer Nik Kershaw, 1.3.58; guitarist Wayne Hussey, 26.5.59 (Mission); journalist Julie Burchill, 3.7.59; Sarah Dallen, 17.12.62, and Keren Woodward, 2.4.63 (they met at school and later moved to London to form Bananarama).

The Montrose Avenue pose on the theatre stage of Normanfield Hospital, Teddington

Adam & The Ants drummer Merrick went to Blackwell Comprehensive; Harriet Wheeler and David Gavurin of The Sundays met at Bristol University; Hugh Cornwell of The Stranglers studied biochemistry at the University; and Bob Geldof's sister was said to have been a teacher at Churchill School.

BRISTOL

Home base for a bewildering array of idiosyncratic bands, like The Cougars, Force West, Johnny Carr & The Cadillacs (all Sixties), Magic Muscle, Subway Sect, Glaxo Babies, Vice Squad, The Cortinas, Essential Bop, The Pigs, Mystery Guests, The Numbers, Private Dicks (all Seventies), The Pop Group, Maximum Joy, Rip Rig And Panic, Pigbag, Electric Guitars, Mark Stewart & The Mafia, Jo Boxers, The Chesterfields, Blue Aeroplanes (all Eighties).

The late Eighties saw The Seers, Brilliant Corners, Rhythm Party ("just like Bros only better looking"), The Driscolls, The Helmets, Rorschach, The Loggerheads, Onslaught, Claytown Troupe, Head, Smith & Mighty, The Flatmates, The Groove Farm and more!

In the early Nineties came a plethora of bands, including The Moonflowers, Beatnik Filmstars, Nautical William, The Herb Garden, Me, Fruit, Strangelove, The Southernaires and Massive Attack (who would become huge in no time at all with a Top Five album *Protection/No*

Magic Muscle in a field near Bristol

(Pete Flanagan)

Protection in '94). Their collaborators, Nellee Hooper and Shara Nelson, would also achieve national prominence.

The Pigs on the now demolished Bristol Docks 1977

In the mid-Nineties came Telstarr, The Eff Word, Up Bustle and Out, Cool Breeze (aka Charlie Laxton), 20-year-old Roni Size & Raprazent (who would take the Mercury Music Award '97), Tricky (aka Adrian Thew - whose Maxinquaye was a Top Three album in '95), The Heads, Hood, Send No Flowers, The Federation (dance), Flynn'n'Flora (drum'n'bass), Movietone and Third Eye Foundation (both lo-fi Flying Saucer Attack offshoots), More Rockers (ex Smith and Mighty), '97 charters Way Out West, The Experimental Pop Band (comprising ex-members of Brilliant Corners – so much family tree potential in Bristol!), and 98's brightest hope Straw.

Local clubs/venues have included Colston Hall in Colston Street (package shows/big deals), Electric Village at the Locarno in Frogmore Street (progressive – like Hendrix in February '67), the Granary at 32 Welsh Back (Seventies/Eighties), the Dugout, the Berkeley Centre, Trinity Hall (new wave), the Anson Rooms at the University (where Massive Attack came home to play four nights in December '98), the Fleece & Firkin, the Louisiana, the Thekla, the Albert Inn, the Blue Mountain Club. Lakota at 6 Upper York Street is a focal point for late Nineties clubbers.

First local group to make waves were The Kestrels, containing Roger Cook, Roger Greenaway and Tony Burrows. Cook and Greenaway wrote millions of hits (like 'I'd Like To Teach The World To Sing') and Burrows was in millions of groups – like The Pipkins, Edison Lighthouse, and The Flowerpot Men.

Acker Bilk formed his Paramount Jazz Band in Bristol in early '58, playing local pubs before moving to London.

A few hours before his fatal car crash, Eddie Cochran played his last gig at Bristol Hippodrome (Easter Saturday, 16.4.60). The previous year, Lonnie Donegan had recorded his hit 'Battle Of New Orleans' there. The same venue saw the start of the Wings tour in May 73 – the first scheduled tour by an ex-Beatle since their last foray in '66.

In September '60 The Shadows played their first gig without Cliff – at Colston Hall. The same venue presented everyone from The Beatles (four times) to Bob Dylan (May '66), who returned there to shoot concert sequences for his unwatchable movie *Hearts Of Fire*, to local heroine PJ Harvey (December '98).

In the early Sixties, American star Big Dee Erwin got lost on his way to Colston Hall. He stopped outside the bowling alley in Kingswood to ask directions and gave a helpful schoolboy half a crown and his autograph!

Jimmy Page played at the Co-op Hall in November '63, as guitarist in Carter Lewis & The Southerners. Tony Prince was resident DJ at the Top Rank before going off to become a star at Radio Luxembourg. The Byrds played the Corn Exchange in August '65. Pink Floyd played the Victoria Rooms in September '67.

In January '64, The Rolling Stones (on tour with The Ronettes) were refused admission to the Royal Hotel on College Green for sartorial irregularities. The Animals subsequently suffered the same fate. In '60, the drunken hooligan Gene Vincent had been allowed to stay – as had Eddie Cochran and Sharon Sheeley, who spent their last night together there.

Ronnie Lane of The Small Faces wrote the lyrics to 'Itchycoo Park' in a Bristol hotel room after perusing a local tourism brochure which spoke of dreaming spires and a bridge of sighs – and a few years later, Andrew Lloyd Webber wrote 'Don't Cry For Me Argentina' while staying at the Unicorn Hotel on the Dockside.

Tricky & Martine (taken on a water tower in Rotherhithe, London)

For a BBC television show in '70, Simon & Garfunkel played an unannounced concert at the Arnolfini Theatre on Narrow Quay.

Away from the glare of dubious publicity, Erasure played their first ever gig at the tiny Western Star Domino Club, off Broadmead, in November '85.

It was while Paul McCartney was in Bristol visiting his girlfriend Jane Asher (appearing at the Old Vic in early '66) that he was drawn to an old clothes shop called Daisy Hawkins. The name inspired a new song, but by the time it was recorded a few weeks later, it had metamorphosed into Eleanor Rigby.

(Bristol Evening Post)

The Colston Hall

Mott The Hoople played one of their earliest gigs (November '69) at the Granary; Marillion made a pre-signing appearance there in November '82; Phil Lynott got up and played after a sold-out Thin Lizzy gig at Colston Hall.

In '87, Tracey Chapman made her UK début at the Bierkeller, third on the bill below Tanita Tikaram and John Martyn. The Bunker Club (late '85 to mid-'87), which presented most of the up and coming C86 bands, was run by Martin Whitehead of The Flatmates – who also operated the local Subway label from 3 Dove Lane.

After various names and guises, the Locarno became the Studio in the late Eighties. The Waterboys walked out of a gig there after complaining that the audience had been packed in too tightly.

The sleeve for Echo & The Bunnymen's second album *Heaven Up Here* was shot on the Severn estuary mudflats; the sleeve of Bunnyman Will Sargeant's '82 solo album *Themes For Grind* was shot at the old Wills Tobacco

warehouses near the Cumberland Basin, and on the railway line near Ashton Gate.

The old Wills Tobacco warehouse

Gary Clail (Top Ten with Human Nature in '91) was said to have been a local scaffolder.

In April '98, Cozy Powell was declared dead on arrival at Frenchay Hospital. The 50- year-old drummer had been driving down the M4 at 104 mph, en route to see his girlfriend in Cardiff, when he lost control of his Saab 9000 Turbo. Told that he'd been drinking, he was not wearing a seat belt and he was using a mobile phone at the time of the accident, an inquest delivered a verdict of accidental death.

Bristol has been mentioned (if not immortalised) in several songs, including 'Bristol Steam Convention Blues' by The Byrds, 'Bristol And Miami' by Selecter and 'Bristol Express' by The (English) Eagles, which was featured in the '62 Clive Donner film *Some People*, set in Bristol.

CLIFTON

On his album *To Whom It May Concern*, Al Stewart sang "I took my love to Clifton in the rain". Whenever he sang it in Bristol, so he says, the audience would burst out laughing!

John Cleese went to Clifton College.

"Lay down thy raincoat and groove": The Bunnymen on the Severn Estuary

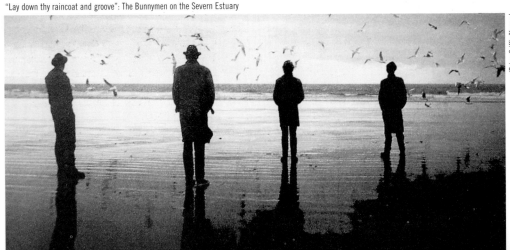

(Brian Griffin/Korova)

BUCKINGHAMSHIRE

AMERSHAM
Birthplace of Butch Baker, 16.7.41 (Barron Knights); Tim Rice, 10.11.44.

ASTON CLINTON
Tamla Motown's first UK outlet was the Oriole label, based in premises opposite the Rising Sun pub on the A41 (later a plastics factory; now derelict).

AYLESBURY
Friars club started in '69, at the British Legion Hall in Walton Street. Genesis and Mott The Hoople (who first played in December '69) were audience faves. Said Ian Hunter: "Mott happened in Aylesbury long before they happened anywhere else."

Later Genesis return to their birthplace

The Borough Assembly Hall in the Market Square was known as the Grosvenor in the Sixties, when everyone from Johnny Kidd to Jimi Hendrix (March '67) played there, and Friars in the Seventies, when the club outgrew its first venue. When Genesis played there in June '71, Peter Gabriel leapt off the stage during an overenthusiastic interpretation of 'The Knife' and broke his ankle. David Bowie previewed his Ziggy Stardust show there in January 72.

1970 contract guaranteeing Genesis £30.00

In August '61, Bill Wyman was on holiday in Aylesbury and was taken to see Dickie Demon & The Barron Knights (as they were then known) at the Grosvenor. What he actually saw was his future; Baron Anthony's bass playing convinced him to go out and buy a bass guitar. He returned to the town as a member of The Rolling Stones in January '64, when they and The Ronettes played the Granada Cinema in the High Street.

When the Assemby Hall was closed for redevelopment, Friars moved to the Reg Maxwell Hall in the Civic Centre and the jollity continued until promoter David Stopps discovered Howard Jones (who first played there in May '82) and quit the club to manage him.

In the late Seventies, the town's biggest star was John Otway; born at 17 Whitehall Street and educated at Queens Park Junior School. He worked for the council as a dustman until fame tapped him on the shoulder.

Otway and his sidekick Wild Willy Barrett caused mayhem on the national new wave circuit until a gig coincided with a World Cup match. Barrett decided to stay at home and watch the game, and the duo split. Otway moved to London to continue his inexorable climb to the top, headlining the Royal Albert Hall in October '98.

Other local residents have included jazz-rock saxophonist Lol Coxhill, Pete Trewavas from Marillion, Bill Drummond from The Timelords and KLF, and Ian Gillan from Deep Purple, who lived for a while in the hinterlands at Cublington.

Other local groups included The Whispering Four (the town's first beat group), The Vice Creems (punks, led by *Zigzag* magazine editor Kris Needs), The Stowaways (guitarist Mick Lister was later in The Truth), Orthi, The Haircuts, The Disco Students, The Blood Oranges, Danny Picasso & The Last Good Kiss, The Robins, The Feckin Ejits, Golden Shower and Big Big Sun (late Eighties Atlantic signing).

In January '77, Keith Richards found himself in Crown Court on drug charges (see Newport Pagnell). After a three day trial he was found half guilty and fined £1,000. Former Mamas and Papas leader John Phillips was his sidekick at the time, though few people in Aylesbury recognized him.

The Coventry Automatics, supporting The Clash at Friars in June '78, changed their name to The Specials on the day of the gig.

The Grange Secondary School was responsible for the education of John Otway, Wild Willy Barrett, Robin Boult (Big Big Sun), Pete Trewavas (Marillion), Kris Needs (*Zigzag*), David Rohoman (Kilburn & The High Roads).

In the Eighties, the town's hottest band was Marillion, who really got going after Fish moved here in January 81. They lived communally at 64 Weston Road, Aston Clinton. Following their first flush of success, they bought houses in the town: Fish lived at 18 Albert Street, Mark Kelly at 42 Willow Road, and Pete Trewavas at 15 Mount Pleasant. All have since moved to more palatial residences.

Their local boozer was Seatons (now closed) at the top of the Market Square – setting for their first hit, 'Market Square Heroes'... inspired by the town's very first punk, known locally as Brick.

Caveman were an early Nineties rap trio.

Home of Nineties indie label Rotator Records, whose acts include Harvey's Rabbit and The Sweeney. The town's hottest late Nineties band are The Debutantes. The Buckingham Arms is just about the only venue for local bands.

BEACONSFIELD

Birthplace of Paul Layton, 4.8.47 (New Seekers).

Operational base of Nineties chart stars and remixers, Fluke.

BLETCHLEY

Birthplace of Spyder Bennett, 28.7.48 (Paper Dolls).

Wilton Hall was a major Sixties venue. The Stones (March '64), Jeff Beck (March '68), The Animals and all the R&B/blues crowd played there – as did Pink Floyd on one of their first provincial forays, in November '66.

During the early Seventies, Bletchley Youth Club in Derwent Drive seemed to attract impossibly big names – such as Mott The Hoople (February '70), Kevin Ayers, etc.

BRILL

Birthplace of drummer Mick Pointer, 22.7.56 (Marillion).

BUCKINGHAM

Former Whitesnake guitarist Bernie Marsden went to Buckingham School and still lives in the town.

Locally based Liquid Gold had two top tenners in '80. Guitarist Sid Twineham later formed The Road Knights, who also went out with Les Gray as Mud. Late Eighties group Horace Cope & The Fortunes saw their future and decided to disband.

CHALFONT ST. GILES

In '98, Chiltern District Council refused permission for Noel Gallagher to instal six floodlights to enable him to play nocturnal soccer at his country retreat.

Also the Nineties home of Mike Oldfield.

CHALFONT ST. PETER

Zoe Ball was educated at the Holy Cross Convent School.

CHESHAM

Art Garfunkel made his UK solo début at the Trap Door folk club, just off the High Street, in '65.

CUDDINGTON

Until he moved to Wales in '88, Labi Siffre lived in the thatched house next to the Crown public house. Heavy Metal group Lone Star also lived in the village during the mid-Eighties.

ELLESBOROUGH

Chequers, the Prime Minister's country retreat, has never seen so many pop idols. Whereas Maggie would entertain statesmen and politicians, and John Major would invite famous sportsmen (like the Bedser twins and Jimmy Greaves), our Cool Britannia PM seems to favour multi-millionaire rock stars – often with bizarre drug backgrounds. Among those to grace his table have been Elton John, Paul McCartney, Mick Jagger, David Bowie and Mick Hucknall. "What do you reckon, Mick? Should I give the order to start bombing Iraq?" As yet, no sign of Linton Kwesi Johnson or Chumbawamba or Shaun Ryder or Shane McGowan.

GERRARDS CROSS
Maurice Gibb of The Bee Gees married Lulu here in February '69.

A newly-born Martha (my dear) with junior McCartney

HIGH WYCOMBE
Birthplace of Martha, 16.6.66 (Paul McCartney's sheepdog).

Students passing through the Royal Grammar School include Tom Springfield (Springfields), Ian Dury and Ted Speight (who were in a skiffle group there and were later re-united in Kilburn & The High Roads), and Howard Jones.

The first floor room above the Nag's Head at 63 London Road has always presented excellent up and coming groups – from Fleetwood Mac to Mott The Hoople (April '70) to Elvis Costello (August '77) and beyond. The ebullient promoter, Ron Watts, intermittently led local R&B/cajun band Brewers Droop – which for a short time contained Mark Knopfler (who auditioned as bassist) playing his first professional role.

Unannounced and uninvited, The Sex Pistols played at the College of Art's Valentine Dance in Feb 76 – supporting Screaming Lord Sutch. Buzzcocks founders Howard Devoto and Pete Shelley travelled down from Manchester to witness their seminal chain-reaction performance. The town was never comfortable with punk: after a Ruts gig at the Students Union Yak Club in '79, fans trashed the place,

smashing the windscreens of cars as they left.

The Town Hall in Queen Victoria Road always presented groups. The Rolling Stones played there several times in '63/4, and it was the first venue for the seminal Bunch Of Stiffs package tour of October '77 – which marked the début of Ian Dury & The Blockheads, and also included Elvis Costello, Nick Lowe and Wreckless Eric. Generation X and The Cure played there in December '78.

While waiting for fame to tap him on the shoulder, Howard Jones was employed in the stock control department at the Perfawrap cling film factory. In the early Seventies, he played electric piano in local group Warrior, who got as far as cutting a demo at Eden Studios and signing a songwriting deal with Carlin Music.

In the Sixties, beat group The Peasants were optimistic; in the late Seventies R&B group Long Tall Shorty looked promising for a while; Thee Hypnotics emerged in the late Eighties.

Among the stars living in the hills beyond the town are Ian Anderson (Jethro Tull), Stewart Copeland (Police) and Sonja Kristina (Curved Air).

Curved Air's Sonja Kristina

Best current local gig is the White Horse at 94 West Wycombe Road, where local stars Born Idol are resident. Other Nineties bands include The Original Sinners, Ragga and The Jack Magic Orchestra (despite some of their number being Icelandic).

LITTLE CHALFONT
Home of quiet and well-behaved heavy metal star Ozzy Osbourne, now installed at the baronial Beel House in Beel Park. The most historically interesting and important residence in the area, it was once occupied by Dirk Bogarde. In November '98, Chiltern District Council asked Ozzy to remove the 17 four-metre high orange floodlights he had installed to facilitate his new hobby, gardening after dark.

LITTLE MARLOW
In September '98, Spice Girl Melanie Brown (Scary Spice) married dancer Jimmy Gulzar at St. John the Baptist Parish Church. To minimise paparazzi intrusion, a canvas tunnel was erected between the church and the Grade II listed Manor House (set in eight acres) purchased by Ms Brown earlier in the year at an estimated cost of £2.25 million.

LONGWICK
Local group The Haircuts immortalised the village hall in 'Do You Remember Longwick?' in '78. Eleven years later, 14,000 revellers converged on the village for a surprise All Night Acid Rave Party, much to the horror of local residents and police.

MARLOW
In December '93, TV star Philip Schofield was in trouble with the local authority for erecting without permission a high fence to exclude prying fans from the ten acre spread he had purchased five months earlier. As well as renovating the house, which once belonged to the Lord of Frawley, Schofield changed its name from Sunnyclose to Great Wood House.

A Harp Beat rock plaque was awarded to singer/songwriter Les Payne, who had a Sunday residency at the Pegasus – to recognise his tenacity and perseverance. Since '56, he had played over 5,000 gigs in his quest for stardom. He's probably well on his way to 6,000 by now.

Genesis 're-form' for a one-off show

MILTON KEYNES
Streets in the Crown Hill area are named after dead rock stars – including Presley Way, Lennon Drive, Orbison Court, Valens Close, Redding Grove, Fury Court, Lynott Close, Vincent Avenue, Bolan Court and Kidd Close.

Milton Keynes Bowl has presented numerous rock concerts, starting with Police in July '80. Status Quo played their 'farewell' gigs' there (they came back, of course) and Michael Jackson blocked roads in all directions in '88. Other Bowlers include U2 and R.E.M. (June '85), The Cult (January '86), Bon Jovi (three times), David Bowie (August '90), ZZ Top and Bryan Adams (July '91), Guns'n Roses (May '93) and Blur (July '95).

The Stables at Wavendon, owned and operated by Johnny Dankworth and Cleo Laine, has long been presenting concerts to suit all musical tastes – from Acker Bilk to Roger McGuinn, The Pasadena Roof Orchestra to Long John Baldry.

The Stables, Wavendon

(Frazer Waller)

Local resident Eddie Stanton got together with Wild Willy Barrett to record 'Milton Keynes We Love You'. The Style Council's '85 tribute 'Come To Milton Keynes' was rather more equivocal.

The video for Cliff Richard's 'Wired For Sound' was shot in the shopping centre, in front of John Lewis.

Home of Acid House executant Jolly Roger.

Once the guitarist with Jethro Tull and Blodwyn Pig, Mick Abrahams moved here to become a financial consultant with Allied Dunbar. In the late Nineties, he was touring as Jethro Tull tribute band 'This Was'.

In the Nineties, Tuesday Strange became the first local band to attract national coverage.

The Woughton Centre has always presented interesting up and coming bands.

In June '89, McDonalds in Midsummer Boulevard was fire-bombed – a day after Chrissie Hynde had addressed a Greenpeace Rainbow Warriors conference and made deprecating comments about the chain.

NEWPORT PAGNELL

In May '76, following a Stones concert at Stafford, Keith Richards' Bentley unaccountably swerved off the M1, burst through a hedge and came to rest in a ploughed field. After being arrested, he was charged with possessing cannabis and cocaine, and with three driving offences. What a naughty boy.

OLNEY

Home of former Foundations frontman Clem Curtis.

PINEWOOD

Film director Michael Winner's first feature was *Play It Cool*, starring Billy Fury and Helen Shapiro.

PRINCES RISBOROUGH

Birthplace of Nigel Harrison, bass player in Blondie. His first group was Farm, whose drummer Paul Hammond replaced Carl Palmer in Atomic Rooster.

During '75, John Otway lived in a tent in the hills near Whiteleaf Cross – chronicled in his song 'Louisa On A Horse'. He later moved to his girlfriend's house in Place Farm Way – the title of another song.

Operational base of late Nineties pop band Tiger.

Tiger, of Princes Risborough, painted by Tiger

STOKE MANDEVILLE

Robert Wyatt was treated at Stoke Mandeville Hospital after fracturing his spine.

Jimmy Savile raises millions for new buildings and equipment, and puts in many hours on the wards.

STOWE

Passing through this exclusive public school were George Melly (more interested in Bessie Smith), Richard Branson, Roger Hodgson (Supertramp) and Crispian Mills (Kula Shaker). There was also a group, The Mongrels, whose single 'I Long To Hear' missed the chart. In December '98, Michael Jackson sent over an emissary to see if the school was suitable for his son Prince Jackson.

A young Mick Abrahams dreams of a future in finance in Milton Keynes

The Beatles played here in April 63. It was the first time they'd even seen a public school and were astonished and delighted that the audience remained seated and silent throughout the entire performance.

Former Whitesnake guitarist Bernie Marsden had his wedding reception here; Cozy Powell was best man.

TINGEWICK

Duran Duran's Andy Taylor played in the village hall in December '88 to raise funds for landscaping the village pond.

WENDOVER

The Well Head pub (now closed) was a cool venue in the late Eighties, when groups like The Housemartins and The Mighty Lemon Drops were regulars.

Marillion men Mark Kelly and Steve Rothery bought homes here when they made a bit of cash.

WESTON TURVILLE

During the Eighties, Noel Edmonds lived here.

WINGRAVE

Ian Dury's band Kilburn & The High Roads lived in the vicarage during their Seventies heyday. Local kids would sit on the railings by the village pond and listen to their rehearsals. Peter Cook lived here too, as a matter of interest.

CAMBRIDGESHIRE

CAMBRIDGE

Birthplace of Syd Barrett, 6.1.46, at 60 Glisson Road, where he lived until his family moved to 183 Hills Road. He attended Morley Memorial Junior School, where Roger Waters' mother was a teacher, and then Cambridge High School For Boys (now Hills Road Sixth Form College: motto *Virtute et Fide*), where he first met Waters (who lived in Rock Road). After moving to London, they formed Pink Floyd, who later paid homage to their roots on 'Grantchester Meadows'.

Ballroom. Also around were Wages Of Sin and Little Women (both featuring Jerry Shirley, later of Humble Pie).

In the Seventies came multifarious eccentric pop rockers including Duke Duke & The Dukes and The Soft Boys, the latter containing Kimberley Rew and led by Robyn Hitchcock, who could often be found busking in Lion Yard.

The Soft Boys recorded for Raw Records at 48 King Street. Also on the label were The Users, The Killjoys, The Unwanted and more.

Grantchester Meadows in 1971

Folk at the Folk Festival

(Dave Peabody)

Barrett later returned to the city to pursue a sporadic solo career and lead ill-fated group Stars. The Barrett Room at Addenbrooke's Hospital is named after Syd's noted pathologist father.

Premier late Sixties local group was Jokers Wild, comprising Dave Gilmour (born here on 6.3.46; later in Floyd), Rick Wills (later in Foreigner) and Willie Wilson (later in Quiver). They were resident at the Victoria

The Cambridge Folk Festival, held annually at Cherry Hinton Hall since '64, has always presented top-line international acts – Arlo Guthrie, Paul Butterfield, Bo Diddley, Jimmy Page and Roy Harper, Stephane Grappelli, Tom Rush, Joan Baez, Nanci Griffith, everyone. Festival organiser Ken Woolard, then a fireman, booked the acts for the first show from the telephone at Cambridge Fire Station in Parkside – lining up a cast which included

The Clancey Brothers, Hedy West and the then unknown Paul Simon. A Harp Beat rock plaque next to the phone celebrates his thirty-plus years of dedication.

1994 festival noticeboard

(Dave Peabody)

Also born in Cambridge were Olivia Newton John, 26.9.48; guitarist Tim Renwick, 7.8.49 (Quiver). He also went to the High School For Boys – as did sleeve designer Storm Thorgeson (Hipgnosis). Tom Robinson, 1.6.50.

University alumni include Nick Drake, Jonathan King, Tim Curry, Kimberley Rew (Katrina & The Waves), Fred Frith and Chris Cutler (Henry Cow), Pete Atkin and Clive James, Simon Boswell (Advertising), Julie Covington, late Eighties singer/songwriters Andy White and John Wesley Harding, Colin Greenwood (Radiohead).

It was at Cambridge Register Office in May '65 that Marianne Faithfull married university student John Dunbar.

Venues come and go, including the Regal Cinema in St. Andrews Street (where The Beatles played twice in '63); the Dorothy Ballroom at 27 Hobson Street (which in September '63 throbbed to The Rolling Stones, and in February '67 resounded to both Pink Floyd and Jimi Hendrix, but is now a restaurant); the Corn Exchange in Market Square (everyone from Syd Barrett's ill-starred Stars in February '72 to The Cowboy Junkies in March '89 and still going!), the Great Northern Hotel in Station Road (which stopped presenting live gigs after noise complaints and later became the short-lived City Limits), the Burleigh Arms in Maid's Causeway (put on The Darling Buds, The Wedding

Present, etc until ubiquitous complaining neighbours caused closure), the Alma Brewery (sporadic local group showcase), and various University halls.

In January '81, Jerry Dammers and Terry Hall of The Specials were each fined £400 plus costs for using threatening words and behaviour likely to cause a breach of the peace at a concert on Midsummer Common.

Eighties groups include The Dolly Mixtures, The Frigidaires, Cri de Coeur, Subculture, Exploding Hamsters, The Great Divide, Perfect Vision, The Poppyheads, Andy Goes Shopping and The Roaring Boys, who extricated a massive advance from CBS and promptly went phut!

Early Nineties faves included The Fruit Bats, The Bible, Jack The Bear and Dina Carroll, who reached the '91 Top Ten with 'It's Too Late'. In the mid-'Nineties came techno/dub reggae act Blue and the promising Donald Elsey's Big Decision. Freeboy graduated to the national circuit in the late 'Nineties.

Spaceward Studio started in a basement at 20 Victoria Street, where early clients included the Soft Boys, Tubeway Army and Stiff Little Fingers.

Late 'Nineties venues include the Boat Race and the Junction.

ELY

Birthplace of Andrew Eldritch, 15.5.59 (Sisters of Mercy).

Operational base of The Look, who reached the '80 Top Ten with 'I Am The Beat'.

First recording by Spaceward Studios was of Syd Barrett, after leaving Pink Floyd, live at the Corn Exchange in 1973

FOXTON

UK residence of Rick Wills, bass player with Foreigner.

GEDDING

Home of former Stones bassman Bill Wyman

GREAT GRANSDEN

Home of keyboard player Don Airey (Ozzy Osbourne, Colosseum, Rainbow, etc).

GREAT PAXTON
Birthplace of Terry Reid, 13.11.49.

HUNTINGDON
Birthplace of drummer Phil Selway, 23.5.64 (Radiohead).

KIMBOLTON
Slow Dog were early Seventies proteges of Terry Reid who looked set for success but never progressed beyond support gigs.

PETERBOROUGH
Birthplace of actor Paul Nicholas, 3.12.45 (he scored hits in the mid-Seventies, but in '64 was playing piano in Screaming Lord Sutch's Savages!); singer Andy Bell, 25.4.64 (Erasure).

Billy Bragg and the rest of the Riff Raff in a Peterborough Photo-Me booth

Local bands included Ginger (Seventies prog rock); Billy Bragg's Riff Raff, The APF Brigade, The Destructors, The Now and The Name (all punk/new wave); The Pleasureheads (late Eighties Peel faves); Shades of Rhythm (early Nineties); Charlie (late Nineties).

Ultimate Records was a late Seventies indie label operating from 41 Long Lodge Drive, Orton Longueville. Acts included The Now and The Dole.

In '78, punk group The Dole dedicated their single 'New Wave Love' to a local vicar's daughter, who was later accused by their manager of being a disruptive influence and breaking up the band! And to pursue this ecclesiastical vein, the Dean of Peterborough's son played bass in Fatima Mansions.

Local outfit A Sudden Sway made one of the great lost albums of the Eighties: *76 Kids Forever*.

Sometime home of Sixties hitmaker Jimmy Justice, blues guitarist/*Melody Maker* Talent Contest winner Lloyd Watson, Gizz Butt (Prodigy) and drummer Mark Heaney, who joined John Squire's Seahorses in summer '98.

The Rolling Stones played a hot gig at the Corn Exchange in September '63.

The Gaslight was an early Nineties indie gig, as was the Shamrock Club. Opened in '95, the Purple Haze Club was soon attracting top flight indie bands.

Local Inland Revenue man Andrew Rigby masterminded Cola Boy's '91 Top Tenner 'Seven Ways To Love' – but wisely didn't give up his day job.

ROYSTON
Operational base of late Seventies band Terra Cotta.

SOMERSHAM
Sometime home of Stranglers' bassist Jean Jacques Burnel.

STAPLEFORD
Birthplace of Stan Cullimore, 6.4.62 (Housemartins).

Julian Cope outside Spaceward Studios recording *World Shut Your Mouth* *(Mercury Records)*

STRETHAM
Second and last home of Spaceward Studio was the Old School House, where Julian Cope, The Bible, and many more recorded. Closed in '88.

THRIPLOW
Operational base for The Fruit Bats and Jack The Bear.

WISBECH
The Rolling Stones' first ballroom gig was at the Corn Exchange, in July '63.

Local lad Simon Scott went Top 40 with 'Move It Baby' in 64.

The Burlesque, at the Rose & Crown public house, was a progressive rock gig; the Angel Hotel is a late Nineties venue.

WITTERING
One-hit wonders Hedgehoppers Anonymous (Top Five in '65 with 'It's Good News Week') were Air Force personnel based at RAF Wittering.

CHESHIRE

Richard Thompson's early handiwork

ALSAGER

Before he started The Thompson Twins, Tom Bailey studied music at Alsager College.

CHESTER

Birthplace of Russ Abbott, 16.9.47; drummer Andie Rathbone, 8.9.71 (Mansun).

Top Sixties groups were Four Hits and A Miss, and the comedy-orientated Black Abbots – led by Russ.

The Beatles' first visit was to the Riverpark Ballroom in Union Street on 16.8.62. Pete Best had been fired that afternoon and The Big Three's Johnny Hutchinson depped. Their next appearance was at the same venue a week later – John Lennon had got married that afternoon and came on stage midway through Group One's support set to berate them publicly for playing numbers popularised by The Beatles! Two further gigs passed without incident. In May '63, The Beatles made a final appearance in Chester, at the Royalty Theatre in City Road.

It was at the Royalty, over Christmas '64, that Herman played the title role in the pantomime *Dick Whittington*. (Can't see Liam Gallagher doing panto).

Before becoming guitar star of Fairport Convention, Richard Thompson was a stained glass designer. An example of his work can be seen in St. Columbus Church.

Quaintways was a top gig in the Sixties and seventies.

The Disco Zombies were late Seventies new wavers.

Having got together at the Fat Cat public house in summer '95, Grey Lantern changed their name to Mansun and reached the Top Twenty a year later with Stripper Vicar.

CREWE

In August '62, The Beatles played twice at the Majestic Ballroom in the High Street. The Rolling Stones played at the Town Hall in November '63.

The first local group to record, Phil Ryan & The Crescents had their press launch at Crewe Station in November '64.

Home of Eighties indie hopefuls Colours Out Of Time and the aptly named Train Set.

Producer Pete Waterman ploughed several of his many millions into the Waterman Rail Heritage Trust Centre, where historic trains are preserved for public display.

Home of Dr. Phibes & The House of Wax Equations – before they relocated to Liverpool.

The Limelight is a cool late Nineties venue.

ELLESMERE PORT
Birthplace of drummer Nigel Olsson, 5.2.49 (Elton John band); bass player Stove King, 8.1.74 (Mansun).

The Beatles played the Civic Hall in January '63 – their one and only appearance here.

Operational base of Merseybeat group The Four Originals, who formed in October '64 and are still going – with only one personnel change!

FRODSHAM
Gary Barlow (Take That) grew up here and played piano at the local British Legion Club.

JODRELL BANK
Brian May was offered a job here, but declined it as his heart was already set on pursuing a rock career.

LYMM
Home of former Stone Roses frontman Ian Brown.

MACCLESFIELD
Birthplace of blues pioneer John Mayall, 29.11.33.

The Beatles appearance at the El Rio Dance Hall in Queen Victoria Street (January '63) was their only visit to the town.

New Order drummer Stephen Morris was expelled from King's School. He auditioned for Warsaw (soon to become Joy Division) after seeing a 'drummer wanted' ad in a local shop window – placed by local resident Ian Curtis. Joy Division's first EP *An Ideal For Living* was issued on the Anonymous label, operating from 52 Ivy Lane.

With Joy Division poised for international recognition, charismatic singer Ian Curtis took his life at his parents' home in Barton Street in May '80.

Home of Gillian Gilbert, who was in punk group The Inadequates before joining New Order.

Home also of The Macc Lads, who started on a Government Enterprise scheme but got thrown off because their album *Beer Sex Chips And Gravy* wasn't considered a worthy pursuit.

Local early Nineties bands include Marion (ex-Ryles Park Comprehensive students; soon signed to Rough Trade) and Big White Stairs.

MERE
While working for his father's concreting firm, Noel Gallagher helped to screed the floor at Mere Golf Club.

NORTHWICH
Birthplace of singer Tim Burgess, 16.6.68 (Charlatans).

The Memorial Hall in Chester Way was a happening Sixties venue. The Beatles played there six times; The Rolling Stones twice; Pink Floyd once.

Home of The Charlatans. Their manager owned Omega Records and the Dead Dead Good label, based at 2 Witton Walk. They celebrated Sproston Green, their M6 turn-off, on their début album.

Home of Nineties label Ozit Records, run by the indefatigable Chris Hewitt.

Operational base of late Eighties indie band The Electric Crayon Set (with future Charlatans singer Tim Burgess); early Nineties hopefuls The Cherrys, The Thrush Puppies and The State of Kate. In the mid-Nineties came Sussed.

POYNTON
Clive Gregson first laid eyes on Christine Collister at Poynton Folk Club.

RUNCORN
The Elite coffee bar was a popular Sixties hang-out – as was La Scala Ballroom in the High Street, where The Beatles played twice in late '62.

SANDBACH
Clive Gregson was a teacher here until he went back to Manchester to start Any Trouble.

Home of aptly named new wavers The Pits.

WARRINGTON
Birthplace of Fifties star Edna Savage; singer Rick Astley, 6.2.66; disc jockey Chris Evans, 1.4.66.

After he made it, George Harrison bought a house for his parents at nearby Appleton.

Home of Sixties psychedelic band Fairytale; recorded for Decca but got lost along the way.

The Fairytale: a Decca press release

Deep Purple made their UK début at the Red Lion Hotel in July '68.

Sometime home of Merseybeats and Creation bass player Bob Garner, who formed Smiley in the early Seventies.

The Carlton Club was a popular Seventies/Eighties venue.

The Steamboat Band were local mid-Nineties hopefuls.

WIDNES
Birthplace of cartoonist and artist Mal Dean, 1941, who went to Simms Cross Primary School, and later designed great sleeves for Pete Brown albums during the Seventies; Spice Girl Melanie Chisholm, 12.1.76 (Sporty Spice). Also hometown of Jackie Abbott, who became featured vocalist in Beautiful South in January '94.

The Queens Hall in Victoria Road is the town's longest-surviving rock venue: The Beatles (September '62 – the day before they recorded 'Love Me Do'), Gerry & The Pacemakers, and all the other Merseybeat groups played there, as did The Stone Roses, in May 89. The Regal Club and Columbia Hall were also popular haunts.

Alan Bleasdale went to Wade Deacon Grammar School, where he was only good at football until his English teacher fired his enthusiasm.

It was whilst waiting for the train on Widnes station, after a local folk club gig at The Howff in September '65 (for which he was paid £12), that Paul Simon – yearning to be back in London in the arms of his beloved Kathy – began writing 'Homeward Bound'. He had been staying at 123 Coroners Lane, the home of club promoter Jeff Speed. Two weeks later, the headlining act was The New Lost City Ramblers – who got £55!

Home base for The Blackwells, who died their hair blond and featured in the rarely shown *Ferry Across The Mersey*, and Sixties also-rans, The Addicts.

The Supercharge song 'Hole Town' was allegedly about Widnes. Of course, I couldn't possibly comment.

Puressence debut album featured Spike Island (where they formed) on the front cover

Spike Island on the Mersey is the setting for an annual summer festival. The Stone Roses played a seminal gig there in March '90, when dealers wandered through the throng asking "Is everyone sorted for Es and wizz?" – inspiration for the controversial Pulp song. The Pond Dwellers, Out and Zen Baseballbat played there in '98.

Late Eighties hopefuls Wake Up Africa evolved into early Nineties hopefuls 35 Summers. Their rival on the local circuit included Fiasco.

WILMSLOW
Pogue Jem Finer was educated at Wilmslow Grammar School.

CORNWALL

ALTARNUN
Home of Tony Butler of Big Country.

BOSCASTLE
Graham Bond's description of nearby Bossiney Waterfall and Rocky Valley inspired Pete Brown to write 'Tickets To Waterfalls' for the first Jack Bruce album. When Bond died, his friend Pete Bailey scattered his ashes here.

BUDE
The Headland Pavilion has promoted weekly Saturday night dances since the early Sixties. The Ebony Combo played summer-long residencies and in '70 achieved a degree of national notoriety under the name Hard Meat.

DAVIDSTOW
Chilli Willi & The Red Hot Peppers cut their album *Bongos Over Balham* at the Lucky Abattoir Studios and Elvis Costello & The Attractions had their first rehearsals in the village hall.

FALMOUTH
Previously the other Aphex Twin, Luke Vibert became a Nineties techno star under the name of Wagon Christ.

FOWEY
Home of The Mechanics (nothing to do with Mike), who were resident session players at Sawmills Studio, South Down, Sandwell, Golant - set in a tidal creek on the Fowey River and approachable only by boat! New Model Army once stated that they'd never record anywhere else! The Stone Roses, Robert Plant, Wet Wet Wet, Oasis, The Verve, Catatonia, Supergrass and many others have enjoyed its facilities.

Gordon Waller - formerly half of Peter & Gordon, and once Sharon Sheeley's fiance - is said to have opened a gift store here when he tired of show-biz.

HELSTON
Home of Ian Dunlop, member of seminal US folk-rock group The International Submarine Band, whose leader Gram Parsons stayed here shortly before his untimely death in September '73. Dunlop's Eighties group, The Muscletones, also contained local resident Terry Clements - former sax player with Janis Joplin's Kosmic Blues Band.

Living in the area in the Nineties was Queen drummer Roger Taylor.

LAUNCESTON
The White Horse Inn was a regular Friday night gig through the early Eighties... favourites were local group Brainiac 5.

Sawmills Studio at high tide

(Sawmills Studio)

LISKEARD
Home of Charlie & The Wide Boys (who made waves on the London pub rock circuit) and Seventies chanteuse Lesley Duncan.

LOOE
Home of legendary (within a five mile radius of here) late Sixties psychedelic outfit Constable Zippo's Electric Commode Band and late ighties bizarros Dan Gleebits & The Bull Bags Boogie Band.

Carlyon Bay beach complex

(Cornwall Tourist Board)

Also the base of A&R Booksearch, who have the biggest stock of rock books on the planet. You could knock over a greenhouse with their catalogue, it's so big. For current or hard to find books, phone them on 01503 220246.

PARR
Paul Whaley, drummer with San Franciscan power trio Blue Cheer, was working in a bakery here during the early Eighties!

PENZANCE
Elvis Costello & The Attractions made their world début at the Garden in July 77.

Home of Danny's Passions (first Cornish band to record), COB (Clive's Original Band... original copies of whose album now fetch astronomical prices) and idiosyncratic pub rockers Brainiac 5 (whose guitarist, Charles Taylor, later ran the Reckless Records empire).

Another Sunny Day (aka multi-instrumentalist Harvey Williams) reached the '88 indie singles chart with 'I'm In Love With A Girl Who Doesn't Even Know I Exist'. Did he manage to attract her attention, one wonders.

Also home town of techno guru The Aphex Twin (aka Richard James).

REDRUTH
The Quasar Coffee Bar was the cool meeting place and the Room At The Top was a folk club presenting the likes of Ralph McTell and Stefan Grossman.

Smile, the trio which burgeoned into Queen, played at the Flamingo Ballroom — where Pink Floyd had appeared in December '67.

ST. AUSTELL
The Cornwall Colisseum at Carlyon Bay is the largest venue in the south west ... used for big national tours. The Smiths played there in October '86.

ST. GERMANS
Siouxsie & The Banshees and The Cure were among headliners at the Elephant Fayre – annual three day mixed media gatherings held on Lord Eliot's estate in the early Eighties.

ST. IVES
Birthplace of drummer Mick Fleetwood, 24.6.44 (Fleetwood Mac).

Donovan, John Renbourn and Ralph McTell were among the early beatnik/ folkie community spending summers here in the early Sixties.

TRURO
From whence came guitarist Keith Lucas, leader of London punk group 999.

Roger Taylor (Queen) was a pupil at Bosvigo School and later the Cathedral School. In March '65, he debuted with Johnny Quale & The Reaction at Truro City Hall – the same venue which Queen chose for their world début on 27.6.70, when Freddie Bulsara adopted the name Freddie Mercury for the first time.

Home of The Famous Jug Band.

WADEBRIDGE
Home of psychedelic group Onyx, who recorded for Pye, CBS and Parlophone but made only local impact.

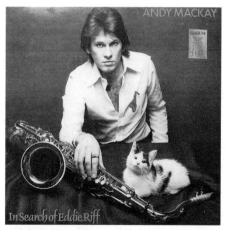

Andy Mackay with cat on sax

Also from Cornwall are guitarist Jon Mark (Mark Almond and John Mayall's Bluesbreakers) and Debbie from My Bloody Valentine... not to mention Roxy Music sax player Andy Mackay, who was born here on 23.7.46.

CUMBRIA

BARROW-IN-FURNESS
Birthplace of bass player Glenn Cornick, 24.4.47 (Jethro Tull).
   Operational base of mid-Sixties group Chapter Five, who recorded for CBS, and Nineties indie band Red Hour.
   Forum 28 is the happening late Nineties venue.

BRAMPTON
Birthplace of Jez Willis, 14.8.63 (Utah Saints).

CARLISLE
Birthplace of singer Mike Harrison, 30.9.42, and bass player Greg Ridley, 23.10.43 (Spooky Tooth). Originally called The VIPs, they moved to London as the first band signed to the Island label. They subsequently changed their name to Art, then Spooky Tooth. When they broke up, Harrison adopted another Carlisle bunch, Junkyard Angel, as his backing group.
   After playing at the ABC Cinema in February '63, The Beatles sought to unwind by attending a dance at the Crown and Mitre Hotel – but were refused admittance for sartorial irregularities (leather jackets). One can only imagine John Lennon's response to the jobsworth who barred their entrance. Jimi Hendrix played the ABC in April '67.

The Cranberries shot 'The Room' on their third album in Grizedale Forest. The band were superimposed later in the warmth of a London studio

Pink Floyd played at the Cosmopolitan Ballroom in July '67. Black Axe were hot in the late Seventies; early Nineties bands included Atlantica.
Home of Beatles biographer Hunter Davies.

EGREMONT
Home of It Bites, who were all schoolfriends. They moved down to London in '86 to hit the Top Ten with 'Calling All The Heroes'. Incidentally, William Wordsworth lived around here too.

KENDAL
Viv Stanshall (RIP) played his last ever gig at the Malt Room in December '93.

PENRITH
Home of vicar's son Timmy Mallett, who (together with Bombalurina) topped the '90 charts with the unspeakable 'Itsy Bitsy Teeny Weeny Yellow Polka Dot Bikini'.

ULLSWATER
Location for Spandau Ballet's 'Musclebound' video.

ULVERSTON
Birthplace of Maude Haley – Bill's mother.

WIGTON
Author and broadcaster Melvyn Bragg played tea-chest bass in Wigton Grammar School's skiffle group.

WORKINGTON
Sugarblast were a Nineties indie band who moved to London and cut singles; Sensitized stuck around and concentrated on the north-west.

DERBYSHIRE

BAKEWELL
Birthplace of Long John Baldry, 12.1.41.

BUXTON
Birthplace of disc jockey Dave Lee Travis, 25.5.45, who reached the '76 Top Five as half of Laurie Lingo & The Dipsticks; Lloyd Cole, 31.1.61 (Commotions).

Scene of the Buxton Rock Festival of July 73, with Chuck Berry, The Sensational Alex Harvey Band and Medicine Head; and of July 74, with The Faces, Mott The Hoople, Man, Lindisfarne and Captain Beefheart. It was Ian Hunter's last UK-mainland gig with Mott.

Echo & The Bunnymen filmed their 'Crocodiles' video at the Pavilion Gardens in St. John's Road – where The Beatles had appeared in April '63 and Wayne Fontana & The Mindbenders parted company in October '65.

CHADDESDEN
After being ejected from the Army as unfit for further service, Terry Dene made an umcomfortable comeback at the Majestic in April '59.

CHESTERFIELD
Birthplace of Tom Bailey, 18.1.54. He left Chesterfield Grammar to attend music college but returned to start The Thompson Twins in late '77. Also the birthplace of drummer Phil 'Filthy Animal' Taylor, 21.9.54 (Motorhead); singer Mark Shaw, 10.6.61 (Then Jerico).

The Victoria Hall (formerly the Regal cinema) was the town's hottest venue in the Sixties, when Cream, The Nice, King Crimson, Mott The Hoople (January '70), etc played there. Another venue was the ABC Cinema – visited by the Jimi Hendrix/Walker Brothers/Cat Stevens package show in April '67.

The Bunnymen recorded and filmed in Buxton

The Fusion Club in Holywell Street was the cool late Seventies hangout; the Queens Park Hotel in Park Road was a late Eighties venue.

Dagaband were early Eighties prog-rockers.

CROMFORD
The sleeve for the Oasis single 'Some Might Say' – their first number one, in May '95 – was shot at Cromford Railway Station.

DERBY
Birthplace of Kevin Coyne, 27.1.44 (who later lived at Normanton); bass player John Wetton, 12.7.49 (King

Crimson/Asia); Peter Hammill (Van der Graaf Generator); Roy Hollingworth (pioneering *Melody Maker* writer).

Charge were a popular early Seventies college band, two of whom joined Arthur Brown's Kingdom Come.

The Sex Pistols were due to play at the King's Hall, but apprehensive local officials insisted on an audition before allowing the gig to proceed. Understandably, the Pistols told them "Don't be silly" and the date was nixed. During this episode, the group was holed up at the Crest Hotel in Littleover.

Legendary line-up for a very wet festival in 1973

Operational base for thrash punks The Enemy – and second-wave punks Anti Pasti, whose 'Six Guns' reached number one on the indie chart.

Nineties group Beyond flickered onto the national chart; grunge trio Bivouac were picked to click – as were The Newcranes, Cable and The Beekeepers.

Local act White Town (actually one guy, Jyoti Mishra) reached number one in '97, with 'Your Woman' – recorded in his home studio. Though born in Rourkela, India, in July '66, he moved to UK as a child and first played in local group Daryl & The Chaperones.

The Wherehouse was a popular Nineties gig.

Home of Imaani – Britain's Eurovision song contest entrant in May 98.

DRONFIELD
Birthplace of Karen Young, 13.4.46, who had a '69 Top Tenner with 'Nobody's Child'.

GLOSSOP
Operational base of Eighties indie band The Bodines, who looked set to make it on Creation but lost momentum.

HAYFIELD
Home of Terry Hall during his Colour Field days.

MATLOCK
Home of Gomez singer and slide guitarist Ben Ottewell.

NEW MILLS
Operational base of early Eighties punks Blitz, who had a Top Three indie album in *Voice Of A Generation*.

RIPLEY
Harry Webb and his group, The Drifters, played their first provincial gig at the Regal Ballroom – operated by Harry Greatorix, who suggested (by all accounts, insisted on) a hipper name. Thus, on 3.5.58, for the first time, they were billed as Cliff Richard & The Drifters.

SWADLINCOTE
Sid Vicious' mother Ann Beverley moved here to get away from it all – but took her life in September '96.

DEVON

ASHBURTON

Once the singer in Reading group Kerry Rapid & His Blue Stars, Alan Hope was later the landlord of the Golden Lion pub in Ashburton. Standing as Monster Raving Loony candidate for the local council, he found himself elected... the party's greatest (possibly only) political triumph! In May '98, the ebullient Hope built on his success by becoming the Mayor. "We don't have a manifesto," he says. "Dog mess is our big issue."

BARNSTAPLE

Local residents include Dave Brock (Hawkwind), Gilli Smyth (Gong) and Harvey Bainbridge (Sonic Assassins).

Most famous band was Spirit Of John Morgan – three turn of the Seventies blues/rock/humour albums.

Yes covered in tomato on Dartmoor

BIDEFORD

Birthplace of Marcus Lillington, 28.2.67 (Breathe).

BRIXHAM

Some locals were not amused when Vic Reeves came to town in December '91 to film the video for his idiosyncratic version of 'Abide With Me'.

DARTINGTON

Before uniting as Marshall Hain – Top Three with 'Dancing In The City' in '78 – Julian Marshall and Kit Hain were students at Dartington Hall College.

DARTMOOR

The sleeve of the Yes album *Tormato* was shot at Yes Tor.

EXETER

Birthplace of singer Tony Burrows, 14.4.42 (Edison Lighthouse). Sometime home of Hawkwind dancer Stacia.

The Beatles played the ABC Cinema in London Inn Square three times in '63/'64.

Principal Edwards Magic Theatre (signed to John Peel's Dandelion label) formed at the University – where Radiohead singer Thom Yorke was a student many years later.

Steve Upton and Martin Turner first met in Dirty Dot's Cafe. There they put together The Empty Vessels, soon to evolve into Wishbone Ash.

In March '75, Ian Hunter played his first post-Mott solo gig at the University in Stocker Road.

Nick Halliwell & The Gift and The Impossible Dreamers (also University students) both cut singles in the Eighties; Flicker Noise were early Nineties dance hopefuls.

GENESIS
WED 19th MAR
Great Hall
8pm

exeter uni. guild of students presents

Genesis play Exeter on their scaled down Duke Tour

In the mid-Nineties came The Frantic Spiders, Psychocandy and Wordbug.

Local Eighties gigs were Routes at 13 Okehampton Street and Tiffanys on the Quay.

EXMOUTH

Birthplace of Pearl Carr, 2.11.23, who with husband Teddy Johnson carried our '59 Eurovision hopes with 'Sing Little Birdie', and disc jockey Ed Stewart, 23.4.41.

Home of excellent *NME* scribe David Quantick.

The Lazy House were Nineties hopefuls.

HOLSWORTHY

The Memorial Hall was a notable Sixties gig – presenting the likes of Them and Jeff Beck's Tridents.

The Old Vicarage in nearby Pyworthy was the home of Hidden Drive Recording Studios, run by former Van Der Graaf Generator drummer Guy Evans.

KINGSBRIDGE

Slade guitarist Dave Hill was born at Fleet Castle, 4.4.46. He moved to the Midlands as a child.

OKEHAMPTON

T V Smith and Gaye Advert moved to London to ride the '77 boom with their punk band The Adverts.

Sometime home of the idiosyncratic Avant Gardener (recorded for Appaloosa and Virgin).

PAIGNTON

In the late Seventies, former rock'n'roller Rory Blackwell was entertainments manager at the Devon Coast Country Club.

PLYMOUTH

When Bill Haley came to town in February '57, the local paper's review was headlined "Moral Victory for Rock'n'Rollers; Good Behaviour is Keynote of City's Vociferous Reception". Similar praise greeted The Beatles in November '63.

Betterdays were a mid-Sixties R&B band whose single became a hot collectors' item – prompting a '93 reunion; Infa Riot were second wave punks.

Van-dike Organisation
Exmouth Hall Exmouth Road
Plymouth Telephone 51326-7
Entertainment Promotion
Recording Design Construction
Photography Advertising

our ref   your ref

FAMILY   24-10-69

Received from the Van Dike the sum of £294 being 70% of gross (£421-7-6)

Family earn £294 in 1969 when Plymouth club owner Greg Van-Dike moves to Exmouth

Opening in summer '68, the Van Dike Club in Albert Road, Devonport (later the Exmouth Social Club) was an important progressive rock venue, presenting everyone from Mott The Hoople (October '69 and several times more) to Derek & The Dominoes (June '70) to Vinegar Joe (with Robert Palmer and Elkie Brooks), who made their début here.

In November '71, Fairport Convention were onstage when 170 police from all over the south west swooped for a drugs raid. Their haul was pitiful: despite a police woman stating that she had seen punters smoking a joint 'nine inches long and one and a half inches wide' (much laughter in court), only one person was convicted and fined for cannabis possession. Such was police paranoia about pot smoking. Also operated by Peter

Vandike, Woods was a primo punk venue. The Pistols played one of their Spots (Sex Pistols On Tour Secretly) gigs here.

Emerson Lake & Palmer made their world début at the Guildhall in August '70.

The Cooperage at the Minerva Tavern gained a reputation as a Nineties venue.

Dub reggae duo Alpha & Omega released albums on their own label.

Persecution Complex emerged in the mid-Nineties as the city's first all-girl band.

SIDMOUTH
Before he moved to Australia, Hank Marvin was resident at Wiscombe Manor near Sidmouth.

TAVISTOCK
Birthplace of bass player Pete Quaife, 27.12.43 (Kinks).

The church at Brentor was pictured on the sleeve of the first McGuinness Flint album.

Local new wavers Amebix made mild national ripples.

TIVERTON
Contrary to what you may have read elsewhere, Paul Simon was not inspired to compose 'Bridge Over Troubled Water' while sitting on the banks of the River Exe. (See the introduction.)

TORQUAY
Birthplace of comedian Peter Cook, 17.11.37 (compere of bizarre TV rock show *Revolver*); bassplayer Martin Turner, 1.10.47 (Wishbone Ash); singer John Matthews, 23.9.67 (The High).

Sometime home of Fifties thrush Ruby Murray, who held the record for most UK top tenners... until Madonna came along 25 years later. Clodagh Rodgers, whose hit run started with 'Come Back And Shake Me' in March '69, later ran a local hotel.

Local groups include The Rustiks (managed by Brian Epstein) and Peter & The Wolves (four late Sixties MGM singles).

Donovan waited table and washed up at the Phyllis Court Hotel in summer '64.

Most successful late Eighties indie band were The Morrisons.

Ultra rare UPC single from Torquay's Peter & The Wolves

TORRINGTON
Operational base of Nineties guitar band The Naked I.

TOTNES
Birthplace of Jimmy Cauty, once in Zodiac Mindwarp's Love Reaction and Brilliant; later half of The Timelords, The Justified Ancients of Mu Mu and KLF.

Late Seventies new wavers Furious Pig released a couple of singles.

DORSET

BEAMINSTER

Origin of electro duo Spooky who moved to London in search of more fertile territory.

BOURNEMOUTH

Birthplace of John Hawken, 9.5.40 (Nashville Teens, Renaissance); Peter Bellamy, 8.9.44 (Young Tradition); Alex James, 21.11.68 (Blur).

Many illustrious stars have appeared here in pantomime – including Adam Faith, who played Aladdin (whilst his Roulettes played Chinese policemen) at the Pavilion in December '62.

The Roulettes: A life beyond panto...

The Beatles played a six night stint at the Gaumont in August '63 and a one-nighter at the Winter Gardens in November '63.

Forgotten (by most people) local groups include Albatross, Dave Anthony's Moods, The Capitta All Stars, The Freebooters, The Future Classics, The G Men, King Harry, Gringo, The Track Marks, Once Bitten, Raw Deal,

Tetrad and Jack-Knife. The Dowlands had a minor hit with The Beatles' song 'All My Loving', but none of The Nite People's eight singles made any impact. The Fuzz recorded for Larry Page's Page One label – after he had changed their name to The Trend. Two thirds of cabaret-jazz trio The Peddlers were from Bournemouth; they scored a Top Twenty hit with 'Birth' in '69. Elias Hulk were a short-lived group whose album is now worth big dosh on the collectors' market.

The first local musician to make a national impression was John Rostill, who moved to London to join The Shadows in October '63.

The same month, Zoot Money moved up to join Alexis Korner's Blues Inc. A well known window cleaner/prankster/R&B fanatic, Zoot had played in numerous local outfits, including The Jan Ralfini Band, The Sands Combo, The Don Robb Band and his own jazz/blues groups. In London he formed The Big Roll Band – one of the era's more spectacular R&B outfits – which through drug metamorphosis became Dantalian's Chariot. Now a musician/actor, he can often be spied in commercials.

Zoot's principal crony in Bournemouth (and London) was Andy Somers, later to become famous as Andy Summers, guitarist in The Police.

Chirpy pirate disc jockey Tony Blackburn – later the first DJ to play a record on Radio One – was a local laddie, best remembered for his early Sixties group Tony Blackburn & The Sabres. Lead guitarist in that ensemble was Al Stewart, soon to make it big on the London folk circuit.

Stewart was one of many locals who visited Strike Music Shop to take guitar lessons from the area's most gifted musician, Robert Fripp, who played in The Ravens (with Gordon Haskell, later vocalist in King Crimson), The League

John Wetton (R) once in "Mogul Thrash" before stardom beckoned

Of Gentlemen (a name he resurrected briefly in the Seventies), and then joined Pete and Mike Giles in Giles Giles and Fripp.

The Giles brothers had served their apprenticeship with the aforementioned Dowlands and Trend Setters Ltd. Their alliance with Fripp began with a month of rehearsal at the Beacon Hotel.

All three moved to London, and in '69 became King Crimson – with the addition of another pal from Bournemouth, Greg Lake. He'd been in local groups like Shame and Shylimbs. After less than two years in King Crimson, he formed one of the Seventies most successful prog-rock supergroups, Emerson Lake & Palmer.

Other Bournemouth luminaries include drummer Lee Kerslake (a stalwart of Uriah heep), John Hawken (Nashville Teens pianist), Richard Palmer James (Supertramp vocalist for a while), bass player John Wetton (graduate of Family, Roxy Music, Asia and various other bands) and Anita Harris (educated at the Convent Of The Cross).

Promoter Mel Bush works from an office in Wolverton Road.

In June '65, David Bowie tried out his new group Davy Jones & The Lower Third at the Pavilion in Westover Road.

The Fall's song 'Bournemouth Runner' was written after they'd stayed in a hotel near the Winter Gardens in Exeter Road. A guy in the next room died while they were there.

Local band Seven seemed poised for stardom, but it wasn't to be; The Cherry Blades and Flood were trying in the early Nineties. They were followed by The Crazy Gods Of Endless Noise, Robert Fripp proteges Camilla's Little Secret, and singer-songwriter Denzil Thomas.

Late Nineties clubbers headed for the Opera House at 570 Christchurch Road.

CORSCOMBE
Childhood home of Polly (PJ) Harvey.

LULWORTH COVE
The video for Ten Pole Tudor's last minor hit, 'Throwing My Baby Out With The Bathwater', was filmed here.

POOLE
In August '65, John Lennon purchased a bungalow in Panorama Road, Sandbanks, for his Aunt Mimi.

New wave band The Tours were signed to Virgin, but dissolved almost immediately. Leader Richard Mazda then formed The Cosmetics, who played Portugal, Japan and various other places with Tom Robinson. Mazda became hot-shot producer of not only Tom but Wall Of Voodoo, Alternative TV, The Fall, and more.

In '93, 18-year-old former Poole Grammar pupil Richard Oakes beat 400 applicants to become guitarist with Suede.

SHAFTESBURY
Mark Price from All About Eve was the short-trousered kid pushing his bike up the cobbled hill (just behind the High Street) in the old Hovis television ad.

Bournemouth's Zoot Money does a double-take

SWANAGE
Big Country shot the video for 'In A Big Country' on Swanage Beach.

WEYMOUTH
In summer '98, local group Electrasy reached the Top Twenty with 'Morning Afterglow'.

WIMBOURNE
Birthplace of Robert Fripp, gentleman and guitarist. Famed for adding intricate decoration to many an album, notably those of King Crimson, a group he has led (on and off) for thirty years. He still resides in the area, in a noble Edwin Lutyens house which he shares with his wife, Toyah Wilcox.

The Martian Schoolgirls were a local punk group.

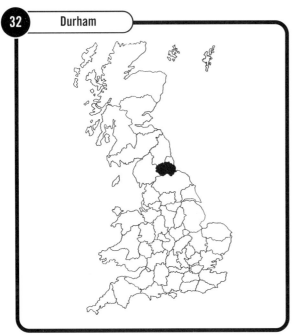

DURHAM

BISHOP AUCKLAND
Home of the splendidly named Flatcap & Whippet label.

Local resident Chris Oddy was bass player in The Humblebums – fronted by Billy Connolly and Gerry Rafferty.

CHESTER LE STREET
Shadows guitarist Bruce Welch lived at 15 Broadwood View and attended Red Rose School.

CONSETT
Longtime rock'n'roll revivalist Freddie Fingers Lee grew up here, having been born in Chopwell on 24.11.37. Also the birthplace of Sixties thrush Susan Maughan, 1.7.42.

A bunch of enterprising locals formed the Consett Music Project, getting grants to build a studio and rehearsal rooms. They taught schoolchildren recording and engineering techniques and other skills appropriate to the post-steelworks era, and they promoted local bands and worthies – like miner/poet/pit-song specialist Jack Purdon.

Hottest late Eighties band was Aiming At America.

The Works and the Stanley Fordham Arms were good Eighties venues... but usually only promoted on giro day.

COXHOE
Sometime home of respected jazz-rock guitarist Martin Holder.

CROOK
Hometown of Bluetones drummer Ed Chesters – previously with Soho.

DARLINGTON
Penetration singer Pauline Murray went to Darlington Art College.

Tom Jones used to cavort at the La Bamba Club at 27 Grange Road – now extinct.

In February '67, The Jimi Hendrix Experience played at the Imperial Hotel.

Sometime home of Vic Reeves, who fronted The Wonder Stuff on the '91 chart topper 'Dizzy'.

Major Accident were early Eighties punks; Sofa Head and Strawberry Story were both early Nineties hopefuls/Peel faves. In the mid-Nineties came Subjugation.

The Imperial Hotel, Darlington 1972

(The Northern Echo)

DURHAM

Birthplace of guitarist Peanut Langford 10.4.43 (Barron Knights); singer Chad Stuart, 10.12.43 (half of Chad & Jeremy); drummer Alan White, 14.6.49 (Plastic Ono Band, Yes); keyboard player Alan Clark, 5.3.52 (Dire Straits); guitarist/singer Paddy McAloon, 7.6.57 (Prefab Sprout); singer Pauline Murray, 8.3.58 (Penetration – who used to rehearse in St. Margarets Church Hall); bassist Martin McAloon, 4.1.62, and guitarist/singer Wendy Smith, 31.5.63 (both Prefab Sprout).

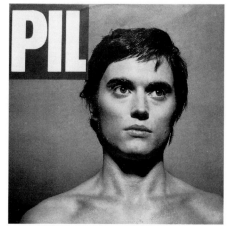

Durham's Martyn Atkins while in PIL

Birthplace also of drummer Martyn Atkins, who lived on the Newton Hall housing estate and went to Wearside School. He played in local Seventies progressive group Mynd until he auditioned for Johnny Rotten and got the job in PIL. Also had his own band, Brian Brain.

Jake Thackray gained an honours degree at Durham University. Equally successful was later student Rod Clements of Lindisfarne.

Prefab Sprout used to play to an average audience of eight at the Brewers Arms (now a nightclub called Brodies) in Gilesgate. "It was as if a spacecraft came through the roof, took them away, and beamed them into stardom," says a local.

Barking Billy & The Rhythm Dogs are R&B executants; The Ray Stubbs All Stars (ditto); Swimmer Leon were tipped as next big local band; Gerbils In Red Wine had the best name!

Local venues have included the Angel (who boast "the loudest juke box in the North East"), the Queens Head, and Fowlers Yard Community Centre.

FATFIELD

Birthplace of Animals organist Alan Price, 19.4.42.

FERRYHILL

Pauline Murray was raised in this wee village, just south of Spennymoor. It was here in '77 that she formed the early punk group Penetration, whose record 'Silent Community' aroused local ire.

HARTLEPOOL

Birthplace of bass player Mod Rogan, 3.2.44 (Roulettes); guitarist Jeremy Spencer, 4.7.48 (Fleetwood Mac).

Guitarist Gordon Smith recorded a couple of albums for Blue Horizon before joining Kevin Coyne's band.

Operational base of early Eighties metal band White Spirit, whose guitarist Janick Gers later joined Whitesnake and Iron Maiden.

Chartbusting techno act Sneaker Pimps originated here – before moving to London, adding Brum vocalist Kellee Dayton, and reaching the '96 Top Twenty with '6 Underground'.

LANGLEY PARK

Former Railway Street resident Paul Ellis moved to London to play keyboards for Hot Chocolate, Billy Ocean and Pepsi & Shirlie.

Despite their album title, Prefab Sprout don't come from here... but Paddy McAloon used to get his hair cut at the barber's shop in Front Street!

A fast-rising/quickly disappearing band that did come from here were called Somebody Famous.

PITY ME

There has to be a bizarre story behind the name of this village, where Terry Gavagan ran the 24-track Guardian Studio... as used by John Miles, among others. The booth was said to be haunted by a little girl, who many claim to have heard!

SEAHAM

Three schoolfriends formed the Reptile House, The Kings of Cotton, and finally The Kane Gang, who made the charts in '84.

STOCKTON-ON-TEES

A skyline of tall chimneys belching smoke into the overcast sky was undoubtedly the inspiration for 'Stars Fell On Stockton', the B-side of The Shadows' '62 chart topper 'Wonderful Land' (which it became after the Clean Air Act).

The Hippodrome presented star-studded pantomimes since the year dot. Marty Wilde was memorable in *Babes In The Wood*; Cliff Richard remembers how lonely the beach was (well it was January!).

Buddy Holly & The Crickets played the Globe Cinema in the High Street in March '58; The Beatles played there in November '63 and again in October '64.

Birthplace of singer/songwriter Lesley Duncan.

In October '68, The Kinks – whose agent thought their future lay in cabaret – played a week at the Club Fiesta at 395 Norton Road.

It was at Tito's in Brunswick Street that a thoroughly demoralised Elton John played his last gigs with Bluesology, backing Long John Baldry for a week over New Year '68 as revellers ate and drank. They played a set here, then rushed to

Early Reg Dwight composition and performance, pre-Sir Elton John, that is

South Shields to play a set there –every night for seven nights.

Sometime home of techno/DJ/remixer CJ Bolland, who also records under the name of Ravesignals.

WITTON GILBERT

This is where Prefab Sprout actually hail from. They used to run the local garage and filling station while planning their international breakout. Petrol purchasers were invited inside to buy second hand albums.

Lesley Duncan single much sought after due to Kate Bush contribution!

ESSEX

(including boroughs in Greater London area)

BARKING

Birthplace of Brian Poole, 2.11.41; guitarist Ricky West, 7.5.43 (Tremeloes); Billy Bragg, 20.12.57; guitarist Dave Evans, better known as The Edge, 8.8.61 (U2... born at Barking Maternity Hospital); John Hendy, 26.3.71 (East 17); Shellie Poole, 20.3.72 (Alisha's Attic).

Brian Poole & The Tremeloes were the town's hottest act in the Sixties (replacing The King Brothers who ruled in the Fifties). Brian Poole and Alan Blakely (whose daughter Claudie is a rising actress) went to Park Secondary Modern. Poole's daughters, Shellie and Karen, continued the family tradition by forming Alisha's Attic and starting a chart run with 'I Am I Feel' in August '96.

Other Sixties groups were Freedom (formed by two ex-Procols), The Sean Buckley Set, and Johnny Milton & The Condors, who changed their name to The Symbols for a couple of hits. In the early Eighties came Wasted Youth.

Billy Bragg (who pre-fame lived at 146 Park Avenue), acclaimed far and wide as the Bard of Barking, was a pupil at the Abbey School — as were members of politico band McCarthy, noted for such indie hits as 'Frans Hals' and 'Should The Bible Be Banned?'

BASILDON

Birthplace of Vince Clarke, 3.7.60, Andy Fletcher, 8.7.60, and Martin Gore, 23.7.61 — all three of whom (together with Chigwell born Dave Gahan) formed synth-pop group Depeche Mode. They had become friends at St. Nicholas School. Also the birthplace of Scott Robinson, 22.11.79 (5ive).

Clarke soon split to start Yazoo with Alison Moyet, another Basildon native (formerly fronting Southend band The Screaming Abdabs).

Throughout '63, The Dave Clark 5 were resident at the Locarno.

Local lad Perry Balmain became a roadie for Cure and later joined the band on keyboards.

The Paramounts outside an approximation of Southend's "Shades Club"

BILLERICAY

Born here in 1942, Ian Dury drew on local knowledge to pillory typical suburban swag-artist Billericay Dickie — self-satisfied all mouth-and-trousers brickie. Among his conquests were Janet from the Isle of Thanet and a nice bit of posh from Burnham on Crouch... but hopefully not Alison Moyet, born here on 18.6.61.

Sometime home of Culture Club star Roy Hay.

BRAINTREE

Liam Howlett was a DJ with local hip hop band Cut To Kill before forming The Prodigy and bursting into the '91 Top Three with Charly.

The Barn was a pioneering acid house club during the late Eighties, when Mr C was resident DJ. Liam Howlett attended his first rave there.

Mantaray are late Nineties nouveau mod Britpoppers.

BRENTWOOD

Birthplace of singer Sonja Kristina, 14.4.49 (Curved Air), who attended the Ursuline Convent.

Paul Simon made his UK début at the Railway Inn folk club in April 64. There he met Kathy, soon to become his girlfriend and the inspiration behind such songs as 'Homeward Bound' and 'America'.

Honey Bane completed her formal education at the St. Charles Youth Treatment Centre.

CANVEY

The rock'n'roll era opened with a 21-year-old greengrocer's assistant from Canvey winning the national Best Dressed Teddy Boy contest in August '54.

The Fix, Pigboy Charlie, Southside Jug Band, The Flowerpots and The Roamers distilled into Dr Feelgood in 72, and they put Canvey firmly on the rock'n'roll map. The Admiral Jellicoe was their local hostelry. Manic guitarist Wilko Johnson split to form his own group, The Solid Senders; heroic singer Lee Brilleaux died from cancer in April '94. In November '93, the group opened their own pub, the Dr Feelgood Music Bar at 21 Knightswick Road. Their label, Grand, operates from 107a High Street.

Dr Feelgood down by the jetty ...

In the Sixties, Wilko (then with The Heap) was the first man on the island with shoulder length hair; ten years later, he was the first with short back and sides! The Goldmine was a popular new wave/new romantics haunt.

CHELMSFORD

The Corn Exchange was the hottest Sixties venue. Jimi Hendrix played there in February '67; Pink Floyd in September '67.

... and Sade on the beach

Home of Tracie Young, and James Vane, who worked as a hairdresser at Silhouette du Barry. Lee Brilleaux once worked here as a solicitors' clerk; Hazel Dean as a secretary.

The Accidents were a late Seventies mod revival band.

Barry Martin studied Medical Laboratory Science at the College — which has no doubt been very useful in his career as guitarist and singer with Britain's most popular and hardworking pub-rock band The Hamsters.

The Prodigy's Keith Flint grew up here; glam-rock queen Suzi Quatro lives in the hinterlands.

Sunscreem were the second rave act to break out of Essex, with Pressure in February '92.

Mid-Nineties band Elemental Child were obviously Bolan fans — taking their name from a T. Rex track.

CHADWELL HEATH

Birthplace of Karen Poole, 8.1.71 (Alisha's Attic).

CHIGWELL

Birthplace of singer Dave Gahan, 9.5.62 (Depeche Mode).

Joe Brown lived in Chigwell Village during the Seventies.

CLACTON

Cliff Richard & The Drifters played a four week residency at Butlin's Holiday Camp in August '58. Whilst there, his first single 'Move It' began to climb the national chart. Dave Dee Dozy Beaky Mick & Tich had a residency six years later — just prior to getting their record deal. In the mid-Seventies, Kevin Rowland (Dexy's) had a summer job there... washing up!

Operational base for Sixties beat groups Peter Jay & The Jaywalkers (featuring vocalist Terry Reid) and Dave Curtiss & The Tremors.

Charles Blackwell, who arranged the orchestration on hits by John Leyton and other Joe Meek acts, later opened a guest house on the sea front.

Most famous Eighties resident was Sade, who grew up there – having been born in Nigeria. Also home for Blockhead sax man Davey Payne.

Local resident David Lea issued techno singles under such pseudonyms as Joey Negro and Raven Maize.

COLCHESTER

Birthplace of drummer John 'Twink' Alder, 29.11.44 (Pretty Things, Tomorrow); Dave Rowntree, 8.5.64 (Blur); Darren Day, July 58 (Cliff Richard soundalike who starred in stage show *Summer Holiday* and reached the '96 Top Twenty with 'Summer Holiday Medley').

Music hall comedian (and friend of The Beatles) Arthur Askey made his stage début at the Electric Theatre in March 1924.

Twink's first group, the Colchester based Fairies were hot on the mid-Sixties London R&B scene.

The sleeve photo on Fairport Convention's *What We Did On Our Holidays* was taken in their dressing room during a gig at Essex University – where R.E.M. played in November '84.

Before launching Cockney Rebel, Steve Harley worked on the local newspaper and lived over a bakery on Sheregate Steps. Another journalist was founder member of RCA group The Cleaners From Venus, Giles Smith (born here in '62), who went on to write for *Mojo*, *Q* and *The Independent*, among others.

A Colchester sitting room with modern English parents

The most famous Colchester composition was probably 'Twinkle Twinkle Little Star', written by Jane and Ann Taylor of 11 West Stockwell Street in 1806.

The most famous Colchester group is Blur (formerly known as Seymour), who broke out with '91 top tenner 'There's No Other Way'. Guitarist Graham Coxon went to Stanway Comprehensive and the Art College. Both he and drummer Dave Rowntree had played in local group Idle Vice.

Sometime home of Peter Astor, leader of The Weather Prophets – also of Edwin Pouncey, who led Seventies punk group The Art Attax and did music-press journalism and

Edwin Pouncey sleeve for his band, 1977

cartoons under the name of Savage Pencil. Not to mention Rebecca Wellerd, the Fire Water Queen.

Looking to follow Blur in the mid-Nineties were Imperial, Junk, and Hirameka Hi-Fi.

Venues include the Twist and the Arts Centre.

An essential guide to growing up with music in Essex

Home of hard-working Seventies heavies Alma Mater, and Eighties hopefuls Modern English, who recorded for 4AD and Sire. More commercially successful was Nik Kershaw, who paid his dues/developed his flight plan while playing with local group Fusion in the pubs around Colchester. In '82, punk band Special Duties had a Top Ten indie single in 'Bullshit Crass'.

DAGENHAM

Birthplace of bass player Alan Howard, 17.10.41, and drummer Dave Munden, 2.12.43 (both of The Tremeloes); Keith West, 6.12.43 (Teenage Opera); Sandie Shaw, 26.2.47; Mike Nolan, 17.12.54 (Bucks Fizz).

Vera Lynn could hardly be described as a rock act, but she did make her public singing début at a Dagenham working man's club.

Pianist/comedian/actor Dudley Moore grew up in Monmouth Road, Becontree.

Following his chart career, Heinz worked at the Ford factory.

Tony Rivers & The Castaways were the hot local break-outs in the Sixties. They became Harmony Grass, who mutated into Capability Brown.

Some Bizzare svengali Stevo attended Eastbury Comprehensive.

The Roundhouse in Lodge Avenue was a good venue at the turn of the Seventies, when the likes of Led Zeppelin (April '69), Bowie, Jethro Tull and Mott The Hoople (October '70) would play.

The Stranglers immortalised Dagenham Dave on their album *No More Heroes*.

The Ejected were early Eighties punks; The Absolute Pictures were early Nineties hopefuls.

A young Charles Shaar Murray from Harlow caught writing for *Schoolkids' Oz* in 1970

EAST MERSEA
Yes made their début well away from the public glare at East Mersea Youth Club in '68.

EPPING
Birthplace of singer David Byron, 29.1.47 (Uriah Heep); actor/singer Nick Kamen, 15.4.62.

'The Battle Of Epping Forest' was discussed by Genesis on the album *Selling England By The Pound*.

In '86, following the modification of UK tax laws, Rod Stewart ended his Los Angelean exile and bought an Elizabethan mansion in Epping Forest.

Greg Ridley lived in North Weald during his Humble Pie days.

Operational base of hippie band Gnidrolog, Seventies/Eighties revolutionaries Crass, and Eighties punks Anti-Establishment.

Groovesville at the Wake Arms on the A10 was a popular Seventies venue.

FRINTON
Birthplace of singer/actor John Leyton 17.2.39. One of producer Joe Meek's hottest acts, he topped '61 charts with 'Johnny Remember Me'.

Between March '64, when Radio Caroline came on the air, and August '67, when the Government shut them down, most of Britain's pirate radio fleet floated in the calm waters off Frinton — just beyond the three mile territorial limit. After Caroline came Atlanta, London, England and 355.

In January '65, gales snapped Caroline's anchor chain and she drifted onto Frinton beach - with the Dutch captain hanging over the bow, shouting "Mayday" at bemused spectators!

GIDEA PARK
Home of multi-instrumentalist and producer Adrian Baker, who released his '81 Top Thirty hits under the name of Gidea Park.

HALSTEAD
Respected Radio 1 disc jockey Steve Lamacq spent his youth here.

HARLOW
The Naturals were one-hit wonders in '64. They should have known better — but brothers Norman (Blockheads) and Garth (East of Eden) Watt-Roy went on to better things.

Mark Knopfler and Charles Shaar Murray were both journalism students at Harlow Tech; guitarist Jim Cregan (Cockney Rebel/Rod Stewart) went to Harlow Art School.

At an outdoor gig in summer '74, Harlow was the setting for the first large-scale outbreak of Bay City Rollermania.

Sometime home of Attila The Stockbroker, Stephanie de Sykes, Glenn Hoddle and guitarist Gypie Mayo, who played in White Mule and Concrete Mick before joining Dr. Feelgood.

Operational base of The Newtown Neurotics, The Sullivans and mid-Eighties popsters Roman Holiday.

Top early Nineties band was The Sweeney, a trio who cut two CDs and several singles, including the John Peel favourite 'Why?' Also on the scene: The Indestructible Rhythm, The Tender Trap and rap-metal act Snowblind, who were generously described as "The sound of angry young Harlow". Collapsed Lung took their multi-racial thrash metal/rap fusion into the indie charts; local DJ Sasha was acclaimed as the first techno remixer of note.

Cornershop made their southern début here in September '92, and were signed to the Wiiija label within minutes of coming off the stage.

Local mid-Nineties hopefuls included Travis Cut.

HAROLD HILL
The Albemarle Youth Centre was a primo early Seventies venue, presenting such up and comers as Thin Lizzy, UFO and Alex Harvey.

HOCKLEY
Birthplace of Lesley Wood, 25.1.58 (Au Pairs).
Operational base of mid-Nineties hopefuls Understand.

HORNCHURCH
Home of Fifties stars The King Brothers, mod group The Little Roosters, and 14- year-old schoolgirl Judith Coster – who signed with Pye in August '64 and recorded as Tammy St. John.

ILFORD
Birthplace of trad-jazz trumpeter Kenny Ball, 22.5.31; drummer Jet Black (real name Brian Duffy), 26.8.38 (Stranglers); chanteuse Kathy Kirby, 20.10.40.

Brian Poole & The Tremeloes decided to turn professional after winning a talent competition at Ilford Palais in '60.

Sometime home of Pirate Mick Green. Also of original Small Face Jimmy Winston and Pink Fairies roadie/Sex Pistols confidante Boss Goodman, both of whom were no doubt familiar with the Mocha coffee bar – an early Mod stronghold. Boss lived at 32 Goodmayes Lane.

Local resident Ian Page started a Mod revival with his band Secret Affair; Laurie Wisefield and Cliff Williams were both in Sugar, then Home; Carl Putnam became singer in Cud.

Other local groups include The Cymbaline (pirate radio faves), The James Boys (rather Osmondish), Serendipity (featuring the ubiquitous not to mention famous Sean Buckley), Jerry The Ferret and The Knack – who covered The Lovin' Spoonful's 'Did You Ever Have To Make Up Your Mind?' for Pye.

The Angel Folk Club in the High Street was cool in the late Sixties, when Roy Harper, Jackson C Frank, Sandy Denny et al appeared there.

The late Jackson C. Frank now worth a fortune

Venues included the Il Rondo Club (where Sam Apple Pie were local heroes) and The Room At The Top, which favoured R&B of the Geno and Georgie persuasion.

Disco Inferno were early Nineties hopefuls.

Hometown of Louise Wener, singer with Sleeper, who started a hit run with 'Inbetweener' in January '95.

LEIGH-ON-SEA
Birthplace of bass player Paul Gray (Eddie & The Hot Rods, The Damned).

Sometime home of Viv Stanshall (Bonzo Dog Band), record producer Peter Eden (Donovan, GT Moore), Dave Bronze (Dr. Feelgood/Eric Clapton).

Operational base of early Nineties Peel faves Foreheads In A Fishtank.

LOUGHTON
During the mid-Sixties boom, the Mother Hubbard on Valley Hill hosted a weekly folk club.

Before Dire Straits got going, Mark Knopfler was a lecturer at Loughton Teachers Training College.

Sometime home of Matt Johnson (The The), son of a local publican.

MALDON
Techno-folk (!) duo and Robert Wyatt collaborators Ultramarine rose from the ashes of local band A Primary Industry.

RAYLEIGH
Culture Club made their UK début in October '81, at Crocs – a club which attracted name bands like The Cure (June '79) and was made famous by Depeche Mode (who were spotted there by Stevo from Some Bizzare). It was later called the Pink Toothbrush.

ROCHFORD
Home of Eddie & The Hot Rods, one of the '75 bridges between pub-rock and punk.

ROMFORD
Birthplace of Fifties singing pin-up Yana (Pamela Guard); R&B star Graham Bond, 28.10.37; songwriter Chris Andrews, 15.10.42 (also scored a hit of his own, 'Yesterday Man'); bass player Cliff Williams, 14.12.49 (AC/DC); singer Pauline Black (Selecter).

Larry Parnes, the Fifties manager famous for his "Stable of Stars", had a dress shop here before he discovered the attractions of rock'n'roll.

The Beatles played the ABC cinema in March '63 and the Odeon six months later.

The Kings Head in the Market Place was a hot gig in the late Sixties, when Family, T. Rex, Black Sabbath, etc used to party on Monday nights.

Mott The Hoople made their inauspicious UK début at the Polytechnic, supporting King Crimson in September '69.

It was at the Electric Stadium in Chadwell Heath that Marillion (then largely unknown) first saw keyboard player Mark Kelly – and lured him away from the headline band, local hot-shots Chemical Alice. Fish could be a very persuasive guy.

Most successful local group is Five Star, from Rush Green, who had six Top Tenners in the mid-Eighties.

Morning changed their name to T2 for a progressive album on Deram; The Purple Hearts were neo mods;

The Blackboard in Colchester

The Wolfhounds looked like breaking out – but didn't.

Sometime residents include David Essex, guitarist Ray Fenwick (Spencer Davis Group) and guitarist Len Tuckey (who played in local Sixties group The Chasers before backing and marrying Suzi Quatro).

I Q Procedure were a hot mid-NIneties techno act.

SAFFRON WALDEN
In June 66, following the attempted takeover of his pirate station Radio City, owner Reg Calvert visited the home of rival Oliver Smedley – who reacted to his threatening

behaviour by taking down his shotgun and blowing him away. The judge and jury subsequently agreed that he acted in self-defence and acquitted him.

Tom Robinson was a pupil at the (Quaker) Friends School... until his expulsion.

Sometime home of Roger Whittaker – after he decided to leave old Durham town.

Original notebook for Genesis' 'Battle Of Epping Forest'

These christian soldiers fight to protect the poor – East End Heroes got to score in ...

The great Steve Marriott (Small Faces, Humble Pie) died when his cottage (in the nearby village of Arkesden) burned down in April '91.

SEVEN KINGS
Local group Spectrum released a couple of singles but went nowhere. However, their drummer Keith Forsey went on to Eurodisco megabucks as Giorgio Moroder collaborator/producer of Donna Summer, Billy Idol, Simple Minds, etc.

SOUTHEND-ON-SEA
Birthplace of bass player Chris Copping (Procol Harum); singer Nigel Benjamin, 12.9.54 (Mott The Hoople, English Assassin); guitarist Roy Hay, 12.8.61 (Culture Club); Danielle Dax (Lemon Kittens); Jake Shillingford, 15.5.66 (My Life Story).

Larry Parnes signed Joe Brown after an audition at the Odeon in the High Street in September '59. He was soon a ubiquitous backing guitarist and a star of TV show *Boy Meets Girls*. The Beatles and the Stones both appeared at the Odeon in '63.

The local rock scene has heaved with vitality since the Fifties, when groups like The Barracudas, The Rockerfellers, The Whirlwinds, Force Five, The Avengers and The Monotones ruled the roost.

In the Sixties, The Paramounts and The Orioles reigned. The former gradually mutated into Procol Harum while Orioles leader Micky Jupp amassed a cult following in the Seventies. The Fingers were a Peter Eden discovery who recorded for Columbia.

When The Paramounts foundered, leader Gary Brooker formed a songwriting partnership with East Ender Keith Reid, who would send lyrics to his home at 15 Fairfield Road in Eastwood. Among the first batch was 'A Whiter Shade Of Pale'.

A very early 4-piece, Talk Talk

Venues included the Jacobean and the Capri (coffee bars), the Studio, the Nightlife, Shades (a mod club on the seafront), the Cricketers pub and the London Hotel. Queen played an early gig at the Kursaal, supporting Mott The Hoople in December '73.

Members of groups like The Tradewinds, Saints And Sinners, The Fugitives, Surly Bird, Glory, Cow Pie, Thomahawk, and The Bread And Cheese Hillbillies coalesced into The Kursaal Flyers in '73. They were resident at the Blue Boar until breaking nationally.

Half of Talk Talk came from Southend, as did Arthur Comics (late Seventies), Tonight ('78), The Steve Hooker Band (R&B), Levi Dexter & The Rip Chords (rockabilly) and The Leepers (mods).

Bonzos leader Vivian Stanshall went to Southend Grammar and then the Art School.

The pirate station Radio Essex broadcast from Knock John Tower in the Thames estuary, 18 miles off Southend. A successful Post Office prosecution removed it from the air in January '67.

Depeche Mode played their first ever paid gig at Scamps in '80.

In April '87, Stiff recording star Lew Lewis was jailed for seven years after robbing a post office in Westcliff. He tried to make his getaway on a bicycle!

Local early Nineties groups included The Cuckoos, The Golden Section and The Knights Of The Occasional Table. In the mid-Nineties came Heck and (some of) Menswear.

'Southend-on-Sea was a '96 single by ex-American Music Club frontman Mark Eitzel.

My Life Story leader Jake Shillingford was previously in local bands 8 Miles High and Rare Pleasures. His parents both lectured in Fine Art at the local Poly.

STANFORD LE HOPE

Guitarist Roy Hay trained and worked as a hairdresser here until Culture Club took off. He lived with his parents in nearby Corringham.

STEEPLE BUMSTEAD

In March '98, guitarist Laurie Wisefield (Home, Wishbone Ash) was asking £265,000 for his five bedroom, 16th century house Rylands Cottage. It had two acres of land, a stable yard and an attic studio.

TILBURY

In the wake of Gandhi's successful campaign for home rule, six-year-old Cliff Richard (born in Lucknow, 14.10.40) set foot on English soil for the first time. He and his family had sailed from Bombay on the *Ranchi*, a P&O passenger liner making its first voyage after conversion back from a wartime troop carrier. After a 20 day voyage, they arrived at Tilbury on 13.9.48.

Pink Floyd played one of their least memorable gigs at the Railway Hotel in April '67.

UPMINSTER

On his '81 album, Ian Dury adopted the persona of Lord Upminster.

WALTON-ON-THE-NAZE

In February '91, a Harp Beat rock plaque was presented to the lifeboat station by former pirate radio disc jockeys Johnnie Walker and John Peel, whose colleagues were often assisted and rescued in times of sickness and distress.

WEELEY

This village was the unlikely setting for an August '71 hippie rock festival featuring T. Rex, Lindisfarne, Mott The Hoople, Curved Air, Caravan and other fashionable acts.

WESTCLIFFE-ON-SEA

Home of top club/festival trio The Hamsters.

Mott The Hoople played the Palace Theatre in April '71.

WIVENHOE

Birthplace of folksinger Keith Christmas, 13.10.46.

It was here, in the late Eighties, that The Cleaners From Venus developed their plan for global stardom, which was abandoned after two albums on German RCA. Singer Martin Newell later made a solo album, produced by Andy Partridge of XTC.

WOODFORD

Birthplace of bandleader John Dankworth, 20.9.27; folkie Johnny Coppin, 5.7.46 (Decameron); singer/actor Nick Berry, 1961 (*East Enders, Heartbeat*), who scored a '86 number one with 'Every Loser Wins'.

In early '59, skiffle star Lonnie Donegan had a house built to his own specification for £15,000.

Deep Purple made a stealthy visit to an Episode Six gig here in July '69 and managed to lure away Ian Gillan and Roger Glover.

Bark Psychosis were early Nineties indie hopefuls; in the mid-Nineties came ambient/drum'n'bass artist T-Power (aka Mark Royal); in the late Nineties Headswim.

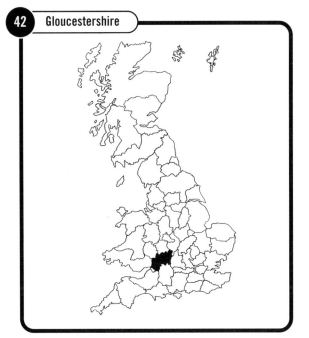

GLOUCESTERSHIRE

AUST

On 17.2.95, a silver Vauxhall Cavalier belonging to missing Manics' guitarist Richey Edwards was discovered, parked up at the service station. Its proximity to the Severn Bridge, which the newspapers invariably described as "a favourite suicide spot", led to speculation that he may never return.

CHELTENHAM

Birthplace of Rolling Stones founder Brian Jones, 28.2.42 (at Park Nursing Home). He grew up in Hatherley Road, attending Dean Close Public School in Shelburne Road and Cheltenham Grammar on the Bath Road. An avid R&B fan playing sax in local rock 'n' roll band The Ramrods, he encountered Alexis Korner at the town's jazz club (held in the clubroom at the back of the Alstone Baths) and was encouraged to move to London. Fans still make pilgrimages to his grave in Cheltenham Cemetery.

Brian Jones: R.I.P.

Also the birthplace of Robert Fisher, 5.11.59 (Climie Fisher); singer Jaz Coleman, 26.2.60 (Killing Joke); guitarist Ian Dench, 7.8.64 (EMF); guitarist Dominic Chad, 5.6.73 (Mansun).

Barry Miles, later founder of the Indica Gallery and Paul McCartney's biographer, was student union secretary at the Art College in the early Sixties – and for dances, would book Brian Jones' band, The Ramrods.

In November '63, The Beatles played the Odeon in Winchcombe Street – their first and last visit to the town; The Rolling Stones played there several times in '63-65. In February '67, The Jimi Hendrix Experience played an early gig at the Blue Moon; in March '79 The Cure played an early gig at the Plough Inn.

Singers Elkie Brooks and Robert Palmer embarked on solo careers after Vinegar Joe's last gig – at St. Paul's College in March '74.

During his years in the slow lane, Steve Winwood lived in the locality and played a few outdoor benefits near Andoversford.

Local singer-songwriter Roy Hill was unsuccessfully promoted as a British Springsteen in the late Seventies.

New wave group Index were based here; multi-instrumentalist Troy Tate later joined The Teardrop Explodes. Progressive band 9.30 Fly released one album and promptly vanished. Late Eighties heavies Taliesin did Radio 1 *Friday Rock Show* sessions.

Erstwhile Shadow Jet Harris, bankrupt and down on his luck, was fined £150 and banned for a year for driving under the influence in February '89.

Chrysalis boss Chris Wright invested some of his Blondie profits in a Cotswold stone country residence, the Glebe House – incorporating a 250 acre stud farm.

Nineties indie label Ochre has impressive space-rock/acid ambient roster incorporating Paul Simpson's Skyray, Will Sergeant's Glide and the Azusa Plane, whose '98 single was called 'Cheltenham'.

Echo & The Bunnymen headlined the Summer Festival at Cox's Meadow in August '91.

Madonna is said to have put her daughter Lourdes on the waiting list for Cheltenham Ladies College.

The Rowdies celebrate in the snug of "Gold Diggers" in 1974

Local Nineties bands included This Picture, Nilon Bombers and Girl Of The Year. The Acorn Centre provided a local showcase.

Local guitarist Wurzel (Mick Burston) joined Motorhead in '90.

In recent years, the annual Cheltenham Literary Festival has offered a stage to cult group Damn Right I Got The Blues — featuring author Ken Follett on bass and vocals.

CHIPPING SODBURY

Birthplace of singing journalist Cath Carroll, 25.8.60 (Miaow).

CINDERFORD

Birthplace of disc jockey Jimmy Young, 21.9.23, who topped the charts twice in '55; singer James Atkin, 28.3.69 (EMF).

Operational base of EMF, who opened with 'Unbelievable' in '90 and took Reeves and Mortimer to number three with 'I'm A Believer'. Most of the band had attended Heywood School and they débuted at the Bilson public house.

CIRENCESTER

Drummer Cozy Powell learned his trade with local Sixties beat group The Sorcerers.

CLEARWELL

In Autumn '73, Deep Purple took over Clearwell Castle to write and rehearse their album Burn. In May 78, Led Zeppelin moved in to work out the set for their imminent tour. Other groups taking advantage of the comfort and setting include Bad Company, Whitesnake and Badfinger. It was subsequently turned into a hotel for the bourgeoisie, replete with peacocks.

COLD ASTON

Home of original Duran Duran drummer Roger Taylor.

GLOUCESTER

Birthplace of bassplayer Zak Foley, 9.12.70 (EMF).

In February '58, Gloucester magistrates fined rocker Terry Dene £155 after he pleaded guilty to wilful damage/drunk and disorderly charges.

The Beatles/Chris Montez/Tommy Roe package tour visited the Regal Cinema in St. Aldate Street in March '63.

After his driving ban, local resident Jet Harris could often be seen riding around town on his bike.

In '87, Ashley Hutchings and his Albion Band released the album By Gloucester Docks I Sat Down And Wept.

Apple Mosaic were late Eighties hopefuls who kind of divided into the Lucid Dream and EMF; jazz rappers Galliano moved to London and ran up a list of hits, starting with Skunk Funk in '92. Other Nineties hopefuls were Bedazzled, Doyenne and Reverb.

LYDNEY

The Town Hall was the venue for a Beatles gig in August '62.

NEWENT

Birthplace of pioneer producer Joe Meek, 5.4.29, who lived at 1 Market Square. A local group, The Saxons, were one of his less successful acts.

STOWE-ON-THE-WOLD

Who bassist John Entwistle lives nearby, in a Gothic pile featured in The Who's bio-pic The Kids Are Alright. Various name bands have recorded in John's home studio where the resident engineer is long term Who sound genius Bobby Pridden.

STROUD

For their second southern excursion, in March '62, The Beatles played the Jaybee Club at the Subscription Rooms in George Street. The newspaper ads were emphatic: "At the request of the Council — no teddy boys... and ladies, please do not wear stiletto heels". It must have been a successful gig: The Beatles returned for a second engagement six months later.

Operational base for idiosyncratic cult band Blurt, whose albums bore titles like A Fish Needs A Bike.

Clearwell Castle after post-Zep refurbishment

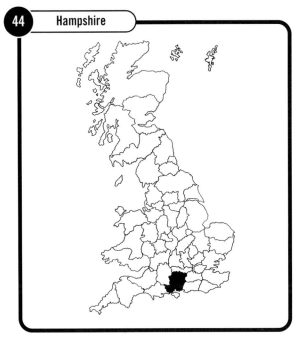

HAMPSHIRE

ALDERSHOT

Birthplace of producer Mickie Most, June '38; drummer Dinky Diamond, December '50 (Sparks).

The Beatles ventured south for the first time in December '61, when they played the Queens Road Palais on the corner of Perowne Street. As he was not known to them, the local newspaper refused to accept Liverpool promoter Sam Leach's cheque for an advertisement, and as he neglected to leave his telephone number with them, his ad was not run. A quick run round the local coffee bars asking people to come to a free dance resulted in an audience of 18 people.

(Aldershot News)

Miles & Miles Removal Co. later to become The Palais De Dance

The town held unpleasant memories for their manager Brian Epstein. In December '52, he had reported to the Royal Army Service Corps to undergo basic training at the start of his National Service.

Sixties groups included Kevin Manning & The E Types, Kerry Rapid & His Blue Stars, and The Bandits.

The Mega City Four's '92 album *Sebastopol Road* was named after their local rehearsal studio. Other Nineties bands included Trousershock BC.

ALTON

Local legend Clive "Slim" Pain won *NME*'s playful Ian Dury Blockhead of the Year competition in '78 and was later the accordian-playing mainstay of several London pub-circuit bands, including The Boothill Foot Tappers, The Balham Alligators and The Blubbery Hellbellies. Damned nice chap.

ANDOVER

Birthplace of drummer Mike Hugg, 11.3.40 (Manfred Mann).

The Troggs put Andover on the rock'n'roll map with their immortal rendition of 'Wild Thing'. Three of their number were born and raised in the town... drummer Ronnie Bond, 4.5.42, bass player Pete Staples, 3.5.44, and singer Reg Presley, 16.6.44. They originally rehearsed in a room above the Copper Kettle, a tea and scones café at 12 High Street (last seen as a Woolwich Building Society office), where a Harp Beat rock plaque celebrates their tenacity. Their '92 album featuring R.E.M. was called *Athens Andover*.

The only other group laying claim to "the Andover Sound" seems to have been The Loot.

And speaking of loot: The Damned signed their contract with Bronze here – just so they could say "Andover the cash".

When the Hatfield-based Gods folded, Ken Hensley moved to Andover and created a new version of the group.

Two-thirds of mid-Nineties indie band Scarfo are local – but they moved to London.

BASINGSTOKE
A schoolgirl one week, a star the next! Tanita Tikaram (born in Munster, West Germany, on 12.8.69) left Queen Mary's Sixth Form College with three A levels. She played two gigs here in town – a Labour Party benefit at Moose Hall and a support spot at Rucstall Hall – and one at the Mean Fiddler... where she was discovered and turned into an overnight success!

Local groups include Go Go Amigo, Papa Brittle (who backed Tanita on her first demos) and The System.

BEAULIEU
Lord Montague's estate was the pastoral setting for annual jazz festivals at the turn of the Sixties... until drunken, lewd, unruly fan behaviour put the lid on them.

(National Motor Museum)

Palace House, Beaulieu

BOTLEY
His Cessna low on fuel, Gary Numan (described by *The Sun* as "the Biggles of the pop world") made an emergency landing on the A3051 Botley to Winchester Road in summer '81. Miraculously, there were no injuries.

COSHAM
Family home of guitarist Mick Jones (born 27.12.44), who began in Nero & The Gladiators and ended up in Foreigner.

DROXFORD
When not cavorting on Monkees reunions, Davy Jones breeds horses on his local farm.

EASTLEIGH
Sometime home of Heinz – the blue-eyed, blond-haired protege of producer Joe Meek. Bass player in The Tornados during their 'Telstar' heyday, he soon went solo to reach the Top Five with his Eddie Cochran tribute 'Just Like Eddie'.

FARNBOROUGH
Local groups included Ace & The Cascades, The Emeralds, The Modern Art Of Living, and The Sound Of Time (whose drummer, Dinky Diamond, was later in Sparks).

In the early Nineties, The Mega City Four broke out with a string of minor hits.

In the mid-Nineties came Who Moved The Ground?

FORDINGBRIDGE
Balls, a Brummie supergroup containing Denny Laine and Steve Gibbons, rehearsed here in a farmhouse during '69 before falling flat on their face.

GOSPORT
Mark Andrews & The Gents were often described as Gosport's answer to Elvis Costello & The Attractions when they made their national bid in the early Eighties... but even they fared better than other local groups like The Classics and The Meddyevils.

The area's most notable export was probably Hookfoot, who backed Elton John at the turn of the Seventies and cut five albums for the DJM label. Guitarist Caleb Quaye and drummer Roger Pope became hot session men.

HAYLING ISLAND
Birthplace of singer songwriter Julia Fordham, 10.8.62.

In '64, fifteen-year-old Rick Parfitt played a summer season at the Sunshine Holiday Camp – just him and his guitar. There he met "a couple of birds" and the three of them formed The Highlights, with whom he toured until joining Status Quo in August '67.

(courtesy of John Owen Smith)

Headley Grange, pre-Led Zep

HEADLEY
During summer '70, Led Zeppelin wrote and recorded some of their third album at Headley Grange, and went on in '71 to record virtually all of their fourth 'Untitled' album there too. 'Stairway To Heaven' was penned on the premises, albeit recorded in London. The group purchased a share in the property three years later. Help Yourself and Bad Company also recorded there.

In '70, Fleetwood Mac paid out £23,000 for Benifold, a nine bedroomed late-Victorian mansion which had previously been used by a religious order (whose vibes were obviously still around). They lived there communally, through their most dispiriting phase, until uprooting and moving to Los Angeles in '74, when their fortunes began to improve dramatically. In December '98, the property was on the market for £1.25 – a snip!

(courtesy of John Owen Smith)

Benifold in Headley, home to Fleetwood Mac

LYMINGTON
Home of Adamski – number one with 'Killer' in '90.

PORTSMOUTH
Birthplace of saxophonist Lol Coxhill, 19.9.32 (Kevin Ayers & The Whole World); singer Paul Jones, 24.2.42 (Manfred Mann); singer Roger Hodgson, 21.3.50 (Supertramp).

England's first touring rock'n'roll group, Tony Crombie & The Rockets, made their début at the Theatre Royal in September '56. The Beatles played the Guildhall twice in '63.

Local groups include Aubrey Small, Autumn, Blackout, Cherry Smash, The Eyes, The Frames, Gold Dust, Jumbo Root, Last Orders, The Lesser Known Tunisians, Shy, Smiling Hard and The Warm Jets... but the city has produced bigger names too.

First group to make it on a large scale was Manfred Mann – originally a modern jazz cum R&B octet called The Mann Hugg Blues Brothers. Their commercial peak came in '64, when 'Do Wah Diddy Diddy' topped both the UK and US charts. Paul Jones was local (but was studying at Oxford) while the others had been drawn to Pompey from such distant places as Johannesburg and Andover.

The most famous Portsmouth resident of the Eighties was Joe Jackson, who fronted Arms And Legs before going for the big one. Another local lad, Brian Howe, replaced Paul Rodgers in the re-formed Bad Company and was later (in '98) part of a consortium involved in buying Portsmouth FC.

The Foster Brothers looked set to break out... but broke up.

The Portsmouth Sinfonia enjoyed the patronage of Brian Eno, who produced two eyebrow raising testaments. Their ever changing composition included some of Deaf School, Alan Clayson (leader of The Argonauts) and Gavin Bryars – who continued working with Eno.

The Psylons were late Eighties Peel faves, but the most newsworthy group of '89 were E-Coli (medical term for bugs up the bum), who were based in Cowplain and attracted attention for their peculiarities rather than their music.

The Cranes broke out for minor chart success in the mid-Nineties. The name of rival band SKAW was an acronym for something kind-a wonderful – but they mutated into the more earthy Pusherman. Other local Nineties outfits included Red Letter Day, The Firework Party, The Amazing Windmills and Emptifish.

Mike Oldfield celebrated the city on his '76 single 'Portsmouth'.

ROMSEY
After marrying a local girl, Stu James re-located his Liverpool group The Mojos, who saw out the Sixties doing cabaret work. Bassist Duncan Campbell later endeare himself to Southampton football club supporters when he wrote and recorded 'The Saints Song'.

SOUTHAMPTON
In February '57, after days of seasickness, a much relieved Bill Haley, hailed as the King of Rock'n'Roll, stepped off the *Queen Elizabeth* to start his first UK tour. Five thousand fans lined Southampton dock to greet his 17-strong party, which included wives, kids and someone's 77-year-old mother! As Haley arrived, Ronnie Scott's jazz band was waiting to board the *Queen Elizabeth* for a US tour – but drummer Phil Seaman was not allowed up the ramp; instead he was arrested for possession of heroin.

Years earlier, in July '44, the great folksinger Woody Guthrie sailed across the Atlantic to France as galley hand on the troop carrier *Sea Porpoise*. After the 3,000 soldiers has been landed, the ship struck a mine and was towed to Southampton. During his few days in Britain, he recorded a session for BBC Children's Hour and took the train to Glasgow, where he boarded a New York-bound ship.

Birthplace of Benny Hill, 21.1.25 ('71 chart topper with 'Ernie'); Mike Vickers, 18.4.42 (Manfred Mann); singer Jona Lewie, 14.3.47; singer Howard Jones, 23.9.55 (in Hythe); bass player Gary Stonedage, 24.11.62 (Big Audio Dynamite).

The most famous local manager and impressario was Reg Calvert, who started out as proprietor of the Band Box, a cellar record shop.

In December '66, Geno Washington & The Ram Jam Band and The Jimi Hendrix Experience shared the bill at a Guildhall concert.

Over the years Southampton has spawned literally hundreds of bands, but few have made waves beyond the immediate vicinity. In the Sixties local faves included Brother Bung, Brownhill Stamp Duty, Chances R, The Daisies, Footprints, Globeshow, Barrie James & The Strangers, Midnights, and Tex Roberg, while the Seventies saw Agnes Strange, Alco, Big Brother, Bitter Lemmings, The Blazers, Brandy Pope & Sundown, Combustion, Ebony, Ebony Rockers, Games To Avoid, Happy Tobacco, Honky, Iguana, King Rock, Lip Moves, Refugee, Rusty Nail, Rye Whisky, Smacky Davis, Strate Jacket, Sweet

Poison, Timepiece, Trader and many more trying their luck.

Among those who gained at least a modicum of national recognition were The Brook Brothers (Everly types who hit the Top Five with 'Warpaint' in '61), Fleur De Lys, Fresh (managed by Simon Napier-Bell), Heaven, The Quik, The Soul Agents (most famous for their five minute stint as Rod Stewart's backing group), Danny Storm & The Strollers, Jakki Whitren and Wishful Thinking.

For many years, Fifties rocker Rory Blackwell held the world record for non-stop drumming – a record he had set in Southampton.

Two of Sigue Sigue Sputnik went to Redbridge Community School – Ray Mayhew and Chris Kavanagh. During their brief flicker of fame, they caused a near riot when they appeared at the Gaumont in Commercial Road – as had The Beatles in May '63, December '63 and November '64.

Eighties group most likely to succeed were The Men They Couldn't Hang, who not only came from Southampton but sang about it... as in 'Dancing On The Pier' and 'Island In The Rain' (which was about the Isle of Wight). Singer Paul Simmons went to Weston Park Boys School with England footballer Graham Roberts.

Nineties bands include Trip, The Cropdusters, Accrington Stanley, Gunk, Dry Riser, Smog and Jane Pow. Some of The Family Cat were also from here – hence the line "and the Saints are playing at home" on their single 'Steamroller'.

Local lad Jon Carter moved to London to establish himself nationally – both as a disc jockey and leader of dance act Monkey Mafia.

SOUTHSEA

Birthplace of Peter Sellers, 1925 (The Goons); Sarah-Jane Owen, 1957 (Belle Stars), who worked briefly as a lifeguard in Portsmouth.

Larry Parnes' rocker Vince Eager made his variety début at the Kings Theatre in Albert Road in April '58. The Beatles played the Savoy Ballroom on South Parade in April '63; the Stones played there five months later.

The three Shulman brothers – Ray, Phil and Derek – lived in Eastney Road. (Ray was born in Portsmouth; the other two moved down from the Gorbals as kids). Their first group was The Howling Wolves, who evolved into Simon Dupree & The Big Sound ('67 top tenners with 'Kites'). By '70, they'd mutated into progressive rock band Gentle Giant.

The Mann Hugg Blues Brothers, later Manfred Mann, made their début at Butlins in '62.

In April '74, Southsea was the location for some of the movie *Tommy*, directed by Ken Russell. At one stage, the pier mysteriously caught fire, adding immeasurably to the excitement of the film. The funfair scenes in *That'll Be The Day*, starring David Essex and Ringo Starr, were also shot in Southsea.

WATERLOOVILLE

Look Back In Anger were local early Eighties goths.

WINCHESTER

Birthplace of Mike Batt, who attended Peter Simmons College and played in various local groups before finding acclaim as Wombles musicmaster.

In January '59, rocker Terry Dene was called up for national service and sent to Winchester Barracks, where he proceeded to have a nervous breakdown. After three months of psychiatric scrutiny he was ejected as unfit for service.

The Rolling Stones came to town to play the Lido Ballroom in December '63.

Original Troggs drummer Ronnie Bond died at the Royal Hampshire County Hospital in Romsey Road in November '92.

Brian Eno studied at Winchester Art School, where he formed heavy rock group The Maxwell Demon!

The city's magnificent cathedral inspired at least two vinyl excursions. In '66, The New Vaudeville Band sold a million copies of their quaint 'Winchester Cathedral' (no group existed at the time; it was sung by session singer John Carter) and ten years later Graham Nash wrote 'Cathedral' for CSN – after exploring the edifice on an LSD trip, and stumbling across the grave of a soldier who had died on his (Nash's) birthday.

Fairport Convention wrote and rehearsed their classic album *Liege And Lief* in a Queen Anne mansion at Farley Chamberlayne.

The only local Seventies/Eighties groups to have made any impact are The Life (signed by EMI but immediately dropped!) and Thieves Like Us.

Robyn Hitchcock mentions the city in his song 'Element Of Light', and former *Whistle Test* presenter/*Q* mag editor Mark Ellen went to school here.

Local Nineties groups included Revolver (who moved to London).

'Twyford Down' was the title of a '93 Galliano single about the M3 extension.

YATELEY

The three popsters who comprise '88 chart stars Breathe all dwelt here.

(Courtesy of Tracks)

BIG BEAT SESSIONS
AT
THE PALAIS BALLROOM
ALDERSHOT

EVERY SATURDAY
commencing this Saturday
9th DECEMBER

Presenting a "Battle of the Bands"

LIVERPOOL v LONDON

LIVERPOOL'S No. "1" BAND
Direct from Their German Tour
THE BEATLES
VERSUS
IVOR JAY & the JAYWALKERS
Plus Two Other Star Groups
7-30 p.m. to 11-30 p.m.
BAR   BUFFET
ADMISSION 5/-
Everyone Welcome—Tell Your Friends

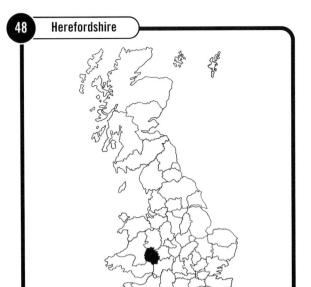

HEREFORDSHIRE

BROMYARD
Future Mott The Hooplers Mick Ralphs (who grew up in nearby Stoke Lacy) and Overend Watts first went professional with the locally-based Buddies in November '65.

HEREFORD
Birthplace of guitarist Mick Ralphs (31.3.44), who went to the Technical College, and home of organist Verden Allen, who worked at Belmont Road garage. They played together in several local groups, including The Shakedown Sound and Silence, before they moved to London in '69, added vocalist Ian Hunter and found fame as Mott The Hoople.

Ten years later, three more locally born musicians – James Honeyman Scott, 4.11.56; Martin Chambers, 4.9.51; and Pete Farndon, 12.6.52 – moved to London, added Akron, Ohio-born vocalist Chrissie Hynde, and found success as The Pretenders.

It was at the town's Municipal Ballroom in March '65 that P J Proby was ordered offstage for an act described by the wife of a Tory alderman as "disgusting and obscene".

In the Sixties, the 1600 Club was the cool venue; local groups included The Ups'n'Downs, The Inmates and The Astrals. In the Seventies, the Market Tavern was a local gig; Karakorum a local band.

Influenced by Seventies dub reggae, Dubmerge emerged in the mid-Nineties.

HERGEST
Mike Oldfield called his second album *Hergest Ridge* – after the hill facing his rural retreat.

LEDBURY
A Green Lane To Ledbury is the title of an atmospheric album by Mike Simmons.

ROSS-ON-WYE
Birthplace of drummer Dale Griffin, 24.10.48 (Mott The Hoople), who went to Walford County Primary and Ross Grammar – where he met Overend Watts. Together they played in school group The Anchors, who were resident at the town's Hope & Anchor pub. They evolved into Wild Dog's Hell Hounds, The Soulents, and Silence. As well as playing all over Europe, they played the town's Top Spot Ballroom and the Ross Rhythm Club.

TITLEY
The Mission spent the summer of '91 holed up here writing their album *Masque* (and complaining that the nearest pub was six miles away).

Terry Thomas samples a brew in Titley's "Bingo" for his legendary solo album

HERTFORDSHIRE

ALDBURY

Owned by ex-Playboy emperor Victor Lownes, the Stocks Country Club was the setting for videos by Madness ('It Must Be Love'), Fun Boy Three ('Summertime'), and Kajagoogoo ('Hang On Now'). The sleeve of the Oasis album *Be Here Now* was also shot here.

Stocks Country Club overun by pop royalty

(Stocks)

BARNET

Birthplace of bass player/songwriter Chris White 7.3.45 (Zombies); singer Andrea Simpson, 12.9.45 (Caravelles); guitarist Pete Banks, 7.7.47 (Yes); Elaine Paige, 5.3.51.

Lois Lane of The Caravelles was educated at St. Martha's Convent; Kenny Morris (Banshees) went to Barnet College of Further Education.

Ian Dury recorded the demos for *New Boots And Panties* at Livingston Studios, 32a East Barnet Road, New Barnet.

An early Toyah release was the splendidly titled *Sheep Farming In Barnet*.

Operational base of the splendid Road Goes On Forever label (PO Box 12).

BERKHAMSTED

Birthplace of Chris Farlowe, 13.10.40, who topped the '66 chart with 'Out Of Time'.

Home of former Kinks keyboard player John Gosling – later the manager of Graham Webb Music, just off the High Street.

Sometime home of Sarah Brightman.

Druid won the *Melody Maker* talent contest in '74 but didn't happen; drummer Ced Sharpley later joined Gary Numan.

BISHOPS STORTFORD

Birthplace of Bill Sharpe, 19.11.52, instigator of locally based Shakatak. That group developed out of Tracks, whose bass player was Trevor Horn. Also the birthplace of drummer Kenny Morris, 1957 (Banshees).

The Rhodes Centre was a popular early Seventies venue.

Operational base of punk band The Epileptics – famous for their indie hit 'Last Bus To Debden'. From their ashes rose Flux Of Pink Indians.

Three And A Half Minutes were set to break out in the early Nineties – but didn't. Instead they evolved into Inaura, who rode the '96 Romo wave.

The Haberdashers' Aske's School, Borehamwood, educating Pink Floyd and Yes men

(M. A. Gilbertson, Haberdashers')

BOREHAMWOOD

Pink Floyd keyboard player Rick Wright and Yes bassist Chris Squire both went to Haberdashers' Aske's, a public school in Butterfly Lane.

The Red Lion public house held a popular mid-Sixties folk club, where Mick Softley was resident singer.

BROOKMANS PARK

Birthplace of Tracey Thorn, 26.9.62 (Everything But The Girl).

BROXBOURNE

Birthplace of drummer Bob Henrit 2.5.46 (Roulettes/Argent/Kinks).

BUSHEY

Birthplace of Simon Le Bon, 27.10.58 (Duran Duran).

In his hits heyday, Vince Hill lived at Heathbourne House in Bushey Heath.

The acoustic soft-rock trio America ('Horse With No Name') met here at a school for children of US airforce personnel.

Wham! cohorts George Michael and Andrew Ridgeley met at Bushey Meads Comprehensive. Their backing singer Shirlie Holliman – later of Pepsi and Shirlie – was also a pupil there. The lads inveigled their way into the business by chatting up record company executive Mark Dean in the Three Crowns pub.

Andrew Ridgeley's mum was deputy head teacher at Bushey Mead Junior School.

CHESHUNT

Birthplace of songwriter/guitarist Russ Ballard, 31.10.45 (Roulettes, Argent, solo), who was educated at Cheshunt County Secondary School.

Another pupil (from September '52) was Cliff Richard, whose family had moved into a brand new council house at 12 Hargreaves Close on 11.4.51. After becoming famous

Cliff's early mansion, 1951

(In Press, Herts.)

he returned regularly to perform charity shows at school – this despite the fact that his prefect's badge was confiscated when he played truant to see his hero Bill Haley. As an aspiring rock'n'roller he would take the Green Line bus into London to play at the 2 Is coffee bar, but the travel sickness he suffered provoked a lifelong aversion to buses.

Sixties beat group The Roulettes, originally formed to back Adam Faith, were Cheshunt based – as were their descendants Unit 4 Plus Two. The latter outfit's winsome frontman Tommy Moeller resurfaced briefly as Whistling Jack Smith on the '67 Top Five hit 'I Was Kaiser Bill's Batman'.

Other local groups included Dave Sampson & The Hunters (who once backed Cliff at the London Palladium when the Shads were indisposed) and Buster Meikle & The Daybreakers. The Mark Four (containing Cliff Richard's original guitarist Norman Mitham) evolved into psychedelic pop-art group Creation.

Also the birthplace of drummer Andy Parker, 1952 (UFO).

The Who played the Wolseley Hall in December '65. Such a lot going on in such a small place!

CODICOTE

Kim Wilde married Hal Fowler at St. Giles Church in September '96. The honeymoon was delayed to allow her to promote her latest single 'Shame'.

CUFFLEY

Birthplace of Zombies guitarist Paul Atkinson, 19.3.46.

ELSTREE

Many popsters made a tentative transition from vinyl to celluloid at Elstree Studios – including Cliff Richard (his first film was *Serious Charge*, with Andrew Ray and Wilfred Pickles). After failing to make it as a skiffler cum coffee bar rocker, Adam Faith worked in the studio's cutting rooms until the television show *Drumbeat* made him a star.

Queen's groundbreaking video for 'Bohemian Rhapsody' was made here in only four hours; The Buggles' last chart single was 'Elstree'.

GOFF'S OAK
Birthplace of Spice Girl Victoria Addams, 7.4.75 (Posh Spice).

HADLEY WOOD
Home of Shadow Bruce Welch.

HARPENDEN
Sometime home of Keith Marshall, who reached the '81 Top Twenty with 'Only Crying'; Martin Gore of Depeche Mode; and Rupert Parkes (alias techno whiz Photek). An article about him in *Wire* described Harpenden as "an almost supernaturally genteel commuter village".

Also former home of reclusive film director Stanley Kubrick, who (until his death in 1999) lived at Childwickbury Manor, set in 175 acres. In recent times, house guests included *Eyes Wide Shut* stars Tom Cruise and Nicole Kidman, who could be spotted swanning around the town. Nothing to do with rock, except that Kubrick's movies have been an inspiration to Bowie, The Byrds, and others too numerous to mention.

HATFIELD
Birthplace of folk colossus Martin Carthy, 21.5.40; vocalist Colin Blunstone, 24.6.45 (Zombies); guitarist Mick Taylor, 17.1.48 (Rolling Stones... he lived at 27 Lockley Crescent); singer Sal Solo, 5.9.54 (Classix Nouveaux).

Among those spending their teenage years in this humdrum new town were Zombies drummer Hugh Grundy and folk troubadour Donovan, whose appearances on *Ready Steady Go!* catapulted him to overnight stardom in '65. He lived in Bishops Rise and went to Onslow Secondary Modern – as did Mick Taylor.

Local Sixties groups included The Favourite Sons (produced by Mike Hurst) and The Gods, who lost their momentum when guitarist Mick Taylor went off to join John Mayall. The latter also included Ken Hensley (later of Uriah Heep) and John Glascock (later of Jethro Tull). Glascock (or Brittle Dick, as the Tull guys called him) began his pop career in The Juniors – famed only for their appearance on television's *5 O'Clock Club*.

Progressive group Babe Ruth originally formed in Hatfield in '71, and Free guitarist Paul Kossoff used to live here.

Another local resident was Barbara Gaskin, who teamed up with Dave Stewart to cut the number one hit 'It's My Party' in '81.

Balls was the absurd name of a much touted '69 Brum supergroup led by Denny Laine. They made their début here, at Breaks Youth Club.

Hatfield's "Breaks Youth Club" the day after a sonic attack by Hawkwind in 1970

Adam & The Ants made their 'Stand And Deliver' video at Hatfield House.

Local schoolfriends The Marine Girls (including Tracey Thorn) had an '83 indie hit with their album *Lazy Ways*.

One of the most bizarre accidents in rock history occurred here in January '70, when Keith Moon accidentally ran over and killed his chauffeur Neil Boland while trying to get away from a gang of skinheads. He had been doing his celebrity bit, opening a disco at the Red Lion pub. Despite having no driving licence, no insurance and being pissed, he was given an absolute discharge – but Boland's death would haunt the otherwise carefree drummer for the rest of his life.

HEMEL HEMPSTEAD
Home of Sixties folkie Mick Softley and underrated soulsters The Q Tips. Andy Powell from Wishbone Ash also lived here, as did Banshees guitarist John McKay.

Damned vocalist Dave Vanian is said to have worked in a local shoe shop while formulating his plan of attack.

Hottest local band of the late Eighties was The Rainmen, which included Peter Bilk (Acker's son) and Steve Rodford (Jim's son).

Made famous by the BBC television series, the Pie In The Sky restaurant in the old town was formerly the Spinning Wheel, where Mick Softley ran an early Sixties folk club. The great Rambling Jack Elliott once played there.

HERTFORD
Operational base for mid-Sixties poppets The Mirage. Six singles failed, but bass player Dee Murray later joined Elton John's first band.

Home of mid-Nineties drum'n'bass pioneer Rob Haigh, who records as Omni Trio and runs a local record shop.

HITCHIN

Home of Sixties beatsters The Clearways and hardcore punks Chron Gen. In '66, identical twins Eric and Derek Massey recorded for CBS as The Twins.

The Hermitage Ballroom was the place to be in the Sixties (Cream played there in September '66), but a skinhead venue to avoid in the Seventies.

Paul Simon, Wizz Jones, Bert Jansch et al played the Railway Tavern, where a thriving folk scene developed in the mid-Sixties. During the same period, the nearby Ship (now the Millstream) was a rock'n'roll pub featuring local stars The Jay Bee Four and such Luton groups as Les Fauves.

Strobe were baggy hopefuls in the early Nineties; three local lads moved to London to establish The Flamingos in '95.

HODDESDON

It was in March '58, while playing at the Five Horseshoes public house in Burford Street, that Cliff Richard was spotted by his first manager, John Foster.

KNEBWORTH

During the Seventies, the extensive grounds of Knebworth House were frequently transformed into a concert site. The Allman Brothers played there in July '74, Pink Floyd in July '75, The Rolling Stones in August '76, and Led

Spot Oasis on stage, Knebworth 1996

(Mike Hutson)

Zeppelin played their final UK shows there in August '79 – collecting a fee said to be "the highest ever in the history of rock entertainment".

Support group to The Stones was 10cc, whose set was preceded by a guy who casually strolled to the front of the stage, removed his clothes, masturbated and climaxed to the cheers of the crowd before being roughly bundled off by stewards, who finally realised he wasn't part of the show!

Brian Eno while lecturing at Hitchin Priory, October 1976

Although they weren't to know it at the time, Queen's Knebworth show on August 9, '86, was to be their last ever public performance.

Tears For Fears shot their 'Mad World' video at Knebworth House.

LETCHWORTH

The Sting Rays got together at St. Christopher School. Other pupils included bass player Neil Murray (Whitesnake, Black Sabbath, Brian May Band), pianist Anthony Moore and guitarist Peter Blegvad (both would later form Slapp Happy), synth player Hoagy Davies (son of television Maigret, Rupert Davies; later in Leeds University group She's French with future Buggle Geoff Downes), saxman Dave Winthrop (Supertramp, Secret Affair) and Victoria Barnes (Rising Stars).

Also from Letchworth were late Sixties group The Original Dyaks.

Mott The Hoople played one of their earliest gigs at Leys Youth Club in October '69.

Hometown of lovers rock starlet Carroll Thompson.

LITTLE BERKHAMSTED

Sometime home of Donovan and Adam Ant.

LITTLE HADHAM

In '70, Fairport Convention moved into an old Ind Coope pub on the A120. Their idyllic life here ended abruptly when a lorry ploughed through Dave Swarbrick's bedroom one Sunday morning. A Dutch driver, anxious not to miss

(Brookmans Park Advertiser)

Dutch driver dies in crash

A Dutch lorry driver was killed and his passenger was seriously injured when the lorry ploughed into the home of the Fairport Convention pop group in Little Hadham, Hertfordshire, yesterday. Eight people in the house, including the four-man pop group, escaped unhurt.

Mr. Johanne Van Der Houwen, the injured passenger, was taken to hospital at Bishop's Stortford.

the Harwich ferry, had fallen asleep at the top of the hill approaching the village. Still, they did write *Full House* there.

LONDON COLNEY
Late Fifties home of guitarist Ian Samwell, who wrote Cliff's first, seminal hit 'Move It' while riding on the Green Line bus from here to Cheshunt in June '58.

MARKYATE
The Zombies used to rehearse in a room over the local grocery store — owned by the father of bass player Chris White.

POTTERS BAR
The Robin Hood hosted a popular mid-Sixties folk club; Farx was a hot progressive rock venue during the Seventies.

RADLETT
Sometime home of guitarist Hank Marvin (Shadows, in case you didn't know) before he moved to Australia; guitarist Stuart Taylor (Tornados, Lord Sutch); George Michael; and — until he electrocuted himself in the early Seventies — bassist John Rostill (Shadows), who lived in The Avenue.

RICKMANSWORTH
Jackson Recording Studio has turned out several hits, the biggest being '2-4-6-8 Motorway' by Tom Robinson. UFO cut their first album there over six evenings in '70; Eddie & The Hot Rods and Dr Feelgood recorded here; Joe Strummer's first studio experience was here, as a member of The 101ers.

During his Led Zep heyday, John Paul Jones lived at Straw Hat, Whisper Wood, off Trout Rise in Loudwater. During the early Seventies, the town was also home to pub rockers Brinsley Schwarz.

Punk band Anorexia seems to be all this town could muster.

ROYSTON
New wave groups included Terra Cotta and The Dogma Cats.

Rare pic sleeve for Anorexia (Rickmansworth) in 1978

ST. ALBANS
Birthplace of singer/song writer/keyboard man Rod Argent

No. 4 Liverpool Road, hub of '70's and '80's music shenanigans

14.6.45 (Zombies/ Argent), bass player Jim Rodford 7.7.45 (Mike Cotton Sound/Argent/Kinks).

Most celebrated local group was The Zombies, four of whom were mates at the Abbey School while singer Colin Blunstone was a sports fanatic from the Grammar School. Between them they racked up 50 GCEs before 'She's Not There' announced their seductive charm. Despite their academic record, they mis-spelt the title of their finest album *Odessey And Oracle*!

Other local stars were Maddy Prior (later of Steeleye Span) and Rod Argent's post-Zombies band Argent.

Donovan, Mick Softley and Mac Macleod were among the crowd of folkies and beatniks who hung around The Cock in St. Peters Street during the mid-Sixties.

Local musicians included bass player Paul Dean, who joined X-Ray Spex, and guitarist Steve Forrest, who joined Silverhead. Local lecturer, poet and writer Jeff Cloves led early Seventies group Stardust, who recorded for Sonet.

A great Sixties venue (Who, Graham Bond, Small Faces, etc), the Market Hall is no more... and nor are the Co-op Hall, the Faulkner Hall, or the Civil Defence Hall. But they still have the odd gig at the City Hall.

The Pistols played one of their earliest gigs at the art school, and the White Riot tour played the City Hall — after which Joe Strummer was arrested for nicking hotel towels.

The Pioneer Youth Club, next to the fire station in Alma Road, presented all manner of groups — from Arthur Brown to Mott The Hoople to The Average White Band.

The Horn of Plenty in 1977 prior to a fire started at a Nigel Simpkins gig

The Horn Of Plenty pub on the corner of Victoria Street presented up-and-coming talent... like The Street Band (with Paul Young) who played there a couple of times a month before their hit. Later a rocking venue for the likes of The Groundhogs and Steve Marriott. While an art student in St. Albans, Kim Wilde worked as a barmaid there.

A dozen or so local new wavers found a vinyl outlet on Waldo's and Bam Caruso — labels launched by Cally and Phil Smee, who also designed sleeves and CD inserts for many companies. Originally at 4 Liverpool Road, the operation moved to 9 Ridgmont Road, which was also the office for the glorious but short-lived *Strange Days* magazine.

Source Direct were late Nineties drum'n'bass pioneers.

SOUTH MIMMS

Deep Purple first got together and rehearsed at Deeves Hall, a local farmhouse.

Deeves Hall, the birth of The Purps

STEVENAGE

Overspill new town which provided an ideal location for adolescent sex romp *Here We Go Round The Mulberry Bush*. Another film, *Quadrophenia*, was dedicated to the kids of Stevenage.

The Rolling Stones came to town in April '64, when they appeared at the Locarno.

Uriah Heep stalwart Ken Hensley went to Alleynes Grammar School where he fronted Ken & His Cousins. His first professional stab was with The Jimmy Brown Sound — an R&B outfit named for James Brown. Residents recall that he spent much of the late Sixties living in a van.

During the punk era, the hot local band was Restricted Hours. Though they look as though they lived in Oklahoma a century ago, gothic outlaws Fields Of The Nephilim also have their roots in Stevenage. They often took refreshment at the Pig and Whistle.

The town was also the sometime home of Lesley Woods of The Au Pairs and Sal Solo of Classix Nouveaux.

Coda Music at 51a High Street is one of the most renowned guitar shops in Europe, with The Prodigy and Supergrass among its illustrious clientele.

The leading jungle label, Moving Shadow is based at 55 Conifer Walk.

Local Nineties bands include Transworld Siren.

TRING

Home of bass player Andy Pyle (Blodwyn Pig/Juicy Lucy/Kinks/etc) and former Spooky Tooth frontman Mike Harrison.

Champney's is a local health farm specialising in the rehabilitation of rich fatties. Horrified by his enormity, EMI dispatched Marillion's Fish to Champney's — hoping he would lose half his bodily bulk before meeting various American VIPs.

Through strategies he refuses to divulge, he ultimately emerged weighing more than he did when he went in!

WALTHAM CROSS

Cliff Richard lived here from October '49 to April '51 — next door to Bob Henrit, later drummer with The Roulettes, Kinks, etc. In '56, he regularly attended Holy Trinity Youth Club, where he started singing with a group of friends, The Quintones. Their performance at Holy Trinity School on 14.7.56 was 15-year-old Cliff's first gig.

WARE

Birthplace of Kenny Pickett, 3.9.43, who fronted Creation and later co-wrote Grandad.

Kim Wilde went to school here; Chas & Dave lived here in the early Eighties.

Watford's Bears photographed in Gaston Tesco

WATFORD

Birthplace of Chris Britton, 21.6.45 (Troggs); Bruce Gilbert, 18.5.46 (Wire); JD Nicholas, 12.4.52 (Heatwave, The Commodores); Shirlie, 18.4.62 (Pepsi And...); Spice Girl Geri Halliwell, 6.8.72 (Ginger Spice) – who attended Watford Girls Grammar School.

Home of minor league R&B group Cops And Robbers – inspired by The Rolling Stones, who they saw at St. John's Hall in September '63.

Rick Wakeman was resident organist at the Top Rank ballroom – and was fired three times.

In February '70, at the Register Office, Jethro Tull's Ian Anderson married Chrysalis press officer Jennie Franks.

Knox, who led punk group The Vibrators, was a student at Watford Art College, where he fronted Knox & The Nightriders.

Rudimentary Peni were a punk trio who had a Top Three indie chart album in Death Church; Sad Lovers & Giants were post-punk popsters.

Local lad Steve Waddington found late Eighties success as half of The Beloved.

When Hayley Mills took 11-year-old son Crispian to the Hare Krishna Temple here, she unwittingly laid the foundation for his success as leader of Kula Shaker.

In December '89, Elton John was made Life President of Watford FC.

The Teaset have tea in Cassiobury Park

WELWYN GARDEN CITY

Birthplace of jazz trombonist/Marquee Club owner/pioneer R&B promoter Chris Barber, 17.4.30. His 'Petite Fleur' was a worldwide hit in '59; Lonnie Donegan recorded 'Rock Island Line' whilst a sideman in his trad jazz band. Also born here was Alan Williams, 22.12.50 (leader of The Rubettes); bass player Mat Osman, 9.10.67 (Suede).

Jazz and rock pub the Cherry Tree hit a glamorous peak in April '69 when Led Zeppelin played there.

A satellite village is the home of the rocking Wilde family... Marty, Joyce, Ricky and Kim. Popsters all!

The punk explosion saw The Astronauts and Johnny Curious & The Strangers releasing singles. For them, it was a case of Welwyn Garden City Blues – as recorded by Home on their album *Pause For A Hoarse Horse*. Local punks Anthrax reached the '83 indie Top Ten with their album *Capitalism Is Cannibalism*.

In '94, local anarchistic punks S*M*A*S*H began to make waves nationally.

ISLE OF MAN

DOUGLAS

Birthplace of Barry Gibb, 1.9.47 (Bee Gees).

Also from the island... singer Christine Collister.

In August '64, when The Rolling Stones played the Palace Ballroom, the island's only police dog – on duty to help control thousands of shrieking fans – reacted to the noise and started snarling at the crowd. She recovered after several days of cossetting with Winalot and Chum. The Stones returned to the same venue in September '65 – without incident.

It was at the Palace in July '74 that Ian Hunter played his last UK gig with Mott The Hoople.

Christine Collister

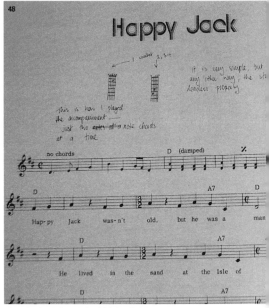

(Reproduced by kind permission of Fabulous Music)

RAMSEY

Radio Caroline North took up position off Ramsey in July '64, transmitting from an old Dutch passenger ferry.

Residents who have benefited from the island's lower rate of personal taxation include John Coghlan (Status Quo), songwriter Mitch Murray ('How Do You Do It?'), Go West, The Sutherland Brothers, and Rick Wakeman – and as we all know, Happy Jack lived in the sand at the Isle of Man.

ISLE OF WIGHT

For a mind-bogglingly thorough examination of the island's musical history, I recommend *Isle Of Wight Rock* by Vic King, Mike Plumbley and Pete Turner (published by Isle of Wight Rock Archives).

BINSTEAD

Growing up here, Nicholas Dingley (later better known as Razzle) was the Island's first punk. He played in local bands The Underdogs and Thin Red Line before joining Hanoi Rocks. He was killed in a car accident in Los Angeles and is buried in Binstead cemetery.

FRESHWATER

The third Isle of Wight festival brought half a million punters to East Afton Farm in August '70. The astonishing bill included The Doors, The Who, Chicago, John Sebastian, Kris Kristofferson, Joni Mitchell, Tiny Tim, Miles Davis, Leonard Cohen and Jimi Hendrix. Rumours of a VD epidemic and LSD in the tapwater proved unfounded.

Local lad Snowy White started out in island groups The Blueshades, The Outer Fringe and Perception, before graduating to Thin Lizzy and Pink Floyd.

GODSHILL

The first Isle of Wight festival was held at Hayles Field in August '68 – with 14 bands, including Tyrannosaurus Rex (who cost £40) and Jefferson Airplane (£1,000). Local band Halcyon Order started the proceedings.

NEWPORT

Birthplace of erstwhile milkman Craig Douglas (real name Terry Perkins), 12.8.41, who reached number one with 'Only Sixteen' in '59. He started his career in a talent contest at the Medina Cinema.

Rock'n'roll sessions started at the Cameo Ballroom in Crocker Street in February '57 and later at the Queens Hall in the High Street.

Three of Level 42 – drummer Phil Gould, guitarist Boon Gould and bassist Mark King (born in Gurnard, 20.10.58) – grew up together on the island. Strangely, Mark King was a milkman too.

'A Trip To Newport Hospital' is a track on Egg's '71 album *The Polite Force*. It mentions Ryde's Castle Hotel and skirmishes with skinheads.

Local groups have included Stormtrooper and Skip Bifferty – when they were hiding from their manager! Early Seventies folk-rockers Shide and Acorn cut an album now worth hundreds on the collectors' market.

The Jefferson Airplane lands on the island

Plans to start a group were discussed by Dave Wakeling and Andy Cox while on holiday here. They co-opted local lad David Steele and returned to Birmingham to form The Beat. Steele (later in The Fine Young Cannibals with Cox) was born here on 8.9.60.

Local Nineties band Sweet Tooth were at the forefront of the short-lived progessive rock revival; Universal Being made waves on the Nineties dance scene.

RYDE

Starting in October '56, the island's first rock'n'roll rendezvous was the Seagull Ballroom at the end of the pier – run by author Philip Norman's father (read *The Skater's Waltz*). Instruction on rock'n'roll jiving was given at the St. John's Ambulance Hall in Newport Street.

In the late Fifties, the trendsetting John Mowbray was the first milkman turned rocker – playing the Ryde pubs as Johnny Vincent.

The Nomads (formed at Portsmouth Art College) won the Island skiffle group competition in May '57 at the Commodore cinema. Their local rivals included The Sapphires, The Cherokees, The Signal Box Five and the Wheatsheaf Rhythm Group.

The Commodore not only presented movies like *Rock Around The Clock* and *Rebel Without A Cause* (both April '56), but became a package tour venue for the likes of Lonnie Donegan, Tommy Steele and Jim Dale. In the Sixties, it was the primo gig for such local groups as The Crescents, The Meteors, The Knights and The Shamrocks – as well as visiting chart stars like The Searchers and Dusty Springfield. The other hot venue was the Flamingo Club in Union Street.

The Rolling Stones played at the Pavilion in March' 64.

La Boheme coffee bar in George Street offered a touch of bohemian romance. The Mayfair Café was owned by the parents of film director Anthony Minghella – who would one day be roundly acclaimed for *Truly Madly Deeply*, but in the Seventies played keyboards in local band Dancer. They recorded an album at Olympic, produced by Tony McPhee, which was never issued.

SANDOWN

Early Sixties group The Zodiacs were managed by the projectionist at the Queen's Cinema.

In the late Sixties, the Manor House at Lake became Middle Earth – presenting such up and comers as The Nice and Colosseum.

SHANKLIN

Birthplace of guitarist Boon Gould, 4.3.55 (Level 42).

In '72, Viv Stanshall fronted The Temperance Seven for a "delightfully awful" summer season at the Pier (destroyed by the '87 hurricane). It was in the Pier Café that he began writing his masterwork *Sir Henry At Rawlinson's End*.

Sequences for the '73 movie *That'll Be The Day* were shot on the beach (where David Essex was a deckchair attendant) and on the Pier. (Other bits were filmed at Sandown Grammar School, the White Lion at Arreton, the Caribou coffee bar in Cross Street Ryde, and the holiday camp at Puckpool). Many islanders were used as extras in the film and have great tales about Keith Moon and Ringo Starr.

VENTNOR

Rock'n'roll dancing was banned at the Winter Gardens in September '57. Late Fifties skiffle groups included The Satellites, The Demons, The Homing Birds and The Alley Cats – who became Johnny Vincent's backing group. (Bass player Stuart Hobday would become a BBC producer).

During the Sixties, the 69 Club operated at the Winter Gardens – presenting everyone from Johnny Kidd to The Who, Screaming Lord Sutch to David Bowie. In '68, the scene moved to the Royal York Hotel, where progressive era circuit bands strutted their stuff.

WOOTTON

The August 69 venue for the second Isle of Wight festival – headlined by Bob Dylan and The Band, whose fee was $50,000. Dylan (who, along with Sara and three year old Jesse, crossed the Atlantic on the *QE2*) stayed and rehearsed at Forelands Farm in Bembridge.

The bill also included The Who, The Nice, Eclection, Bonzo Dog, Family, Free, Joe Cocker, The Moody Blues, Tom Paxton and loads more. Beatles Harrison, Lennon and Starr attended the festival – as did Francoise Hardy, Jane Fonda, Elton John and Bob Willis (among many thousands more).

YARMOUTH

Robyn Hitchcock (born in West Sussex) lived here during the late Eighties. His song Airscape was inspired by Compton Beach. His father, a noted novelist, grew up in Ventnor.

Elaborate festival tickets

(Geoff Ulph)

KENT

ASHFORD
Operational base of Nineties band The Beautiful Losers.

BECKENHAM
Birthplace of Peter Frampton, 22.4.50; pianist Django Bates, 2.10.60 (Earthworks); Nick Heyward, 20.5.61.

Bill Wyman's formal education was completed at Beckenham Grammar School. Early in their marriage, he and his wife Diane lived at 40 Birbeck Road. Later, they moved to 9 Kenilworth Court, opposite Beckenham Grammar – where Herd and Status Quo man Andy Bown was also a pupil.

In '69, David Bowie was a co-founder of the Beckenham Arts Lab, held at the Three Tuns pub in the High Street. Guests included The Humblebums (Gerry Rafferty and Billy Connolly), Robin Scott (later M of Pop Music fame), and local group Comus. During this period, Bowie lived in Foxgrove Road, but by the end of the year, he and Angie had moved into flat 7 of Haddon Hall, a Victorian town house at 42 Southend Road. Other residents included producer Tony Visconti and Bowie's latest backing musicians, The Spiders From Mars.

At home with the Bowie's, 42 Southend Road

(Rex Features)

In summer '69, Bowie also organised Beckenham Free Festival – held at Croydon Road recreation ground, next to the hospital.

Nick Heyward, Les Nemes and Graham Jones all went to Kelsey Park School, where they laid plans for Haircut 100.

Local venues included the Mistrale Club, next to the station, which played host to Geno Washington and Desmond Dekker; and the Eden Park Hotel, which presented the likes of Free and Juicy Lucy in the early Seventies.

BELTRING
Among the London families who spent their summers picking hops for Whitbreads was that of Chas Hodges – now half of Chas & Dave.

BEXLEY
Boy George was born in Bexley Hospital on 14.6.61. In July '69, Marianne Faithfull entered the same establishment to cure her heroin addiction.

Also the birthplace of guitarist Tony Oliver, 21.10.55 (*Zigzag* magazine and The Inmates).

The Black Prince has been a jazz and rock venue forever. Its heyday was during the Sixties R&B boom, when such stars as Little Walter (October '64) appeared, but it converted to meet underground/progressive tastes. Mott The Hoople played there in March '71.

In the early Nineties, local act Midway Still looked set to break out.

BEXLEY HEATH
Kate Bush was born at Bexley Heath Maternity Hospital on 30.7.58.

BROADSTAIRS
Birthplace of Bob Calvert, poet and vocalist with Hawkwind.

Operational base of Nineties tribute band the LA Doors.

BROMLEY
Birthplace of drummer Alan Blakely, 7.4.42 (Tremeloes); drummer Topper Headon, 30.5.55 (Clash); Norman Cook, 31.7.63 (Housemartins, Fatboy Slim).

Between '57 and '69, David Bowie's home was his parents' house at 4 Plaistow Grove, Sundridge Park. He attended Burnt Ash Junior Mixed, in Rangefield Road, before moving on (September '58) to Bromley Technical High School, in Oakley Road, Keston (now Ravensbourne School for Boys). Other pupils at the latter were Peter Frampton (whose father was Bowie's art master), George Underwood (who recorded a single under the name of Calvin James and did artwork on Bowie sleeves), Billy Idol and Steven Severin (Banshees).

Mark Wynter (nine early Sixties hits) lived on the Flower House Estate in Downham and went to Rangefield Road School.

Beatles manager Brian Epstein and disc jockey Brian Matthew planned to build a recording studio/theatre complex in the town during the mid-Sixties but were thwarted by the local council.

The town's hottest Sixties R&B/rock club was the Bromel at Bromley Court Hotel on Bromley Hill. Jimmy Reed, John Lee Hooker and Memphis Slim all appeared there during '64; Jimi Hendrix played there in January '67.

Also popular was the Bal Tabarin, adjoining the Tavern in Downham Way, where you could see Marmalade, Arthur Brown or Procol Harum – or dance to Tommy Jackson's Electronic Trio after the bingo session finished. It was resurrected as the Warehouse in the late Eighties, presenting The Blues Band, Fields Of The Nephilim, and the like.

The Star and Garter public house held a weekly folk club during the mid-Sixties, hosting such names as Alex Campbell and Martin Carthy.

David and Angela Bowie were married at the Registry Office in Beckenham Lane on 20.3.70.

Tintagel were local rock-orientated folkies who made ripples in the Seventies.

Among the earliest followers of punk rock were the Bromley Contingent, whose garb and street theatre attracted much press coverage. Two of their number, Siouxsie and Steve (who cemented their friendship in Bromley's dole office), formed The Banshees, while William Broad soon became famous as Billy Idol. Their initial inspiration was a Sex Pistols gig at Bromley Tech in January '76.

Home of new wave group The Acid Drops.

BURWASH
When The Who made it big, Roger Daltrey bought Holmshurst Manor in East Burwash – a Jacobean mansion set in 35 acres. Within the grounds is Lakedown Fishery, where affluent rod-men may take their pick of four lakes stocked with rainbow and brown trout ranging from 24 ounces to 16 pounds. Leo Sayer recorded his début album *Silverbird* in Roger's studio there.

CANTERBURY
Former Canterbury Cathedral choirboys include Fifties rocker Dickie Pride, Terry Cox (drummer in Pentangle), and teen balladeer Mark Wynter.

During the Sixties, the city spawned a plethora of groups: The Earl Gutheridge Explosion, The Four Methods, The Corvettes, The Insect, The Rojeens, and The Wilde Flowers... out of whom sprang The Soft Machine, Caravan, Kevin Ayers & The Whole World, Matching Mole, Gong, Hatfield & The North, and several more!

Robert Wyatt, Mike Ratledge, Hugh Hopper, David Sinclair and various other instigators of the group scene first met at Simon Langton Grammar School.

Guitarist Steve Hillage went to the University of Kent – as did Seventies punk poet Attila The Stockbroker. Robert Wyatt went to Canterbury College of Art... where one of the tutors was Ian Dury. Two of his pupils later joined him in Kilburn & The High Roads – Humphrey Ocean and Keith Lucas (then in Canterbury group Frosty Jodpur; later the leader of punk group 999).

Because of the length of their hair, The Wilde Flowers were banned from the Three Compasses public house in St. Peter's Street. In February '65, Canterbury Magistrates Court fined Kevin Ayers (then of 4 Russell Drive, Swalecliffe) £5 for carrying a passenger on his scooter while still a learner.

Teenager Deena Webster released a few singles in the late Sixties; the local Fiddler's Dram took a day trip to the Top Three in '80.

Warner Brothers shot footage for The Great Medicine Ball at a July '70 gig featuring The Grateful Dead, The Faces, Mott The Hoople and Pink Floyd.

In November '78, Joy Division played their very first southern gig at the Odeon – and returned to play the University in March '79.

Local Nineties acts include Playground and Omar.

CHATHAM
In January '63, the day after the release of their second single 'Please Please Me', The Beatles played the Invicta Ballroom in the High Street. The Stones played there in March '64.

The Jimi Hendrix, Pink Floyd, Nice, Move, Amen Corner package show visited the Central Hall in December '67.

The Milkshakes down by the jetty

The Milkshakes made waves and cut records; so did The Prisoners. The former even recorded a song called 'Chatham Drive'. Singer Billy Childish (real name Steven Hamper) later went solo.

Other local groups include Thee Mighty Caesars, The Dentists, The Pop Rivits, The Del-Monas, The James Taylor Quartet, The Prime Movers and The Len Bright Combo – led by former Stiff star Wreckless Eric, who lived here during the Eighties, when he also worked as roadie for visiting US country star George Hamilton IV! In the Nineties, Eric moved to rural France, where he leads The Hitsville House Band.

Adam Faith and 'beat girls'

CHISLEHURST

Singer Joan Regan moved here in '58, to become a neighbour of her agent Leslie Grade.

Chislehurst Caves, which can be seen in the Adam Faith movie *Beat Girl*, opened up as a rock venue in the Sixties. Bill Wyman's group The Cliftons played here regularly; Jimi Hendrix played here in December '66. On October 31, '74, the Caves were the venue for the UK launch of Swan Song Records, Led Zeppelin's custom label. All of Zep were in attendance plus Bad Company, Maggie Bell and new signing, The Pretty Things. Alan Freeman, Bob Harris and Roy Harper also attended and music was provided by Bob Kerr's Whoopee Band and John Chiltern's Feetwarmers with George Melly. Topless ladies, cigar chewing monks and girls dressed as nuns

mingled with the guests, making it a hedonistic Hallowe'en celebration in the grand Zeppelin tradition. Siouxsie of The Banshees spent her schooldays here.

Peter Grant's Swan Song

CLIFTONVILLE

Home of Nineties neo-psychedelic experimenter Paul Roland.

CRAYFORD

Birthplace of bass player John Stax, 6.4.44 (Pretty Things).

The Town Hall was a popular venue during the Sixties – music, fights and sexual intrigue.

DARTFORD

Birthplace of Rolling Stones Mick Jagger, 26.7.43, and Keith Richards, 18.12.43 – both at Livingstone Hospital, East Hill. They attended Maypole County Primary and Westhill Infants respectively, before meeting up at Wentworth County Primary. At 11, Mick went to Dartford Grammar while Keith displayed dwindling enthusiasm for lessons at the Technical College. Rapport was only established in '61, when they chanced to meet on Dartford Station and Keith noticed that Mick was carrying a London American single: Chuck Berry's 'Back In The USA'/'Memphis Tennessee'.

Jagger used to live in The Close, Wilmington.

Another graduate of Dartford Grammar was Dick Taylor, original bass player in the Stones and later instigator of The Pretty Things. Taylor, 28.1.43, and singer Phil May, 9.11.44, were also born in Dartford – as was bassist Rick Huxley, 5.8.42 (Dave Clark Five); artist/sleeve designer Peter Blake, 25.6.32 (*Sgt Pepper*, Band Aid); brothers Phil, 9.1.64, and Paul Hartnoll, 18.5.68 (both of techno pioneers Orbital).

Gene Vincent and Margie Russell were married at Dartford Register Office on 23.1.63. She was five months pregnant.

Tim Hinckley (Jody Grind, Vinegar Joe) grew up here – as did Joe Leeway of The Thompson Twins.

After his deification in London, Rusty Egan became the groovy disc jockey at Flicks: "From the Blitz to the sticks – Mondays at Flicks".

Oasis played their first southern gig in the Students Union at Dartford Poly in April '92, supporting Oldham band The Ya Yas.

DEAL
Birthplace of singer Glen Dale 2.4.43 (Fortunes).

Jimmy Page played the Strand Palace in December '63, when he was guitarist with Carter Lewis & The Southerners.

DOVER
Birthplace of Alan Clayson, 3.5.51 (Clayson & The Argonauts); Jane Summers, 4.4.61 (Bodysnatchers); top sax session man Gary Barnacle.

Home of Vashti, Sixties hopeful managed by Andrew Oldham.

For some reason a favourite of American doo-wop groups, 'The White Cliffs Of Dover' was also recorded by The Righteous Brothers.

Jimmy Cliff wrote 'Many Rivers To Cross' in Dover, when he spent a week here sleeping rough.

In May '71, Richard Branson spent a night in a cell at Dover Police Station after being charged with defrauding Customs & Excise in connection with his mail order record business.

Local lads Robin File and Sean McCann moved to Manchester to form Audioweb, who reached the '97 Top Twenty with a cover of The Clash's 'Bankrobber'.

ERITH
Birthplace of Sixties singer Bern Elliott, 17.11.42 (original leader of The Fenmen, and later The Clan).

FOLKESTONE
Birthplace of bassplayer Noel – born on Christmas Day, hence Noel - Redding, 25.12.45 (Jimi Hendrix Experience). His mid-Sixties local group was The Loving Kind. Other local musicians, Neil Landon (Flowerpot Men) and Jimmy Leverton (Juicy Lucy), joined Redding in his post-Hendrix group Fat Mattress.

Also the birthplace of drummer Pete Kircher, 21.1.48 (Honeybus, Status Quo).

Tofts at 35-39 Grace Hill was a popular Sixties hang-out. A showcase for local talent, it was also a regular venue for Ron Wood's Birds and The Freddy Mack Big Band.

The Rolling Stones played Leas Cliff Hall in April '64.

The Medium Wave Band got as far as London in the late Seventies; The Skydogs were early Nineties hopefuls; The Mystreated were a mid-Nineties garage band. Kula Shaker keyboard player Jay Darlington learned his chops with local

late Eighties garage band The Sheds.

The Metronome gained a reputation as the town's best Nineties gig.

GILLINGHAM
Birthplace of Peter Hewson, 1.9.50 (Chicory Tip).

Wang Chung broke through internationally in '83, but Acker & The Nice Boys found only local acclaim.

Alvin Purple were a mid-Nineties neo-mod band.

GRAVESEND
During the early Sixties, *The Royal Daffodil* would sail for Calais under the banner Rock Across The Channel! Various groups, from Acker Bilk to The Shadows, would provide music for the revellers.

Guy Darrell & The Midniters signed with Oriole in '64 but went nowhere.

Fantasy were local heroes when they released their '72 album – which sold zilch but is now a rare and valuable collectors' item.

HERNE BAY
Birthplace of Kevin Ayers, 16.8.45 (Soft Machine); Richard Coughlan, 2.9.47, and David Sinclair, 24.11.47 (both Caravan).

The Last Resort were early Eighties punks.

Status Quo's Richard Coughlan, a spell in the Army doing him no good

HYTHE
Supertramp formed, lived and rehearsed at Botolphs Bridge House on Burmarsh Road, West Hythe in summer '69.

KESTON
Bill Wyman moved here in June '66.

MAIDSTONE
Home of Seventies popsters Chicory Tip – chart toppers with 'Son Of My Father'. Before, and after, they were famous they used to play at the London Tavern in Week Street.

The Granada was a Fifties/Sixties package show venue where everyone from Sam Cooke to Screaming Lord Sutch played.

The Royal Star Hotel in the High Street (replaced by a shopping arcade) was a trad jazz/rock'n'roll stronghold; the Rat Trap was a coffee bar where the likes of Albert Lee would play.

Peter Bellamy, singer in seminal folk group The Young Tradition, attended Maidstone School of Art.

Beatsters The Manish Boys became one of David Bowie's backing groups; aspiring new wavers included Stark and The Performing Ferret Band; Alkatrazz were popular in heavy metal circles.

It was over the nearby village of Detling in December '76, that the Civil Aviation Authority lost contact with Pink Floyd's 40-foot long, helium filled, floating pig. It had become a hazard to air traffic after breaking away from its mooring at Battersea Power Station, where it was part of a promotion for their album *Animals*.

In November' 87, former Clash drummer Topper Headon was jailed for 15 months at Maidstone Crown Court, for supplying heroin to a man who later died.

Jefferson Airhead emerged in the early Nineties, kindly pointing out to local spliff-heads that Maidstone is an anagram of "I am stoned".

Starclub were early Nineties, Beatles influenced; Sonar Nation were mid-Nineties movers.

After an advert in The Stage, seeking "five girls who can sing and dance", drew together The Spice Girls, they were billeted communally here, in a three bedroom house.

ORPINGTON

Birthplace of singer/songwriter Ralph McTell, 3.12.44.

RAMSGATE

Local new wave group The Record Players attracted modest national attention.

Hometown of Paul Daley – half of top techno act Leftfield.

ROCHESTER

Birthplace of drummer Ronnie Verrell, 21.2.26 (Tommy Steele, Frank Skinner).

Home of late Sixties pop group Vanity Fare, who reached the Top Ten with 'Early In The Morning'.

The Love Family were early Nineties hopefuls.

ST. MARYS CRAY

One of the earliest instances of rock'n'roll style mayhem happened in April '54, when two gangs of teddy boys met in violent confrontation. 55 were arrested.

A hot Sixties gig was the Iron Curtain Club, which presented the likes of The Move.

SEVENOAKS

Birthplace of drummer Bill Bruford, 17.5.50 (Yes, King Crimson).

(Andy Earl)

Maidstone's Starclub, now members of Echo & The Bunnymen, Rialto and Oasis

MARGATE

As immortalised by Chas & Dave on their '82 hit.

In July '63, The Beatles played six nights (two shows a night) at the 2,000 seater Winter Gardens in Fort Crescent. It was in panto at the same venue, in '64, that Lonnie Donegan met his second wife, Jill Westlake, who was playing Cinderella to his Buttons.

The Rolling Stones played Dreamland in August '63.

Home of another Bowie backing group, The Lower Third, and Eighties cult singer/writer Paul Roland.

(Jane Bown, Camera Press Ltd)

The Beatles filming

The promotional film clip for 'Strawberry Fields Forever' saw The Beatles cavorting around a dead tree in Knole Park. They arrived in four matching Austin Minis with blacked-out windows. John Lennon, snooping around local antique shops during a break in filming, bought the old circus poster which inspired 'Being For The Benefit Of Mr Kite'.

Local resident Peter Skellern wrote his instrumental 'Cold Feet' after his tootsies turned into blocks of ice during intense bell ringing practice at the parish church.

Named with M25 deference or revulsion, synth band Orbital emerged in '90 with 'Chime', the first of many hits.

The Pied Piper (aka Mike Hazell) was an early Nineties rave figure.

SIDCUP

Birthplace of bassist/producer John Paul Jones, 3.1.46 (Led Zeppelin).

In March '57, Joan Regan was ambulanced to St. Mary's Hospital with three cracked ribs and a fractured knee-cap after her Vauxhall Velox skidded into a lamp-post and overturned.

Keith Richards attended Sidcup Art College after being expelled from Dartford Tech for truancy. Other pupils included Dick Taylor and Phil May, who started hot R&B group The Pretty Things there. In December '62, the embryonic Stones (pre Bill and Charlie) played at the Art College.

SNODLAND

Home of the late Judge Dread (Alex Hughes), who charted several rude reggae ditties in the Seventies – including Big Six, Big Seven and The Winkle Man.

STURRY

In spring '66, Daevid Allen and Kevin Ayers moved into the Old Coach House, where The Soft Machine would soon come together and start rehearsing.

SWANLEY

Birthplace of Sixties popster Crispian St. Peters, 5.4.44.

TENTERDEN

Local papers praised the public spirited Paul McCartney who, driving home to Rye, stopped to offer assistance at the scene of an accident on the Appledore Road.

At 16, Tom Robinson was sent to Finchden Manor, a readjustment centre for wayward youths. It was there that he formed his first group, Davanq, in '71.

TONBRIDGE

Birthplace of Shane MacGowan, 25.12.57 (Pogues), who would move to Tipperary with his family at a tender age.

K-Creative and Conemelt were Nineties techno outfits.

TUNBRIDGE WELLS

Birthplace of Tony Colton, 11.2.42 (leader of Sixties R&B group The Crawdaddies). Before taking up singing, he'd been a film extra – appearing in all Cliff Richard's early films.

The Rolling Stones played at the Assembly Hall in March '64. In October '64, The Dixie Cups made their UK début at the Essoldo – a package tour venue which also played host to Dionne Warwick and The Isley Brothers (among many others).

Home base for Sixties pop groups Tony's Defenders, Jason Crest, High Broom, Holy Mackerel – and Kippington Lodge, who became Brinsley Schwarz in '69 after five singles had missed the charts. They namecheck the town on 'Ebury Down': "Guess I'll go back to Tonbridge and re-form my band".

The controversial Anti Nowhere League topped the' 81 indie chart with their blitzkrieg reading of 'The Streets Of London'.

Sid Vicious attended Sandrock Road Secondary Modern.

Marillion shot the video for 'Garden Party' at Groombridge House.

Local early Nineties bands included Joeyfat and Sulphur.

WELLING

First local act to record was the Simmons – two brothers who cut mid-Sixties singles for Pye.

Kate Bush grew up in a 350-year-old farmhouse, not far from Woolwich cemetery.

Hometown of Steve Hillier, who moved to Newcastle to form mid-Nineties chart-makers Dubstar, and drum'n'bass artist Jay D'Kruze.

WEST MALLING

In the early Sixties, Gene Vincent lived here with his wife Margie.

Scenes for The Beatles' *Magical Mystery Tour* were shot here, at the aerodrome and in the High Street, in September '67.

WHITSTABLE

Birthplace of Bette Bright (singer in Deaf School; later married Suggs from Madness).

Derelict gun towers on Shivering Sands, nine miles off the Whitstable coast, became the base for pirate broadcasters Radio Sutch in May '64. Gunboats failed to dislodge him, prompting the news headline "Sutch Turns Back The Navy!" Sutch later sold out to his manager Reg Calvert and the station became Radio City.

In June '64 Radio Invicta began operating from an adjacent fort. Six months later its owner, Tom Pepper, was mysteriously drowned leaving the station. As Radio 390 it continued broadcasting until the passing of the Marine Offences Act.

Seminal Kent group The Wilde Flowers made their world début at the Bear And Key Hotel in January '65.

In summer '93, indie newcomers Salad (of unknown provenance) released their début single Kent – about the reactionaries inhabiting the commuter belt.

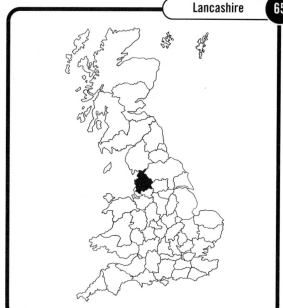

LANCASHIRE

ACCRINGTON
Birthplace of Jon Anderson, 25.10.44. He went to St. Johns Catholic School before forming The Warriors, whose drummer, Ian Wallace, was later in Bob Dylan's band. Anderson moved to London in '67 and ultimately formed Yes.

The Cybermen were late Seventies power-poppers.

BAMBER BRIDGE
A popular Seventies gig was the Pear Tree Hotel.

Operational base of techno/rave duo Dream Frequency, who assaulted the early Nineties charts.

BLACKBURN
Birthplace of Lionel Morton, 14.8.42 (Four Pennies); Tony Ashton, 1.3.46 (Ashton Gardner & Dyke); Karen Kay, 18.7.47.

Tony Ashton went to St. Georges Secondary Modern.

Operational base of The Four Pennies — '64 chart toppers with 'Juliet'.

In September '56, the town's Watch Committee banned local screenings of the Bill Haley film *Rock Around The Clock* — in case it provoked teenage riots and crime.

In January '67, a council survey revealed some 4,000 holes in the town's roads — a fact noted by John Lennon in The Beatles song 'A Day In The Life'. There is also a mention in the film *Yellow Submarine*: adrift in a land full of holes, one character remarks, "It reminds me of Blackburn, Lancashire". The Beatles' only appearance in Blackburn had been at King George's Hall in Northgate, back in May '63.

The Boomtown Rats made their UK début at the Lode Star pub in '77, getting 70 quid for their efforts.

Best punk era group was The Stiffs, whose 'Inside Out' was a Peel fave. Also around were Direct Hits and IQ Zero.

In the early Eighties, the town was in the tabloids as a result of ubiquitous acid house parties in the derelict cotton mills.

Local lad Rich Phillips released several mid-'Nineties jungle singles under the pseudonym Advantage.

BLACKPOOL
Birthplace of Cynthia Lennon, 10.9.39; Graham Nash, 2.2.42 (Hollies/CSN); Andy Summers, 31.12.42 (Police); Julie Grant, 12.7.46 (minor mid-'Sixties hits); John Evan, 28.3.48 (John Evan Smash); John Rossall, 26.11.48 (Glitter Band); Robert Smith, 21.4.59 (Cure); Coleen Nolan, 12.3.65 (Nolans); David Ball, 3.5.59 (Soft Cell); Chris Lowe, 10.10.59 (Pet Shop Boys).

"In an upstairs room in Blackpool, by the side of the northern sea; the army had my father, while my mother was having me," sings Graham Nash on 'Military Madness', lead track on his first solo album.

Russ Hamilton – Top Three with 'We Will Make Love' in '57 – was a redcoat at Butlins Holiday Camp.

It was at the Royal Pavilion, Manchester Square, that Lonnie Donegan recorded his '61 hit, 'Michael Row The Boat'.

Sixties R&B groups included Johnny Breeze & The Atlantics, and The Executives (featuring future *NME* writer Roy Carr)... but The Blades, who made their début at the Holy Family Youth Club in '63, were to become the most successful. By '66, they had evolved into The John Evan Band, specialising in blues and soul. They split when singer Ian Anderson and bassist Glenn Cornick (both local lads) moved to Luton in late '67. There they formed Jethro Tull... soon to include Blackpool pals John Evan, Jeffrey Hammond-Hammond and Barriemore Barlow. Anderson mentions his old home town on the Tull song 'Going Up The Pool'.

Also calling Blackpool home were Roy Harper, The Rockin' Vickers (a wild Sixties group through which passed pre-Hawkwind Lemmy), The Wheels (transplanted Belfast R&B merchants), Complex (whose early Seventies prog-rock album is worth big dosh to collectors), Anti Social and Skrewdriver (belligerent late Seventies punks) and John Sykes (Thin Lizzy, Whitesnake). The Rockin' Vickers attracted notoriety for activities at their farmhouse in Garstang Road; leader Harry Feeney later ran a Datsun showroom in Devonshire Road. Complex leader Steve Coe later masterminded Monsoon, who went Top Twenty with 'Ever So Lonely' in '82.

During an early Sixties tour, Tommy Roe's van broke down en route to a Blackpool gig. As he stood there looking anxious, a coach bringing Blackpool's football team home pulled up and transported him to the venue.

In July '64, the Empress Ballroom was the setting for Britain's biggest rock riot to date. At a Rolling Stones concert, a disruptive element in the audience (mainly pissed-up Glaswegian holidaymakers) demolished fixtures and fittings, smashed equipment, wrecked a Steinway piano, ripped curtains and generally rampaged. Fifty fans needed hospital treatment.

The Beatles played in Blackpool nine times during '63/4 – either at the ABC theatre, the Queens Theatre or the Opera House. In autumn '80, U2 played at the Clifton Hotel – to an audience of about 50.

Locally hot in the mid-Seventies, Mistress, led by Denise Gibson, were one of UK's first professional all-girl rock bands.

In the early Eighties, the town's biggest star was Dave Ball... half of Soft Cell. He went to Arnold School (where Chris Lowe was also a pupil – obviously a school for synth players) and then on to Blackpool Tech. Lowe was in local

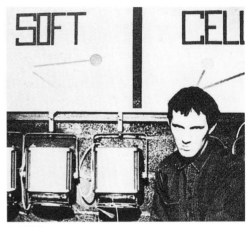

David Ball

group One Under The Eight and was apparently a glass collector in a bar on Central Pier.

Making it onto vinyl in the Eighties were The Membranes (whose bassplayer/singer John Robb published the fanzine *Blackpool Rox* and later authored books), The Fits, Tunnel Vision, Scala Tympani, Crackous Rock'n'Roll, Vee Vee V, Section 25 and The Denise Gibson Band.

The basement of the Railway in Talbot Road was a prime venue in the early Seventies, when The Groundhogs and Wishbone Ash visited. Decent bands also played at the Norbreck Castle on Queens Promenade and Tiffanys in Central Drive. Nineties venues include Your Father's Moustache and Sequins.

On July 29, '89, The Stone Roses performed at the Empress Ballroom, a truly wonderful gig that was captured on video.

Local early Nineties hopefuls include The Sunday Trips, The Sheds, Nick Unlimited, The Glow Worms, The Reason Why, Big Red Bus and The Nature Things.

Section 25 single photographed in the Blackpool dunes

Local laddie Nick Brown started the successful indie label Clawfist.

In April '91, resiliant star PJ Proby suffered a heart attack at the Lansdowne Hotel and recuperated at the Victoria Hospital in Whinney Heys Road.

Blackpool was a track on Roy Harper's '66 début album *The Sophisticated Beggar*; 'Oh Blackpool' was a track on The Beautiful South's '89 début album *Welcome To The Beautiful South*. The Sweet's 'Ballroom Blitz' is said to have been written about an incident at the local Mecca.

BRIERFIELD
Birthplace of Bernie Calvert, 16.9.42 (Hollies); Alan Buck, 7.4.43 (Four Pennies).

BURNLEY
Birthplace of Eric Haydock, 3.2.43, and Bobby Elliott, 8.12.42 (both Hollies); Tex Comer, 23.2.49 (Ace... in fact their hit, 'How Long', was written about him: he was considering a defection to another group, Quiver).

The Dolphins were an early Sixties beat group; two of their number, Tony Hicks and Bobby Elliott, later joined The Hollies.

Sixties groups included The Glass Menagerie (whose keyboard player Lou Stonebridge was later in Paladin and McGuinness Flint); Slack Alice were locally popular in the Seventies; punk groups included The Not Sensibles.

Nineties chartsters The Milltown Brothers (from Colne) are often to be seen at Turf Moor, supporting their beloved Burnley FC.

In the Nineties, several bands emerged, including Beware The Green Monkey and Bus K.

Former Rossendale Road resident Nigel Hunter (now known as Danbert Nobacon of Chumbawamba) gained notoriety by throwing a bucket of ice-water over John Prescott at the '98 Brit Awards.

CHORLEY
Birthplace of John Foxx, who lived in Eaves Lane before he moved to London in '74 and formed Ultravox. Under their original name of Tiger Lily, they played their first try-out gig in Chorley.

Lloyd Cole's dad was secretary at Shaw Hill Golf Club.

Shaw Hill Hotel, Chorley

(Shaw Hill Hotel)

Lloyd went to Leyland Runshaw College and formed his first band here.

Home of early 'Nineties Peel faves The Krispy Three.

COLNE
The local Milltown Brothers began their chart run with 'Which Way Should I Jump' in February '91; The Hate Syndicate are still looking to start theirs.

DARWEN
Birthplace of Bryn Haworth.

In January '63, The Beatles headlined 'The Greatest Teenage Dance' at the Co-operative Hall in Market Street. Support groups were The Electones, Ricky Day & The Mustangs and The Mike Taylor Combo. The gig was promoted by the Baptist Church Youth Club.

In the Sixties, the best record shop in town was Nightingales.

Operational base of the Nineties Peel faves The Levellers Five (albums on Probe Plus), who became The Calvin Party to avoid confusion with The Levellers.

LEVELLERS 5
springtime

(Probe Plus)

Peel favourites The Levellers Five

DEEPLY VALE
The Ashworth Valley was the setting for a free festival which ran annually from '74 to '79, presenting such acts as Steve Hillage, The Ruts, The Fall and The Frantic Elevators. The '78 festival ran for seven days had over 40 bands!

EARBY
Residents still recall the day in '64 when The Four Pennies honoured a contract to play the village youth club – even though their record 'Juliet' had shot to number one. Utter pandemonium!

FLEETWOOD
Early Eighties group The Tins didn't happen; late Nineties group One Way System are hoping for more.

Boat builder and Ormskirk resident, Les Pattinson

KIRKHAM

In October '98, singer Ian Brown started a four month sentence here – at the Category D, low-risk open prison. He was later transferred to Strangeways in Manchester and released on Christmas Eve after serving eight weeks.

LANCASTER

Birthplace of drummer Aynsley Dunbar, 10.1.46 (Mayall, Mothers, Starship); John Waite, 4.7.54 (Babys, Missing You).

China Street attracted some national attention in the late Seventies.

The Sugar House was a popular gig.

Cottonmouth were hot mid-Nineties Brit-poppers.

LYTHAM ST. ANNE'S

Birthplace of folkie and journalist Andrew Cronshaw, 18.4.49.

The Voice of America were local hopefuls, as were The Buggs (whose their drummer joined Alien Sex Fiend).

MORECAMBE

Birthplace of broadcaster and writer Charlie Gillett, 20.2.42. Also home to the late Beatles publicist Tony Barrow.

The Beatles played at the Floral Hall Ballroom on the Promenade in August '62 and January '63; The Rolling Stones appeared there in September '63.

Local late Seventies band Shrink recorded for Charlie Gillett's Oval label.

Sometime home of singer and journalist Simon Dudfield (Fabulous).

NELSON

Birthplace of guitarist Tony Hicks, 16.12.45 (Hollies); drummer Mark Price, 10.8.59 (All About Eve).

The Imperial Ballroom in Carr Road hosted every major Sixties group from The Beatles (May' 63) to the Stones (May '64) to Bo Diddley (September '65) to Jimi Hendrix (May '67) to Pink Floyd (September '67).

ORMSKIRK

Birthplace of Les Pattinson, 18.4.58 (Echo & The Bunnymen).

As a child, Marianne Faithfull lived in Greetby Hill and attended Ormskirk Church of England Infant School.

PRESTON

Birthplace of Keef Hartley, 8.3.44, who played drums for Rory Storm and Freddie Starr before moving to London to join John Mayall and ultimately form his own band. He played at Woodstock but missed inclusion in the movie!

It must be a drummers town... also spawning Paul Varley of The Arrows and Fred Kelly of Rare Bird.

One of the most famous natives was that man with the golden trumpet Eddie Calvert, born 15.3.22. At the age of 11, he was already principal cornet player in Preston Town Silver Band.

After the riot which exploded at their Blackpool gig in July 64, The Rolling Stones stayed at the Bull & Royal Hotel – heavily patrolled by police.

Local groups include David John & The Mood (Sixties R&B), The Puppets (produced by Joe Meek), Little Free Rock and Stoned Rose (Seventies progressive), The Blank Students and The Disco Zombies (late Seventies hopefuls), and Dandelion Adventure (early Nineties).

Starting in September '69, the Amethyst Club in Old Cock Yard presented the likes of Genesis, Supertramp and Renaissance (all of whom played for less than 75 quid), while the Seventies scene was centred around the Dog & Partridge in Friargate.

Formerly a dress-regulated disco, the Warehouse became the focus of punk activity – but no local bands made it out. Coolest Nineties venues are the Adelphi and the Charter Theatre.

Singer/songwriter Kevin Coyne worked at Whittington Mental Hospital – its influence surfacing in many of his songs.

Preston also gets a mention in Cheap Day Return, from Jethro Tull's *Aqualung* album.

After leaving school, Les Pattinson – soon to become bass player in Echo & The Bunnymen – was an apprentice boatmaker at Douglas Yard.

In March '85, The Stone Roses played their first northern gig at Clouds; in June '94, in their biggest concert to date, Oasis played Avenham Park – supporting The Boo Radleys.

Tjinder Singh and Ben Ayres (Cornershop) met at the Poly, where they formed General Havoc. Later, as founders of Cornershop, they returned to record their first two EPs at West Orange Studios.

Local bands emerging in the early Nineties included Dreamland, Gary Hall & The Stormkeepers, The Xentrix ("thrash-metal with a social conscience"), Pastel Collision and Bass Culture (techno). In '96, Formula One received ecstatic reviews for their first London gigs — and lo-fi teen bands Good Morning Canada and Presley were both warmly received in '97.

ST. ANNE'S-ON-SEA

Harry Epstein and Queenie Hyman met here on holiday in 1932 and married the following year. Brian Epstein would be their first son.

In August '57, Tommy Steele was asked to leave the Majestic Hotel. His crime was banging on a xylophone at 2 am.

The first Cornershop E.P. in Deeply Vale

UP HOLLAND

Richard Ashcroft and Nick McCabe — soon to become the core of The Verve — met at Up Holland Comprehensive.

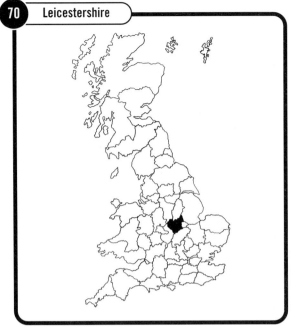

LEICESTERSHIRE

CASTLE DONINGTON
Setting for annual Monsters Of Rock festival, which has featured every heavy metal band ever invented – from Rainbow in '80, through AC/DC and Blue Oyster Cult in '81, Bon Jovi and Anthrax in '87, Motley Crue and Metallica in '91, Kiss and Ozzy Osbourne in '96. Biggest attendance was 97,800 in '88 when the headliners were Iron Maiden – who were also the loudest band to play there. Before the '95 bash, the Rev Brian Whitehead held a special service at St. Edwards Church to repel occult forces which he believed might radiate from the stage during White Zombie's set.

ENDERBY
In late '65, John Deacon's school group The Opposition played at the Co-op Hall – their most prestigious gig to date. During the next four years, they would play every venue within a ball of twine's distance from Leicester.

HINCKLEY
Sally Barker & The Rhythm worked their way onto the national pub/R&B circuit.

Hometown of Damon Baxter – aka dance act The Deadly Avenger, who scored an *NME* Single of the Week in '98.

LEICESTER
Birthplace of keyboard player Jon Lord, 9.6.41 (Deep Purple); singer Roger Chapman, 8.4.42 (Family); drummer Brian Davison, 25.5.42 (Nice); bassist Rod Allen, 31.3.44 (Fortunes); drummer Barry Jenkins, 22.12.44 (Nashville Teens, The Animals); keyboard player Tony Kaye, 11.1.46 (Yes); drummer Rob Townsend, 7.7.47 (Family); bass player John Illsley, 24.6.49 (Dire Straits); drummer Rob Gotobed, 1951 (Wire); bass player John Deacon, 19.8.51 (Queen);

saxplayer Anthony Thistlethwaite, 31.8.55 (Waterboys); singer Phil Oakey, 2.10.55 (Human League); guitarist John Ashton, 30.11.57 (Psychedelic Furs).

Arnold George Dorsey – later to become famous as Engelbert Humperdinck – grew up here and still has family in the area.

Roger Chapman and Rob Townsend went to Ellis Avenue Boys School; Charlie Whitney went to the Art College, where The Farinas made their début in '62. John Deacon went to Gartree High School and later to Beauchamp Grammar.

The Farinas and The Roaring Twenties coalesced into the city's most famous late Sixties export, Family. Their fame was eclipsed by Showaddywaddy, who emerged in '74 and racked up ten Top Ten hits.

Family: Leicester's finest   *(Michael White)*

Other local groups include The Dallas Boys (stars of Fifties TV show *Oh Boy!*); Pesky Gee, who made a radical change of direction to succeed as Black Widow (early Seventies gothic/ sorcery); Le Gay, who moved to London in the progressive Seventies and made some headway as Gypsy; progressive band Spring (including Pick Withers,

Gypsy: Leicester's second finest wisely changed their name from Le Gay

later of Dire Straits, and Pat Moran, later a producer at Rockfield), whose album is now a big dosh item at collectors' fairs; Chrome Molly (headbangers); Amber Squad, Atrocious Ghastly, The Disco Zombies and The Sinatras (all new wave).

Son of a local factory owner, Bruce Woolley fronted Camera Club and wrote The Buggles' number one hit 'Video Killed The Radio Star'.

Making headway in '89 were hot EMI signing Diesel Park West – once known locally as The Filberts. Singer John Butler previously led mid-Seventies group Widowmaker. Also hot for a while were Crazyhead (who recorded for Food) and Gaye Bykers On Acid (whose Nosedive Karma was a number one indie hit). Yeah Yeah Noh were Peel faves in the mid-Eighties. Bomb Party, The Numatics, Pookha Makes Three, The Swinging Laurels and The Fire Next Time cut records in the Eighties, when the Princess Charlotte at 8 Oxford Street first gained a reputation as the town's best gig.

The De Montfort Hall in Granville Road has always been a popular concert/package show venue. Buddy Holly & The Crickets played here in March '58, The Beatles in March '63 (and twice again), Dylan in May '65, Donovan a few weeks later, and The Who played here three times, the first time also in May '65 on a package tour that also included Tom Jones and Marianne Faithfull. Over the years, just about everyone famous enough has appeared here – including The Damned (June '85), The Stone Roses (December '95), Ocean Colour Scene (October '96).

Former Family, Blind Faith and Traffic bass player Ric Grech died of kidney failure at Gwendolen Road Hospital in March '90.

Most famous Nineties band is Cornershop, who formed here in '92. Also trying hard were Blab Happy, Storyville, The Flamingos, Company For Henry (indie janglers), Gonzo Salvage (post-modern beatbox), Prolapse (half Scottish) and Kevin Hewitt (early Factory signing making a comeback bid after ten year hiatus).

In the mid-Nineties came highly rated indie bands Perfume (ex-Blab Happy), Slinky, Angelica and Delicatessen – two of whom (Neil Carlill and Will Foster) won '98 chart success with side project Lodger.

Though he spent time in Florida, Mark Morrison (number one with 'Return Of The Mack' in '96) is considered a native of Leicester.

LOUGHBOROUGH

Birthplace of skiffle star Bob Cort, 20.12.29; maverick drummer Viv Prince, 9.8.44 (Pretty Things); Paul Brindley (Sundays).

The Celebrated Artists Band released singles in the Seventies but went nowhere.

Suzi Quatro made her UK début at the Students Union Building in Ashby Road in '72.

MALLORY PARK

The Bay City Rollers went nova at Radio One's Fun Day in May 75, when 40 weeping girls were fished out of the lake having failed to swim across to their idols. The group was helicoptered out without performing. Some 50,000 fans were beside themselves.

MARKET HARBOROUGH

Birthplace of Simon Park, whose Eye Level reached number one in '73.

Harborough Horace (aka Adrian Croasdell) is a famous soul DJ and CD compiler.

OAKHAM

Operational base of Nineties group The Waiting List, who describe themselves as 'Rutland Rock' – and since they seem to be the only exponents of that genre, I hope they won't mind me listing them under Leicestershire rather than Rutland.

The De Montfort Hall

(De Montfort Hall)

Due to the enormous wealth of talent and plethora of venues, this section is necessarily compressed. To get a fuller picture, your attention is drawn to *The Beatles & Some Other Guys* by Pete Frame (Omnibus Press).

The Strawberry Fields gates unmolested even in 1978

Birthplace of (just a few) comedian Ken Dodd, 8.11.29 (fifteen Sixties hits!); manager Brian Epstein, 19.9.34; singer Michael Cox, 19.3.40 (Joe Meek protege); rocker Billy Fury, 17.4.40; guitarist John McNally, 30.8.41 (Searchers founder); singer/guitarist Gerry Marsden, 24.9.42 (Gerry & The Pacemakers); singer Cilla Black, 27.5.43; drummer Jim McCarty, 25.7.43 (Yardbirds); drummer Aynsley Dunbar,

LIVERPOOL

10.1.46 (Journey, Whitesnake); drummer Snowy Fleet, 16.8.46 (Easybeats); singer David Garrick, 12.9.46; singer Carol Decker, 10.9.57 (T'Pau); guitarist/singer Pete Wylie, 22.3.58 (Wah!); keyboard whiz Henry Priestman, 21.7.58 (Yachts, Christians); guitarist/singer Ian Broudie, in Penny Lane on 4.8.58 (Big in Japan, Lightning Seeds); singer Ian McCulloch, 5.5.59 (Echo & The Bunnymen); singer Pete Burns, 5.8.59 (Dead or Alive); singer Colin Vearncombe, 25.6.62 (Black); singer Paul Draper, 26.9.72 (Mansun).

First local chart stars were Frankie Vaughan, Lita Roza, Michael Holliday, and teenage balladeer Russ Hamilton, who lived at 158 Beacon Lane, Everton.

Then came pre-Beatle boom rockers like Lance Fortune, The Vernons Girls (who worked for Vernons football pools in Aintree), Johnny Gentle, Janice Peters, Michael Cox, and Billy Fury, who was discovered in Marty Wilde's dressing room (see Birkenhead). The most influential gigs were Buddy Holly & The Crickets at the Philharmonic Hall on Hope Street in March '58, and the Gene Vincent/ Eddie Cochran package at the Empire in March '60.

Also, Roy Rogers rode Trigger from the Adelphi Hotel down Lime Street to the Empire Theatre... and it was only weeks later that poor old Trigger died!

Beatles landmarks: Ringo Starr was born in the Dingle at 9 Madryn Street (off High Park Street) in Liverpool 8, on 7.7.40. While still a toddler, he moved around the corner to 10 Admiral Grove, where he stayed until moving to London in '64. A sickly child, he spent many months in the Royal Children's Hospital in Myrtle Street. He was educated at St. Silas Primary in Pengwern Street and Dingle Vale Secondary Modern. His local pub was the Empress in High Park Street – as pictured on his album *Sentimental Journey*.

John Lennon was born at Oxford Street Maternity Hospital (just across the road from the Roman Catholic Cathedral) on 9.10.40. His early boyhood was spent at 9 Newcastle Road, Liverpool 15 (just around the corner from Penny Lane) and he later moved – with Aunt Mimi and

John's house, Menlove Avenue

Uncle George – to Mendips, 251 Menlove Avenue, Woolton, Liverpool 25 (just around the corner from Strawberry Fields).

He went to Dovedale Primary in Dovedale Road, Liverpool 18, and Quarry Bank Grammar in Harthill Road. He started at the Art College in Hope Street in '57, meeting Bill Harry (*Merseybeat* publisher), Stuart Sutcliffe (Silver Beetle) and Cynthia Powell – soon to become his wife.

The Registry Office, 64 Mount Pleasant

After their Register Office wedding at 64 Mount Pleasant, he and Cynthia honeymooned/lived in Brian Epstein's flat at 36 Falkner Street. Their son Julian was born at Sefton General in Smithdown Road on 8.4.63.

Paul McCartney was born at Walton Hospital in Rice Lane, Liverpool 9, on 18.6.42. As a baby, he lived at 10 Sunbury Road, Anfield, but later lived at 20 Forthlin Road, Allerton... his home until moving to London. He went to

Joseph Williams Primary in Naylorsfield Road, Belle Vale, Liverpool 25 and then Liverpool Institute in Mount Street, where he met George.

George Harrison was born at 12 Arnold Grove, Wavertree, Liverpool 15. For a while he lived at 174 Mackets Lane, Hunts Cross, Liverpool 25. (see also Speke).

Stuart Sutcliffe had a studio/flat in the basement of 7 Percy Street. He also shared a flat with Lennon at 3 Gambier Terrace.

7 Percy Street   No.3 Gambier Terrace

Pete Best (born in Madras, India) attended Collegiate Grammar School in Shaw Street, Liverpool 6. His mother operated the Casbah Club in the cellar of their house at 8 Hayman's Green, West Derby.

Brian Epstein was born at 4 Rodney Street. His famous NEMS Record Shop and management office was at 12

The old NEMS shop became Rumbelows in 1979

Whitechapel, where a commemorative Harp Beat rock plaque (since disappeared) was presented by Gerry Marsden in July '91. (It's now a sex shop; punters now seek ten inch vibrators rather than ten inch singles). The Epstein family home was at 197 Queens Drive in Childwall. He is buried at the Kirkdale Jewish Cemetery, Longmoor Lane, Liverpool 9.

The Quarrymen made their début at a Roseberry Street open air carnival in May 57, and later played at St. Barnabus Church Hall in Penny Lane, and the Broadway Conservative Club in Broad Lane, Norris Green, Liverpool 11.

John and Paul first met at a Quarrymen gig at St. Peter's Church Hall in Church Road, Woolton in July '57.

Complete with barber shop and bank, Penny Lane is in Liverpool 18 – though souvenir hunters have convinced the council not to erect any more signs.

Strawberry Fields is a Salvation Army Children's Home in Beaconsfield Road, Liverpool 25.

"The shelter in the middle of the roundabout ..."

A statue of Eleanor Rigby can be seen in Stanley Street. The sculptor was former rock'n'roller Tommy Steele, who charged half a sixpence for his work (but never got it!).

The ferry across the Mersey, as advertised by Gerry & The Pacemakers, leaves from the Landing Stage – as did the Royal Iris, often used for rock cruises.

Beatles contemporaries included The Searchers, Kingsize Taylor & The Dominoes, Rory Storm & The Hurricanes, The Big Three, Gerry & The Pacemakers, The Swinging Blue Jeans, Cilla Black, The Remo Four, Faron's Flamingos, The Dennisons, The Merseybeats, Billy J Kramer & The Coasters, Lee Curtis & The All Stars, The Fourmost, Freddie Starr & The Midnighters, and loads more... over 400 groups by the end of '62.

Most famous of all the venues in Liverpool (and possibly the world) was the Cavern at 10 Mathew Street – where The

Second to Abbey Road, the most famous of street signs

Beatles are said to have played 292 times. A trad-jazz/skiffle stronghold, it first succumbed to The Beatles in March '61. Public Health officials shut it down in February '66. It reopened from July '66 to May '73 and was then redeveloped. A new building, Cavern Walks, describes itself as Liverpool's ultimate shopping and entertainment experience! It was at the Cavern in '61 that Tommy Steele met the writers and backers of *Half A Sixpence* and agreed to play in it.

The Razamataz Club, ex-The Blue Angel

Other Merseybeat venues included the Blue Angel Club at 108 Seel Street (operated by sometime Beatles manager Allan Williams, who is said to have thrown Judy Garland out for not paying for her drinks). It was here that Cilla Black was spotted by Brian Epstein. Formerly the Wyvern, it was the scene of the famous Larry Parnes audition when The Silver Beetles were selected to back Johnny Gentle. Then there was the Casanova Club in Dale Street; the Black Cat Club above Sampson & Barlow's Restaurant in London Road (later the Peppermint Lounge); the Iron Door Club at 13 Temple Street; St. George's Hall in Lime Street; Silver Blades Ice Rink in Prescot Road; the Locarno and Grafton Ballrooms in West Derby Road, Liverpool 6; Knotty Ash Village Hall, East Prescot Road, Liverpool 14; Blair Co-op Hall in Walton Road; the Holyoake Hall in Smithdown Road; the Pavilion Theatre in Lodge Lane; and the Rialto Ballroom, where the enterprising Oriole Records recorded ten groups in May '63.

Popular coffee bars and clubs included the Jacaranda at 23 Slater Street; the Zodiac (later the Scorpion) at 98 Duke Street; the Odd Spot at 89 Bold Street; Streates in Mount Pleasant; the Lantern at 144 Aigburth Street; the Castle at 70 South Castle Street. One of the city's first black clubs was the Colony at 80 Berkley Street, featuring Beatles' friend Lord Woodbine.

A Hard Day's Night had its Northern premiere at the Odeon in London Road, as did *Give My Regards To Broad Street*... on the same day that Paul McCartney was given Freedom of the City.

The Empire Theatre in Lime Street was the major package tour venue. The Beatles supported Little Richard here in October '62 and played their last Liverpool concert in December '65. They also did their *Juke Box Jury* show from here.

Popular pubs were Ye Cracke in Rice Street, the Philharmonic in Hope Street, the White Star in Rainford Gardens, and – most famous of all – the Grapes in Mathew Street. Cavern disc jockey Bob Wooler has been a regular here since December '60.

The *Merseybeat* newspaper was published from an office at 81a Renshaw Street.

The old *Merseybeat* offices

Hessy's guitar shop

Top musical instrument shops were Frank Hessy's at 62 Stanley Street, Bradley's at 26 Lord Street, and Rushworth's in Whitechapel.

Favoured tailors included Eric's at 9 Commutation Row and Duncan Classic Tailors at 29 London Road.

In July '64, when the Lord Mayor welcomed back The Beatles from their triumphant US tour, a quarter of a million fans lined the route from Speke Airport to the Town Hall in Water Street.

"The Jac", 23 Slater Street

The individual Beatles were incorporated into street names on the Kensington Fields Estate, built by Wimpey Homes in '81.

Other pupils at the Institute included Don Andrew and Colin Manley (Remo Four), Les Chadwick (Pacemakers), Stu James (Mojos). With financial and spiritual assistance from Paul McCartney, it was turned into the Fame-style Liverpool Institute of the Performing Arts.

Cilla Black went to St. Andrews Secondary Modern and Anfield Commercial College.

The Everyman Theatre in Hope Street was a favourite poetry venue. Adrian Henri later formed The Liverpool Scene (famous for 'The Entry Of Christ Into Liverpool'), while Roger McGough formed Scaffold (Number One in '68 with 'Lily The Pink'). Willy Russell's play *John Paul George Ringo & Bert* had its world premiere here in '74.

The Spinners were kingpins of the folk scene, but Paul Simon played a gig at the Cross Keys pub in '64.

Bob Dylan played at the Odeon in '65 and '66. Scenes in *Don't Look Back* ('65) show him chatting to fans outside the venue. A live recording of his '66 concert with The Band became a popular bootleg – but one track, 'Just Like Tom Thumb's Blues', appeared officially as the B-side of his single 'I Want You'.

Hundreds of groups sprang up following the success of The Beatles, but after '63 the only new ones to make the charts were The Mojos, The Escorts, Tommy Quickly, and The Cryin' Shames.

Milked dry by the recording industry, Liverpool spent the next 12 years in the doldrums. The only rock groups to make any sort of progress were Liverpool Express, Arrival, Supercharge, Nasty Pop, Strife and Afraid of Mice.

Then, in the late Seventies, came the second deluge – centred on Eric's Club in the very same Mathew Street, right opposite the site of the Cavern. On the wall above the door was Arthur Dooley's statue (erected in '74) to remind bands and fans of their heritage.

The Beatles statue, Mathew Street

Between its opening in October '76 and its police closedown in March '80, Eric's rejuvenated Liverpool. Pistols and Clash gigs inspired local lads; Madness made their provincial début there in June 79; Devo made their UK début there in July '79.

First local group was Deaf School (containing future producer Clive Langer and Bette Bright); first punk band was Big In Japan (containing future entrepreneur and Timelord Bill Drummond and Holly Johnson). The floodgates were opened by Echo & The Bunnymen, The Teardrop Explodes, Wah, The Yachts, Pink Military, Orchestral Manoeuvres In The Dark, and less successful outfits like The Spitfire Boys (with Budgie and Paul Rutherford) and The Mystery Girls (with Pete Burns and Julian Cope).

The first wave also included Dalek I Love You, White & Torch, Those Naughty Lumps, Ellery Bop, Nightmares In Wax, and Hambi & The Dance (with Wayne Hussey). Hambi later opened the Pink Museum Studio, where Oasis recorded their first single 'Supersonic'.

First local labels were Zoo, based in Whitechapel and Inevitable, at 4 Rutland Road, Liverpool 17.

A favourite meeting place was Probe Records in Rainford Gardens. There Geoff Davies would bombard incipient bandleaders with weird and wonderful sounds. Pete Wylie, Pete Burns, Julian Cope and Paul Rutherford all worked behind the counter at various times, and Gary Dwyer (later The Teardrop's drummer) was employed as a bouncer when it got overcrowded! The shop later moved to its current premises in Wood Street and the Probe Plus label operates from 12 Buckingham Avenue.

The Grapes became top boozer with the new generation as well as the old, and the first floor café (O'Hallaghan's Tea Room) over Aunt Twacky's Bazaar (just across the road) was always teeming with guys anxious to become famous. It was here that the creative nucleus of the late Seventies scene (Jayne Casey, Bill Drummond, Holly Johnson, Paul Rutherford, etc) first met each other. It was later turned into the Armadillo Tea Rooms – another café-cum-meeting place for street dreamers.

Pete Wylie, Ian McCulloch (who had both been to Alsop Comprehensive in Walton) and various others shared a flat in Penny Lane.

The early Eighties saw more quirky bands with strange names... The Icicle Works, Frankie Goes To Hollywood, Modern Eon, A Flock Of Seagulls, China Crisis, The Lotus Eaters, The Room, Pale Fountains, Dead Or Alive.

Eric's had now re-opened as Brady's. Other gigs were Plato's Ballroom, held weekly at Pickwicks in Fraser Street (off the London Road); the Royal Court in Roe Street, which had once been the province of Laurence Olivier and Margaret Rutherford but had now fallen prey to the punk horde; the Warehouse in Wood Street; and the System (the old Iron Door Club modified) where Club Zoo became groovy for a while.

Frankie Goes To Hollywood made their début at Pickwicks, supporting Hambi & The Dance.

Another famous band haunt was Brian's Cafe in Stanley Street – a greasy spoon so atmospheric that from ten yards away, people could tell that you'd just been there!

The mid-Eighties brought The Reverb Brothers, Here's Johnny, Black, It's Immaterial (their hit 'Driving Away From Home' was about a journey down the M62 to Manchester, where they used to live), Doctor (of The Medics) and Rolo McGinty (leader of The Woodentops).

Late Eighties faves included The La's, The Christians, 16 Tambourines, The Reynolds Girls, Benny Profane, Rain and Up And Running.

Both Deep Purple (March '76) and Deaf School (April '78) played their last gig at the Empire – though the former later re-formed – and Aerosmith made their UK début there in October '76.

The Grapes, a meeting place then and now

The Bluecoat Gallery in School Lane presented Captain Beefheart's first UK exhibition in '72; a retrospective of Stuart Sutcliffe's work in '90; a Mal Dean retrospective in '93; and the first gallery shows of John Hyatt (ex Three Johns), *NME* photographer Pennie Smith, and Pete Frame's *Rock Family Trees* (in '90 and '98). It was here also that Yoko Ono received her first real fee for a performance – of Music for the Mind in September '67. It's the oldest and most beautiful building in Liverpool (if not the world) and is always worth a visit.

(The Bluecoat Gallery)

Captain Beefheart at The Bluecoat, 1972

The Old Iron Door Club

Following John and Stu into Liverpool Art College were the instigators of Deaf School and The Yachts, Bill Drummond (Big In Japan, KLF), Budgie (Spitfire Boys, The Slits and The Banshees), and John Campbell (It's Immaterial). Sleeve designer Mal Dean was already there. Radiohead's Phil Selway went to the Poly. Pete Wylie was a student at the University until rock'n'roll got the better of him.

Architecture students at the Uni included Chris Lowe (Pet Shop Boys) and Jarvis Whitehead (It's Immaterial).

Vic Christian, the original keyboard player in The Christians, quit rather than give up his job as music teacher at Quarry Bank Grammar, where Holly Johnson was a pupil... and that brings us full circle!

The Royal Court continued to present bands: it was a favourite venue for R.E.M., who played there in November '84, October '85 and May '89; locally based Space played there for two nights in December '98.

A plethora of bands emerged in the Nineties, including Ian McNabb (ex Icicle Works), Magic Clock, Dead Men's Suits, The Stairs, Where's The Beach?, Fishmonkeyman, Spontaneous Cattle Combustion, Breed, Connie Lush, The Wizards of Twiddly (who also backed Kevin Ayers on tour), The Muffin Men (Zappa devotees, playing his compositions), Oceanic ('91 chart breakers with Insanity), Mr Ray's Wig World (Peel faves), The Onset, The Tidemarks, Mazey Fade, Cast ('95 breakout with 'Finetime'), The Kachinas, Pele, Electrixion (Bunnymen spin-off), Space ('96 breakout with 'Female Of The Species'), Waist (Rain spin-off), Cecil, Livingstone, Apollo 440 (made the '95 Top Forty with a techno version of 'Don't Fear The Reaper'), Steve Roberts (ex 16 Tambourines), Mike Badger (ex The La's), Ism, Surreal Madrid, Ooberman, Ricky Spontane – they keep coming, but as yet the long awaited third tidal wave shows no sign of gathering momentum.

Cool Nineties venues include the Cosmos, Planet X, Quadrant Park, Le Bateau, the Krazyhouse in Wood Street (where Oasis first played in town), the Lomax in Cumberland Street and the larger L2 in Hotham Street, the Mardi Gras in Bold Street and Nation in Wolstenholme Square (haven for Cream clubbers).

Songs include 'Cavern Stomp' by The Big Three, 'Going Down To Liverpool' by The Bangles (not to mention Katrina & The Waves), 'Ferry Cross The Mersey' by Gerry & The Pacemakers, 'Up Here In The North Of England' by The Icicle Works. "Liverpool's where I belong," sang The Stone Roses on their '89 track 'Mersey Paradise' – even though they were from Manchester.

LONDON

(by postal district)

E1 Wapping, Whitechapel, Shoreditch, Stepney

Birthplace of songwriter Lionel Bart, 1.8.30; Georgia Brown, 21.10.33; Des O'Connor (three top tenners); Kenny Lynch, 20.3.39 (he lived in Watney Street); rock'n'roller Neil Christian, 14.2.43; singer Denis Dalziel, 10.10.43 (Honeycombs); drummer Kenney Jones, 16.9.48 (Small Faces; he lived in Arbour Square); guitarist Andy Powell, 8.2.50 (Wishbone Ash); Billy Ocean, 21.1.52; drummer Terry Chimes, 1956 (Clash); Samantha Fox, 15.4.66 (at Mile End Hospital); singer Damon Albarn, 23.3.68 (Blur); Tony Mortimer, 20.10.70 (East 17).

Micky Finn & The Blue Men were early R&B/bluebeat merchants from Mile End Road.

In '64/65, Paul Simon was living at Judith Piepe's council flat in Dellow Road, off Cable Street (famous for the Oswald Mosely race riots of 1936). He wrote 'The Big Bright Green Pleasure Machine' in a nearby all-night launderette. Other house guests included Al Stewart, Sandy Denny, occasionally Art Garfunkel and – years later – Nick Laird-Clowes of Dream Academy. It was left to Southampton group The Men They Couldn't Hang to come up with 'The Ghosts Of Cable Street'.

Underground bizarros The Social Deviants lived in Princelet Street.

Robert Wyatt's 'Shipbuilding' video was made at St. Katherine's Dock – near Tower Bridge.

Jarvis Cocker recalled his few months local residence on the Pulp B-side 'Mile End'.

The Spitz at 109 Commercial Road established itself as a cool late Nineties venue.

In June '95, Tower Bridge was raised to allow a 10-metre high statue of Michael Jackson to sail upstream, promoting his album *History*.

On New Year's Eve '98, the over-anxious Frank Butcher ran into and killed Tiffany Grant outside the Queen Victoria public house in Albert Square – allowing actress Martine McCutcheon to pursue her pop career single-mindedly.

E2 Bethnal Green

Birthplace of Laurie London, 19.1.44 (one-hit teen wonder, star of *6.5 Special*); Helen Shapiro, 28.9.46; Peter Green, 29.10.46 (Fleetwood Mac); Cheryl Baker, 8.3.55 (Bucks Fizz).

The video for Culture Club's 'Time (Clock Of The Heart)' was shot at the Ship And Blue Ball in Boundary Street.

E3 Bow

Birthplace of Steve Marriott, 30.1.47 (Small Faces); Taffy, 14.2.52 ('I Love My Radio'); Tina Charles, 10.3.55 (number one with 'I Love To Love' in '76).

In April '55, Lonnie Donegan married Maureen Tyler at St. Luke's Church.

(Rex Features)

Michael Jackson squeezes beneath some bridge or other

Mile End Stadium, off Burdett Street, was the venue for a '95 celebration of Britpop featuring Blur, Pulp and The Boo Radleys.

Three Mills Island Studios in Three Mills Lane was a favourite late Nineties rave venue.

E4 Chingford
Birthplace of singer Paul Di'Anno, 17.5.59 (Iron Maiden)

Home of Sixties group The Druids and mid-Eighties indie band The Kick.

E5 Clapton
Birthplace of Fifties star Mike Preston, 14.5.34; guitarist Dave Murray, 23.12.58 (Iron Maiden).

Helen Shapiro was educated at Clapton Park Comprehensive; she and Marc Bolan both went to Northwold Primary.

Late Sixties group Springfield Park were named after a local park.

Howard Werth and The Audience in Dalston

E6 East Ham
Birthplace of Vera Lynn, 20.3.17 (she went to Brampton Road School); guitarist Bert Weedon, 10.5.20.

Lonnie Donegan grew up here, which accounts for the cockney chirp rather than a Glaswegian growl.

In October '62, Phil Everly took the stage of the Granada (281 Barking Road) at the start of a UK tour – but Don was missing. He was ensconced at the Middlesex Hospital, strung out on speed. He flew home, leaving Phil to complete the tour alone.

The Beatles started their second UK tour at Granada in March '63. Tommy Roe and Chris Montez shared the bill.

Locally based groups include Wasted Youth (early Eighties) and McCarthy (late Eighties).

E7 Forest Gate
The Upper Cut at the Forest Gate Centre in Woodgrange Road, owned by boxer Billy Walker, was opened by The Who in December '66. It was hot for a few years, but eventually

became a bingo and social club. Otis Redding blew the place apart and Jimi Hendrix wrote 'Purple Haze' there.

Bill Curbishley, manager of The Who, grew up here; his brother Alan played for West Ham and manages Charlton Athletic.

E8, 9 Dalston, Hackney
Birthplace of Anthony Newley, 24.9.31; Gary Brooker, 29.5.45 (Procol Harum); Marc Bolan, 30.9.47; Graham Parker, 18.11.50; Nicko McBain, 5.6.52 (Iron Maiden); Leee John, 23.6.57 (Imagination); Phil Collen, 8.12.57 (Def Leppard); Nicola Summers, 13.5.59 (Bodysnatchers), Mel, 11.7.66, and Kim Apleby, 8.8.61. Most were born at Hackney Hospital, 230 Homerton High Street.

Formed in November '63, local group The Sherabons found fame after a name change to The Honeycombs. Oddly, The Honeybus were also from here.

In the mid-Sixties, the Double D Club was a hot venue above Burtons at 372 Mare Street. Bands like The Cheynes and Zoot Money would appear.

Local lads Howard Werth and Keith Gemmell formed progressive band Audience, who found a cult following on Charisma; Alan Williams found fame leading The Rubettes; Ray Cooper became Elton John's longtime percussionist.

Before his adoption as a punk idol, Sid Vicious studied at Hackney College of Further Education.

The Desperate Bicycles were a pioneering indie band whose '77 single 'The Medium Is Tedium' described the process of DIY records.

'The Medium Is Tedium'

(Michael Werner)

Several members of Bad Manners were local – as indicated by their B-side 'Night Bus To Dalston'. Throbbing Gristle offshoots Chris & Cosey lived at 50 Beck Road.

The Clash, Tom Robinson and Sham '69 headlined an inspirational Rock Against Racism concert in Victoria Park, April '78. Paul Weller appeared there in August '98.

The Prodigy made their début at the Labyrinth.

Rapper Overlord X made waves in the early Nineties – as did indie bands Animals That Swim and Springheel Jack.

In the mid-Nineties, drum'n'bass maestro Square Pusher (Tom Jenkinson) found national acclaim. Working similar territory were Krome and Time.

The Creation label went through tricky times in their offices on the second floor at 8 Westgate Street – but were ultimately able to move to Hampstead.

Asian Dub Foundation made their début at a benefit concert at the Empire in '94.

E10 Leyton
In the late Fifties, teenager Joe Brown played guitar and sang in The Spacemen, a skiffle group, whose early gigs were at The Lion & Key public house. The Antelope was also a skiffle pub. Russ Sainty (later leader of The Nu Notes) first appeared in public there, guesting with The Buddy Monroe Five.

Sounds Incorporated made their début at Leyton Baths in '61. The Beatles played there in April '63.

Home of The Leyton Buzzards, who eventually mutated into Modern Romance.

Iron Maiden founder and rapper Duke Baysee (Top 30 with 'Sugar Sugar' in '94) both attended Leyton County High School.

E11 Wanstead, Leytonstone
Birthplace of bass player Steve Harris, 12.3.57 (Iron Maiden), who lived at 40 Steele Road.

Lonnie Donegan was living here at the time of his first hit, 'Rock Island Line'.

The Red Lion in Leytonstone High Road was a popular late Sixties venue. The Who played there in December '64;

The Red Lion, 1900. The Who not in shot

(Vestry House Museum)

such up and comers as Jethro Tull and Fleetwood Mac a few years later.

Sometime home of new wave troubadour Patrik (sic) Fitzgerald and Blur frontman Damon Albarn.

On release of their '93 début album *Patriot Games*, Gunshot were described as Britain's best rap group.

Head On A Stick were frontliners in the mid-Nineties M11/squat protest.

Home of late Nineties tabla king Talvin Singh – born into a Ugandan Asian family evicted by Idi Amin.

E12 Manor Park
Steve Marriott and Ronnie Lane formed The Small Faces after meeting at the J60 Music Bar, where the former was employed as a salesman. He also went to school locally – at Sandringham Secondary Modern.

The Small Faces used to rehearse at the Ruskin Arms, 386 High Street North – where Iron Maiden often gigged in their pre-fame days.

Rap duo Definition of Sound broke out with '91 hit 'Wear Your Love Like Heaven'.

E13 Plaistow, West Ham
Birthplace of Ronnie Lane, 1.4.46 (Small Faces); Cliff Anderson, 30.1.51 (Cure).

As a child, Joe Brown lived at The Sultan pub in Grange Road, where his uncle was landlord. He went to Hilda Road Primary School and then Plaistow Grammar – until he was relegated to Pretoria Road Secondary Modern.

Operational base of hardcore punks Smak and The Cockney Rejects, whose West Ham anthem 'I'm Forever Blowing Bubbles' went Top 40 and whose album track 'Oi Oi Oi' became a genre classification.

Home of Peter 'Sketch' Martin, bass player in early Eighties duo Linx.

The Ian Dury song 'Plaistow Patricia' concerns a junkie whose "tits had dropped and arse had spread", but she still married a wealthy Chinaman.

E14 Tower Hamlets
The London Arena in Limeharbour Way is the area's biggest venue.

E15 Stratford
Birthplace of organist Jimmy Winston, 20.4.45 (Small Faces); singer Graham Bonney, 2.6.45; drummer, songwriter, journalist Will Birch, 12.9.48 (Kursaal Flyers, The Records); comic/folkie Richard Digance, 24.12.49; Joe's daughter Sam Brown, 7.10.64.

Lonnie Donegan met his future wife Maureen when he played a gig at her father's pub, the King Alfred in Locksley Street.

Fronted by David Essex, The Everons were regulars at the Eagle in Chobham Road. It was here, in '64, that Essex was discovered by his future manager Derek Bowman.

Other local groups include Dr Marigold's Prescription and Chords Five (average age 15).

Refused entry to the loo at the Francis Service Station at 176 Romford Road, three of The Rolling Stones were forced to urinate against a convenient wall. In June '65, local magistrates fined them five quid each.

A prime late Sixties blues club was the Bottleneck, held at the Railway Tavern in Angel Lane.

Iron Maiden made their world début at the Cart & Horses public house at 1 Maryland Park in early '76.

E16 Canning Town

David Essex was educated at Star Lane Primary and Shipman Road County Secondary.

In '59, 16-year-old Georgie Fame was working as a pub pianist at the Essex Arms near Silvertown Bridge when he was seen by Lionel Bart, who sent him along to manager Larry Parnes for an audition.

The Bridge House has always been an interesting venue. It was here that Blancmange were spotted by Stevo and Depeche Mode were discovered (in December '80) by Daniel Miller of Mute Records. The Blues Band made their début here in April '79; Billy Bragg came second in a talent contest final in July '82.

E17 Walthamstow

Birthplace of saxplayer Denny Payton, 11.8.43 (Dave Clark Five); guitarist Mick Box, 8.6.47 (Uriah Heep); guitarist Steve Hillage, 2.8.51 (Gong).

The Granada in Hoe Street was a big Sixties venue. Johnny Burnette and US Bonds played there in May' 62; The Beatles and Roy Orbison in May '63. James Brown made his UK début there in March '66.

In '61, Ian Dury was a student at Walthamstow School of Art. His tutor was Peter Blake. Dury's first band, Kilburn & The High Roads, played their last gig at the Town Hall in June '76. Support groups were The 101-ers and The Stranglers.

Local groups include Sam Apple Pie (late Sixties bluesers), The Wasps (late Seventies) and Eighties/Nineties psychedelic flagwavers The Bevis Frond. Local lads Malcolm Morley and Dave Charles made international cult impact with Help Yourself (trippy Seventies prog rock).

Local lad Mick Box played football for London Schoolboys before forming rock groups like The Stalkers and Spice. (The Spice Girls were originally going to be called Spice – proving that Box was 30 years ahead on a visionary level). He made it big in Uriah Heep, who are still going and have played in more places around the world than any other band. (If Michael Palin goes somewhere, you can bet your arse that Uriah Heep beat him to it).

Operational base of late Seventies indie label Small Wonder (Patrik Fitzgerald and The Leyton Buzzards), who operated from 162 Hoe Street, and of Co-Co – our '78 Eurovision song contest entrants with 'The Bad Old Days'.

Premier pub rock venue was the Royal Standard.

In the early Nineties, Some Have Fins and The Cuckoos emerged; Hefner were late Nineties indie hopefuls.

East 17, E17 boys

(All Action)

No group put the area on the map like East 17. They all went to St. George Monoux Secondary School – and went Top Ten with first single 'House Of Love' in '92. The next year, their début album Walthamstow entered the chart at number one.

EC1 Clerkenwell, Holborn

Birthplace of Gary Kemp, 16.10.59 (Spandau Ballet) – at Barts Hospital.

Anthony Newley, Steve Marriott, Andrew Oldham discovery Adrienne Posta, Millie and Eternal founders Louise Nurding and Kelle Bryan were among those learning stagecraft at the Italia Conti Academy of Theatre Arts at 23 Goswell Road.

Cat Stevens was educated at Hugh Myddleton School and then Northampton Secondary Modern in Old Street.

Spandau Ballet, their manager Steve Dagger, and Chris Foreman of Madness all attended Dame Alice Owens Grammar School in Owens Row.

The interim office of Creation Records was 83 Clerkenwell Road.

Turnmills at 636 Clerkenwell Road and the 333 Club at 333 Old Street were popular late Nineties clubbers' venues.

The Italia Conti Academy

EC2 City, London Wall, Moorgate

Among students passing through the Guildhall School of Music in the Barbican were Bernie Watson (John Mayall's Bluesbreakers), Andy Mackay (Roxy Music), producer George Martin, John Cale (Velvet Underground), Peter Skellern, Matthew Fisher (Procol Harum), Ian Mosley (Marillion) and Phil Gould (Level 42).

Live at The Hope, Islington

(Dai Davies)

EC4 Holborn, Fleet Street

In the Sixties and early Seventies *Melody Maker's* offices in the IPC building at 161-166 Fleet Street attracted a slew of popsters anxious to be interviewed, including Paul and Linda McCartney, Ringo, The Walker Brothers, Georgie Fame, Alan Price, Marianne Faithful and Jimmy Page. In '62 Bob Dylan wandered in, announced that he was an American folksinger visiting London and was promptly shown the door. Mick Jagger, too, was turned away by an aggressive doorman at the rear of the building.

Many *MM* interviews took place in the Red Lion pub, now demolished, in Red Lion Court; Steve Winwood, Spencer Davis, The Bee Gees, Marc Bolan, Peter Frampton, David Bowie, Arthur Brown, Steve Howe, Peter Gabriel, Phil Colins, Viv Stanshall, Neil Innes, Ronnie Lane, Ornette Coleman, Peter Noone, Mitch Mitchell, Neol Redding and dozens more all explained themselves there between pints of ale.

Disc & Music Echo magazine was in the same building as *MM*.

Britannia Row Studios without Pink Floyd

(Brit Row)

N1 Islington

Birthplace of drummer Charlie Watts, 2.6.41 (Rolling Stones); singer Tony Hadley, 2.6.60 (Spandau Ballet); bassist Mark Bedford, 24.8.61 (Madness); singer Shaznay Lewis, 14.10.75 (All Saints), who went to Mount Carmel School.

Rehearsals for the TV show *Oh Boy!* were held at the Four Provinces of Ireland Club in Canonbury Lane. There a nervous Cliff Richard prepared for his television début in September '58 – shaving off his sideburns at the insistence of producer Jack Good.

It was at the Mildmay Tavern on Newington Green that The Sherabons were spotted by songwriters Howard and Blaikley, who changed their name to The Honeycombs, provided them with 'Have I The Right', and watched them zip to Number One.

The Hope & Anchor at 207 Upper Street was pub-rock mecca for more than a decade. Before he made his name at Stiff, Dave Robinson ran a recording studio here. Among many provincial bands making their London début in the dank cellar were Joy Division in December '78, Dexy's in June' 79, and U2 in December '79. In October '82, Frankie Goes To Hollywood made two promotional videos there – 'Relax' and 'Two Tribes'. Arista, who financed the venture, passed on the band. After many financial problems, it closed down in December '84 – but has recently reopened as a venue.

Madness played their first gig at a party in the back garden of 8 Compton Terrace (directly opposite the Hope & Anchor) in June '77 and their third at the City and East London College in Pitfield Street in February '78.

The Clash played their first public gig at the Screen On The Green on 29.8.76, over The Buzzcocks (making their London début). Headliners were the Pistols, who were looking for a label... but record company A&R men were too intimidated to enter!

Operational base of early Eighties Anglo-African act Orchestra Jazira, who lived in Balls Pond Road.

R&B group Juice On The Loose were all bar fixtures at the Kings Head in Upper Street. The Pied Bull at 1 Liverpool Road was another longtime music pub, often used for rehearsals/auditions. In the Seventies, when groups like Mott The Hoople (January '70) played there, it was known as the Barn. When it alchemised into the Powerhaus in the late Eighties, it showcased such up and comers as The Stone Roses and Blur – who were spotted there by perspicacious Food label exec, Andy Ross.

Pre-Spandau teenagers Martin and Gary Kemp acquired acting skills and social graces at the Anna Scher School at 70 Barnsbury Road, as did Phil Daniels – mod star of *Quadrophenia* and leader of The Cross.

The 2-Tone label had their offices at 285 Pentonville Road; Bronski Beat made their début in autumn '83 at the Bell pub at 259 Pentonville Road.

At 35 Britannia Row are Pink Floyd's studios, which have been used by everyone from Tori Amos to Maxi Priest, Erasure to Motorhead. Among the first albums to emerge were *Animals* by Pink Floyd (January '77) and *Music For Pleasure* by The Damned (January '78).

The Blue Note at 1 Parkfield Street and the Goodsway Depot off York Way were both popular late Nineties clubbers' venues.

N2 East Finchley, Fortis Green

Fairport Convention were so named because they assembled at a house called Fairport in Fortis Green – formerly a surgery where Simon Nicol's late GP father Dr EB Nicol was in partnership.

N3 Finchley

Birthplace of George Michael, 25.6.63; Spice Girl Emma Bunton, 21.1.78 (Baby Spice).

Chas Smash of Madness went to Finchley High School.

In '67, The New Vaudeville Band scored a hit with their execrable novelty 'Finchley Central'.

Local bands include early punks Eater, whose precocious 14-year-old drummer rejoiced in the name of Dee Generate.

N4 Finsbury Park, Stroud Green

When they first moved down from Newcastle, Hank Marvin and Bruce Welch shared digs in a house in Holly Park.

During the Fifties and Sixties, the Finsbury Park Astoria at 232 Seven Sisters Road was a prime package show venue. The Beatles played twice nightly for 16 days over Christmas' 63; The Jeff Beck Group made its début on the same night that Jimi Hendrix set fire to his guitar for the first time in March '67. After refurbishment, it re-opened as the Rainbow in November '71, when The Who filled it for

The Rainbow in its heyday

(Barry Plummer)

three nights. The following month, some pillock pushed Frank Zappa off the stage causing multiple fractures. Eric Clapton made his famous comeback there in January '73. Its subsequent decline as a venue was slow but sure and it closed in '80.

The Hornsey Wood Tavern at 376 Seven Sisters Road was known as Bluesville in the Sixties R&B boom and was still thriving when Led Zeppelin played there in March '69. A sister club operated at the Manor House at 316 Green Lanes – the Stones played there five times in '63. The George Robey, opposite the Rainbow, was on the Seventies/Eighties pub rock circuit.

R&B hero Graham Bond met his death when he leapt in front of an oncoming train at Finsbury Park tube station in May '74.

Free were formed after Paul Kossoff and Simon Kirke saw Paul Rodgers singing at the Fickle Pickle club (wherever that was) in early '68.

Mike Barson of Madness married Sandra Wilson at Finsbury Park Register Office in February '81, and soon removed to Holland.

Finsbury Park itself became a popular open air gig. Over the years, the annual Fleadh has presented such acts as Bob Dylan (twice), Van Morrison, The Pogues, Crowded House, The Corrs and The World Party. The Sex Pistols played there on their '96 reunion tour.

N5 Highbury

Birthplace of David White, 2.6.65 (Brother Beyond).

Pathway Studios

(Pathway)

Pathway Studio at 2a Grosvenor Avenue came into its own during the punk era when every major group cut records there. Nick Lowe's Stiff début 'So It Goes' was made there for £45, Dire Straits recorded their first demos there in '77, and Police cut their first single there.

Wessex Sound Studios at 106 Highbury New Park was where the Pistols recorded their earliest works, where The Clash cut *London Calling* and Abigail Mead made 'I Want To Be Your Drill Instructor'.

In June '77, Johnny Rotten was ambushed and razored when he emerged from the Pegasus pub in Stoke Newington Church Street.

Town & Country 2, at 20-22 Highbury Corner, became the Garage in '93. Upstairs at the Garage was the venue for Bernard Butler's first solo gig in January '98.

N6 Highgate

Rod Stewart was born here on 10.1.45, and lived in a flat over his parents' newsagent's shop in Archway Road (long since pulled down and redeveloped). Also born here was Dave Ambrose, 11.12.46 (bass player in The Brian Auger Trinity and later the EMI exec who signed up Sigue Sigue Sputnik); Steven Severin, 25.9.55 (co-instigator of The Banshees).

Fairport Convention's Simon Nicol worked as a projectionist at Highgate Odeon.

The cover of The Kinks' '71 album *Muswell Hillbillies* was shot inside the Archway Tavern. Archway People was a '93 St. Etienne B-side.

Sting lives in a house once owned by Yehudi Menuhin.

Local mid-Nineties bands included Rosa Mota.

"Fairport" East Finchley

N7, 19 Holloway, Tufnell Park

Birthplace of producer George Martin, 1926; guitarist Steve Howe, 8.4.47 (Yes); Mike West, 27.8.65 (aka The Rebel MC); Terry Coldwell, 21.7.74 (East 17).

Empire Yard at 538 Holloway Road was the operational base of Joe Meek's ill-fated Triumph label, which ran for the first seven months of '60.

In summer '60, Meek took a lease (£7.10.0d a week) on a three storey flat over a leather goods shop at 304 Holloway Road. It was here, in his chaotic studio, that he

cut such classics as 'Telstar' by The Tornados and 'Johnny Remember Me' by John Leyton, and here in February '67 that he blew out his brains (and those of his landlady) with a shotgun he had borrowed from his erstwhile star Heinz.

The gents toilet in nearby Madras Place was a favourite haunt of Meek's. On one of his visits, in November '63, he was arrested for opportuning and subsequently fined £15.

A local group who benefited from Meek's patronage were The Syndicats, featuring guitarist Steve Howe. They had formed at Barnsbury School for Boys and played their first gig at Eden Grove Youth Club.

When he moved down from Northampton in the late Sixties, Ian Hunter lived in a flat in Cheverton Road and worked at Fryer Brothers engineering factory. When he became famous in Mott The Hoople, he recollected days spent in nearby Waterlow Park.

Eddy Grant grew up on a council estate in Hornsey Rise and went to Acland Burghley School, where he formed his first group, The Equals. Another Acland Burleigh pupil was Lee Thompson from Madness (when he wasn't doing time in various detention centres).

In '72, Queen drummer Roger Taylor graduated from North London Polytechnic in Holloway Road with a degree in biology. Ace made their début there in February '73, and Chilli Willi & The Red Hot Peppers played their final gig there two years later.

The Lord Nelson at 100 Holloway Road was a major venue of the Seventies pub rock circuit.

In the pre-fame early Seventies, Bob Geldof lived here, in a filthy decaying squat. During this period, he also helped to construct the M25 – all colourfully detailed in his excellent autobiography.

Johnny Rotten lived in Benwell Road and languished in St. William of York School, Brewery Road, for several years... until his expulsion. His brother Jimmy was in local bands The 4 By 2s and The Bollock Brothers.

Stranglers frontman Hugh Cornwell languished in Pentonville Prison, Caledonian Road, for six weeks after being found guilty of heroin possession (March '80).

A Strangler's account of life inside Holloway

Holloway Jail was discussed on The Kinks' album *Muswell Hillbillies*.

St. Etienne operated from 32 Tytherton Road – also the address of their Ice Rink label.

In the mid-Nineties, local girl band Linus made waves on the indie scene; Baby Fox on the drum'n'bass circuit.

N8 Hornsey, Crouch End

Former students at Hornsey Art School in Crouch Hill (now part of Middlesex Poly) include Ray Davies (Kinks), Danny Kleinman (leader of Seventies pub rock group Bazooka Joe), Stuart Goddard (aka Adam Ant), Lester Square (Monochrome Set), Neal Brown (leader of The Vincent Units), Mike Barson (Madness), Viv Albertine (Slits), Steve Walsh (Manicured Noise), Graham Lewis and Rob Gotobed (Wire), Roger Glover (Deep Purple), Lynsey de Paul, Gina Birch and Ana de Silva (both of The Raincoats, who made their début here in December '78).

In April '78, Madness played what they considered to be a splendid gig at the Nightingale pub – but were refused further bookings after neighbours complained of the noise.

Local residents have included broadcaster Andy Kershaw, songwriter Pete Brown, Sheriff Jack and Momus.

The Kinks' recording studio, known as Konk, is at 84 Tottenham Lane.

Dave Stewart's Church Studio (converted from a disused church) is at 145 Crouch Hill. The first Eurythmics album to be recorded here was Touch in '83, since when it has been used by everyone from Depeche Mode to Bob Dylan. A ghost in the former Belfry area does not disturb motion sensors, but can unbolt heavy oak doors.

In March '57, Cliff Richard played truant to see his hero Bill Haley at Edmonton Regal – the same place Hank Marvin and Bruce Welch made their London début in April '58. They were then in The Railroaders Skiffle Group, in the finals of a national contest – which they failed to win. However, they stuck around London and six months later became part of Cliff's backing group, The Drifters.

The winner of the above contest was The John Henry Skiffle Group, whose leader later emerged as Chris Farlowe.

Jerry Lee Lewis made his UK début at Edmonton Regal in May '58; the Stones and the Everlys played there in October '63.

Local lads Chas & Dave have recorded songs celebrating Edmonton Green and Tottenham Hotspur. Chas went to Eldon Road Junior School and lived in Harton Road. His first day job was apprentice watchmaker at Turners the Jeweller on Edmonton Green (later the title of a track on *Rockney*), but cavorting with Billy Gray & The Stormers at the Kings Head held more appeal.

Cooks Ferry Inn on the River Lea Towpath, Angel Road, was a trad jazz stronghold until the R&B boom when it became the Blue Opera Club, presenting The Animals, Who, Yardbirds and other memorable bands. Led Zeppelin played here in March 69 – and it was still going strong in the Seventies, when two members of Hackensack saved a woman from drowning in the Lea.

At Last The 1958 Rock'n'Roll Show, featuring Freddie Fingers Lee and Ian Hunter, had a residency at the Angel.

Caleb Quaye, an early cohort of Elton John, grew up here.

Bob Dylan signs autographs, Dave Stewart doesn't

(Rex Features)

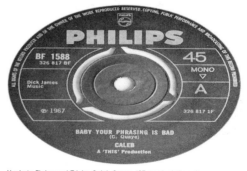

Uncle to Finlay and Tricky: Caleb Quaye, '67 psychedelic rarity

N9, 18 Edmonton

Birthplace of vocalist/organist Mike Smith, 6.12.43 (Dave Clark Five); Chas Hodges, 28.12.43 (Chas & Dave); drummer BJ Wilson, 18.3.47 (Procol Harum); Morgan Fisher, 1.1.50 (Love Affair, Mott The Hoople); Brian Harvey, 8.8.74 (East 17).

N10 Muswell Hill

Birthplace of Ray, 21.6.44, and Dave Davies, 3.2.47 – founders of The Kinks. Eight years after starting out at North Bank Youth Club they immortalised the area on their '71 album *Muswell Hillbillies*. Also born here were Shane Fenton/Alvin Stardust, 27.9.44; Tyger Hutchings, 26.1.45, and Simon Nicol, 13.10.50 (both of Fairport Convention).

Ray and Dave Davies went to William Grimshaw Grammar (now Creighton Comprehensive) in Creighton Avenue – as did Rod Stewart. During their early hit
career, the Davies brothers shared a flat in Connaught Gardens.

As their first hit climbed the charts, Emile Ford & The Checkmates were resident at the Athenaeum Ballroom.

Local group Turquoise were managed by Rolling Stones chauffeur Tom Keylock.

The Stukas were a late Seventies Thamesbeat band.

The indie Compact label (famous for Mari Wilson) operated from 67 Onslow Gardens.

N11 Friern Barnet, Bounds Green

Fairport Convention's Simon Nicol went to Friern Barnet School.

Professor Bruce Lacey (once of trad-jazz vaudeville group, The Alberts), who played The Beatles' gardener in *Help!* and is celebrated on the Fairport's Mr Lacey, lived in Durnsford Road – not a stone's throw from Ashley Hutchings' house.

N12 North Finchley

The Torrington pub at 4 Lodge Lane has always been a popular rock venue.

N13 Palmers Green

Birthplace of Shadows drummer Brian Bennet, 9.2.40, who lived in a council house at 125a Ferndale Avenue and went to Hazelwood Lane School. His first group was local skiffle outfit The Velvets.

Sometime home of pedal steel guitarist BJ Cole, who has played with everyone from Cochise to The Verve, Elton John to R.E.M.

N14 Southgate

In May '59, shortly after his breakthrough, Cliff Richard bought his parents a house here – for £4000.

In October '98, Drugstore, whose singer Isabel Monteiro is South American and who are famous for their song 'El President' (about Salvador Allende – killed during the '73 CIA-backed right wing coup in Chile), discovered that the despotic General Pinochet was undergoing surgery at the Grovelands Priory Hospital in the Bourne – and played a concert outside, to draw attention to his presence.

N15, 17 Tottenham

Birthplace of drummer Dave Clark, 15.11.42; Richard Hudson, 9.5.48 (Strawbs); Mark Hollis, 1955 (Talk Talk). The Dave Clark Five made their début at South Grove Youth Club in January '62, and their local reputation as resident band at the Royal Dance Hall, 413 High Road. When they moved on, another local group, The Migil Five,

Tottenham schoolboy, Mark Hollis' pencil case

took over. David Bowie took over the Royal for most of January '72, perfecting his Ziggy Stardust stage show.

Other local acts include Hello (two mid-Seventies Top Ten hits) and Princess (late Eighties chart star). The former rehearsed in Broad Lane; the latter went to school there (Carlsmead). Charlie were mid-Seventies prog rockers; The Jetset were early Eighties mod revivalists; The Demon Boyz were late Eighties hip-hoppers; Freez were early Eighties Britfunk; Urban Species were mid-Nineties rappers; The AK 47s were mid-Nineties crusties.

Club Noreik in the High Road was a hot mid-Sixties venue, which regularly held All Nite Raves. Stars at these events included Chuck Berry, John Lee Hooker and Gene Vincent.

Michael Oldfield wrote *Tubular Bells* when he was living in a Tottenham bedsitter.

Banshees drummer Kenny Morris went to Tottenham Primary School.

Sometime home of rapper Black Radical II.

Local group The Hinnies are said to have provided the soundtrack for a movie featuring David Mellor's erstwhile lover Antonia de Sanchez.

N16 Stamford Hill, Stoke Newington

Birthplace of Malcolm McLaren, 22.1.46; guitarist Adrian Curtis, 26.6.49 (Gun); Nathan Moore, 10.1.65 (Brother Beyond).

Marc Bolan attended Northwood Primary and then William Wordsworth Secondary Modern.

Sid Vicious lived in Evering Road.

The Rochester Castle was a popular gig on the pub-rock circuit.

The Fire label, based at 21a Maury Road, released the first two albums by Pulp – *Freaks* and *Separations*.

Zip Zip Undo Me were early Nineties eccentrics.

Operational base of Shut Up And Dance label/production team.

N20 Totteridge, Whetstone

Birthplace of Richard Thompson, 3.4.49 (Fairport Convention).

Paul Young moved here in the late Eighties, but the most celebrated local resident is Mickie Most, who lives in a resplendent 30 room Georgian-style mansion.

N21 Winchmore Hill

Shadows drummer Brian Bennett was educated at Winchmore Hill School.

In September '69, Keith Moon laid out £15,000 for a luxury residence in Old Park Ridings.

N22 Wood Green

TV producer Jack Good was educated at Trinity Grammar School.

The first singer in Fairport Convention, Judy Dyble (born 13.2.49), lived in Crescent Rise and worked at Wood Green Central Library.

Everyone from Pink Floyd to Led Zeppelin to Fleetwood Mac has played at the Fishmongers Arms at 287 High Road. A heaving R&B/blues club in the Sixties, it became known as the Village Of The Damned in the progressive Seventies, when Edgar Broughton, Stray, etc played there. The heavy metal band UFO were formed after auditions there in '69. It was here also that Elton John failed an audition to join The Mike Cotton Sound.

In April '67, Alexandra Palace was the venue for the 14 Hour Technicolour Dream – a benefit for the police-beleaguered newspaper *International Times*. Britain's first Be-In, it featured over 20 acts including Pink Floyd, Arthur Brown, The Purple Gang, The Soft Machine and The Deviants. Pete Townshend, John Lennon and Dick Gregory were among the guests.

In June '64, Ally Pally was the scene for an All Night Rave headed by the Stones; The Small Faces played one of their last gigs there on New Year's Eve' 68; Led Zeppelin played two nights there just before Christmas '72; The Grateful Dead played three nights in September '74; The Stone Roses packed it out in November '89; New Order saw in '99. Everyone always complained the sound was rotten.

Bethnal were a late Seventies band lost in the new wave.

Totteridge born Richard Thompson

NW1 Camden, Marylebone

Birthplace of Dickie Valentine, 4.11.29 (Fifties crooner); Adam Ant, 3.11.54.

Pupils at St. Marylebone Grammar School include Adam Ant, Benny Green, Julian Temple, Peter Bardens (Cheynes, Them, Camel), Barry Blue and Allan Mostert (captain of the rugby team and later guitarist in Quintessence).

In the Fifties/Sixties, the coaches taking package shows around Britain would always collect the stars and musicians in Allsop Place, behind Madame Tussauds. Even the *Magical Mystery Tour* coach started from here. Scenes for The Beatles' movie *A Hard Day's Night* were shot just up the road at Marylebone Station.

In the late Fifties, Cliff Richard, Hank Marvin and Bruce Welch shared a flat at 100 Marylebone High Street.

The Royal Academy of Music
(Suzie Maeder)

Several students at the Royal Academy of Music in Marylebone Road opted for rock music rather than classical... Nicky Hopkins (Jeff Beck, Quicksilver), Geoff Goddard (wrote hits for John Leyton and other Joe Meek acts), John Gosling (Kinks), Kerry Minnear (Gentle Giant), producer Chris Thomas, Annie Lennox (Eurythmics), Karl Jenkins (Soft Machine), David Bedford (Kevin Ayers), Steve Nieve (Attractions), Joe Jackson and Elton John.

One of London's most famous rock landmarks is the Roundhouse in Chalk Farm Road. The first gig was an all-night hippie rave to launch/raise funds for the underground newspaper *The International Times* in October '66. It had been going derelict for years and was dank, filthy, cold and grim but the audience – including Paul McCartney, Jane Asher, Marianne Faithfull, Antonioni, Monica Vitti and other celebs – all enjoyed the event. Pink Floyd and Soft Machine were headliners, and groovy punters rolled naked in a 56 gallon jelly, cast in a bathtub. The power supply was less than the average kitchen, so fuses were blown continually.

Other significant Roundhouse gigs include Hendrix in February '67; The Doors/Jefferson Airplane in '68; Led Zeppelin's London début in November '68 (they got 150 quid); the legendary David Bowie & The Hype performance in February '70; and The Who's last full performance of *Tommy* on December 20, '70, when they were supported by Elton John. Michael Nesmith and John Stewart shared the

John Tobler & Pete Frame in association with Charisma Artistes present at the
ROUNDHOUSE CHALK FARM LONDON NW1
on Sunday April 28th 1974
from 3.30 till 10.30
THE ZIGZAG FIFTH ANNIVERSARY
SUPER WAHOO EXTRAVAGANZA
starring
Michael Nesmith & Red Rhodes
John Stewart
Chris Darrow
Help Yourself
Chilli Willi & the Red Hot Peppers
Starry Eyed and Laughing
Kilburn & the High Roads
THIS IS YOUR GIG...PLEASE COME EARLY
WE WANNA SEE YOUR FACE
IN THE PLACE
only £1.50 plus vat

Pete Frame's Roundhouse bash

stage at *Zigzag* magazine's fifth birthday party in April '74; Man played three nights (with ex-Quicksilver guitarist John Cipollina) in May '75; Patti Smith made her UK début there (May '76), as did The Ramones (July '76).

Just down the road at Camden Lock is Dingwalls – a favourite pub-rock stronghold and hip-rock showcase since the early Seventies. R.E.M. made their UK début there in November '83; Blur made theirs (as Seymour) in '90; Lynden David Hall appeared there in October '98.

In the railway yards between (opposite Hartland Road, now redeveloped) was the warehouse where The Clash got their act together. It was there that they did their first gig, a media only preview (in August '76), and shot their first album sleeve. In September '76, the first experimental line-up of Siouxsie & The Banshees rehearsed there, prior to their performance-art début at the 100 Club Punk Festival – and later in the year, Sid Vicious rehearsed his never-to-fly group The Flowers Of Romance. In March '78, police cars and a helicopter swooped on Topper Headon and Paul Simonon, who were using air-guns to take pot-shots at pigeons – but were thought to be shooting at passing trains.

Just up the road is Chalk Farm underground station, where Madness posed for the sleeve of their album *Absolutely*. The '84 Madness hit 'One Better Day' was about the down-and-outs rehabilitation centre Arlington House, in Arlington Road (the author of this book was in the video). Eleven years later, singer Suggs had a solo hit with 'Camden Town'.

Former XTC keyboard player Barry Andrews immortalised his residence on a single, 'Rossmore Road'. In the Nineties, the road became famous as the address of the Sylvia Young Theatre School – among whose pupils were Nicole and Natalie Appleton and Melanie Blatt (later to become three quarters of All Saints) and Billie.

Fashionable venues included the Electric Ballroom at 184 Camden High Street, where Sid Vicious played his last UK gig (a benefit concert billed as Sid Sods Off in August '78) and Elastica played one of their first (February '94). The first of many Smiths bootlegs was recorded there in December '83. Down the road, was Steve Strange's venture Camden Palace, at 1a Camden Road. Once a BBC television theatre, where *The Goon Show* was recorded, it was known as the Music Machine in the Seventies.

The Brecknock at 227 Camden Road was a major pub-rock venue; the Dublin Castle at 94 Parkway still is. Blur played a memorable gig there in May '95. The Monarch saw the début of Ultrasound in October '95.

The Falcon at 234 Royal College Street has been a cool venue for a decade. Up the road at 271 is the office of Ultimate Records (home of The Candyskins, among others).

Operational base of several Nineties bands, including Silverfish, Th' Faith Healers, Sun Carriage, Gallon Drunk (up from Guildford) and the Earls of Suave. Wirral band Half Man Half Biscuit summed up a genre with their '98 track 'Four Skinny Indie Kids (drinking weak lager in a Camden boozer)'.

My Life Story ran into a spot of bother with London Transport when they appropriated their logo for the '95 single 'Mornington Crescent' (a recently re-opened tube station).

The Clash in Chalk Farm

Madness in Camden Town

The Jazz Café, which opened at 5 Parkway in December '90, presents jazz, soul, R&B and greying rockers like Eric Burdon and Roger Chapman.

The Magistrates Court at 181 Marylebone Road has dealt with such miscreants as Keith Richards (June '73), John and Yoko (October '68), Sid and Nancy (May '78) and Jimmy Page (October '84)... all on offences related to drugs. In June' 73, Mick Jagger was there answering the

The Camden Palace

(Camden Palace)

charge that he had sired Marsha Hunt's child. During the mid-Sixties, Jagger had lived at Harley House in Marylebone Road, where Who manager Bill Curbishley had offices in the Eighties and early Nineties.

The Register Office at Council House has witnessed the weddings of Paul McCartney and Linda Eastman (March' 69), and Ringo Starr and Barbara Bach (April '81), among others.

In '76, Neil Murray (Whitesnake) and Annie Lennox lived in the same house in Gloucester Crescent. She was playing flute in Redbrass and singing Joni Mitchell songs at the harmonium.

While trying to establish The Birthday Party in summer '80, Nick Cave worked at London Zoo, washing up in the cafeteria and collecting litter. In May '89, The Zoo was used for the press reception to launch the latest album by 10,000 Maniacs – Blind Man's Zoo.

Pink Floyd launched their *Dark Side Of The Moon* album at the London Planatarium in March '73 but forgot to turn

up. Guests listened to their meisterwerk at megavolume while gazing at the stars.

Before finding fame with Blur, Damon Albarn worked briefly at Beat Factory Studios at 1 Christopher Place, Chalton Street. He was soon the star of Food Records, operating from 172a Arlington Road.

The late Nineties offices of Creation Records are at 109 Regents Park Road and their artists have been known to take refreshment at the Pembroke Castle at 150 Gloucester Place. In October '98, Liam Gallagher was arrested after a

The Jazz Café

(The Jazz Café)

confrontation with paparazzi outside this establishment but no charges were brought.

NW2 Cricklewood, Dollis Hill
In '64, Bill Leader's Broadside folk club operated at 30 Park Avenue. Guests included Memphis Slim, Davy Graham and Little Walter – backed by Bert Jansch!

Bow Wow Wow singer Annabella L'Win went to Hampstead Comprehensive in Westbere Road.

Mike Barson of Madness went to Cricklewood Secondary.

During their hits period, Dublin trio The Bachelors lived at Clarendon Court in Sidmouth Road.

Sometime home of maverick critic Everett True, who recorded for Creation under the name of The Legend. Also home to The Kays, an embryonic version of Kula Shaker – and to top dance act 4 Hero.

A tourist's eye view of the Planetarium

Madness on Primrose Hill

Sometime home of Boy George – and Noel Gallagher, who lived in Steeles Road (at the house with all the photographers outside).

Primrose Hill was the location for several album sleeve photos, including *Between The Buttons* by The Rolling Stones, *Nicola* by Bert Jansch and *Rise And Fall* by Madness.

More madness on Primrose Hill by the band Trees

NW3 Hampstead
Birthplace of Shadows drummer Tony Meehan; Marianne Faithfull, 29.12.46; guitarist Paul Kossoff, 14.9.50 (Free); Rhoda Dakar, 1960 (Special AKA).

Local song references include 'Swiss Cottage Manoeuvres' by Al Stewart; 'Hampstead Incident' by Donovan; 'Hampstead Girl' by Dream Academy.

While waiting for stardom (and Dave Stewart) to tap her on the shoulder, Annie Lennox worked at Pippins restaurant.

As a schoolboy, Pink Floyd's Roger Mason lived in Downshire Hill; Mick Jagger and Keith Richards shared a flat at 10a Holly Hill in summer '64.

The Country Club, approached through an alleyway at 210a Haverstock Hill, was an excellent underground/progressive venue in the grounds of the Globe Tennis Club. The Stones played there in February '64; Mott The Hoople made their London début there in summer '69, and Elton John once appeared in tennis gear, straight from the court after a summer evening game.

Folk rock stars Chad (Stuart) and Jeremy (Clyde) met at the Central School of Speech And Drama at 64 Eton Avenue. Another pupil was Jon Lord, later of Deep Purple.

The Tinkers Club, held at the Three Horseshoes in Heath Street was a famous folkie venue in the Sixties, when Paul Simon and Ralph McTell would appear.

Following his mandrax overdose, Kenny Everett was rushed to the Royal Free Hospital, where he was successfully resuscitated.

Respecting Post Office advice, punk comedian Johnny Rubbish used the postcode on his '78 Pistols piss-take single 'NW3 4JR'.

In the early Nineties, George Martin converted a church in Lyndhurst Road into his new Air Studios – among whose clientele have been Elton John, Beverly Craven and Dire Straits.

Madness singer Suggs was educated at Quinton Kynaston School in Swiss Cottage; Melanie Blatt of All Saints went to Fitzjohn's Primary.

NW4 Hendon
Birthplace of drummer Andy Steele, 2.8.41 (Herd).

Twelve-year-old John Entwistle made his public début at Hendon Town Hall, playing french horn with the Middlesex Youth Orchestra.

Mik Kaminski, leader of one-hit wonders Violinski, lived in Queens Road.

Dire Straits made the video for 'Twisting By The Pool' at the swimming pool in the Copthall Sports Centre.

Snuff were a hot hardcore band in the late Eighties.

As Slaughter Joe, Joe Foster made a name for himself as artist and producer in the early Nineties.

NW5 Gospel Oak, Kentish Town
Birthplace of Bam King, 18.9.46, (Ace); Lee Thompson, 5.10.57 (Madness).

Air Studios, Hampstead

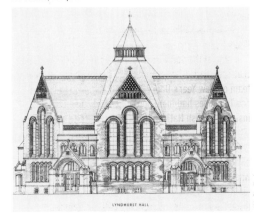

LYNDHURST HALL

(Air Studios)

Former pupils of William Ellis School in Highgate Road include Richard Thompson, Gerry Conway (Fairport), Hugh Cornwell (Stranglers), Mark Bedford (Madness).

Former pupils of Gospel Oak Primary in Gordonhouse Road include Mike Barson, Lee Thompson and Chris Foreman. All were reunited in Madness, whose first rehearsals were at Mike's mother's house in Chetwynd Road.

Local groups include The Action, Mighty Baby, Ace – and Gospel Oak. In '74, Ian Matthews released an album called *Journeys From Gospel Oak*.

Scottish prog-rock band Writing On The Wall shared a house in Burghley Road, which is celebrated on their compilation album of the same name.

The Tally Ho (later Hudsons) at 9 Fortress Road was the venue which precipitated the mid-Seventies pub rock circuit. The first groups to establish it as such were Eggs Over Easy, Bees Make Honey, Brinsley Schwarz and Ducks DeLuxe, who made their UK début there in August '72. Another perenniel pub gig is the Bull & Gate, where The Hype showcased up and comers like Voice Of The Beehive in the late Eighties.

Photos on the sleeve of *Muswell Hillbillies* show the Kinks cavorting in Retcar Close.

The Town And Country Club at 9-17 Highgate Road became one of the hottest/coolest late Eighties London venues. Van Morrison played the final night in May '93 – and the first night, in May '93, when it reopened as the Forum. The Velvet Underground played there in June '93; Oasis in August '94.

NW6 Kilburn, West Hampstead

Birthplace of Tom, 2.7.36, and Dusty Springfield, 16.4.39 (Springfields).

The State Theatre at 195 Kilburn High Road was a prime rock venue in the Fifties. Buddy Holly appeared there in March 58 and Jerry Lee Lewis two months later. The Rolling Stones played here in November '63, The Beatles in October '64 – and Ron Wood chose it for his solo début in July '74.

Pre-Led Zeppelin session man John Paul Jones lived at 7 Priory Road.

It was at the Decca studio at 165 Broadhurst Gardens that The Beatles failed to impress the company's A&R team on New Year's Day '62. They thought Brian Poole & The Tremeloes had more potential and signed them instead. English National Opera took over the building in '80.

The Railway Hotel (next door) at 100 West End Lane was better known as Klook's Kleek during the Sixties R&B boom when groups like Led Zeppelin (April '69) played there. In '65, John Mayall was given a rare opportunity to record a live album here – by suspending cables through the

The Railway Hotel

windows to Decca's studio, where engineer Gus Dudgeon was able to tape it!

In the Seventies, it became the Moonlight Club, presenting punk and new wave acts. Joy Division played three nights in April 80, less than a month before the death of their singer. It was here also that The Stone Roses made their world début (supporting Pete Townshend) in October '84 and that PJ Harvey played her first London gig in August '91.

Island Records' first operational base was 108 Cambridge Road.

Shadows drummer Tony Meehan and Bow Wow Wow singer Annabella L'Win were both educated at Beckford Primary in Dornfell Street.

Drummer Keef Hartley gave one of his albums the enigmatic title *Battle Of NW6*.

In the mid-Nineties, T Rex fans contributed to a tombstone for Marc Bolan's erstwhile partner Steve Peregrine Took, who was buried in Kilburn Cemetary in October '80.

Sidelining his pop career, Cat Stevens changed his name to Yusuf Islam and now operates the Islamia Schools Trust at 8 Brondesbury Park.

It was in a Kilburn launderette that the pubescent Annabella L'Win was discovered by Malcolm McLaren, who immediately installed her in Bow Wow Wow.

Home of Nineties chart stars Bush – who moved to the States – and hardcore band Headbutt.

The Rhythm King label operates from 121 Salisbury Road.

NW7 Mill Hill

The duo Twice As Much, who recorded for Andrew Oldham's Immediate label, first met as pupils at Mill Hill public school.

Ed Ball, former luminary of early Eighties pisstakers The Television Personalities, later recorded Another Member of the Mill Hill Self-hate Club.

Abbey Road Studios

(Barry Plummer)

NW8 St. John's Wood

Birthplace of Martin Lamble, 28.8.49 (Fairport Convention).

Tony Meehan attended Regents Park Central in Lisson Grove.

EMI have long maintained their studios at 3 Abbey Road, but it was The Beatles who put the road and the zebra crossing on the rock map with their '69 album. The graffiti on the low white wall outside the studio is cleaned off every three months — but not before a photograph has been taken. One day EMI plans to publish a book of collected Abbey Road Beatles graffiti. It's safe to say that Abbey Road Studios is the single most visited rock landmark in London, and after Graceland probably the world, and fittingly too, since in a rush of creativity yet to be emulated the fab four recorded their soundtrack to the Sixties there between '62 and '69.

So did dozens of others, of course, including Cliff Richard, Pink Flord, Kate Bush and many many more.

In April '65, Paul McCartney paid out 40 grand for a house at 7 Cavendish Avenue, not far from the studio.

No. 7 Cavendish Avenue, McCartney's Home

(Barry Plummer)

Here The Beatles met to plan their recordings and many Lennon/McCartney songs were born on the premises.

In late '66, Keith Moon, his wife Kim and daughter Amanda moved out of his parents' Wembley house and into an elegant flat in Ormonde Terrace (next door to Scott Walker) — until noise complaints precipitated further moves to Maida Vale, Highgate and Winchmore Hill.

During the Seventies, Kenny Everett lived in a flat in Charles Lane, next to a restaurant.

Mickie Most's RAK Studios are at 42-48 Charlbert Street. From here emerged not only hits by Suzi Quatro and Hot Chocolate, but also records by Simply Red, The Pet Shop Boys, Paul McCartney and many others.

Sometime home of Nineties chartsters Lush.

NW9 Colindale, Kingsbury

Birthplace of Shadows bass player Jet Harris (in Honeypot Lane), 6.7.39; bassist Chris Squire, 4.3.48 (Yes); singer Mari Wilson, 29.9.57.

Rolling Stone Charlie Watts was educated at Tylers Croft Secondary Modern — now part of Kingsbury High School in Princes Avenue. Other pupil were Sixties thrush Julie Rogers and George Michael.

Local groups include rockabilly hopefuls, The Polecats.

NW10 Harlesden, Kensal Green, Neasden, Willesden

Birthplace of Larry Parnes, 1930; Valerie Murtagh, 1936 (Avons); dynamic rocker Johnny Kidd, 23.12.39; saxophonist Davey Payne, 11.8.44 (Blockheads); Keith Moon, 23.8.46 (at Central Middlesex Hospital in Acton Lane); Mick Tucker, 17.7.49 (Sweet); Twiggy, 19.9.49.

Twiggy (who reached the '76 Top Twenty with Country Joe's 'Here I Go Again') lived at 93 St. Raphael's Way and went to Bridge Road Primary School, then Kilburn High School for Girls.

Twig the wonderkid

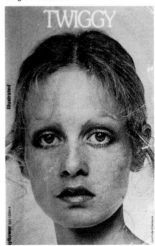

Keith Moon (secretly) married Kim Kerrigan at Willesden Register Office in March '66.

In summer '66, Cream first got together at Ginger Baker's house in Braemar Avenue. When he moved on, the next tenants had to put up with his highly psychedelic interior decor.

At the time of her Top Five hits, Clodagh Rodgers was living in Dobree Avenue. Also local were The Young Idea, a duo who reached the '67 Top Ten with their cover of 'With A Little Help From My Friends'.

Trojan Records operated from a makeshift building in Neasden Lane; producer Lee Perry maintained a UK residence in the area; Aswad emerged from Harlesden in '76.

During his schooldays, Sex Pistol Glen Matlock lived at 18 Ravensworth Road.

Edgar Broughton Band recorded at Morgan Studios (pictured) in 1972

Morgan Studios at 169 Willesden High Road High Road were hot in the late Sixties/Seventies. Among those who recorded albums here were Mott The Hoople, Rod Stewart, Paul McCartney and The Cure. Mike Hedges (later producer of The Cure, Manics, Texas, etc) started here as a tea boy. In the same building are the offices of Zomba and Silvertone Records.

Punk group The Slits made their début supporting The Clash on their memorable gig at the Colosseum in March '77.

Local lass Mari Wilson became known as the Queen of Neasden.

The Mean Fiddler at 28a High Street, Harlesden, acquired a reputation as one of the best London venues for rootsy, ethnic, interesting, honest, real music. Van Morrison and Paul McCartney have played tour warm-ups there; Roy Orbison played his last UK gig there in '88.

From Battery Studios at 1 Maybury Gardens came hits by Paul Weller, Lisa Stansfield, Neneh Cherry, The Stone Roses and many more.

Pioneering UK funk band Atmosfear cut 'Dancing In Outer Space' a perennial club favourite since the end of the Seventies.

Famous rapper Young MC (Marvin Young) was born here but moved to the States as a child; General Levy stuck around and reached the '94 Top Ten with 'Incredible'. Also home to brothers and sisters hip-hoppers Eusebe – and former East Enders actress Michelle Gayle, who reached the '94 Top Five with 'Sweetness'.

NW11 Golders Green

Fairport Convention made their world début at St. Michael's Hall, Golders Green Road, on 27.5.67 – with a set incorporating 'Seven And Seven Is', 'My Back Pages' and 'Johnny B Goode'.

The Paul Butterfield Blues Band made their UK début at briefly popular R&B venue the Refectory at 911 Finchley Road in December '66. Hendrix played there the following month.

The Hippodrome was a longtime BBC concert venue.

At the height of his Radio One disc jockey fame, Noel Edmonds lived at 35 Brookland Hill.

The illustrious indie label Mute started at 16 Decoy Avenue – with a single by The Normal.

A '97 CD of the late Pete Ham's work was named after his home at 7 Park Avenue. All of Badfinger lived here in the early Seventies.

At Golders Green Chapel, friends bade farewell to Marc Bolan in September '77, and Keith Moon in September '78.

SE1 Borough, Lambeth

Due to the unprecedented clamour of fans at Waterloo Station in February '57, the press described Bill Haley's arrival into London (by train from Southampton) as "the second battle of Waterloo".

Waterloo Station, Bridge and Underground were the setting for The Kinks' hit 'Waterloo Sunset' (featuring Swinging London icons Terry Stamp and Julie Christie), and Bob Geldof's '86 follow-up 'Love Like A Rocket'.

The underground train sequence on Steve Miller's 'Children Of The Future' was recorded on the Bakerloo line, between Oxford Circus and Waterloo.

The Trocadero Theatre (torn down long ago) at the Elephant & Castle was renowned for its critical Teddy Boy audience who threw pennies at Cliff Richard, jeered Bobby Darin, but idolised Duane Eddy! Two policemen were injured trying to disperse "juvenile delinquents" who were letting off steam after seeing *Rock Around The Clock* there. Buddy Holly & The Crickets made their UK début there in March '58... Des O'Connor was the compere!

Fifties rock'n'roller Terry Dene was born in a flat above a sweetshop in the Elephant & Castle on 20.12.38 – in Lancaster Road, which has long since been bulldozed and redeveloped. He was educated at St. Johns and All Saints Secondary Mixed in Waterloo Road. Also born in Lambeth was guitarist Ian Samwell, 19.1.38, who wrote 'Move It' for Cliff Richard and 'Whatcha Gonna Do About It?' for The Small Faces.

At a house in Waterloo Road known variously as the Cave and the Yellow Door, three unknowns formed a group called The Cavemen... Tommy Steele, Lionel Bart and Mike Pratt (subsequently the television star of *Randall & Hopkirk Deceased*).

Fifties rocker Dickie Pride was "discovered" singing at the Union Tavern in the Old Kent Road, and Long John Baldry made his début at the World Turned Upside Down in '58. The Thomas A Becket at 302 Old Kent Road has been a rock pub since the Sixties (The Delinquents, featuring future Clash star Mick Jones, played an early gig there in late '74), and the Ambulance Hut was a hardcore venue presenting such bands as The Butthole Surfers. On one of their most memorable gigs (November '84), The Jesus & Mary Chain trashed the place.

The reputation of the Workhouse Studio at 488 Old Kent Road was established by albums like *New Boots And Panties* (Ian Dury) and *No Parlez* (Paul Young).

The Royal Festival Hall in 1964

(Eric De Maré)

The Royal Festival Hall in Belvedere Road on the South Bank has presented suitably sedate gigs. Dylan played his first formal UK concert here on a Sunday afternoon in May '64, as did Peter Paul & Mary. Three years later, flocks of colourful hippies came to see Emily play at the adjacent Queen Elizabeth Hall when Pink Floyd presented their seminal Games For May.

Birthplace of Susan Dallion, 27.5.57 (better known as Siouxsie) at Guy's Hospital in St. Thomas Street, London Bridge; late Eighties star Roachford, 22.1.65; Eighth Wonder vocalist/film actress and pop stars' wife Patsy Kensit on 4.3.68. Other residents have included Dennis Greaves (Nine Below Zero, The Truth); Chris and Peter Coyne (Sid Presley Experience, The Godfathers).

The immensely successful PWL label was based at 4-7 The Vineyard, off Sanctuary Street. In the late Eighties, Rick Astley and Kylie Minogue both started their careers with a Number One; Jason Donovan had three Number Ones in a row. As Nick Lowe sang: "Do you remmber Rick Astley? He had a great big hit – it was ghastly!"

During the Nineties, the Ministry of Sound at 103 Gaunt Street became London's best known club.

Asian Dub Foundation have their roots at Community Music, where Dr Das was a tutor.

SE2 Abbey Wood
Kate Bush was educated at St. Joseph's Convent.

SE3 Blackheath
Birthplace of fifties star Marty Wilde, 15.4.39; ace guitarist Albert Lee, 21.12.43; drummer Jon Hiseman, 21.6.44; Virgin boss Richard Branson, 18.7.50 (at Stonefield Maternity Home); ivory tickler Jools Holland, 24.1.58 (Squeeze).

Led Zeppelin's John Paul Jones was educated at Christ College.

Local mid-Nineties bands include Appleberry Crescent.

Local twins Ben and Scott Addison have played together in various local bands, including Brigandage, Boys Wonder and mid-Nineties acid jazz group Corduroy.

Hilly Fields and Nick Nicely

(Harvest Records)

SE4 Brockley
Fifties star Gary Mills was went to Brockley County School, as did Sandie Shaw's husband Jeff Banks; soul singer Mica Paris grew up in Brockley. The title of Nick Nicely's '82 single 'Hilly Fields' (among the first to use scratching) was said to have been inspired by the local park.

The Rivoli Ballroom in Brockley Road is a favourite location for video shoots – including 'I Guess That's Why They Call It The Blues' by Elton John, 'I'll Sail This Ship Alone' by Beautiful South and 'Private Dancer' by Tina Turner.

SE5 Camberwell
Birthplace of Peter Perrett, 8.4.52 (Only Ones) – at Kings College Hospital.

A '64 flash in the charts, The Joy Strings, formed at the Salvation Army training college in Denmark Hill.

Syd Barrett was a student at Camberwell Art School when he and his mates formed Pink Floyd. A bunch of Barrett disciples formed the locally based neo-psych group House Of Love and broke out with '90 Top Ten album Fontana. Banshees drummer Kenny Morris also studied graphics at the Art School.

After a booze binge at the Camden Music Machine in February '80, AC/DC singer Bon Scott spent the night asleep in a car, outside his friend's house. When he could not be roused, he was driven to Kings College Hospital in Denmark Hill, where he was pronounced DOA. The coroner recorded a verdict of "death by misadventure".

Home of Jon Marsh, half of late Eighties duo The Beloved.

Early Nineties bands include Back To The Planet and Flinch — who won Best Newcomers award at Manchester's In The City in '94. That same year, The Camberwell Butterflies made waves on the techno/dance scene and JX charted with 'Son of a Gun.'

SE6 Bellingham, Catford

The Hippodrome in Brownhill Road (now replaced by Eros House) was a variety show venue in pre-rock'n'roll days, presenting Eddie Calvert, Dorothy Squires, Billy Cotton and their ilk.

Further along Brownhill Road is Catford Boys School, where David Sylvian (Japan) was educated. Francis Rossi and Alan Lancaster (later of Status Quo) met at Sedgehill School in Sedgehill Road.

Lewisham Theatre, Rushey Green, has been a popular venue since 1932. Everyone from Eartha Kitt to Suzi Quatro

The Lewisham Theatre and an undamaged floor

(Lewisham Theatre)

has appeared here. During the Fifties, at the weekly jiving sessions, girls were given rubber tips to slip over the heels of their stilettos to prevent damage to the floor. The Raisins, a black group from Catford, played their final gig here in March '69, supporting Stevie Wonder.

The Savoy Rooms at 75 Rushey Green, was a Fifties dancehall; it became the Witchdoctor in the Sixties, and Mr Smiths in the Seventies. The Rolling Stones played there in May '64.

In '57, overnight star Tommy Steele was able to move his parents out of Bermondsey and buy them a house in Ravensbourne Park.

Many of The Bonzo Dog Band's early gigs were at the Tigers Head (later renamed The Squire) in Catford.

Sometime home of Pentangle singer Jacqui McShee.

Squeeze made their début at Catford Girls School in Bellingham Road.

Natural Life were early Nineties hopefuls; percussionist Shovel later joined M People.

SUMMER OF '74   20p

the **Who**

AND FRIENDS

**LOU REED
HUMBLE PIE
BAD COMPANY
LINDISFARNE
MAGGIE BELL**

**SATURDAY 18TH MAY
CHARLTON ATHLETIC
FOOTBALL CLUB**

The Who play Charlton

SE7 Charlton

Marty Wilde was educated at Charlton Central School, but left at 15 to work in a factory until he became famous!

The Who drew 50,000 fans to Charlton Athletic's ground, the Valley, in May '74, and did an action replay in May '76.

The Blood were early Eighties punks.

SE8 Deptford

Formed in '74, Squeeze put the area on the rock map when their first release appeared on the Deptford Fun City label.

During spring '77, Mark Knopfler and his mates sat in their flat at Farrar House, on the Crossfields Estate, and settled on Dire Straits as the name for their new group. Their first gig was that July, on the greensward behind the block. After another early date, at the Oxford Arms (later The Birds Nest) in Deptford Church Street, the local paper called them "a poor man's JJ Cale". A mural on the wall of Drake House in Creekside, titled Love Over Gold, inspired the album of that name.

Other commendable local groups have included The Rejects, The Electric Bluebirds, The Fabulous Poodles, The Flying Pickets and The Bicycle Thieves.

Dee C Lee was raised in Deptford and worked in a boutique there until joining The Style Council.

Mark Perry published his famous punk fanzine *Sniffin'*

The Albany Empire

Glue from 24 Rochfort House in Grove Street, and in March '77 formed Alternative TV.

The Albany Empire theatre in Creek Road became a hip new wave venue in the late Seventies, until closed and pulled down for road widening. A new Albany in Douglas Way continued to present all manner of acts, from Christy Moore to Misty In Roots.

The Kings Head became a well known venue after groups like The Chords – local Mod revivalists with several hits on Polydor – attracted a following in '79.

Twisted Sister shot the video for 'Can't Stop Rock'n'Roll' at St. George's Wharf.

Allison Phillips, drummer with Deptford girl band Taboo, used to name roads for Lewisham Borough Council.

SE9 Eltham

As a lad, Boy George lived with his parents at 29 Joan Crescent. He subsequently attended Eltham Green School

Deptford (SE8) and its most famous of record companies

in Queenscroft Road – until September '75, when he was deemed impossible to control. Glen Tilbrook (Squeeze) was asked to leave the same institution after a confrontation about the length of his hair.

The Falcon Hotel in Rochester Way was a popular Sixties venue presenting chart stars.

Local punk band Conflict topped the '83 indie chart with their album *It's Time To See Who's Who.*

Les 'Fruitbat' Carter of Carter USM went to Crown Woods Comprehensive and was set for a footballing career (he was an England schoolboy) until rock intervened.

In '95, J Pac were signed by Tom Watkins, who had previously managed The Pet Shop Boys and Bros.

SE10 Greenwich

Birthplace of The London Boys, Edem (1963) and Dennis (1964) – introduced by the '89 Top Five hit 'Requiem'.

Marty Wilde's first school was Halstow Road Primary.

Mark Knopfler wrote his first hit after seeing jazz band The Sultans Of Swing playing at the White Swan in Blackheath Road.

Squeeze's Chris Difford lived in King George Street, as recalled on the '85 album *Cosi Fan Tutti Frutti.*

Sidi Bou Said have been described as "Greenwich's answer to The Pixies"; A1 People are a hotly tipped late Nineties techno act.

SE11 Kennington

The Who filled the Oval cricket ground in September '71. Also on the bill were America, Lindisfarne and The Faces. Frank Zappa brought his Grand Wazoo Orchestra to the same venue in September '72.

The Cricketers pub has long been a venue for up and comers. Ian Dury used to live next door in Oval Mansions.

SE12 Lee

During their Sixties heyday, both John Mayall and Manfred Mann lived in Southbrook Road. Max Wall, who cut *England's Glory* for Stiff, lived in Marvels Lane.

Mica Paris developed her style as a member of Lee-based gospel group The Spirit Of Watts.

HUGE STOCK OF
ALL BAND INSTRUMENTS
FROM 3/6 WEEKLY
PART EXCHANGE
NEW AND SLIGHTLY USED

LEN STILES
233/235, LEWISHAM HIGH ST.
Telephone: LEE 8018

SE13 Hither Green, Lewisham

Birthplace of bass player Bill Wyman, 24.10.36 (Rolling Stones); drummer Ginger Baker,19.8.40 (Cream); drummer Pete Gavin, 9.8.46 (Vinegar Joe, Joe Cocker); organist Pete Gage, 31.8.47 (Ram Jam Band); Sid Vicious, 10.5.57 (Sex Pistols); singer David Sylvian, 23.2.58 (Japan); the Goss twins, Matt and Luke, 29.9.68 (Bros). Also of Eternal founder Louise (Nurding), 4.11.74 (went solo for '95 Top Tenner' Light Of My Life') – who later moved to Eltham, then Croydon.

Val Doonican was married at St. Saviours Church in April '62; Bonzo Dog and Rutles mainspring Neil Innes lived in Slaithwaite Road; Crispian St. Peters lived in Molesworth Street; Peter Skellern lived in Springbank Road; Splodgenessabounds incubated in Bonfield Road and made their début at the Leemore Centre. Also local were Sixties group Kenny Bernard & The Wranglers.

Cinema smashing and onstreet hooliganism greeted the showing of *Rock Around The Clock* at Lewisham Gaumont, in Loampit Vale, in September '56. Over 1500 Teddy boys ran berserk in what the press described as a rock'n'roll

riot. It later became a package show venue: fans halted traffic when Cliff Richard appeared there in April '59; Georgie Fame's audition for Larry Parnes was being shoved onstage, completely unrehearsed, at one such show in October '59. It was renamed the Odeon in '62, and the package shows continued with such beat-boom acts as The Beatles, Chuck Berry, Little Richard and the Stones, through to punk heroes The Clash and Ian Dury. It was backstage, in November '63, that Duane Eddy and The Shirelles learned of President Kennedy's assassination; a youthful Jimmy Page was there too that night, playing guitar with Carter Lewis & The Southerners. The Odeon was demolished in '81 to make way for the nice new town centre.

In the Fifties, aspiring local musicians bought their instruments from Len Stiles, whose shop at 233 High Street boasted a huge stock of new and slightly used gear, from only 3/6d weekly.

El Partido was a primarily black club at 8-12 Lee High Road, hosted by Duke Lee. Acts ranged from local favourites to Clarence Frogman Henry and Bo Diddley.

Kate Bush played her first gigs fronting The K.T. Bush Band at the Rose of Lee (later called Sports), a pub in Lee High Road.

In the early Nineties, teenager Blade was described as the best British rapper ever.

Making ripples if not waves in the mid-Nineties was The Sea, a folk/reggae/rock hybrid.

SE14 Deptford, New Cross

Alumni of Goldsmiths College in Lewisham Way include John Illsley (Dire Straits), John Cale (Velvet Underground), Neil Innes (Bonzos), Malcolm McLaren (Sex Pistols manager), Steve Mackey (Pulp), Graham Coxon and Alex James (both Blur).

Stone Idol was an early Seventies band formed by pupils at Addey & Stanhope School. Their drummer Chris Blackwell went on to play with Toyah and Robert Plant. He was obviously hoping to emulate another ex-pupil, Jon Hiseman.

Linton Kwesi Johnson's New Craas Massakah described the January '81 turning point in south London policing and Government attitudes.

Reggae singer and Shardeloes Road resident Winston Groovy wrote the '83 UB40 hit 'Please Don't Make Me Cry'.

'The Only Living Boy In New Cross' was a Top Ten hit for Carter USM in April '92.

Operational base of early Eighties scrap-metal percussionists Test Department, Nineties funk metallers The Atom Seed, and indie act The Belltower.

The Venue in Clifton Rise is one of UK's top indie clubs.

SE15 Peckham

Birthplace of Alan Lancaster, 7.2.49 (Status Quo).

Sixties R&B club The Bromel had a Peckham branch at the Co-op Hall in Rye Lane.

The Newlands Tavern in Stuart Road was a primo venue on the Seventies London pub-rock circuit, presenting the likes of Ian Dury and Dr Feelgood.

The operational base of Charley Records (at 155 Ilderton Road); early Eighties bizarros Splodgenessabounds (famous for their '80 Top Tenner 'Two Pints Of Lager'); and rap group The Three Wise Men.

While a student at St. Martins, Jarvis Cocker lived at 59 Lyndhurst Grove – as recalled in the eponymous '93 Pulp song.

Back To The Planet played their earliest gigs at the Dolehouse, the former DHSS office-cum-squat.

Local ragga star CJ Lewis reached the '94 Top Three with 'Sweets For My Sweet' – the first in a series of hit revivals – and Connor Reeves reached the Top Twenty in '97.

SE16 Bermondsey, Rotherhithe

Birthplace of Britain's first rock'n'roll star Tommy Steele, 17.12.36... not to mention his brother, Colin Hicks. They lived at 52 Frean Street, and Tommy went to Bacon's School for Boys. Coffee bar rocker Wee Willie Harris was also born in Bermondsey, as was Sixties chart star Julie Rogers, 6.4.43 (Top Three with 'The Wedding' in '64).

Max Bygraves was born in Rotherhithe, 16.10.22, and went to St. Josephs School. He first hit the charts with 'Cowpuncher's Cantata' in '52!

Setting for the video of The Specials' hit 'Ghost Town'... which was about Coventry!

Home of mid-Nineties techno dj/remixer Ashley Beedle.

Cathy Bush

(J.C. Bush)

SE18 Plumstead, Woolwich

Birthplace of Fifties rocker Terry Wayne, 24.9.41 (loads of publicity but no hits); Kate Bush, 30.7.58 (loads of publicity and loads of hits!); drummer Chris Kavanagh, 4.6.64 (Sigue Sigue Sputnik, Big Audio Dynamite).

An appearance in a contest at the Granada Cinema in Powis Street climaxed the career of Bellingham skiffle group The Hells Angels. The Beatles played there on a package with Gerry & The Pacemakers and Billy J Kramer & The Dakotas in June '63.

The Black Cat was a mid-Sixties R&B club at 5 Vincent Road. Sonny Boy Williamson played there in December '64.

Sometime home of teenage singer/songwriter Rosa Ania.

A hotbed of mid-Nineties teenage girl groups, including Shampoo and Oval.

SE19 Crystal Palace, Norwood

Crystal Palace Bowl became a rock venue in the Seventies, when acts like Pink Floyd, The Beach Boys, Rick Wakeman (who suffered an onstage heart attack), Santana, Bob Marley and Elvis Costello headlined... and was still going in the Nineties, when groups like The Pixies and Ride would appear.

Des'ree, who first charted with Feel So High in August '91, was a former pupil at Norwood Convent.

SE20 Penge

Bill Wyman went to Oakfield Junior School. He married for the first time in October '59, at Christ Church. He and Diane had their first home in Woodbine Grove.

Operational base of new wave hopefuls Tennis Shoes.

SE21, 22 Dulwich

Birthplace of Fifties favourite Anne Shelton, 10.11.23; bass player Kim Gardner, 27.1.46 (Ashton Gardner & Dyke); Belouis Some, 12.12.59.

Status Quo (then called The Spectres) used to rehearse in the ATC headquarters in Lordship Lane. Their first professional gig was at the Samuel Jones Sports Club in '62.

Quiet Sun was an early Seventies progressive group formed at Dulwich College. Guitarist Phil Manzanera went on to Roxy Music.

SE23 Forest Hill, Honor Oak

Birthplace of Francis Rossi, 29.5.49 (Status Quo).

The Glenlyn, at 15 Perry Vale (behind the station) was a popular Sixties venue, presenting The Kinks, The Animals, John Mayall, etc on Friday and Saturday and bingo on the other nights. Later became Crystals Snooker Club.

Forest Hill was the operational base of two Seventies bands: Peter Perrett's Only Ones and David Sylvian's Japan (who used to rehearse in Elsinore Road).

Peter and his pets: The Only Ones

Maxi Priest was a pupil at Roger Manwood Secondary School in Brockley Rise and later worked with Dennis Rowe's Catford-based Saxon Sound System.

Operational base of early Eighties dud reggae band Basement 5 – led by *NME* photographer Dennis Morris and produced by Martin Hannett.

Reggae star Desmond Dekker was living in Devonshire Road in August '93, when Camberwell magistrates fined him £1,250 and imposed a five year ban for driving with nearly two and a half times the legal alcohol limit.

SE24 Herne Hill
Brockwell Park was the setting for a Rock Against Racism gig in September '78. Elvis Costello, Aswad and Sham 69 entertained.

SE26 Sydenham
Operational base of Seventies blues band Killing Floor and Eighties indie band (Kid Jensen favourites) Colour Box.

SE27 West Norwood
Birthplace of John Coghlan, 19.9.46 (Status Quo); keyboard player Barry Andrews, 12.9.56, (XTC/Shriekback: he went to Hitherfield School).

Operational base of Terraplane, who mutated into Nineties chartbusters Thunder.

Thunder in a W1 back street

SW1 Belgravia, Pimlico, Westminster
Birthplace of keyboard player Peter Bardens, 19.6.44 (Camel); Kirk Brandon, 3.8.56 (Theatre of Hate, Spear of Destiny).

It was at Buckingham Palace that The Beatles received their MBEs in October '65 and Bob Geldof his knighthood in July '86. Paul McCartney, Tim Rice, Elton John and Cliff Richard are among those to have been similarly honoured. In March '77, The Sex Pistols signed their A&M contract on a table outside the front gates. In less than a week, they were dropped from the label, £75,000 richer. The Palace's incumbent, with a safety pin through her mouth, would soon grace the picture-sleeve of 'God Save The Queen'.

Roxy Music's Andy Mackay was educated at Westminster City Grammar; Peter & Gordon first met as pupils at Westminster School – where Shane McGowan was later a reluctant student.

Pop stars of every generation, Larry Page to Adam Faith to Ringo Starr to Eric Burdon, have married at Caxton Hall in Caxton Street.

On moving down from Liverpool, George Harrison and Ringo Starr shared flat 7 at Whaddon House, William Mews; Brian Epstein also lived here, in flat 15.

In '64, Brian Jones shared a flat with The Pretty Things at 13 Chester Street. The address became the title of a Pretty Things album track. In early '68, Jones lived in Chesham Place.

13 Chester Street after a total renovation

When they first moved to London in summer '69, Mott The Hoople shared a flat at 20b Lower Sloane Street before moving to Earls Court.

John Lennon first met Yoko Ono in November '66, during a preview for the latter's show *Unfinished Paintings And Objects* at Indica Gallery (opened in January '66 by Barry Miles and John Dunbar, with assistance from investors Paul McCartney and Peter Asher) at 6 Masons Yard, off Duke Street. A stones-throw away at number 13 Masons Yard was the Scotch of St. James, a swinging-London split-level disco for in-crowd groovers, which opened in

March '65. It was here that The Jimi Hendrix Experience made their world début on 25.10.66 – and that Kit Lambert and Chris Stamp signed them to a record deal.

It was at the Birdland Club in Jermyn Street, in September '66, that Eric Burdon auditioned applicants for his New Animals – including Noel Redding, who was passed over but hired by Hendrix, who happened to be present. A week later, Mitch Mitchell auditioned here for Jimi, and The Experience was complete.

In April '67, Marianne Faithfull launched her acting career playing Irina in Chekhov's *Three Sisters* at the Royal Court Theatre in Sloane Square. She was living at 29 Lennox Gardens, where she and Mick Jagger were enjoying the early months of their affair.

In August '67, Brian Epstein took a drug overdose in his flat at 24 Chapel Street, Belgravia. His butler discovered his lifeless body the next morning.

Launched from the House of Commons in November '85, Red Wedge was a left wing fundraising alliance put together by Billy Bragg, Jerry Dammers, Paul Weller and ex-*NME* editor Neil Spencer.

In '67, The Troggs recorded a song 'Number 10 Downing Street'. 22 years later Elvis Costello expressed his contempt for the current incumbent in 'Tramp It Down', as did The Beat with 'Stand Down Margaret'. Whereas Margaret Thatcher invited statesmen to Downing Street, and John Major famous sportsmen, Tony Blair shocked the media by inviting Creation mogul Alan McGee (who had donated £50,000 to the Labour Party) and his flagship band Oasis.

The ICA (Institute of Contemporary Arts) at 12 Carlton House Terrace (Pall Mall) has frequently presented rock nights – usually of an avant garde nature. Adam & The Ants made their début there in May '77; Everything But The Girl made theirs in January '83; Tindersticks played a five night season in November '96. The Venue, a Virgin/Branson operation at 160 Victoria Street, was a top showcase gig in the late Seventies/early Eighties. The variety of presentation can be gauged by the roster for September '83, which included The Smiths, Stevie Ray Vaughan, The Poison Girls and Sun Ra.

Haircut 100 played their first date at the Ski Club in Eaton Square – operated by Nick Heyward's parents.

The sleeve of his album *New Boots And Panties* shows Ian Dury and his son Baxter standing outside Axton's at 306 Vauxhall Bridge Road. He used to wait for the bus there and often popped in "to buy his two tone crotchless panties".

SW2 Brixton

Following a drug conviction in June '67, Mick Jagger spent a night in Brixton prison. The prison was also the setting for Simon & Garfunkel's first British concert (in '65, some months before they became famous) and for 'Sonny's Letter', a police fit-up story by Linton Kwesi Johnson, rock's most articulate and authoritative spokesman in the fight against police and NF racism.

Before joining Fleetwood Mac, guitarist Danny Kirwan led local blues group Boilerhouse.

When they moved to London from Wales in the late Sixties, The Bystanders – soon to change their name to Man – lived together at 66 Tierney Road.

The Hot Chocolate Band formed here in '70 and cut a single for Apple before signing with Mickie Most's RAK label as Hot Chocolate.

Mick Jones (Clash) lived at Christchurch House and went to the Strand Grammar School. Poly Styrene of X-Ray Spex also grew up locally.

Joe Strummer's group The 101-ers played their first gig at the Telegraph pub at 228 Brixton Hill in September '74 – a benefit for the Chile Solidarity Campaign, headlined by Matumbi.

The Fridge in Town Hall Parade was (and is) a cool venue, presenting everyone from Eartha Kitt to The Fall, Take That to Courtney Pine.

Operational base for late Seventies new wavers The Skunks; early Eighties band The Expressos; Nineties grunge band Headcleaner; indie band Joyride.

SW3 Chelsea

In '67, Mick Jagger paid a reported £40,000 for 48 Cheyne Walk, overlooking the Thames, while Brian Jones moved into Royal Avenue House on the Kings Road. Police tracked him down and found cannabis concealed in a ball of wool. "I don't knit," said Brian.

During '67, Eric Clapton lived above the Pheasantry at 125 Kings Road – once the residence of Nell Gwynne, so it is said. Another tenant was Martin Sharp, a psychedelic poster artist who also designed Cream's *Disraeli Gears* sleeve. Italian film director Michelangelo Antonioni held a party here to select cool-looking extras for his movie *Blow Up*.

In his mid-Sixties heyday, PJ Proby could afford to live at 5 Cheltenham Terrace, off the Kings Road.

Pre-fame Sandy Denny was a nurse at Brompton Hospital.

It was at Sound Techniques Studio in Old Church Street that Pink Floyd recorded their first single, 'Arnold Layne'; that Richard Thompson met his future wife Linda Peters (she was recording a cornflakes commercial!).

The cover of Richard Thompson's album *Hand Of Kindness* was shot on a deserted Chelsea Embankment.

In May '65, at Chelsea Register Office, 250 Kings Road, Marianne Faithfull married ex-Vibrators bass player Ben Brierley.

Chelsea Art School *(Chelsea)*

(Chelsea College of Art and Design)

It was at Chelsea Art School that John Martyn first encountered his future wife Beverly. Alexei Sayle was a student here in the late Seventies, when he missed a seminal gig by The Sex Pistols. He'd never heard of them, so went home "to drink cocoa and watch Department S on his black and white telly". John Deacon (Queen) also studied here.

Three distracted pupils of the Oratory in Stewarts Grove formed post-punk band The Television Personalities, who stormed the indie charts with such gems as 'Where's Bill Grundy Now?' and 'I Know Where Syd Barrett Lives'.

The Pet Shop Boys are said to have first met each other in a Kings Road music shop.

Fifteen-year-old Boy George worked at Shades, a clothes stall in Chelsea Antique Market. The punk group Chelsea were led by Gene October. 'I Don't Wanna Go To Chelsea' was a '78 hit for Elvis Costello.

SW4 Clapham

Birthplace of Dennis Waterman, 24.2.48 (Top Three in '80. He starred in *Up The Junction*, set locally, and Squeeze later sang about it); Mick Jones, 26.6.55 (Clash, Big Audio Dynamite), at the now-closed South London Women's Hospital.

Among Clapham's residents have been Bob Geldof and Paula Yates, Kevin Coyne, Thunderclap Newman (his dog used to do tricks in the local pubs!) and Murray Head.

Sting, Sade, Peter Gabriel, Billy Bragg and Boy George were among those singing for an estimated audience of half a million at an Anti Apartheid concert on Clapham Common in June '86.

Local groups include Bontemps Roulez (Seventies pub rockers) and Rock Goddess (early Eighties heavy metal, who mutatated into the much more famous Girlschool). Second Hand turned into Seventh Wave; The Wee Papa Girl Rappers went Top Ten with 'Wee Rule' in '88.

Dave Angel was a rising mid-Nineties techno star – his sister had a string of cool tempo hits under the name of Monie Love.

SW5 Earls Court

The Troubadour at 265 Old Brompton Road has been a coffee house/folk venue since the Fifties. In December '62, Bob Dylan gave a handful of impromptu performances on his first London visit – as did Bert Jansch and Robin Williamson (later of The Incredible String Band) on theirs.

In '66/'67, Pink Floyd and other underground scene-makers shared 101 Cromwell Road. It was here that Syd Barrett began to display strange behaviour. "Acid in the coffee every morning," was said to be a contributory cause.

Guitarist David O'List (Nice, Roxy Music) grew up in Trebovir Road.

Initially famous for The Lurkers, The Doll and Tubeway Army, the Beggars Banquet empire began to flourish at 8 Hogarth Road.

Earls Court Exhibition Centre has presented various rock music extravaganzas: Led Zeppelin did five nights in May '75; Pink Floyd played and built *The Wall* there for six nights in August '80; Bob Dylan filled it for six nights in June '81. Others who have played there include Eric Clapton, The Who, Genesis, Rod Stewart and Oasis. At the Brit Awards ceremony in February '96, Jarvis Cocker indicated his displeasure with Michael Jackson's obnoxious display by taking the stage and protruding his arse audiencewards.

SW6 Fulham, Parsons Green

Birthplace of Fifties rocker Duffy Power, 9.9.41; guitarist David O'List, 13.12.48 (Nice, Roxy Music); singer Simon Climie, 7.4.60 (Climie Fisher).

Fleetwood Mac held their first rehearsals at the Black Bull in Fulham Road. The Golden Lion at 490 Fulham Road and the Cock Tavern at 360 North End Road were pub rock venues. The Kings Head was thriving in the Nineties.

Before they were Sex Pistols, Glen Matlock and Paul Cook used to play football at Lillie Road recreation ground.

Late Seventies indie outlet The Label (started by Pistols producer Dave Goodman and noted for Eater) operated from 106 Dawes Road.

In April '80, during their first attempts to infiltrate the London scene, The Birthday Party lived in squalor and penury at 39 Maxwell Road.

Fulham Fallout was the only chart album by The Lurkers.

The Royal Albert Hall, SW7

Never Stop "Discotheque" / Echo & The Bunnymen

SW7 South Kensington

The Royal Albert Hall has presented prestigious rock gigs since the Fifties. Janis Joplin made her UK début there, The Nice burnt an American flag, and Cream said goodbye, but boisterous fans and bizarre groups saw policy changes in '71 when Frank Zappa (for oscenity) and Mott The Hoople (for causing riots and damage) were both banned. Rock was again deemed permissible in the Eighties, when groups like Siouxsie & The Banshees (originally the wildest, most untutored punks of all) drew well-behaved audiences – and John Otway realised his dream by headlining there in October '98. The most ubiquitous performer is Eric Clapton, whose residencies (of up to 24 nights) have been an annual event for over a decade.

The Royal College of Music in Prince Consort Road has educated such rock luminaries as Darryl Way (Curved Air), Tony Kaye and Rick Wakeman (Yes), Davy O'List (Nice), Steve Nieve (Attractions), Richard Harvey and Brian Gulland (Gryphon), and Mike Moran (writer/arranger).

Ian Dury, John Foxx (Ultravox) and Sarah Jane Owen (Belle Stars) all made it to the Royal College of Art in Kensington Gore. Peter Blake was a tutor there at the time he designed the sleeve for *Sgt Pepper's Lonely Hearts Club Band*.

When John and Cynthia Lennon moved down to London in early '64, they took a flat at 13 Emperors Gate.

In summer '66, Brian Jones and Anita Pallenberg shared a flat in Courtfield Road; and Dana Gillespie lived in Thurloe Square. That same year, Donovan had an album track called 'Sunny South Kensington'.

Al Stewart used to live in "a run down basement" in Elvaston Place – recalled in a '71 song of that name.

Brian May studied astronomy at Imperial College, where his band 1984 supported The Jimi Hendrix Experience in May '67. His later trio Smile played the first of many gigs here on 26.10.68, supporting Pink Floyd.

A popular Sixties night spot was Blaises, a basement club at 121 Queens Gate. Jimi Hendrix made an early appearance here in September '66, guesting with The Brian Auger Trinity.

Equally thronging was the Cromwellian at 3 Cromwell Road... described as "three floors of fun"! It was here that Long John Baldry asked Elton John if Bluesology would be his backing group.

The Elizabethan Room of the Gore Hotel in Queensgate was the setting for the press launch of the Stones album *Beggars Banquet* in December '68. Everyone threw food around. How jolly.

29 Exhibition Road is home of British Museum annexe, the National Sound Archive.

SW8 Battersea

In December '76, during a photo shoot for Pink Floyd's album *Animals*, a 40 ft inflated pig, moored to Battersea Power Station, broke loose, floated heavenwards, bewildered pilots, and was never seen again. The Power Station was also used as the backdrop to Toyah's video of 'Brave New World'. First act to see its potential was Juniors Eyes, who called their '69 album *Battersea Power Station*.

The Who's Ramport Studio was at 115/7 Thessaly Road.

The Cannibals were the first (and possibly last) act on late Seventies label Big Cock Records, operating from 13 Silverton Road.

Club Coliseum at 1 Nine Elms Lane is the womb of local late Nineties drum'n'bass culture.

SW9 Brixton, Stockwell

David Bowie was born at 40 Stansfield Road on 6.8.47.

One of the most famous of all Sixties R&B/soul clubs was the Ram Jam at 390 Brixton Road, owned by Geno Washington's manager and named after his band. From here, the cry of "Geno! Geno!" spread throughout the land. Mayall, Hendrix, Cream and all other important bands played here.

The title of Eddy Grant's '83 Top Three hit was inspired by the local Electric Avenue.

Hottest current venue is the Academy, 211 Stockwell Road. All the great acts from Dylan to The Fun Lovin' Criminals have played there. The Smiths played their final UK gig there in December '86; The Alarm said goodbye there in June '91.

Briefly, while waiting for Queen to happen, Brian May taught English at Stockwell Manor Comprehensive.

Residents have included Nico; local groups include Local Heroes SW9 (!) and Under Neath What, who lived in a squat in Barrington Road.

The Swan has long been an Irish music/pub-rock venue, presenting everyone from Rolf Harris to The Balham Alligators. The Dogstar at 389 Coldharbour Lane was a fashionable late Nineties venue – as was The Brix (refurbished as Mass in September '98) at St. Matthews Church.

Operational base of mid-Nineties rap act Katch 22 and indie band The Sunkings.

SW10 Chelsea

During the gestation of The Rolling Stones, Mick Jagger, Brian Jones and Keith Richards shared a gruesome flat at 102 Edith Grove, bereft of food, furniture or heat. They used to rehearse in a room above the Weatherby Arms at 500 Kings Road – where Bill Wyman successfully auditioned.

During the Sixties, Lionel Bart lived at 3a Seymour Walk.

After taking acid in '67, Yes bass player Chris Squire

spent two days in St. Stephens Hospital. In September '77, Keith Moon was rushed here after a fit. Doctors predicted he might not survive – but he lasted another year.

In '71, Malcolm McLaren and Vivienne Westwood opened Let It Rock at 430 Kings Road. After a brief spell as Too Fast To Live Too Young To Die, it became Sex in '75. It was here that Chrissie Hynde and Glen Matlock worked, Johnny Rotten was discovered, and The Sex Pistols were created.

The grooviest shop of the psychedelic era was Granny Takes A Trip at 488 Kings Road.

During The Sex Pistols' heyday, Johnny Rotten lived at 45 Gunter Grove.

SW11 Battersea

Birthplace of one of Britain's earliest rock'n'rollers, Rory Blackwell. Terry Dene and Georgie Fame both made their professional débuts in his band.

One of London's earliest blues clubs was the Blue Horizon, which ran at the Nag's Head at 205 York Road. Producer Mike Vernon was the promoter. Free played their first gig here in May '68; Alexis Korner, who named them, was in the audience.

Whilst The Who's roadie Cy Langston was inside Battersea Dogs Home buying a guard dog in September '65, a thief stole their van and scarpered with 5,000 quids worth of equipment. Elton John got his dog Thomas from Battersea Dogs Home.

Reggae pioneers Matumbi emerged from Battersea in '72, and the Pasadenas appeared in '88.

The 101 Club at 101 St. John's Hill was a popular late Seventies/early Eighties gig; the Grand (a converted theatre) opened just up the road in '92, with acts ranging from Jamiroquai to The Kinks, The Manic Street Preachers to Suede.

Famous for The Sugarcubes and Bjork, the idiosyncratic One Little Indian label is based at 250 York Road. Their roster also included Drive – containing Mel Blatt, later of All Saints.

SW12 Balham

Birthplace of Captain Sensible, at St. James Hospital on 24.4.54 (Damned); Dee C Lee, 6.6.61.

Chilli Willi & The Red Hot Peppers called their album *Bongos Over Balham*, and a bunch of pub rock cajuns call their group The Balham Alligators.

Olympic Studios

(Olympic Studios)

SW13 Barnes

The Rolling Stones' first official recording session took place at Olympic Studios at 117 Church Road in May '63, yielding top 30 hit 'Come On'. In October 68, Led Zeppelin recorded their first album there – in 30 hours, for a mere £1700! And in May '71, The Who recorded *Who's Next* there.

In '69, before they formed Queen, Freddie Mercury, Roger Taylor and Brian May shared a flat in Ferry Road. On 29.5.76, Brian May married Chrissie Mullen at St. Osmund's Church in Castlenau.

In September '77, a purple mini GT driven by Gloria Jones went out of control crossing Barnes Common. It veered off the road and smashed into a tree, killing the passenger, Marc Bolan. Fans still visit the spot to lay flowers beside the tree. In the mid-Sixties, Bolan had lived not far away in Lonsdale Road.

The seeds for Subway Sect were sown by Vic Godard and fellow pioneer punk pupils at the Sheen School.

In December '83, at a reception at The Old Rangoon Restaurant following his first solo concert, former Led Zeppelin guitarist Jimmy Page threw a glass of wine over journalist John Blake. "You are the scum of the earth," he said. "Kneel down before me and apologise."

Sometime home of Ben Watt, half of Everything But The Girl.

The Bull's Head at Barnes Bridge has been a music pub forever.

Marc Bolan's fatal call to nature, SW13

The Half Moon, Putney

SW14 East Sheen, Mortlake

Birthplace of singer/songwriter Bridget St. John.

Paul Cook completed his apprenticeship as an electrician at Watney's Brewery just as The Sex Pistols got going.

SW15 Putney, Roehampton

In July '67, Rolling Stone Brian Jones booked himself into the Priory, a psychiatric hospital in Priory Lane, for 20 days. "I need treatment," he told doctors. Another famous patient, Brian Epstein, had just moved out – having spent May and June there, recuperating from insomnia and depression.

Hedonistic behaviour at the mid-Sixties home of The Moody Blues in Roehampton made sex-and-drugs style headlines in the Sunday papers.

Peter Green lived in Putney; he went to Ronald Ross Primary and Elliot Secondary School.

In the early Seventies, Elvis Costello and his band Flip City shared a house at 3 Stag Lane.

The Pontiac Club in Zeeta House, 200 Upper Richmond Road was a R&B/mod venue decorated in classic Sixties op-art style. It was here that Peter Green blagged his way into John Mayall's Bluesbreakers.

Rather more enduring is the Half Moon at 93 Lower Richmond Road – a jazz/folk/blues/rock stronghold forever.

Police played their first headlining gig at the Railway Hotel in Putney in May '77.

Sandy Denny, who died in April '78, is buried in Putney Vale Cemetery.

SW16 Streatham

Birthplace of Dave Kelly, 13.3.47 (Blues Band).

In the Fifties, the Dolphin was the place to be, but the action had crossed the road by the Sixties when punters could carry on skating at the Silver Blades Ice Rink (386 Streatham High Street) while bands like Cream and The Pretty Things entertained them!

When Eden Kane hit number one with 'Well I Ask You' in '61, he was living in Norbury Crescent. His brother, Peter Sarstedt was still living there eight years later when he reached Number One with 'Where Do You Go To My Lovely'.

SW17 Tooting

Birthplace of Phil Lithman, 17.6.49 (Chilli Willi, The Residents); singer Jill Saward, 9.12.53 (Fusion Orchestra, Shakatak).

The Beatles appeared at Tooting Granada, 50 Mitcham Road, which was a popular late Fifties/early Sixties package tour venue (later converted into a bingo hall). In May '58, after his appearance here, Jerry Lee Lewis' UK tour was aborted by theatre chain moguls who were incensed that his wife (his third one!) was only 13.

Pat Boone made his UK début at the same venue on Boxing Day '56, as did Gene Vincent in December '59. During his act, Gene suddenly swung his steel-braced leg over the microphone, pole-axing guitarist Joe Brown as he leapt forward to take a solo.

Three years later, Vincent was treated at St. Georges Hospital in Blackshaw Road when he aggravated his dodgy leg. Brian Jones was also treated at St. Georges – for nervous exhaustion in '67; Cilla Black had her babies here;

and Keith Moon had a hernia operation. In June '95, guitarist Rory Gallagher died here after complications resulting from a liver transplant.

When he left school, Marc Bolan worked in Edgar's, a clothes shop on Tooting Broadway.

In December '80, Sting played two gigs in a sardine-packed 5000 capacity tent on Tooting Bec Common.

The Castle has been a pub-rock venue forever, presenting Mott The Hoople (April '70), Free, The Groundhogs and perennial locals The Tooting Frooties.

The Castle, Tooting, in 1940 (The Groundhogs on that night)

(Young & Co.'s Brewery PLC Archive)

SW18 Wandsworth

Birthplace of bandleader Ted Heath, 30.3.02 (at 76 Atheldene Avenue); Jon Moss, 11.9.57 (Culture Club).

Adam Faith made his professional début with The Worried Men Skiffle Group at a boys' club in Wandsworth.

Johnny Rotten first rehearsed with The Sex Pistols at the Rose And Crown public house.

As a member of Flip City, Elvis Costello gigged for the inmates of Wandsworth Prison – as did The 101ers, three times in early '76. Included in their set were 'Jailhouse Rock' and 'Riot in Cell Block Number Nine'.

Faces keyboard player Ian McLagan married Kim Moon (formerly Mrs Keith Moon) at the Register Office in October '78.

SW19 Wimbledon

Birthplace of guitarist Tom McGuinness, 2.12.41 (Manfred Mann); guitarist Peter Thorp, 25.5.44 (Roulettes); Sandy Denny, 6.1.47; guitarist Porl Thompson, 8.11.57 (Cure); keyboard player Mick Talbot, 11.9.58 (Style Council).

Jeff Beck went to Wimbledon Art College, where punk group The Art Attacks made their début in summer '76. Publicist and former rock group manager Max Clifford went to All Saints Junior School.

In December '63, The Beatles played a special Fan Club concert at Wimbledon Palais, a once-famous ballroom in High Street, Merton. The Rolling Stones played there three times in '64. Punters no longer go there to dance, but to buy sofas: it's now called Furnitureland!

The Yardbirds cut their early singles at R G Jones Studios in Beaulah Road. Twenty five years later, Cliff Richard cut 'Mistletoe And Wine' here.

Wimbledon Common is the ancestral home of The Wombles – television puppets who scored top tenners under Mike Batt's direction. Notorious rock manager Don Arden also lived there before moving to the States. Local groups have included The Outsiders (new wave) and The Merton Parkas (neo-mods).

Before he started Sham 69, Jimmy Pursey worked at Wimbledon Greyhound Stadium.

Having started in Malvern, the late Seventies indie label Cherry Red moved to London to set up shop at 199 Kingston Road.

Over the years, the basement of the Labour Party Club at 267 The Broadway has been used as a club. In the hippie era, it was the Hobbits' Garden – recently it became a rave venue, the Watershed. The Cube Club, based at the William Morris Club in Broadway, was closed down in the early Nineties after noise complaints.

The 100 Club, Oxford Street, W1

W1 West End, Mayfair, Soho

Oxford Street... the 100 Club has survived every fashion from trad jazz to whatever's happening this week. Britain's first punk festival was held here in September '76, when Siouxsie & The Banshees and The Subway Sect made their débuts. The Damned also made their début there, in July 76 – supporting The Sex Pistols. Oasis played there in March '94.

The Marquee Club was originally at 165 Oxford Street, underneath the Academy Cinema; The Rolling Stones made their world début there on 12.7.62, helping to convert it from traditional jazz to R&B and solid rock.

Opening in April '64, at number 79 (on the corner of Dean Street) was the subterranean venue Beat City (where the Stones played in the stifling heat of July '64). In February '66, it became Tiles – when Jeff Dexter was the disc jockey and persuaded the owner to book cool acts like Wilson Pickett (March '66) and Pink Floyd (June '67).

At 119 was Dryden Chambers, approached through an alleyway. Here, in labyrinthine offices, were the Miles Copeland empire, *Sniffin' Glue*, *Zigzag* magazine, John Sherry Enterprises, and various other rockbiz enterprises.

At 214 are Air Studios, tucked away on the fifth floor near Oxford Circus. George Martin is the most visible co-owner.

Since time immemorial, HMV's record shop at number 363 has been a hub of rock activity. Terry Dene worked here; Cliff Richard cut his first demos ('Breathless' and 'Lawdy Miss Clawdy'); The Beatles had acetates made – which led to their EMI contract and, within two years, global fame.

Old Compton Street... the 2Is coffee bar at number 59 was mecca to Fifties teenagers. Among those who played or got their big break there were Tommy Steele, Terry Dene, The Vipers, Cliff Richard, Hank and Bruce, Mickie Most, Tony Sheridan, Adam Faith, Joe Brown, Lance Fortune and Emile Ford. BBC-TV broadcast a live *6.5 Special* from here and Wee Willie Harris celebrated the place on 'Rockin' At The 2Is'. The distinctive murals were executed by regular patron Lionel Bart. Track Records.

Other Fifties rock'n'roll venues were Vince Taylor's Top Ten Club in Berwick Street, and the Condor Club, where Marty Wilde was discovered.

Other coffee bar/skiffle clubs in the locality were the Heaven And Hell (next door to the 2Is) at 57 Old Compton Street, the Freight Train at 44 Berwick Street (owned by skiffler Chas McDevitt and later turned into Musicland record shop, where Elton John is said to have worked), the House of Sam Widges at 9 D'Arblay Street, the Partisan at 7 Carlisle Street, Russell Quaye's Skiffle Cellar at 49 Greek Street, Le Macabre at 23 Meard Street (the tables were shaped like coffins!), and the Breadbasket at 65 Cleveland Street (where The Vipers first got going in early '56).

By the mid-Sixties, the Skiffle Cellar had become Les Cousins – the best folk club in Soho. The likes of Bert Jansch and Al Stewart made it famous.

Good too was the Ballads & Blues Club at the Black Horse, 6 Rathbone Place. That was started in '53 by Ewan McColl – author of 'First Time Ever I Saw Your Face' and father of Kirsty.

Folkies and beatniks drank in Finch's in Goodge Street – the setting for Donovan's 'Sunny Goodge Street' – and sang at the King and Queen, a pub on the corner of Foley Street. It was here, on his first visit to London in late '62, that Bob Dylan made several impromptu appearances.

Heddon Street... David Bowie was photographed here in January '72 for the sleeve of *Ziggy Stardust*.

Exceedingly rare RCA Records sampler album cunningly titled after their W1 address

Wardour Street... the second and most famous home of the Marquee Club was at number 90 – opened by The Yardbirds in March '64. Everyone from the Stones to The Who to Bowie to Marillion played here in their hungry years. It was at an early 'happening', The Spontaneous Underground in March '66, that Pink Floyd were spotted by future manager Peter Jenner. Led Zeppelin débuted at the Marquee as The New Yardbirds in October '68, and returned there for a chaotic gig in March '71. The Stones filmed a TV special there around the same time and after many delays and false starts threw out their invitation-only audience because they preferred to stay in the bar than watch the band!

Just up from the Marquee was La Chasse (number 100), a private drinking club in a mangy, smoke filled first floor room containing a bar and sundry bullshitters. Plans for Yes were hatched here in May '68, when Jon Anderson was a barman. Keith Moon once arrived at La Chasse via the fire escape, having climbed over the rooftops from The Who's offices in Old Compton Street. A more traditional meeting place/watering hole was nearby pub the Ship. It's difficult to find a muso who hasn't stuck his head in here at some time or another.

The Ship Pub

(Nikki Lloyd)

The Wag Club

Crackers was a mid-Seventies funk disco at the top end of Wardour Street (number 201). In '76, it became the Vortex to catch the punk boom. Sham 69 played at the opening ceremony; Jimmy Pursey was arrested and fined 30 quid for breaching the peace. In July '77, a memorable Salford night showcased The Buzzcocks, The Fall and John Cooper Clarke. In August '77, dumb-ass provincial punks cheered when news came through that Elvis Presley had died. Danny Baker (then a *Sniffin' Glue* correspondent) took the stage and lectured them on his importance.

The 101ers played occasionally at the nearby St. Moritz (number 159) in late '75, immortalising the owner on Sweety of the St. Moritz. It became a primo New Romantics haunt a few years later.

The Roundhouse (not to be confused with the Chalk Farm venue) was a pub at '83 Wardour Street – the mid-Fifties home of the London Skiffle Centre, run by Alexis Korner and Cyril Davies, who modified it to the Blues and Barrelhouse Club in '58. Thirty years later, you could pay three quid to see "Live Show: Male And Female In Bed", but it has now reverted to licensed premises.

The Flamingo, a cellar at 33 Wardour Street, was a great Sixties jazz/R&B stronghold originally populated by hookers, black GIs, gangsters and cool fans. The too-white Rolling Stones failed there (in November '62), but Georgie Fame was welcomed with open arms. During the hippie/underground era, it became The Temple – a grisly unwelcome hole if ever I saw one. In the late Fifties/Sixties, the first floor housed one of London's first discos, the Whiskey A Gogo, where the press reception was held for Buddy Holly's UK tour of March '58. Special guests Denis Compton and Godfrey Evans were there to give a cricketing flavour! In the early Eighties, it was turned into the oh-so-trendy Wag Club – Wag being an acronym for Whiskey A Gogo.

The Rolling Stones held their first rehearsals in a room over the Bricklayers Arms, on the corner of Broadwick Street and Duck Lane – no longer a pub, but still recognizable.

The pre-Bill and Charlie Stones were among the early R&B groups to play at Giorgio Gomelsky's short lived Piccadilly Club, which operated in late '62, in Ham Yard at 41 Great Windmill Street. In '63, it was taken over by Lionel Blake and Ronan O'Rahilly (soon to float Radio Caroline) and made famous as the Scene Club – patronised by the Who/Stones/R&B/mod elite. Monday was R&B night with manic disc jockey Guy "too fast to live" Stevens. Punters divested themselves of dubious possessions when the police waded in one night, shouted "don't nobody move", and found the place knee-deep in pills!

The Ad Lib Club was a mid-Sixties in-crowd haunt on an upper floor of 7 Leicester Place. Guy Peellaert's painting, contained in his book *Rock Dreams*, depicted some of its patrons. In the basement was the short-lived London Cavern, where The Small Faces got their act together and were discovered by producer/ songwriter Ian Samwell. It subsequently became known as the Notre Dame Hall and is still used for gigs. The Revillos made their London début there in September '79.

Regent Street... upper crust revellers at the Cafe Royal were amused by Tommy Steele's novel rock'n'roll act in '56; David Bowie held his star-studded "retirement party" there in July '73. Pink Floyd instigators Nick Mason, Roger Waters and Rick Wright were all students at Regent Street Polytechnic's School of Architecture – where in October '66, the newly arrived Jimi Hendrix got up on stage at a Cream gig.

Tottenham Court Road... Bill Haley & his Comets made their UK début at the Dominion Theatre in February '57, and Buddy Holly attended Chris Barber's benefit concert for Big Bill Broonzy there in March '58. Van Morrison played eleven nights at the same venue in May '83, and in '86 it was the setting for Dave Clark's musical *Time*, with Cliff Richard (and later David Cassidy) in the lead role. The Pentangle's first gig was at the Horseshoe pub next door (number 264) in October '67.

London's first and best flower power/underground club was UFO, which happened on Friday nights in the basement of 31 Tottenham Court Road (normally occupied by the Blarney Club). Opened in December '66, it presented the likes of Pink Floyd, Soft Machine, Jimi Hendrix and Procol Harum. It was here that Pete Townshend saw Arthur Brown and signed him to Track; that Joe Boyd saw Fairport Convention and signed them to Witchseason. Closed after lurid drug exposés in the Sunday papers.

The offices of pirate ship Radio London were at 17 Curzon Street.

Carnaby Street... Pet Shop Boy Neil Tennant (editor at *Smash Hits*), Ian Matthews (shoe seller at Ravels) and Boy George all worked here. John Stephen's clothes shop at number 41 was the first of many which would transform it into the centre of Swinging London during the mid-Sixties.

Lord John in Carnaby Street

(Rex Features)

As such, it was celebrated on 'Dedicated Follower Of Fashion' by The Kinks and' Carnaby Street' by The Jam.

One of central London's first black clubs was the Roaring 20s in the basement of 50 Carnaby Street. Opened in '61, it featured Count Suckle playing bluebeat on his (pre-discotheque era) sound system. Georgie Fame was one of the few white acts to gig there regularly.

In its Seventies heyday, the *NME*'s editorial offices were at 5-7 Carnaby Street, while over the road at number 52-55 was *Smash Hits*. *Mojo, Q, Kerrang* and other EMAP empire publications are published from 4 Winsley Street.

Argyll Street... home of the Palladium (at number 7), which has been presenting rock shows since the days of Johnnie Ray and Frankie Lymon & The Teenagers. The TV show *Sunday Night At The London Palladium* featured many rock acts, including The Beatles in October '63. Many commentators have cited this event as the birth of Beatlemania, since fans blocked Argyll Street and spilled over into Gt. Marlborough Street. The chaos was covered by the tabloid press who used the term 'Beatlemania' for the first time. The Rolling Stones caused national indignation in January '67, when they refused to wave from the revolving stage in the traditional TV show finale.

Brian Epstein had his NEMS Enterprises offices in Sutherland House next door to the Palladium, at number 5-6 Argyll Street.

Opening in July '81, the Limelight Club, in a converted church, became a honey pot for famous neo-popsters. The first line-up of Yes rehearsed in a basement under the Lucky Horseshoe Cafe. Dire Straits mention Shaftesbury Avenue in 'Wild West End' (not to mention the number 19 bus!).

When youth fashion flowered in the Fifties and Sixties, the hippest shops were Austin's (favoured by Justin de Villeneuve, The Yardbirds, etc) and Cecil Gee (at number 39), both in Shaftesbury Avenue.

The Rock Circus at 3 Piccadilly was previously the site of the Pavilion cinema, where *A Hard Day's Night, Help!* and *Yellow Submarine* were all premiered.

The Prince of Wales Theatre at 31 Coventry Street was one of the traditional venues for the annual Royal Command Performances, which featured every major rock act considered famous and genteel enough for royal inspection – including Tommy Steele, The Beatles ('63 – "Just rattle your jewellery"). In the late Nineties, it was the venue for Smokey Joe's Café, showcasing the music of songwriters Leiber and Stoller.

Kajagoogoo heart-throb Limahl once worked as a drinks waiter at the Embassy Club, 6 New Bond Street.

Baker Street... The Beatles' boutique Apple was at number 94. It opened December '67, and closed in July '68. Gerry Rafferty wrote his most enduring hit while staying with friends in Baker Street.

The Speakeasy, Margaret Street

Billy's, 69 Dean Street

20 Manchester Square housed EMI, self-styled World's Greatest Recording Organisation, from '60 until they moved out to Hammersmith in the Nineties.

Margaret Street... the Speakeasy, which opened in December '66 in the basement of number 50, was a primo groover/star-watchers hangout for a decade or so – even though some observers likened it to an upholstered sewer. It was here that Yes successfully auditioned for Atlantic Records, that Thin Lizzy made their English début (December '70), and that a drunken roadie urinated into Tony Stratton Smith's supper. Hendrix would jam (he also tried to pull Marianne Faithfull under the eyes of Mick J), people would be gay. New York Doll Billy Murcia spent the last hedonistic night of his life here in November '72.

Kingly Street... the Bag O'Nails club at number 9 found favour with the Sixties rock elite. It was here that John McVie proposed to Christine Perfect, and that Paul McCartney first encountered Linda Eastman. Down the road at number 62 was La Valbonne, a fashionable niterie often used for record company press receptions. The Blues Bar at number 20 was a fashionable late Nineties haunt.

The Revolution Club at 14-16 Bruton Place and Annabel's at 44 Berkeley Square were also trendy late Sixties/early Seventies rock biz watering holes. On New Years Eve '66/'67 George Harrison and Patti, Brian Epstein, Eric Clapton and others were refused admittance to Annabel's because George was not wearing a tie. He refused the one offered to him by the doorman and they saw in the New Year at the Lyon's Corner House Restaurant on Coventry Street.

Louise's in Poland Street was the home of the early punk set and Rusty Egan's Bowie Nights (March '79) drew peacock punters to Billy's at 69 Dean Street. Later, both Le Beat Route (number 16) and Le Kilt (number 60) in Greek Street fostered the class of '81 new romantics. The Gargoyle Club in Meard Street was the first home of the ghoul'n'gothic Batcave in October '82. Spandau Ballet made their 'Chant No 1' video at Le Beat Route; Culture Club filmed 'Do You Really Want To Hurt Me' at the Gargoyle.

The Gargoyle Club   (Nikki Lloyd)

After operating from 95 Wigmore Street, The Beatles moved their Apple/business offices to 3 Savile Row, which they purchased in June '68. All five floors were carpeted in apple green and the street outside was a magnet for screamers known as Apple Scruffs. It was on the roof, at lunchtime on 30.1.69. that the Fab Four gave their last, brief public performance.

Paul McCartney's MPL empire is based at 1 Soho Square; Charisma Records was over the road at number 34. CBS was at 17/19 Soho Square but moved to more spacious accommodation at 10 Gt. Marlborough Street in the early Nineties.

Headquarters of Macca's empire, Soho Square

(Nikki Lloyd)

In July '74, Mama Cass died in flat 9, 12 Curzon Place – of a heart attack induced by excessive drug use. In September '78, Keith Moon died in the very same room having overdosed on the prescription drug Heminevrin. The flat was Harry Nilsson's London base.

Ringo Starr took a lease on the ground floor flat at 34 Montagu Square in early '65. When he moved to stockbroker country, he sublet it to Jimi Hendrix and his manager Chas Chandler (from December '66 to March '67). In July 68, John and Yoko became the latest tenants – and it was here that the brain-police and their sniffer dogs busted them for pot possession in October '68. This gave the landlords ample excuse to terminate Ringo's lease.

Hendrix and Chandler lived at 43 Upper Berkeley Street from March '67 to June '68 – after which Jimi moved in with girlfriend Kathy Etchingham at 23 Brook Street. Although this residence bears a blue plaque, he lived here only until March 69, when to all intents and purposes he relocated to the States.

It was in Pye's studio at 40 Bryanston Street that The Who recorded 'I Can't Explain' and that Graham Nash met David Crosby for the first time, in March '67.

In June '67, David Bowie moved into the home of his manager, Ken Pitt, at 39 Manchester Street. During this period, Bowie would often visit his mentor, the mime artist Lindsay Kemp, at his flat above a strip club in Bateman Buildings.

Charles Dickens was a cub reporter at Gt. Marlborough Street Magistrates Court (opposite the end of Carnaby Street), which later saw many rock stars pass through its portal – including Brian Jones, Mick Jagger, Marianne Faithfull, Keith Richards and Johnny Rotten. One of Britain's most historic courtrooms, it was closed in April '98 – deemed too old fashioned to serve justice any longer.

It was from a stall on the corner of Dean Street, in the early Seventies, that Bob Geldof embarked on an abortive career as a hot dog salesman. Further down Dean Street, within the Nellie Dean pub, ex-pop stars with beer guts would lie about their lives. The Good Earth Studio at number 59 was designed by Tony Visconti. Off Dean Street, at 17 St. Anne's Court was

Headquarters of Stevo's old empire, St. Anne's Court

(Nikki Lloyd)

Trident Studio (closed for redevelopment in '90), where everyone from Bowie to Queen recorded, and house producers John Anthony, Roy Thomas Baker and Ken Scott learned their craft. In a rare excursion away from Abbey Road, The Beatles recorded 'Hey Jude' and some songs for the *White Album* there in autumn '68.

Gerrard Street once boasted Happening 44 (a psychedelic club at number 44 – now a Chinese super market) and the first location of Ronnie Scott's Jazz Club (number 39). The latter building subsequently housed the offices of Anim Management, who looked after The Animals and Hendrix – while down the street at number 47 was the Rik Gunnell Agency – England's biggest R&B booker with the likes of Mayall, Price, Fame, Farlowe, Geno, Zoot on his list. Warren Zevon sang about the Lee Ho Fook restaurant on 'Werewolves Of London'.

Ronnie outside his club

(Ronnie Scott's)

Ronnie Scott moved his jazz club to 47 Frith Street, where it has since remained. The Who gave their first performance of *Tommy* there in May '69 and Jimi Hendrix gave his last public performance (16.9.70), getting up to jam with Eric Burdon and War. Just across the street at number 23b is Angelucci's wonderful coffee shop – which Mark Knopfler visited in the first line of 'Walking In The Wild West End'.

The Moka at 29 Frith Street was (in '53) the first coffee bar in London with an Espresso machine.

At 70 Old Compton Street were the offices of Track Records, and at number 63 was Dougie Millings & Son, 'Tailors to the Stars'. When you could afford to get togged out there, you were considered to have made it.

Madness dancer/singer Carl Smyth was born on 14.1.58 at the Middlesex Hospital in Mortimer Street – where Keith Moon was pronounced dead on arrival in September '78. Not far away, at 97 Charlotte Street, are the offices of Fiction Records (made wealthy by The Cure). Joe Boyd's Witchseason Productions used to be along here too.

Before he bought his St. John's Wood gaff, Paul McCartney lived with Jane Asher's parents and brother Peter at 57 Wimpole Street.

The offices of the Music of Life label were originally at 22 Hanway Street. In '89, four of its five stars had been imprisoned within the past twelve months, mostly for herbal irregularites!

Bananarama's Siobhan and Sarah studied at the London College of Fashion, 20 John Princes Street. Another student was Jane Eugene of Loose Ends.

Radio One is transmitted from Egton House in Langham Street, just around the corner from the BBC's Broadcasting House in Portland Place. Tony Blackburn opened the station in September '67, playing 'Flowers In The Rain' by The Move. Former studio managers include Alexis Korner (Blues Inc) and Bill Sharpe (Shakatak).

Up the road at 35 Portland Place was IBC recording studio, where Joe Meek worked as an engineer when he first came to London in '56. He was responsible for the great sound on 'Bad Penny Blues' by Humphrey Lyttelton and 'Last Train To San Fernando' by Johnny Duncan. The Rolling Stones made their first tentative recordings here in March '63 (a couple of Bo Diddleys, a couple of Jimmy Reeds and a Muddy Waters). The Who recorded *Tommy* there. Over the years, it has housed Chas Chandler's Barn Records and George Peckham's (Porky's Prime Cuts) Master Room – which later removed to 55-59 Shaftesbury Avenue.

The Langham Hilton Hotel in Portland Place was previously a BBC building. The Chukka Bar was formerly Langham 1, where Joan Armatrading (October '72), Queen (February '73), Bob Marley & The Wailers (May '73) and The Chameleons (June '81) recorded their first sessions for Radio One shows.

Fee paying guest wonders how his loons will fit through the doors of the old Wardour Street Marquee Club, 1973   (Barry Plummer)

Another BBC Radio studio was at 201 Piccadilly, where The Beatles, Tim Hardin, Joe Cocker and many others recorded memorable sessions.

The CBS Studio at 31-37 Whitfield Street was taken over by Stock Aitken & Waterman, who produced billions of hits here.

The Borderline in Orange Yard, off Manette Street, has been a cool venue since the early Eighties. Legendary gigs include Lenny Kravitz's UK début in December '89, R.E.M.'s appearances with Billy Bragg and Robyn Hitchcock (May '89 and March '91), and the Oasis 'Cigarettes And Alcohol' video shoot and gig (September '94).

In June '84, The Jesus And Mary Chain made their London début at the Living Room (operated by Alan McGee) above the Roebuck pub in Tottenham Court Road (now called something improbable).

The Fool: painters and decorators to Apple Boutiques,1967

(Rex Features Ltd)

W2 Bayswater, Paddington

Birthplace of Jerry Lordan, 1933 (he wrote The Shadows hit 'Apache'); Mike Sarne, 6.8.39 (he and Wendy Richard had a '62 number one hit with 'Come Outside'); drummer Ian Mosley, 16.6.53 (Marillion); Elvis Costello, 25.8.54; Pepsi, 10.12.58 (Shirlie And...); Seal, 19.2.63; John McKay (Banshees).

In May '65, Bob Dylan spent a few days in St. Mary's Hospital, recuperating from a stomach bug he'd picked up in Portugal.

Rolling Stone Brian Jones was briefly employed as a salesman at Whiteley's department store in Queensway; Sex Pistol Glen Matlock was a sometime salesman; and Madness drummer Dan Woodgate worked in their design department for a spell.

Hyde Park free concerts drew fans from all over Britain. The first show, in June '68, featured Pink Floyd and Jethro Tull; Blind Faith made their début there in June '69; The Rolling Stones bade adieu to Brian Jones and welcomed Mick Taylor in July '69, drawing Britain's biggest audience. In June '96 The Who, Bob Dylan and Eric Clapton played a Prince's Trust gig.

The Cue Club in Praed Street was a great Sixties reggae/black music venue.

Also in Praed Street (number 113, opposite the hospital) was the Paddington Kitchen, where Mick Jones and Tony James planned their prototype punk group London SS, auditioning such future punk stars as Rat Scabies, Paul

Simonon and Bryan James. They used to rehearse in the basement of the pub on the corner, the Fountains Abbey. Mick Jones worked for the DHSS at 5 Praed Street and lived at 111 Wilmcote House, on the Warwick Estate.

32 Alexander Street was the home of both Blackhill Enterprises (managers of Floyd, T Rex, Dury, etc) and Stiff Records. It was here that the likes of Wreckless Eric and Elvis Costello brought their demo tapes and daydreams, and here that Marc Bolan charmed his future wife June, who worked as a secretary for Blackhill.

Fairport Convention recorded their haunting 'The Lord Is In This Place' at St. Peter's Church in Westbourne Grove.

During the late Sixties, Richard Branson lived at 44 Albion Street, from which address he also published his magazine *Student*. Premises in South Wharf Road became the first HQ/warehouse for his Virgin Records mail-order business.

In November '68, at a flat in Moscow Road, where they were living together, Crosby Stills & Nash planned the trio they would form as soon as Nash quit The Hollies.

During the first half of '76, Joe Strummer and Palmolive shared a squat at 42 Orsett Terrace. The former would leave The 101ers for The Clash; the latter would form Flowers Of Romance, who rehearsed in the basement during that hot summer.

In late '80, a confused Marvin Gaye was resident in London – at a flat in Hyde Park West, off Kendal Street.

In June '89, the marriage of Bill Wyman and Mandy Smith was blessed at St. John the Evangelist Church in Hyde Park Crescent. Spike Milligan gave the bridegroom a walking frame.

In September '66, Jimi Hendrix spent his first nights in England at the Hyde Park Towers Hotel at 41 Inverness Terrace; The Manic Street Preachers' freshly shaven-headed frontman Richey Edwards was last seen alive when he checked out of the Embassy Hotel on 1.2.95.

A favourite haven for such visiting bands as The Teardrop Explodes and The Mission, the Columbia at 95-99 Lancaster Gate acquired a reputation as the primo rock'n'roll hotel.

The Columbia Hotel, Bayswater   *(The Columbia Hotel)*

W3 Acton

Birthplace of Adam Faith, 23.6.40, at 4 Churchfield Road East. He went to Derwent Water School, John Perring Junior in Long Drive, and Acton Wells Secondary.

Former pupils of Acton County Grammar include Pete Townshend, Roger Daltrey and John Entwistle (all of The Who), Ian Gillan (Deep Purple).

In '68, the newly formed Deep Purple shared a house at 13 Second Avenue, Acton Vale.

While formulating plans, future punk stars Mick Jones, Paul Simonon, Viv Albertine and Sid Vicious all shared a first floor squat at 22 Davis Road.

The White Hart at 264 High Street was a popular Sixties/Seventies venue. It was here, in February '63, that John McVie played his first gig with John Mayall's Bluesbreakers. The Nice came together here – during auditions for PP Arnold's backing group.

Clear Blue Sky were early Seventies hopefuls with a non-selling Vertigo album; Whirlwind were late Seventies rockabilly revivalists.

The splendid Rykodisc group of labels operate from 78 Stanley Gardens.

Operational base of Nineties indie band Big Boy Tomato.

W4 Chiswick

Birthplace of John Entwistle, 9.10.44; Pete Townshend, 19.5.45; Davy O'List, 13.12.48 (Nice); Phil Collins, 30.1.51; Kim Wilde, 18.11.60; Ian Spice, 18.9.66 (Breathe).

Residents have included Midge Ure, Bruce and Pete Thomas (Elvis' Attractions), Rat Scabies, Nick Lowe, Jack Good, John Spencer (Home Service), Robyn Hitchcock and Peter Blake – noted painter, but also *Sgt Pepper* and Band Aid sleeve designer.

In December '57, Lonnie Donegan played Wishee Washee in the panto *Alladin* at the Chiswick Empire.

Steve Marriott wrote 'Lazy Sunday' after protracted disagreements with his middle class neighbours in Chiswick Walk.

When he tired of touring, Mott The Hoople's bass player, Overend Watts, opened an antique shop (the Duke of Bedford Park) on the corner of Southfield Road.

The most memorable gig in the area seems to have been at the Town Hall (on the Green) in '66, when sundry mod/skinhead thugs from Devonshire Road (now trendy middle class) invaded the stage and attacked The Graham Bond Organisation. Observers recall Ginger Baker and Jack Bruce defending themselves with their instruments while the yobbo horde took the place apart.

Elvis Costello's biggest hit, 'Oliver's Army', was recorded at Eden Studios, 20-24 Beaumont Road. So were Shakin Stevens' chart toppers 'This Ole House' and 'Green Door'. Studio engineer Roger Bechirian recorded under the alias Blanket of Secrecy.

The Chiswick label was based in Camden Town.

Metropolis Studios in Chiswick

W 5, 7, 13 Ealing

Birthplace of pianist Nicky Hopkins, 24.2.44; singer/writer Speedy Keen, 29.3.45 (Thunderclap Newman); guitarist Ian Gomm, 17.3.47 (Brinsley Schwarz); drummer Mitch Mitchell, 9.7.47 (Jimi Hendrix Experience); bass player Tony Butler, 13.2.57 (Big Country).

London's first rhythm & blues club was in a cellar below the ABC teashop in Helena Chambers, Ealing Broadway. Started by Alexis Korner and Cyril Davies in March '62, it was a source of inspiration to a generation of R&B groups. It was here that Mick Jagger and Keith Richards first met Brian Jones and Paul Jones. The Stones played here 22 times between July '62 and February '63.

Star pupils from the Ealing Art School in St. Marys Road include Ron Wood, Roger Ruskin Spear, Thunderclap Newman, Freddie Mercury, and Pete Townshend, who met his wife Karen Astley there.

Rick Wakeman attended Drayton Manor Grammar School in Hanwell; Bluetones guitarist Adam Devlin went to Gunnersbury Catholic School.

Operational base of Sixties bands Second Thoughts and July, some of whom found cult acclaim in their next enterprise, Jade Warrior. Local singer-songwriter Tom Newman found fame as Mike Oldfield's producer.

Local funk/rap outfit The Brand New Heavies scored a run of hits, starting with 'Never Stop' in October '91; Jamiroquai topped the '93 album chart with 'Emergency On Planet Earth'.

Bonzo Dog's Roger Ruskin Spear

W6 Hammersmith

Birthplace of Cat Stevens, 21.7.47; Paul Cook, 20.7.57 (Sex Pistols); Gary Numan, 8.3.58; Mikey Craig, 15.2.60 (Culture Club).

Disc jockey Pete Murray was a pupil at St. Pauls School for Boys. As a boxing contender, he was matched against future jazz band leader Mick Mulligan, who beat him on points.

Whilst looking to get Roxy Music off the ground, Bryan Ferry taught ceramics at a private school for girls in Hammersmith. Among the pupils at St. Pauls School for Girls was singer/songwriter Bridget St. John.

Even as 'Release Me' was zooming to number one in '67, Englebert Humperdinck was living in a flat above Times Furnishing in King Street.

After outgrowing its offices at Basing Street, Island Records moved their HQ to a stately town house at 22 St. Peters Square. Bob Marley's UK residence was tucked away behind it in British Grove.

The old Island Records' office (now moved to New Kings Road)

(Ken Hallett)

Hammersmith Odeon when it still had a "Mighty Compton Organ" as played on by Keith Emerson

The Hammersmith Odeon in Queen Caroline Street has always been a top rock showplace. The Rolling Stones and The Everly Brothers played here in November '63; Chuck Berry in May '64; The Beatles presented their Christmas Show here for 20 nights in December '64; Bruce Springsteen made his UK début here in November '75. Currently has the unfortunate name of Labatt's Apollo.

The Hammersmith Palais at 242 Shepherds Bush Road was a premier dancehall (supposedly the largest in Britain) and later a fashionable rock'n'roll haunt — celebrated on the '79 Clash single 'White Man In Hammersmith Palais'. Mick Hucknall's first London appearance was here — in The Frantic Elevators, supporting The Skids in August '79. R.E.M. played two nights in October '85.

The first offices of Charley Records were at 9 Beadon Road.

The Greyhound at 175 Fulham Palace Road has always presented rock groups. On their London début in November '74, The Jam supported Thin Lizzy — and later supported Stackridge, whose idiosyncratic yokel fans threw turnips at them. The Only Ones made their début here in January '77.

The Red Cow at 157 Hammersmith Road is a similar establishment. Appropriately enough, The Hammersmith Gorillas often played here.

Sex Pistols guitarist Steve Jones grew up in Benbow Road. Drummer Paul Cook lives nearby in Carthew Road.

The Clarendon Hotel in Hammersmith Broadway was a popular Eighties venue for up and coming bands. Stiff boss Dave Robinson had his wedding reception here in August '79... Madness provided the music.

The Riverside Studios is a huge TV studio/rehearsal room/theatre complex/cinema in Crisp Road. The Beatles taped videos for *Top Of The Pops*; The Sex Pistols rehearsed here; Chris Evans' *TFI Friday* beamed out from here.

43 Brook Green is the current home of the EMI Records Group; 1 Sussex Place house Polygram; 72 Black Lion Lane is home to Go! Discs.

W8 Kensington

Birthplace of Paul Hardcastle, 10.12.57 (Number One with '19' in '85); Betty Boo, 6.3.70.

Jimi Hendrix was pronounced dead on arrival at St. Mary Abbots Hospital in September '70.

Pink Floyd's début was in late '65, at the Countdown Club in Palace Gate. They got 15 quid.

It was in October '70, at a gig at the College of Estate Management in St. Albans Grove (where the author of this book once vainly toiled), that John Deacon saw the embryonic Queen – which he would join within four months.

The New York Dolls made their UK début at Bibas in Kensington High Street in November '73.

Jimmy Page's bookshop of the black arts cunningly disguised as a gift shop to lure in old lady

Jimmy Page was owner of the Equinox, an occult bookshop at 4 Holland Street. It closed in '79.

Cat Stevens, now Yusuf Islam, married Fouzia Ali at Kensington Mosque in September '79.

In Kensington High Street, Kensington Market was where Sigue Sigue Sputnik first got together, where The Cult's Billy Duffy worked between gigs, and where promoter Harvey Goldsmith used to flog posters in the Sixties. Other famous stall holders have included Freddie Mercury and Roger Taylor, who had a clothing emporium there during the early non-remunerative days of Queen. When Taylor returned to college, Mercury took on new partner Alan Mair – later of The Only Ones.

Kensington High Street was immortalised by Sixties band Dead Sea Fruit, and a late Sixties American group had the temerity to call themselves Kensington Market.

46 Kensington Court is the home of East West Records; 28a Kensington High Street houses WEA.

In '80, Freddie Mercury paid over £500,000 for 1 Logan Place, whose high walls have been covered in graffiti since his death there in November '91.

Byam Shaw School under repair after Paul Simonon

Clash bassplayer Paul Simonon attended the Byam Shaw School Of Art at 70 Campden Street. So did Dave Ambrose, who played bass in Brian Auger's Trinity and, as an A&R man, signed The Sex Pistols to EMI and Transvision Vamp to MCA.

Bill Wyman's Sticky Fingers restaurant is at 1a Phillimore Gardens.

Following his bum-waggling protest (see SW5) against Michael Jackson's Christ-like performance at the '96 Brit Awards, Jarvis Cocker was arrested and taken to Kensington Police Station to be interrogated until the early hours. No charges were brought.

W9 Maida Vale, Westbourne Grove

Birthplace of drummer Dan Woodgate, 19.10.60 (Madness).

The Zigzag Club flourished very briefly at 22 Great Western Road. It opened in November '81 with Bow Wow Wow – who also flourished very briefly. Regulars reckon the best gig was in July '82, when The Birthday Party and Sisters of Mercy played.

The Windsor Castle at 309 Harrow Road was a highly popular pub-rock gig. The Bodysnatchers made their début there in November '79.

Equally popular was the Chippenham in Chippenham Road. The 101ers had a residency from December '74 to April '75; it was later a staple gig for The Derelicts, and The Modettes made their début here.

The Foundations got together and rehearsed at the Butterfly Café in early '67.

In the early days of Pink Floyd, their truck driver June Child (later Bolan), their light-show guy John Marsh, and their managers Peter Jenner and Andrew King all shared a house at 41 Edbrooke Road – the first office of Blackhill Enterprises.

In summer '74, various squatters at 101 Walterton Road formed The 101ers; in the early Eighties, Nick Cave and Tracy Pew (Birthday Party) lived in a squat in the same road.

More commodious accommodation in the area has housed John Otway, Dave Edmunds, Tommy Vance, Gary Shearston, Marc Bolan, Jimmy McCulloch and others too numerous to mention. Richard Branson lived on two houseboats on the Regents Park Canal: the *Alberta* (early Seventies) and the *Duende* (late Seventies). The Floyd's Dave Gilmour owns what estate agents might call a 'desirable residence' in Little Venice.

Every rock act in the universe has recorded at the BBC Studios in Delaware Road, as an examination of Ken Garner's brilliant book *In Session Tonight* will reveal. It had been the Maida Vale Roller Skating Palace before the BBC bought it in 1934 and turned it into the largest studio in the country. Since Radio One started in September '67, it has been the principal studio for John Peel, Andy Kershaw, Tommy Vance, etc sessions... by everyone from BB King to The Orb to The Fall to Nirvana.

Maida Vale Studios

(Barry Plummer)

W10 Kensal Rise

The Acklam Hall in Westbourne Park became a popular post punk venue favoured by the likes of The Vincent Units, The Derelicts, Prag Vec and The Raincoats. It was here in November '78 that Madness, supporting The Tribesmen, were attacked by iron bar and razor wielding skinheads – as re-enacted in their film *Take It Or Leave It*.

Hit group The Passions lived in a squat in Latimer Road – as did activist group The Derelicts. Future Clash bass player Paul Simonon was a pupil at Isaac Newton School in Wornington Road.

Oxford Gardens has been home to Richard Branson, late Sixties group Quintessence and bassplayer Pete Farndon (Pretenders), who was found dead in his flat in April 83.

Dexy's Midnight Runners shot the video for 'Celtic Soul Brothers' around the Kensal Rise Canal.

Subterania at 12 Acklam Road is a popular venue for such happeners as Shakespears Sister, Beats International and Paul Weller. John Peel held his 50th birthday party there. Also happening is the Station Tavern.

The offices of Mute Records are at 429 Harrow Road; those of Virgin at 553-579. Chrysalis are in Bramley Road.

W11 Notting Hill

By the mid-Sixties, the population of 'the Gate' and 'the Grove' included a strong black and white intermingling of liberals, creatives, poets, beats, middle class graduates, new age traveller prototypes, graffiti philosophers, drug visionaries and longhairs. The Free School in Powis Terrace was an early hippie idea that didn't get off the ground, but All Saints Hall (off Westbourne Park Road) became a focus for community-welding activity. Here the nascent Pink Floyd were able to experiment to their heart's content (several gigs in November-December '66); Hawkwind also débuted here in July '69; as did Quintessence, who recorded 'Getting It Straight In Notting Hill Gate' on their first album.

In the late Fifties/early Sixties, the Rio on Westbourne Park Road (at Ledbury Road) was a black hang-out where incipient beats could score dope.

All Saints Road, Lancaster Road and St. Lukes Road were locations used for Ringo's solo explorations in *A Hard Day's Night*.

In late '67, the first office of Release (operated by Caroline Coon) was at 52 Princedale Road, which was also the mail order address of *Oz* magazine. Their main office/studio was up the road at number 70, which was also a subsequent Release office.

Portobello Road... Sixties flower power stars bought flamboyant clothes there – some bands still do; Cat Stevens sang about it on the B-side of his first single; Virgin Records had their offices in adjacent Vernon Yard during their Seventies/Eighties heyday; the Mountain Grill café was favoured by blacks, hippies, navvies, arty types and even Bolan and Bowie. Regular noshers Hawkwind named their fifth album after the place – *Hall Of The Mountain Grill*. Hippie music magazine *Friends* was published from number 305.

Basing Street was the title of a dramatic Nick Lowe song about the 1977 racial disturbances. Island Records had their HQ here (8-10) in the Seventies, when classic Traffic and Mott albums were recorded in their studios. When Island moved to Hammersmith, Trevor Horn took the place over for his ZTT/Sarm set up. Multi-million sellers by Frankie Goes To Hollywood and Band Aid were recorded here – not to mention the first Dire Straits album, which cost all of twelve grand.

Mick Farren's Social Deviants made their début at the Artesian Well public house; Joe Strummer's group The 101-ers had a residency at the Elgin from May to December '75.

Basing Street Studios, ex-Island Records HQ

Van Morrison lived in Ladbroke Grove during the heyday of Them (as recalled in 'Slim Slow Slider'). Other residents have included Hawkwind, Skin Alley, The Third Ear Band (though most of them lived the other side of the Westway in W10), Aswad and Marc Bolan, who lived at 57 Blenheim Crescent in his Tyrannosaurus Rex days.

41b Blemheim Crescent was the headquarters of Miles Copeland's group of labels: Deptford Fun City, Step Forward, Illegal.

In 1958/9, Joe Meek was studio manager/engineer at Dennis Preston's Lansdowne Studio at 2 Lansdowne House, Lansdowne Road. There he engineered 'Sea Of Love' by Marty Wilde and produced 'Mr Blue' by Mark Wynter.

Jimi Hendrix spent his last night on earth (17-18.9.70) in Monika Danneman's basement flat at 22 Lansdowne Crescent.

On 12.5.77, Malcolm McLaren visited Richard Branson's house in Denbigh Terrace to contract The Sex Pistols to Virgin.

The great Rough Trade record shop is now at 130 Talbot Road, having moved from 202 Kensington Park Road.

In the Nineties, All Saints Road became highly fashionable and famous as a result of the phenomenally successful All Saints, formed by Melanie Blatt and Shaznay Lewis who had both worked as backing singers at Metamorphosis Studio (once housed in All Saints Road, now defunct). At number 19 is Nation Records – home of The Asian Dub Foundation.

W12 Shepherds Bush

Birthplace of Roger Daltrey, 1.3.44; Chip Hawkes, 11.11.46 (Tremeloes); Yasmin Evans, 19.5.60 (better known as Yazz).

Cliff Richard was first seen by agent George Ganjou, playing a Saturday morning show at Shepherds Bush Gaumont on 14.6.58. For the first time, girls screamed at him – encouraging Ganjou to pay for the demo which won Cliff his EMI contract.

The Shepherds Bush Empire became the BBC Television Theatre between '56 and '91. Home of *Juke Box Jury*, *Wogan*, *Cilla*, and billions of other shows. In the Nineties, it reverted to a theatre/music venue, perfectly sized for presenting the likes of The Mavericks and Eddi Reader.

The Townhouse at 150 Goldhawk Road was Virgin's studio. It was here that Phil Collins recorded *Face Value*, Sting recorded *Ten Summoner's Tales* and Pulp recorded *Different Class*.

The Social Club at 205 Goldhawk Road, now the Goldhawk Club, was an early Who stronghold. Roger Daltrey's childhood home was around the corner at 15 Percy Road, and Roger's first ever gig with a band was at the Sulgrave Road Boys Club on Goldhawk Road, just past the Seven Stars roundabout, in '62. He called his group The Detours and after a few personnel changes it mutated into The Who.

Wormwood Scrubs prison was the temporary residence of two Rolling Stones, Keith Richards (June '67) and Brian Jones (October '67) – both found guilty of dope possession. "We've got to make an example of those long-haired drug fiends." While serving nine months there for drug possession in '68, producer Guy Stevens read *Mott The Hoople* – an American novel by Willard Manus. On release, he returned to Island Records and bestowed the name on his first signing.

In May '74, David Cassidy was popular enough to fill White City Stadium. Many over-excited fans required first aid treatment and six were hospitalised. One subsequently died.

It was at Warwick Nightingale's house in Hemlock Road that future Sex Pistols Steve Jones, Paul Cook and Glen Matlock first rehearsed together. They had been at local schools (St Clement Dane's and Christopher Wren) with elements of the earlier prog-rock group Stray. Andy Fraser (Free, Sparks) was also a former St. Clement Dane pupil.

Late Seventies indie label Butt Records (Kevin Coyne, Bill Nelson) operated from 27 Aylmer Road.

The BBC studios in Lime Grove (now redeveloped) and the BBC Television Centre in Wood Lane have been home to *Top Of The Pops, The Old Grey Whistle Test, Rock Family Trees* and other rock programmes too numerous to mention.

Pupils at Hammersmith Art School at 40 Lime Grove included Cat Stevens, Mick Jones (Clash) and Viv Albertine (Slits).

Television Centre, BBC Studios

The BBC Transcription Service at Kensington House in Richmond Way was used to record sessions for radio shows until the late Seventies. Memorable visitors at the legendary Studio T1 included Genesis (May '71), David Bowie (September '71) and Roxy Music (January '72).

Local rapper Darkman reached the '94 charts with 'Yabba Dabba Doo'; grunge rockers Bush found an audience in the States; hot indie band Symposium (formerly pupils at Cardinal Vaughan Roman Catholic Comprehensive) emerged in '97.

W14 West Kensington
A prime venue on the Seventies pub rock circuit was the Kensington in Russell Gardens.

More prestigious was the Nashville Rooms at 171 North End Road. Every pub rock group played here, every punk group worth its salt. Rockpile made their début here in February '77.

When they first moved to London, The Animals lived in Fitz James Avenue – in a mansion block flat owned by one of the partners in the Scene Club. Heavyweight Led Zeppelin manager Peter Grant was their roadie!

During their Kensington Market days, Roger Taylor and Freddie Mercury shared a flat in Sinclair Road.

The Central School of Art   (The London Institute)

WC1 Bloomsbury
The Central School of Art in Southampton Row has fostered many a musician – including Legs Larry Smith and Vivian Stanshall (Bonzo Dog Band), Dick Taylor (Pretty Things), Joe Strummer (Clash), and Lene Lovich. Not to mention Caroline Coon, the *Melody Maker*'s punk specialist. The Pistols played their second ever gig here in November '75, and Generation X débuted here in December '76.

On their first London trip, to audition for Decca on New Year's Day '62, The Beatles stayed at the Royal Hotel, 38-52 Woburn Place.

In December '62, Bob Dylan made a pre-fame appearance at Ewan MacColl's folk club, held at the Pindar Of Wakefield pub at 328 Grays Inn Road – the same venue The Pogues made their début in October '82. Now rather grandiosely named the Water Rats Theatre, it continues to present interesting music.

Around the corner in Sidmouth Street, Johnny Rotten met Jah Wobble when both were students at Kingsway College. A few years earlier, broadcaster Charlie Gillett had been a lecturer there (his only proper day job!)

Both Ringo Starr (November '64) and George Harrison (February '69) had tonsillectomies at University College Hospital in Gower Street – the birthplace of guitarist Chris Foreman, 8.8.55 (Madness); frontman Mark Moore, 12.1.65 (S'Express); and singer Melanie Blatt, 25.3.75 (All Saints).

Along the road at the Royal Academy of Dramatic Art (number 62), Brian Epstein was quickly disillusioned about any future on the stage. Another student was future disc jockey Brian Matthew.

At Dick James Music, 71-75 New Oxford Street, as the founder luxuriated in the mountain of money he had made from publishing the music of The Beatles and other beat groups, Elton John and Bernie Taupin (hired as staff writers in January '68) were in the demo studio working on the first songs of a catalogue which would make him another fortune. James' label, DJM Records, initially operated from this address.

Collett's old record shop

Over the road, at 70 New Oxford Street, was Collett's wonderful record shop – the only place in England which stocked all the classic Elektra and Vanguard imports.

Euston Tower, on the corner of Hampstead and Euston Roads, housed Capital Radio. "They say they're in tune with London," said Clash leader Joe Strummer in May 77, "but they're in tune with Hampstead. They've turned their back on the whole youth of the city." He underlined this view by spraying White Riot on the station's ground floor windows and writing the withering 'Capital Radio'.

A short-lived Seventies venue was Kings Cross Cinema, where Mott The Hoople and Iggy & The Stooges (their only UK gig) played in July '72. 'Kings Cross' was a track on The Pet Shop Boys album *Actually*. Test Department and The Mutoid Waste were among a buch of groups that did word-of-mouth gigs in the disused Kings Cross Bus Station. Eighties indie band Eat lived in a Kings Cross squat, and the Bloomsbury Set (the band, not the literary crowd) were also local residents.

It was at the Scala Cinema in Pentonville Road that Janet Street Porter and London Weekend made the documentary which rocketed Spandau Ballet into public consciousness in April '80.

When they first stayed overnight in London, The Stone Roses used to book into the YMCA in Great Russell Street – until they were banned.

Opened in November '95, the End at 18 West Central Street was a groovers' paradise operated by Mr C (ex The Shamen).

WC2 Covent Garden

It was at The Gyre And Gimbal, a basement coffee bar in John Adam Street, that Larry Parnes laid eyes on Tommy Steele – his first protégé and the cornerstone of British rock'n'roll.

Many musicians have dragged their sack of woe to the High Court in the Strand... among them The Kinks, The Troggs ('67), The Beatles ('71), Fleetwood Mac ('74), Gilbert O'Sullivan, Sting, Hazel O'Connor ('82), Ray Jackson, Elton John ('85), The Sex Pistols ('86), Holly Johnson ('88), Kirk Brandon ('94) and The Stone Roses ('95). In December '97, Morrissey was famously described by the trial judge as being "devious, truculent and unreliable" when he was ordered to pay about £1 million to former Smiths drummer Mike Joyce. Bruce Springsteen, suited and tied, won back the rights to some early recordings in '98.

At Bow Street Magistrates Court, in July '62, Ricky Valance was fined £15 for disturbing the peace in a coffee bar fracas. The Bo Street Runners (the "w" was dropped in deference to their hero, Mr. Diddley) won a *Ready Steady Go!* talent contest – and promptly disappeared.

Dylan behind the Savoy, WC2

(Nikki Lloyd)

Originally an upper crust stronghold, the Savoy Hotel in the Strand learned to accept nouveau riche rock stars as soon as Bill Haley set foot in the country in February '57. Bob Dylan's ructions with the management were captured in *Don't Look Back* and his video for 'Subterranean Homesick Blues' was shot in the street behind the hotel... he and Donovan had sat up all night writing out the caption boards. Elton John also had trouble with the management; he left a bath tap running when he phoned his wife and caused £5,000 worth of damage! In his speech at an awards ceremony, Albert Lee said his presence was proof that gypsies were now allowed into the Savoy.

Lennon in the Lyceum. Backstage at the Peace Concert, 15th December 1969. Back row: Jim Price, Bobby Keys, Jim Gordon, Klaus Voorman, Bonnie, Delaney. Centre row: George, Alan White, Keith Moon, Neil Boland, Eric Barrat, Billy Preston, Eric Clapton. Front row: Tony Ashton, John, Yoko

(Barry Plummer)

Around the corner at 9 Villiers Street is the Griffin, where Pogues singer Shane MacGowan was a barman during the mid-Seventies. Just down the street, within the arches, was gay disco Heaven, where Spandau Ballet and Eurythmics played seminal gigs, and numerous provincial bands made their London début... like Southern Death Cult in '81 and Erasure in December '85. In early '83, loaded on "various substances", regular visitor Bernard Sumner was inspired to write New Order's seminal 'Blue Monday'. Heaven was previously known as the Global Village, an early Seventies progressive club.

Around another corner is the Lyceum ballroom, where every band worth its salt played during the Sixties and Seventies. Derek & The Dominoes made their world début there in June '70. It was here in spring '84, at the *Daily Mirror* Rock and Pop Awards, that Bill Wyman first met future wife Mandy Smith. He was there to present a special award to Alexis Korner's widow.

Both Mick Jagger and Robert Elms completed their formal education at the London School of Economics in Houghton Street. In the mid-Sixties, Peter Jenner was an LSE lecturer – until he discovered Pink Floyd and dropped out to become their manager.

A popular Fifties rock'n'roll/beatnik haunt was the Nucleus in the basement of 9 Monmouth Street. Around the corner in Endell Street was the notorious VD clinic. To be "on the slab at Endell Street" was a fear expressed by many a musician.

Studio 51, a cellar club at 10/11 Great Newport Street, was a prime trad jazz/R&B hangout during the early Sixties. The first rock group to play there was The Rockets (led by jazz drummer Tony Crombie) in September '56. Until they got too popular, The Rolling Stones had a Sunday residency (March '63 to September '63) and The Downliners Sect made their first recordings there.

While putting The Rolling Stones together, Brian Jones worked fleetingly at the Civil Service store in the Strand. It was at Regent Sound Studios, 4 Denmark Street, that the Stones recorded 'Not Fade Away' in January '64 (Phil Spector and Gene Pitney were also in the studio) and that Elton John recorded any number of cover versions (mainly during '69-70) for budget labels like Hallmark and MFP. The ground floor currently houses the utterly fabulous Helter Skelter bookshop.

Opposite, along a passage at 22 Denmark Street (next to Andy's Guitar Centre), is the 12 Bar Club (opened in '94), where Bert Jansch had his first London residency since the Sixties and up and comers (like Arnold, February '98) are given a showcase.

The Rolling Stones recorded 'I Wanna Be Your Man' at De Lane Lea Studios, in the basement of 129 Kingsway, opposite Holborn tube station. It was there also that The Animals cut 'House Of The Rising Sun', Hendrix cut 'Hey Joe' and 'Purple Haze', and The Beatles cut 'It's All Too Much'. Ian Gillan was a subsequent co-owner of the place.

Bunjies, 27 Lichfield Street, WC2

Bunjies, a coffee house in the basement of 27 Litchfield Street, was opened in '54 by Peter Reynolds, who named it after his cousin's hamster. (Where else can you find stuff like this?) Though fairly miniscule, it has presented a most extraordinary roster of talent, from Adam Faith and Davy Graham, to Bob Dylan and Paul Simon, Al Stewart and Elvis Costello, Louise Goffin and Jeff Buckley. And it's still going strong!

In January '63, Bob Dylan assisted on a Richard Farina/Eric Von Schmidt album recorded in the basement of Dobell's Record Shop at 77 Charing Cross Road. He used his alias Blind Boy Grunt for the first time.

In May '65, Joan Baez, Donovan, Tom Paxton and the unknown Marc Bolan led an anti-Vietnam War march which ended in Trafalgar Square — as had so many CND marches in the previous few years. In April '68, rock'n'roll revivalist Freddie Fingers Lee, a former steeplejack, climbed to the top of Nelson's Column to promote his latest single.

Studio 9 of Television House, 4-12 Kingsway, was the home of *Ready Steady Go!,* which was broadcast from here between October '63 and spring '65.

The Playhouse Theatre in Northumberland Avenue was a BBC radio studio until the Seventies. The Beatles recorded 13 sessions there during their first year of fame; Hendrix recorded several sessions there in '67; Led Zeppelin in '69.

At 135 Shaftesbury Avenue was the Saville Theatre, which Epstein took over to promote a series of seminal concerts. The Who, Cream, Jimi Hendrix, The Bee Gees (their London début) all played there — as did Fats Domino, on his belated UK début in March' 67. It was converted into a cinema complex in '70.

Denmark Street is London's traditional Tin Pan Alley, thronging with publishers, managers, agents and peripheral hustlers. The first publisher to move here was Lawrence Wright in 1911. Among other things, Wright founded the *Melody Maker* in 1926. The Giaconda snack bar invariably contained daydreaming musicians, waiting for their big break. Any number of people claim to have loaned Tom Jones half a crown so he could buy egg and chips.

Elton John worked as a tea boy at Mills Music, 20 Denmark Street.

The first office of Dick James Music was at 132 Charing Cross Road, where Brian Epstein inked The Beatles to their Northern Songs publishing contract.

Down the road at number 96 was Anello & Davide, which became world famous as a result of supplying The Beatles with their Cuban-heeled Ba-ba boots.

The ageless Astoria at 165 Charing Cross Road continues to present across the spectrum stars from Debbie Gibson to del amitri to Buffalo Tom. It was here in December '94, that Richey Edwards played his last gigs with The Manic Street Preachers.

The Astoria, W1

(Nikki Lloyd)

St. Martins Art School at 109 Charing Cross Road has nurtured many aspiring musicians... like Lionel Bart, Rodney Slater (Bonzo Dog Band), Mick Farren (Pink Fairies), Patrick Campbell Lyons and Alex Spyropoulos (Nirvana), Sade, Lora Logic (X-Ray Spex), Glen Matlock (Sex Pistols), Jarvis Cocker (Pulp), and Pennie Leyton (Belle Stars). Sarah Jane Owen (another Belle Star) was a lecturer there.

The Sex Pistols made their world début at St. Martins in November '75. A horrified social secretary cut the power after five numbers. The band rehearsed and crashed not a stone's throw away, in a seedy two-storey outbuilding tucked away behind 6 Denmark Street, and formerly used by Badfinger. It was subsequently a rehearsal room for Siouxsie & The Banshees and Bananarama.

Break For The Border is a music-orientated Tex-Mex bar and restaurant in Goslett Yard, at 127 Charing Cross Road.

Cat Stevens (who used to live in the flat above his dad's restaurant, the Moulin Rouge at 49 New Oxford Street, WC1), went to Drury Lane Roman Catholic School.

The Arts Lab at 182 Drury Lane (the first of several in Britain) was a late Sixties hippie hangout run by Jim Haynes. The Third Ear Band started there. Genesis played five nights at the Theatre Royal, Drury Lane in January '74. A Drury Lane squat, subjected to heavy police eviction, was commemorated on the '69 Fairport Convention track 'Genesis Hall'.

Middle Earth

The Roxy (Neal Street) compilation album

Middle Earth was a primo flower power club in the basement of 43 King Street, presenting such great bands as The Byrds (with Gram Parsons, May '68), Captain Beefheart & his Magic Band, etc. It transferred to the Roundhouse in Chalk Farm after continued police and media hassle. 150 cops swooped in for a drug raid in March '68.

At the Africa Centre (38 King Street), The The made their début in May '79. Waggish manager Stevo subsequently got CBS boss Maurice Oberstein to negotiate their contract while sitting on one of the lions in Trafalgar Square! The Africa Centre also saw the unveiling of Ian McCulloch's post Bunnymen venture McCulloch's Mysterio Show in January '92.

A hop, skip and a jump away from the Africa Centre is the Rock Garden at 6/7 The Piazza. A popular venue since the Seventies, it continues to present up and coming bands. The Birthday Party made their UK début here in June '80; The Smiths made their London début in March '83.

Keith Moon's last public appearance was in September '78 at the Peppermint Park, a trendy restaurant on Upper St. Martins Lane – at a party to celebrate the UK premier of *The Buddy Holly Story*.

Chaguerama's at 41-43 Neal Street was popular with the clothes-horse clique in '75 and became the best punk club in London when it re-opened as the Roxy in December '76... with Generation X headlining. Every significant group played there, even though it closed after four months.

The Blitz at 4 Great Queen Street was the favourite haunt of the new romantic poodle people. Both the club and the movement were launched by Steve Strange and Rusty Egan. It opened in June '79 and reached a peak of chic that September when Bowie swooped in with Bob Geldof.

The Sex Pistols celebrated Jubilee Day, June '77, by meeting numerous friends at Charing Cross Pier and taking a boat trip up the Thames. Police interrupted the cruise, arresting Malcolm McLaren and Vivienne Westwood among others.

In '88, the Marquee Club moved to its third location at 105 Charing Cross Road; Kiss played on opening night.

Gomez played their first London showcase at trendy club the Mars Bar, at 12 Sutton Row, on 19.3.98.

The 2I's coffee bar, Old Compton Street (W1)   (Rex Features Ltd)

MANCHESTER, GREATER

ALTRINCHAM

Birthplace of guitarist John Squire, 24.11.62 (Stone Roses) – at Broad Heath.

Kennedy House, 31 Stamford Street, is the current home of Manchester's most illustrious agency, Kennedy Street Management – who looked after Herman's Hermits, Wayne Fontana, Freddie & The Dreamers, The Big Three, 10cc, Sad Cafe, etc, as well as various professional snooker players.

Joy Division played early gigs (the first in March '79) at Bowden Vale Youth Club.

In reports of his High Court case, Morrissey's address was given as Bowden Road.

Stone Roses conspirators Ian Brown and John Squire went to Altrincham Grammar.

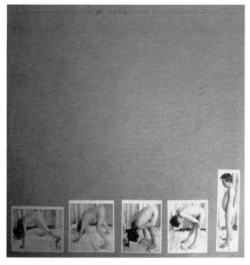

Early Joy Division bootleg album of an Altrincham gig

ANCOATS

Birthplace of Ian Brown, 20.2.63 (Stone Roses).

Sankey's Soap at Beehive Mill in Jersey Street was a hot Nineties venue.

ARDWICK

Birthplace of drummer Alan 'Reni' Wren, 10.4.64 (Stone Roses).

Johnny & The Moondogs played the Hippodrome in Hyde Road in November '59, in a fruitless bid to win recognition in the Carroll Levis *TV Star Search* contest. They returned to play the ABC cinema in Stockport Road three times in '63/'65.

The Apollo on the corner of Hyde Road and Stockport Road (suggesting it may be one of the above venues under a new name – but nobody seems to know!) presented The Rolling Stones in September '66 – and is still going strong, with concerts by Bjork and Squeeze in late '98.

ASHTON-UNDER-LYNE

At 16, Mick Hucknall enrolled as a student at Tameside College of Further Education. While there, he formed punk band The Frantic Elevators.

Clint Boon's 4-track studio/rehearsal space, the Mill, became a stomping ground for all local musicians.

Punk thrashers The Hoax made their début at the Spread Eagle – a Rock Against Racey (the RAK group) gig, which ended prematurely when a van load of mods arrived and proceeded to trash the place.

AUDENSHAW

Mick Hucknall attended the Grammar School – leaving in summer '76 with three O levels.

BOLTON

Birthplace of disc jockey Mark Radcliffe, 29.6.58 (Shire Horses); Mark 'Bez' Berry, 18.4.64 (Happy Mondays).

Local singer Michael Haslam never found a hit but he did support The Beatles on their Hammersmith Christmas season in '64.

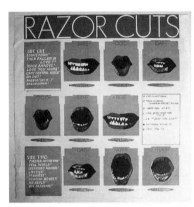

Early Buzzcocks bootleg album including live material from Bolton

The Nevada was such a hot venue in the Sixties/Seventies that Geno Washington & The Ram Jam Band recorded a live album there.

Howard Devoto and Pete Shelley became friends at the Institute of Technology, where they hatched plans for a rock group, the prototype Buzzcocks – who made their début at a college textile students social evening in April '76. Their disciples, Joy Division, played an early gig at the same venue in October '78.

In December '80, the thoroughly knackered and beleaguered Buzzcocks played at the town's Sports Centre – their last UK gig for nine years.

Sometime home of Sixties soul star Wynder K Frogg (Mick Weaver) and 808 State founder Martin Price.

BRAMHALL

ABC 's Martin Fry and his younger brother Jamie (currently in Earl Brutus) grew up in this leafy middle-class suburb.

BURNAGE

Former Durutti Column guitarist Dave Rowbotham was axed to death here in November '91. The Happy Mondays remembered him on Cowboy Dave.

Noel and Liam Gallagher attended St. Bernard's Catholic Primary in Burnage Lane. Pete Garner (Stone Roses) and Aziz Ibrahim (Simply Red) went to Burnage High.

Mr Sifter's local record shop is mentioned on the second Oasis hit, 'Shakermaker'.

BURY

Birthplace of Peter Skellern, 14.3.47.

Machine Gun Feedback were early Nineties indie.

CADISHEAD

Sometime home of genius rock'n'roll cartoonist Ray Lowry.

Operational base of The Lumpen Proles, Mummy's Boys and Ronnie Anonymous (who cut the indie classic 'Ten Pints, A Tennis Racquet And A Mirror'). All honed their craft at the Fingerprint & Firkin.

John Mayall up a tree

CHEADLE

In '63, John Mayall lived in a tree house, 30 feet above the ground, in Acre Lane. He had a record player up there... I'm not sure about a loo.

Birthplace of Jasper Stainthorpe, 7.12.61 (Then Jerico).

CHORLTON

The Oaks was a prime punk venue for a while, presenting such hot acts as Slaughter & The Dogs and The Heartbreakers.

The Stone Roses rehearsed at Spirit Studio, off Barlow Moor Road. While waiting for the band to take off, their guitarist John Squire worked at Cosgrove Hall, making models for television programmes.

Slaughter & The Dogs straight outta Chorlton

CHORLTON-CUM-HARDY
Birthplace of Andy Gibb, 5.3.58.

As children, The Bee Gees lived in Keppel Road and went to Oswald Road Primary School.

Twisted Wheel disc jockey Roger Eagle also ran the great specialist magazine *R&B Scene* from 540 Wilbraham Road.

CHORLTON-ON-MEDLOCK
Birthplace of Mike Joyce, 1.6.63 (Smiths); Johnny Marr, 31.10.63 – at 122 Everton Road (Smiths).

Barbara Mullaney in 1972 prog rock epic

CORONATION STREET
Pop stars with Corrie pedigrees include Peter Noone (Herman's Hermits), Chris Sandford (Top Twenty in '63), Davy Jones (Monkees), Tony Blackburn (can this be true?), Lyn Paul (New Seekers), Jilted John (Top Five in '78), Kevin Kennedy (Paris Valentinos with Johnny Marr) and Melanie Brown (Spice Girls).

CRUMPSALL
Birthplace of bassplayer Gary 'Mani' Mounfield, 16.11.62 (Stone Roses).

DAVYHULME
Birthplace of Peter Noone, 5.11.47 (Herman's Hermits); Steven Morrissey, 22.5.59 (Smiths) – at Park Hospital.

Herman's Hermits, then known as The Heartbeats, were discovered by future manager Harvey Lisberg at a church hall here.

DENTON
Childhood home of Mick Hucknall – first in the village of Bredbury, then at 30 West Park Avenue. He went to St. Lawrence's Junior School. At 16, he took an evening job at Broomstair Working Men's Club in Linden Road. His first band, The Frantic Elevators, would later rehearse there on Sunday afternoons.

Operational base of late Seventies punk band The Hoax – featuring the youthful Mike Joyce on drums.

DIGGLE
Barclay James Harvest got their act together in a remote farmhouse near Saddleworth Moor.

HULME
Tony Wilson's Factory club opened in the premises of the Russell Club in Royce Lane in May '78, with Joy Division, Big In Japan, Durutti Column and others. The Factory label's numerical prefix FAC was used not only on records, but badges and posters too. FAC1 was the poster advertising the first club gig.

Steven Morrissey attended St. Wilfred's Primary and Junior Schools, then St. Mary's Secondary School in Renton Road.

The mighty (and forgotten) King of the Slums

Local Eighties bands included King Of The Slums, The Ruthless Rap Assassins, Tools You Can Trust, Big Flame and The Inca Babies. In the Nineties came Sexus.

During the early Eighties, Ian Brown lived in Charles Barry Crescent and Mick Hucknall lived in Otterburn Close.

Home of maverick Edward Barton – perpetrator of The Jane indie singles.

HYDE
Late Eighties indie band the Paris Angels rehearsed at the old Police Station before signing with Virgin.

LEIGH
Birthplace of Georgie Fame, 24.6.43. He went to Windermere Road Secondary Modern until he left at 16 to work in a local cotton factory. Also of keyboard player Mike O'Neal, who started playing at the Globe public house in The Wabash Skiffle Group before moving to London to form Nero & The Gladiators in the early Sixties. He played alongside Albert Lee in Heads Hands & Feet a decade later. Also of guitarist and singer Pete Shelley, 17.4.55 (Buzzcocks). He went to the Boys Grammar.

LEVENSHULME

Home of Tony McCarroll; Paul 'Bonehead' Arthur lived at nearby West Point. When Liam Gallagher joined their band Rain, he insisted on a name change to Oasis. They rehearsed at the Grove – a club in Plymouth Grove, Longsight – and then at the Red House in Ancoats.

MANCHESTER

Quite impossible to list everyone who was born here, but here are a few: Freddie Garrity, 1940 (& The Dreamers); Roy Harper, 12.6.41; Eric Stewart, 20.1.45 (10cc); Wayne Fontana, 28.10.45 (Mindbenders); Davy Jones, 30.12.45 (Monkees); John Cooper Clarke, 25.1.49; Robin and Maurice Gibb, 22.12.49 (Bee Gee twins); Martin Price, 26.3.55 (808 State); Martin Fry, 9.3.58 (ABC); Stuart Adamson, 11.4.58 (Big Country); John Maher, 21.4.60 (Buzzcocks); Mick Hucknell, 8.6.60 (Simply Red); Noel Gallagher, 29.5.67, and Liam Gallagher, 21.9.72 (Oasis).

The best Sixties R&B club was the Twisted Wheel at 30 Brazennose Street. John Mayall was resident there in '62/3 but every act worth its salt played there – from Alexis Korner to Little Walter, Graham Bond to Screaming Jay Hawkins.

Hottest pop venue was the Oasis in Lloyd Street, where The Deltas changed their name to The Hollies (after seeing holly in the Christmas decorations, December '62), where The Beatles played four times (starting in February '62), where the Stones played in August '63, where Wayne Fontana was spotted and signed, and where Dave Lee Travis learned his trade, spinning discs for a quid a night. Other Sixties venues were Mr Smiths in Brazil

Street, the Three Coins in Fountain Street (where The Beatles played in January '63), and the Manchester Cavern.

Groups would also meet in various coffee bars – Guys and Dolls in Kennedy Street being most fondly remembered – and at Barrett's Music Shop, 86 Oxford Road.

The Bee Gees in a psychedelic field of their own

The Bee Gees made their world début at the Gaumont Theatre in December '56. Jimmy Page first appeared locally at St. Bernadette's Youth Club and the Science of College & Technology in November '63 – as guitarist in Carter Lewis & The Southerners. In November '68, he returned to the latter venue with his brand new outfit, Led Zeppelin.

In January '64, a converted church in Dickinson Road became the first studio for *Top Of The Pops*.

In August '64, twelve girls and two policewomen fainted during riots at a Rolling Stones gig at the New Elizabethan Ballroom in Bellevue, and in March '65 a hysterical girl fell from the dress circle during a Stones gig at the Palace Theatre.

The Sixties group scene threw up international stars in the shape of Wayne Fontana & The Mindbenders, Herman's Hermits and Freddie & The Dreamers. At their peak, in April '65, they held the top three positions on the *Billboard* Top 100 –with 'Game Of Love', 'Mrs Brown You've Got A Lovely Daughter' and 'I'm Telling You Now', respectively. Best of all were The Hollies, who racked up 18 UK Top Ten hits.

Hundreds more failed to make any national impression – like Graham Gouldman's Mockingbirds, or Paul Young's Toggery Five. Lol Creme's dad had a shop in Shude Hill, where his early group The Sabres used to rehearse.

Bob Dylan played (and was famously harangued and bootlegged) at the Free Trade Hall in May '65 and May '66. Local historian CP Lee wrote a superb book about his visits: *Bob Dylan: Like The Night*.

Stackwaddy, pre-"bugger off" sentimental period

In the post-beat/pre-punk era came 10cc, Stackwaddy, Gravy Train, Greasy Bear and Sad Café.

The city's best psychedelic venue was the Magic Village, started by former Twisted Wheel promoter Roger Eagle. Pink Floyd played there in June '68. When Mick Hucknall was putting Simply Red together, he stayed at Eagle's house, absorbing his almighty record collection. Eagle later operated the amazing Eric's Club in Liverpool, and later the two International Clubs in Manchester.

Van Der Graaf Generator formed at Manchester University; where The Chemical Brothers (Ed Simons and Tom Rowlands) also came together; other students included Radiohead's Ed O'Brien and Sleeper's Jon Stewart. Mick Hucknall (Simply Red), Elliot Rashman (Albertos roadie and Simply Red manager), Carmel, Linder (Ludus), John McGeoch (Magazine, PiL) and Buzzcocks sleeve designer Malcolm Garrett all went to Manchester Poly – as did Tom Hingley (Inspiral Carpets). John Mayall attended the Regional School of Art. It sounds apocryphal to me, but multi-millionaire Chrysalis founder Chris Wright is said to have failed his exams at the Manchester Business School.

In case we forget ... Sad Café

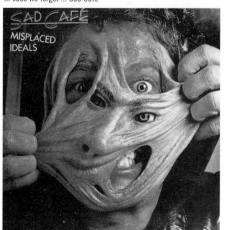

Ian Curtis of Joy Division and Clive Gregson of Any Trouble both worked at the DHSS office.

The late Seventies punk/new wave scene was sparked off by a seminal Sex Pistols gig at the Lesser Free Trade Hall in Peter Street on 4.6.76, promoted by Howard Devoto and Pete Shelley. Their group The Buzzcocks made its official début when the Pistols returned to the same venue on 20.7.76. Most of the audience were inspired to form bands of their own.

Earliest groups on the punk scene included The Buzzcocks, Slaughter & The Dogs, The Fall, Warsaw (later Joy Division), Ed Banger & The Nosebleeds, and The Drones.

Hot on their trail were Durutti Column, Magazine, The Passage, Ludus, Manicured Noise, The Negatives, Spherical Objects, Dislocation Dance, Jilted John, The Diagram Brothers, V2, The Decorators, Bette Lynch's Legs, The Tiller Boys and John Cooper Clarke – not to mention Alberto Y Los Trios Paranoias, who were the bridge between hippies and punks.

Best late Seventies city centre club was the Electric Circus in Collyhurst Street, off Rochdale Road – which was the primo punk venue until the authorities closed it over "fire regulations". The Buzzcocks played there in November '76, and in July '77 signed their United Artists contract on the bar. The Sex Pistols played there in December '76, on the notorious Anarchy tour. Warsaw (billed as The Stiff Kittens) made their début there in May '77; Magazine played there the night it closed in October '77.

Next to open was Rafters in the cellar of 65 Oxford Road. Magazine made their début here in October '77. At an audition here in spring '78, Joy Division failed to impress Stiff execs, but they did impress Factory boss Tony Wilson (who signed them) and club DJ Rob Gretton (who became their manager). Mick Hucknall's Frantic Elevators made their début at Rafters in June '78, supporting Sham 69.

In late '77, Morrissey (Smiths) and Billy Duffy (Cult) made their public début at the Ritz in Whitworth Street, when they were both in The Nosebleeds. The Smiths made their début at the same venue in October '82 (supporting London poseurs Blue Rondo A La Turk).

A popular late Seventies watering hole was the Ranch, a gay bar often "littered with Bowie casualties" in Little Lever Street. The Buzzcocks played an early gig there.

First local label of note was Rabid, started in '77 by flyposter king Tosh Ryan. Operating from 20 Cotton Lane in Withington, it released early singles by Slaughter & The Dogs, The Nosebleeds, Jilted John and John Cooper Clarke.

Ed Banger single with Durutti Column member,
Vini Reilly, in school uniform

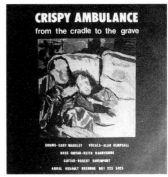

'Overlooked' Crispy Ambulance

Most stylish and successful local label was Factory, started by Tony Wilson in late '78, with premises at 86 Palatine Road. Its roster was breathtaking – from the earliest days of A Certain Ratio and Joy Division to the latter days of New Order and The Happy Mondays. Expansion saw them setting up the Dry Bar in Oldham Street and moving into new, expensively refurbished offices in Charles Street. Sadly, an insoluble cash crisis developed in late '92 and the greatest provincial label in Britain went tits up.

New Order made their début as a trio at the Beach Club (a Wednesday night takeover of Oozit's Club in Shude Hill) in July '80.

The Hacienda club (operated by Factory Records and New Order and given the Factory catalogue number FAC 51) was a self-styled post-industrial fantasy venue, opening in May '82, at 11-13 Whitworth Street West. The Stone Roses first played there in August '85; The Happy Mondays came last in a Battle of the Bands contest in late '84. For years it lost money – subsidised by Factory and New Order – but in the late Eighties, the Hacienda became the womb of acid house, the hub of rave culture, the hippest venue in Britain. (Ecstasy had more influence than acid ever had). Gangster infiltration and drug-war violence caused January to May '91 shut-down – but it reopened and thrived until January '97 closure.

Richard Boon's Buzzcocks management company New Hormones operated from 50 Newton Street. The New Hormones record label roster included The Decorators, Ludus, The Diagram Brothers and The Tiller Boys. The Buzzcocks recorded their *Spiral Scratch* EP at Indigo Studios in Gartside Street, with Martin Hannett producing, in December '76.

A former cotton warehouse in Little Peter Street was converted into TJ's rehearsal studios, used by every local band from The Frantic Elevators to Joy Division to The Inadequates (with Gillian Gilbert) to The Buzzcocks. TJM was a spin-off indie label offering The Distractions, V2, Victim and The Frantic Elevators.

In the Eighties came The Mothmen, The Distractions, A Certain Ratio, Occult Chemistry, Crispy Ambulance, The Freshies, The Smirks, The Blue Orchids, Any Trouble, Quando Quango (featuring Mike Pickering, later of M People), Flag Of Convenience (Buzzcocks spin-off), The Inca Babies, Simply Red, James and two thirds of Swing Out Sister.

Late Eighties groups included King Of The Slums, The Sun And The Moon, Turning Blue, The Waltones, The Happy Mondays, Stockholm Monsters, The High, A Man Called Gerald, Lavolta Lakota, Baby Ford, Northside (from Blackley), Easterhouse (who perversely named themselves after a council estate in Glasgow!), 808 State, Yargo, Electronic and The Stone Roses.

The Gallery in Peter Street (where R.E.M. played in November '84) and the Portland Bar (under the Piccadilly Hotel) were the places to play.

The city's first warehouse rave was a Stone Roses gig in a British Railways arch in Fairfield Street, behind Piccadilly Station in July '85.

The late Roger Eagle, promoter at Manchester's International Clubs and all-round guru

Both the International 1 and the International 2 presented many seminal gigs. The former, which opened in April '85, hosted The Stone Roses several times – including their classic four-piece line-up début in November '87. The latter put on the famous James/Stone Roses gig in May '88, where Liam Gallagher saw his future. This venue had formerly been known as the Astoria – where the Gallagher brothers' parents first met, at a dance in January '64. Meanwhile, the Free Trade Hall (though continually threatened with unpleasant modification) continued to present gigs: Glasgow group Blue Nile made their world début there in September '90.

Early Nineties bands included Mrs Robinson, The Sugar Merchants, That Uncertain Feeling, World Of Twist (charted in '90), The Mock Turtles (charted in '91), Interstella (charted in '91), Ultracynic (charted in '92), Sub Sub (charted big in '93 with Ain't No Love), The Joy (whose début single lasted 27 minutes), The Family Foundation, Flat Back 4, Johnny Dangerously, D-Generation, Harvey's Rabbit, Goldie, Medalark Eleven, Sister Lovers, Strange, The Rain Kings, Too Much Texas, The Lovers, Rig, Mad Jacks, Metal Monkey Machine, One Summer, Chapter and Verse, Revenge (Peter Hook's subsidiary enterprise), Robert Reilly & The Buffalo Club, Weaveworld, JJ, The Slum Turkeys, Eskimos'n'Egypt, Distant Cousins, Slow Bongo Floyd, Zero Zero, Molly Halfhead (chart flicker in '95 with 'Shine'), and Machine Gun Feedback (who mutated into The Space Monkeys and signed with Factory Too).

Take That and M People were the big breakouts of '91, with 'Promises' and 'How Can I Love You More', respectively. The former were conceived as a Mancunian New Kids On The Block but ultimately delivered a Wham-like twist when Robbie Williams emerged as a respected solo artist. The latter were formed by Mike Pickering, DJ and booker at the Hacienda and producer of the first Happy Mondays release. The Happy Mondays offshoot Black Grape topped the chart with their '95 album *It's Great When You're Straight*.

Biggest band in Manchester – and the world – is Oasis, spearheaded by brothers Noel and Liam Gallagher, who were born at 2 Sandycroft Street in Longsight, which was redeveloped soon after the latter's birth – necessitating a family move to Burnage.

Oasis played their first gig (as a quartet) at the Boardwalk in Little Peter Street on 18.8.91 – and their first as a quintet (including Noel, who had recently been made redundant as an Inspiral Carpets roadie) at the same venue on 15.1.92. Several more of their best pre-fame gigs also happened there.

Other hot Nineties venues include the Holy City Zoo in York Street, the Canal Café Bar in Whitworth Street, the Night and Day Café in Oldham Street, the Band on the Wall at 25 Swan Street, the Roadhouse in Newton Street, the Academy in Oxford Road, the Venue in Whitworth Street, the Brickhouse at 66 Whitworth Street West, the Palace Theatre in Oxford Street, and for ginormous bands the Nynex Arena at Victoria Station. Formerly the offices of Factory Records, the Paradise Factory at 112-116 Princess Street became a clubbers' haven.

Late Nineties bands/acts include Solar Race, Jubilee, Northern Uproar, Audioweb (ex The Sugar Merchants), Jealous, Brassy, Sexus, Strange Brew, Lamb, Mr Scruff, Earl Brutus, Gold Blade, Monaco, Brubaker, Kavana and '98 Creation signing One Lady Owner.

In October '98, Manchester Magistrates Court heard how Ian Brown had threatened to chop off the hand of a British Airways stewardess on a flight from Paris to Manchester. He was sentenced to four months in jail, part of which was served at Strangeways.

'Strangeways Here We Come' was a famous Smiths' title; 'The Ballad of Strangeways' was a song by Donovan, who found himself temporarily confronted by prison bars after an unhappy misunderstanding in '64.

The Bard of Salford, John Cooper Clarke directed one of his most biting diatribes at Beasley Street, a remote backwater in Gorton, and he mentions tacky Oxford Road in 'Salome Maloney'.

The legendary Oasis first demo tape with 'Columbia' as the first track

More silly Freshies' product

Meanwhile, Chris Sievey of The Freshies committed to vinyl his plaintive declaration 'I'm In Love With The Girl On The Manchester Virgin Megastore Check-out Desk'! I wonder where she is now?

In '90, London band The Times recorded their tribute – entitled Manchester.

MIDDLETON

The Beatles played at the Co-operative Hall in Long Street in April '63.

Tony Wilson's great late Seventies TV show *So It Goes* was recorded at the Civic Hall.

In '85, Parish Bowman Studio was purchased by Rochdale-based Suite 16 and renamed Suite 8.

Operational base of Eighties band The Chameleons (who rehearsed at Suite 8) and their spin-off The Reegs. Not to mention The Mock Turtles, who broke out with '91 hit 'Can You Dig It?' Previously called Judge Happiness, they were led by Steve Coogan's brother Martin.

Puressence were the next to break out, in the mid-Nineties.

MOSS SIDE

Home of early Nineties rappers MC Tunes (Nicky Lockett) and MC Buzz B (Daryl Braithwaite), Social Kaos, Audioweb singer Martin Merchant and the Higgins sisters – better known as '98 chartbusters Cleopatra.

Former Magazine and Bad Seeds bass player Barry Adamson cut a solo album called Moss Side Story.

Oasis chose Manchester City's ground at Maine Road as the setting for their finest post-fame gigs: two nights in April '96.

OLD TRAFFORD

In July 92, a Simply Red concert drew 45,000 fans to the cricket ground.

OLDHAM

Birthplace of all four members of Barclay James Harvest: Wooly Woolstenholme, 15.4.47; John Lees, 13.1.48; Mel Pritchard, 20.1.48; Les Holroyd, 12.3.48. Also funny man Bernard Cribbins, 29.12.28 (two Top Ten hits in '62!); bass player Ray Jones, 20.10.39, (Dakotas); drummer Chris Curtis, 26.8.41 (Searchers); Phillip Schofield, 1.4.62.

The Beatles appeared at the Astoria Ballroom in King Street in February '63; The Jimi Hendrix Experience played there in January 67.

Home of psychedelic indie band The Inspiral Carpets, who made their début at the Mare And Foal public house in April '86 and broke nationally with '90 hit 'This Is How It Feels'. Other local outfits included Jazz Media, Asia Fields, T'Challa Grid, The Klingons, Hungry Socks, Exit, Wonky Alice and Wheatstone's Bridge – all of whom met to discuss their progress at the Miners Arms.

Oasis played their fifth gig at Club 57 – supporting the latest hot local band The Ya Yas.

OPENSHAW

Mindbenders/10cc guitarist Eric Stewart went to the Technical High School; Monkee Davy Jones went to Varna Secondary Modern.

PRESTWICH

The Happy Mondays headlined the Cities in the Park Festival at Heaton Park in August '91. Other Manchester area bands on the bill included Candlestick Park and Electronic.

RADCLIFFE

Hitless for two years, the once sensational rocker Johnny Kidd was killed here in a car collision on the way to a cabaret gig in October '66. Another passenger, his bass player Nick Simper, went on to play in the first line-up of Deep Purple.

Barclay James Harvest

ROCHDALE

Birthplace of Johnny Clegg, 13.7.53 (who emigrated to South Africa, where he formed Julaka and Savuka); disc jockey and radio journalist Andy Kershaw, 9.11.59; *Razzamatazz* TV show presenter Lisa Stansfield, 11.4.66.

Andy Kershaw's dad was headmaster of nearby Whitworth High School, his mother was Mayoress of Whitworth, and his sister followed him into the world of broadcasting.

Late Sixties Rochdale Grammar School group The Way We Live cut their début album in the attic of sound-man John Brierley's parents' house in Edenfield Road. It is now the most collectable, high-priced record in the Dandelion catalogue. In '73, Brierley opened a two track studio at 179 Drake Street and the band, now called Tractor, cut their local hit 'No More Rock'n'Roll.'

The Way We Live proudly framed on their mother's Rochdale home wall

In late '77, Brierley opened the 16-track Cargo Studio at 16 Kenion Street – with Tractor Music (a PA hire/rehearsal space) on the ground floor. Cargo's clients included Joy Division, Dead or Alive, The Mekons and Gang Of Four. In '85, the studio was taken over by Chris Hewitt and New Order's Peter Hook and renamed Suite 16 (at Tony Wilson's suggestion). The Stone Roses, James, New Order, The Chameleons, and many more flocked in. In the late Nineties, the studio was purchased by Shan Hira – formerly of Factory band The Stockholm Monsters.

The first gig New Order undertook with new keyboard player Gillian Gilbert was at Rochdale College in December '80.

Blue Zone were late Eighties hopefuls, who were convinced to record under the name of lead singer Stansfield and reached number one with 'All Around The World' in '89.

Peter Hook's late Nineties band Monaco (whose début album *Music For Pleasure* went Top Ten) were Rochdale based – and included Suite 16 engineer Dave Potts.

Also local were techno duo Autechre (brief 94 charters) and Asian hip-hoppers The Kaliphz.

Mike Harding hit the '75 chart with 'Rochdale Cowboy'.

RUSHOLME

Birthplace of Steve Diggle, 7.5.55 (Buzzcocks).

'Rusholme Ruffians' was a track on The Smiths' album *Meat Is Murder*.

SALE

Stone Roses founders John Squire and Ian Brown grew up as neighbours in Sylvan Avenue. Their earlier band, The Patrol, made their début at a local youth club called the Annexe.

SALFORD

Birthplace of singer Allan Clarke, 5.4.42 (Hollies); drummer Tony Mansfield, 28.5.43 (Dakotas); guitarist Fritz Fryer, 6.12.44 (Four Pennies); bassist Karl Green, 31.7.47 (Hermits); singer Elkie Brooks, 25.2.48 (Vinegar Joe, solo); John Cooper Clarke, 25.1.49 (the Bard of Salford); Bernard Sumner, 4.1.56 and Peter Hook, 13.2.56 (Joy Division, New Order); Mark Smith, 5.3.57 (Fall); Dave Ball, 3.5.59 (Soft Cell, The Grid). Factory founder Tony Wilson was born here too (his parents owned a local tobacconists shop) – but moved out to Marple at the age of five.

Passing through Salford Grammar School were Graham Nash (Hollies) and Ian Curtis (Joy Division). Elkie Brooks went to Sedgley Park County Primary and North Salford Secondary Modern, where Graham Gouldman and Kevin Godley were also pupils.

When Howard Devoto moved to Salford, The Buzzcocks rehearsed at his flat at 364 Lower Broughton Road and then (after complaints about noise) at St. Boniface's Church Hall in Frederick Road.

New wavers included The Salford Jets. Craig Davies was a late Eighties hopeful.

New Order, the most influential band of the early Eighties, began with Bernard Sumner and Peter Hook experimenting in the former's grandmother's house in Broughton. Later, they rehearsed at the Swan public house.

The Happy Mondays were probably the most influential band of the late Eighties (and I am going to lump everything here, even though I should sub-divide it up into Little Hulton, Swinton, etc – maybe next time). Birthplace of guitarist Mark Day, 29.12.61; singer Shaun Ryder, 23.8.62; bass player Paul Ryder, 24.4.64; drummer Gary Whelan, 12.2.66; keyboard player Paul Davis, 7.3.66. The Ryders went to Ambrose High School; the others went to Wardley High School.

Mid-Nineties breakers included First Offence and Gabrielle's Wish.

STALEYBRIDGE

Any Trouble auditioned for Stiff Records at the Commercial Arms.

STOCKPORT

Birthplace of bass player Eric Haydock, 3.2.43 (Hollies); Ric Rothwell, 11.3.44 (Mindbenders); Richard Darbyshire, 8.3.60 (Living In A Box).

Frankie Vaughan wrote and sang 'I'm Going Back To Stockport'. The song had been commissioned – to improve the town's dull image.

The Merseybeats were managed by Alan Cheetham of Fiveways Corner, Hazel Grove, and booked by the McKiernan Agency at 1 Heaton Moor Road.

Opened in '68, Strawberry Studios at 3 Waterloo Road was soon the hottest studio in Greater Manchester. Co-owners were Graham Gouldman and Eric Stewart (ex The Mockingbirds and The Mindbenders respectively), engineer Peter Tattersall, and the management company Kennedy Street Enterprises. The first hit was

'Neanderthal Man' by Hotlegs, who eventually mutated into 10cc. Late one night, as Paul McCartney was leaving, he found a girl standing at the adjacent bus-stop crying – and promptly took out his acoustic and rattled off a few songs to cheer her up. Simply Red cut their first demos there; The Stone Roses recorded there – both produced by Martin Hannett.

Local bands include The Purple Gang (psychedelicos), The Elite (punk/new wave). Sixties beat group The Toggery Five were named after a clothes shop in Mersey Square – "all the top groups visit the Toggery for their stage and leisure wear" – which was also the setting for 'Rumble On Mersey Square South' by Wimple Winch, who evolved into prog-rock band Pacific Drift

Super-rare pic sleeve from Stockport's Wimple Winch (ex-The Four Just Men)

A short-lived psychedelic club was the Sinking Ship in Royal Oak Yard, Underbank.

Gillian Gilbert took graphics and business studies at Stockport Tech but dropped out after a year to join New Order.

The Grand Hotel, Wigan, home to Buddy Holly for a night

What Noise? and Robinson were early Nineties indie hopefuls.

STRETFORD
From late '64, when his family moved here, until The Smiths took off, Steven Morrissey lived at 384 Kings Road. It was here, in May '82, that Johnny Marr knocked on the door to start their collaboration. Morrissey completed his formal education at Stretford Technical College.

Peter Noone went to Stretford Grammar.

That Uncertain Feeling released singles in the Nineties.

TIMPERLEY
Birthplace of disc jockey Keith Skues, 4.3.39.

The Stone Roses have their roots at South Trafford College, where disenchanted students Ian Brown, John Squire, Andy Couzens and Simon Wolstencroft formed The Patrol.

WHALLEY RANGE
Birthplace of Gillian Gilbert, 27.1.61 (New Order).

Peter Noone was asked to leave St. Bede's College because he was taking off too much time to appear in Coronation Street. Mike Harding was a student there too.

Sometime home of Steve Hopkins (Invisible Girls) and Mark Collins (Charlatans).

WIGAN
Birthplace of songwriter Barry Mason (loads of hits for Engelbert, Tom Jones, etc); singer Limahl, 19.12.58 (Kajagoogoo).

Buddy Holly & The Crickets played the Ritz Theatre in March '58 and stayed overnight at the Grand Hotel in Dorning Street.

The Beatles played at the ABC cinema in Station Road in October '64.

The Long & The Short (two minor hits in '64) were based here.

The small mining village of Bickershaw was the setting for an extremely muddy rock festival in May '72. The Kinks, Grateful Dead, Country Joe, Donovan, Dr John and Captain Beefheart were headliners.

Wigan Casino became the Mecca for Northern Soul in the mid-Seventies; records by Wigan's Chosen Few and Wigan's Ovation capitalised on the scene. In November '77, apprehensive police banned a projected series of weekly punk nights at the Casino.

The Railway Children were big with Peel and Kershaw in the mid-Eighties, and finally got some hits in the Nineties. Peel also admired the locally based Jailcell Recipes and The Tansads.

Biggest band to come out of Wigan were Brit-rock frontrunners The Verve. Their first gig at the Honeysuckle pub in August '90 drew flies; their homecoming gig at Haigh Hall in May '98 drew over 30,000 fans.

In '99, Witness (proteges of Verve guitarist Nick McCabe) released their début album.

Bickershaw Festival memorabilia

WITHINGTON
20 Cotton Lane housed the city's first independent labels, Rabid (featuring Jilted John and John Cooper Clarke) and Razz (featuring the idiosyncratic Chris Sievy & The Freshies).

Vini Reilly (Durutti Column) grew up here – having been born at Heaton Park.

WYTHENSHAWE
Birthplace of Lyn Paul, 16.2.49 (New Seekers), who made her singing début at Wythenshawe Labour Club.

John Mayall was a youth club leader here, which provided adequate facilities for his group The Blues Syndicate to rehearse.

Local lass Joan Carroll wrote the lyrics for 'Just One Look' and was later married to Mothers Of Invention/Captain Beefheart drummer Art Trypp III.

Cult guitarist Billy Duffy (born 12.5.61) was educated at Brookway High School. Johnny Marr (who lived in Baguley) used to watch his school group rehearse, picking up guitar hints. Marr and Andy Rourke (both future Smiths) attended St. Augustine's Grammar – later renamed St. John Pleasington School.

Slaughter & The Dogs were the big confrontational punk band – formed by schoolfriends Mick Rossi and Wayne Barrett. Their rivals were Ed Banger & The Nosebleeds, including Vini Reilly on guitar.

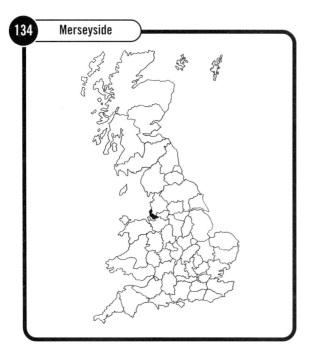

MERSEYSIDE

(excluding Liverpool)

Liverpool, 1963, Beat-mania. Too many groups to mention

The Mojos from Birkenhead, Lewis Collins (right)

AINTREE

Birthplace of drummer Pete Gill, 8.3.64 (Frankie Goes To Hollywood).

The Institute (in Longmoor Lane, next to the Black Bull) and the Orrell Park Ballroom in Orrell Lane were popular early Sixties venues. The Beatles played the former over 30 times between January 61 and January 62.

First wave Merseybeat group Faron's Flamingos sprang from here.

The Scaffold thanked us very much for the Aintree Iron... what was it exactly?

In July '88, Michael Jackson played Aintree Racecourse in what was the biggest ever British concert by a single artist.

BIRKENHEAD

Birthplace of Lewis Collins, 26.5.42 (sometime bass player in The Mojos; later star of TV series *The Professionals*).

It was during a package show at the Essoldo Cinema, Argyll Street, in September '58 that Billy Fury talked his way into Marty Wilde's dressing room and impressed his manager, Larry Parnes, enough to win an invitation to London. Within weeks he was a national star! That's the popular myth... what actually happened was this: Fury's parents had asked Parnes to return his 78 rpm demo of 'Playing For Keeps', and Parnes suggested that Billy call round to the gig. He duly went (with his pal Jimmy Tarbuck!) and performed onstage that same night, joining the tour for the rest of its schedule. He had no job at the time, having just got out of hospital.

The local group venue was the Majestic Ballroom in Conway Street, where The Beatles played 17 times. They also played three times at the Technical College in Borough Road.

Groups often stopped off at Morgan's fish and chip shop on Borough Road, near the Fire Station. Rory Storm was a regular customer, and the proprietor distinctly remembers Sandie Shaw dropping in.

Many Merseybeat groups bought their instruments and amps at R A Strother & Son, 7 Charing Cross.

Elvis Costello and his Attractions

Elvis Costello (whose formative years were spent on Merseyside) paid tribute by snapping the run-down Clockwork Orange Cafe, in Hoylake Road, on the back of his 'Oliver's Army' sleeve.

Home of the heroic, idiosyncratic indie faves Half Man Half Biscuit. Four lads who shook the Wirral, they took their name from local punk group Instant Agony, who were describing Prince Charles. They turned down an invitation to appear on *The Tube* because Tranmere Rovers were playing at home that night!

Also celebrationists of the Wirral are Jegsy Dodd & The Sons Of Harry Cross – famous for songs like 'Downtown Birkenhead', 'Who Killed New Brighton' and 'I'm The Trendiest Man Who Never Got Into Atmosphere' – Atmosphere being "a horrible disco club for pseudo poseurs" according to one observer.

Another local lad is Bill Steers – member of two hardcore bands, Napalm Death and Carcass.

Local Nineties bands include Scorpio Rising and The Co-optimists.

BOOTLE

Birthplace of singer Billy J Kramer, 19.8.43 (Dakotas); bass player Carl Hunter, 14.4.65 (Farm).

Mike Pender and Chris Curtis, later of The Searchers, met as pupils at St. Winifred's School.

A popular early Sixties gig was the Blue Penguin Club at St. Johns Hall.

Operational base of The Farm, who finally broke through with 'Groovy Train' in '90 after a decade of toil.

Local Nineties indie bands The Real People, The Hoovers and People Get Ready also won record deals.

The only Nineties gig appeared to be the Marsh Lane Community Centre.

BROMBOROUGH

Birthplace of Paul Heaton, 9.5.62 (Housemartins).

Crosby: birthplace of Kenny Everett (pictured in his pram aged 2 by his mum)

CROSBY

Birthplace of Kenny Everett, 25.12.44, at his parents' house in Hereford Road. He was educated at St. Edmunds, then at St. Bede's Secondary Modern. Searchers drummer Chris Curtis went to St. Mary's College.

The Jive Hive, held at St. Luke's Hall in Liverpool Road, opened for business in May '59. Less popular was the Alexandra Hall in Coronation Road.

Most interesting late Nineties band is Clinic.

FORMBY

Home of Steve Murray, later known as folkie recording artist Timon, and subsequently (during his dalliance with The Clash) as Tymon Dogg. He was later half of new age folk duo The Frugivores.

GARSTON

Many Merseybeat groups gigged at Garston Baths in Speke Road. Drunken thuggery led to the nick-name Garston Bloodbaths.

Wilson Hall, opposite the bus depot in Speke Road, was an early Quarry Men venue. It was here, in February '57, that George Harrison first saw the group and became interested in joining.

HESWALL

Birthplace of John Peel, 30.8.39 (disc jockey); singer Ian Astbury, 14.5.62 (Cult).

In the midst of Beatlemania, Paul McCartney bought his father a house in Baskervyle Road. The Beatles had played several pre-fame gigs at the Jazz Club, held at the Womens Institute in Barnston Road. It was here, in March '62, that Epstein made them wear suits on stage for the first time.

Home of Andy McCluskey, founder of Orchestral Manoeuvres In The Dark.

The Sisters Of Mercy used the Wirral estuary as a backdrop for promotional shots for their album *Floodlands*.

The Wirral Estuary makes the big-time

HOYLAKE

Brian Epstein's first venture into the family business was running a local store, Clarendon Furnishing.

Cynthia Powell, later Cynthia Lennon, lived in Trinity Road. Her son Julian was educated at Hoylake School. The Beatles had played at the YMCA in Birkenhead Road in February '62 – when they were booed offstage!

Also from here were Stan Hugill (world authority on sea shanties) and Paul Kennerley, who wrote concept albums – like *White Mansions* – and married Emmylou Harris.

Harold Wilson shamelessly endorses late Sixties assault on the pop charts

HUYTON

Prime Minister Harold Wilson was MP for Huyton. In July '66, he presided over the re-opening of the Cavern.

Beatle Stu Sutcliffe attended Park View Primary School. He died in Hamburg in '62, and is buried at the Parish Church Cemetery in Stanley Road.

Primo Sixties gig was at Hambleton Hall in St. Davids Road, Page Moss, where The Beatles played 16 times.

Tom Evans (Badfinger) went to Long View Secondary School.

Operational base of hot Eighties bands The La's and Rain. Mike Badger, who played in and named the former, is now a singer-songwriter and sculptor: he designed the tin robot on the sleeve of Space's hit album 'Tin Planet'.

KIRKBY

Birthplace of Hal Carter, who left the area to work as Marty Wilde's roadie and later managed Billy Fury; Gary Daly, 5.5.62, and Eddie Lundon, 9.6.62, who met at St. Kevin's Comprehensive and later formed China Crisis. Bunnyman Will Sergeant lived at nearby Melling.

Local Sixties beat group The Kirkbys named themselves after the town and the area was later immortalised on the B-side of the first single by Teardrop Explodes – Kirkby Workers Dream Fades! The Glass Torpedoes were an early Eighties indie band.

Julian Cope & The Menace Greeves outside Liverpool heading towards Kirkby

From acorn beginnings, Amazon Recording Studios in Stopgate Lane, Simonswood has attracted everyone from The Smiths to Wet Wet Wet, Dusty Springfield to New Order. Owner Jeremy Lewis started with a 4-track in the cellar of his Woolton home (recording Nasty Pop and Deaf School) and then sold his car to buy this place in the mid-Seventies. He also started (with Pete Fulwell) the Inevitable label and took proteges China Crisis and Dead Or Alive to Virgin... who didn't want Dead Or Alive!

Local Nineties bands include the Pure Morning.

KNOTTY ASH

As made famous by Ken Dodd. The pre-fame Beatles played the village hall in East Prescot Road eight times

Ken Dodd: a hit with the chicks when knot a diddyman

LITHERLAND

During the early Sixties, the Town Hall in Hatton Hill Road was one of the most popular venues on Merseyside. The Beatles' gig on 27.12.60 (fresh back from Hamburg) was widely seen as the turning point in their career.

MAGHULL

Les Pattinson and Will Sergeant (both Bunnymen) went to Deyes Lane Secondary Modern.

The Farm took their name from their local rehearsal rooms, Maghull Farm.

NESTON

Cass & The Cassanovas were the first rock group to put Neston Village Institute in Hinderton Road on the map. The Silver Beetles playeded here six times in summer '60.

NEW BRIGHTON

The Tower Ballroom on the Promenade held up to 5,000 punters. The Beatles played there (27 times), as did everyone from Little Richard to The Rolling Stones – until fire destroyed it in '69.

When big enough to fill one of Liverpool's largest venues, Elvis Costello chose to play the Grand in New Brighton instead... for nostalgic reasons, no doubt.

The Boo Radleys made their début at the Victoria in '88.

NEWTON LE WILLOWS

On leaving Selwyn Jones High School, Rick Astley worked for his father at the Parkside Garden Centre in Southworth Road.

Operational base of bizarre punk band Naafi Sandwich, led by the extraordinary Sir Freddie Viaduct.

The current modest home of Rick Astley

PORT SUNLIGHT

Birthplace of singer Pete Burns, 5.8.59 (Dead Or Alive).

Hulme Hall in Port Sunlight Village (created for his workers by soap magnate Lord Leverhulme) got The Beatles for 30 quid in October '62 – just as 'Love Me Do' carried them into the chart for the first time.

PRESCOT

Before going to the Art College, Stu Sutcliffe went to Prescot Grammar.

Appropriately, Mott The Hoople played CF Mott College in May '70.

Julian Cope started at CF Mott College in September '76 but was soon distracted by the scene revolving around Eric's. In '77, he lived in a top floor flat at 7 Laburnam Road – but moved out when it was over-run by hippies.

ROBY

Home of Colin Vearncombe, who scored a decade of hits under the alias Black.

ST. HELENS

Birthplace of Budgie, 21.8.57 (Slits, The Banshees).

The Plaza Ballroom in Duke Street started featuring local groups in '59.

Gravy Train released a couple of late Sixties prog-rock albums that now change hands for big money on the collectors' market.

Before joining Frankie Goes To Hollywood, Paul Rutherford was at St. Helens Art School.

Local Nineties bands include Poisoned Electrik Head.

SEAFORTH

Lathom Hall in Lathom Avenue was a merseybeat stomping ground. The Beatles played there eleven times.

SOUTHPORT

Birthplace of Dora Bryan, 7.2.24 (hit '63 Top Twenty with 'All I Want For Christmas Is A Beatle'); guitarist Ollie Halsall, 14.3.49 (Patto, Kevin Ayers, etc); Berni Flint (hits in '77); and Marc Almond, 9.7.57 (Soft Cell), who went to Starbeck Infants, King George V Grammar, and Southport Art College.

Lita Roza, UK's top girl singer of '55, began her professional career singing in a Southport restaurant.

Annual pantomimes have always been star-studded affairs... ever since Vince Eager played Simple Simon in Mother Goose ('60).

The Beatles played four times at the Floral Hall, eight times at the Kingsway Club, and once at the Django Club in the Queen's Hotel – all on the Promenade. They also played at the Cambridge Hall and the Odeon Cinema, both in Lord Street. The Stones played the Floral Hall in December '63.

Rhythm & Blues Inc (featuring teenager Ollie Halsall) played the mid-Sixties Merseybeat circuit; Mayhem were the town's token punks.

Comedian Alexei Sayle (a chart star in '84) did a foundation course at Southport School of Art, before moving down to Chelsea.

Noted Merseybeat singer and guitarist Kingsize Taylor dumped music for a butcher's shop in Crown Buildings, Birkdale.

Ainsdale is home of Merseybeat historian Spencer Leigh, and guitarist/singer Paul Stroud of mid-Nineties faves Mint 400. Their song 'Natterjack Joe' acknowledged a rare species of toad found only in the local sand dunes.

Ollie Peacock and Ian Ball left their band Severed to join local mates Tom Gray and Paul Blackburn in Gomez – who became the hottest band of '98. As I write this, they are lined-up for a late '98 homecoming bonanza at the Floral Hall, which is still going strong after all these years.

The Deadlies was another local Nineties band.

SPEKE

Local lad George Harrison made his public début at Speke British Legion Club in Damwood Road, with The Rebels in '56. At age 6, he and his family had moved into a council house at 25 Upton Green.

As a child, Paul McCartney lived at 72 Western Avenue and went to Stockton Wood Road Primary. His family later moved to 12 Ardwick Road. He and George rode the same school bus to the Liverpool Institute.

WALLASEY

Birthplace of Les Maguire, 27.12.41 (Pacemakers); Jackie Lomax, 10.5.44 (Undertakers); bassplayer Timothy Brown, 26.2.69, and singer/guitarist Sice, 18.6.69 (both Boo Radleys).

As a child, Paul McCartney lived briefly at 92 Broadway.

The Silver Beetles/Beatles played the Grosvenor Ballroom, in Grosvenor Street Liscard, 14 times between June '60 and September '61.

Most famous local Merseybeat group was The Undertakers; most famous Nineties group was The Boo Radleys.

WAVERTREE

Birthplace of Holly Johnson, 19.2.60 (Frankie Goes to Hollywood).

In July '61, The Beatles played twice at Holyoake Hall in Smithdown Road – which, as biographer Mark Lewisohn points out, is the closest they ever got to Penny Lane.

WEST DERBY

Pete Best's mother Mona opened the Casbah Club in the basement of her house at 8 Haymans Green. The Quarry Men played the opening night in August '59 – the first of some 44 gigs there.

WEST KIRBY

In February '62, The Beatles played the Macdona Hall on the corner of Banks Road and Salisbury Avenue (above the Thistle Cafe) – their first official booking under Brian Epstein's management.

Home of Paul Humphries, who founded Orchestral Manoeuvres In The Dark with schoolfriend Andy McCluskey.

WOOLTON

John Lennon attended Quarry Bank High School in Harthill Road. His skiffle group The Quarry Men played there in July '57.

It was on 6th July '57, when The Quarry Men played a garden fete at St. Peters Church that John Lennon met Paul McCartney for the first time.

The Undertakers under the shadow of Liverpool's cathedral

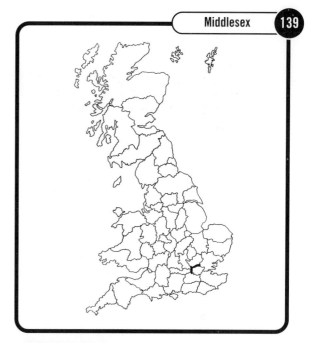

MIDDLESEX

(all within Greater London boundry, but with Middlesex postal address)

Mungo Jerry at the Hollywood Festival

ASHFORD

Birthplace of frontman Ray Dorset, 21.3.46 (Mungo Jerry); singer Chris Thompson, 19.3.57 (Boothill Foot Tappers, Barely Works).

Marc Bolan's T Rex cohort Steve Peregrine Took attempted to kick his heroin habit at the Ashford Hospital in London Road.

BRENTFORD

In the early Sixties, Rod Stewart was an apprentice at Brentford football club... but only briefly!

Home of Demon Records, originally set up by Stiff founder Jake Riviera and Radar founder Andrew Lauder.

CRANFORD

Ian Gillan made his first public appearance at St. Dunstans Youth Club, fronting The Moonshiners.

Brothers Mark and Scott Morriss of The Bluetones attended Cranford Community School.

Two of Twice As Much

EDGWARE

Birthplace of singer Andrew Rose, 12.3.47 (Twice As Much); drummer Dave Mattacks, 3.48 (Fairport Convention); singer Steve Ellis, 7.4.50 (Love Affair, Widowmaker); singer Jenny Haan (Babe Ruth); singer Billy Idol, 30.11.55.

ENFIELD

Birthplace of John Dalton, 21.5.43 (Kinks); Lenny Davidson, 30.5.44 (Dave Clark Five); Johnny Almond, 20.7.46 (Mark Almond).

Cliff Richard worked as a credit control clerk at Ferguson's TV and radio factory on Great Cambridge Road from September '57 until August '58, when (against all advice) he gave up his day job to become a rock'n'roll star!

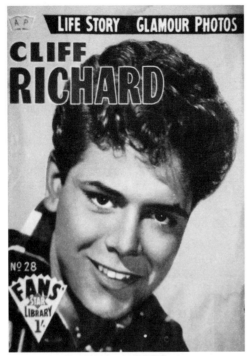

Cliff gives up his day job and goes for the knighthood

Operational base of psychedelic pop-art group Creation (chart stars in '66 and an inspiration to Alan McGee), Hocus Pocus (who changed their name to UFO in summer '69 and ultimately became one of the world's biggest HM draws), and mid-Seventies popsters Chufff (who achieved huge though brief chart success as Kenny).

FELTHAM

Brian May lived at 6 Walsham Road and attended Cardinal Road Infants before moving on to Hanworth Road Primary. Freddie Mercury and his family also lived here, following their flight from Zanzibar in '64.

Local band The Guana Batz topped the '85 indie album chart with 'Held Down To Vinyl – At Last'.

GREENFORD

Birthplace of television producer Jack Good, 7.8.31 (*6.5 Special, Oh Boy!*).

It was at the Oldfield Hotel in Oldfield Lane that Keith Moon managed to talk his way into The Who. He had played the venue many times as drummer with The Beachcombers.

Jeff Beck Group drummer Micky Waller went to Greenford Grammar School.

The Starlite was a hot Sixties venue; Cream played there in December '66.

In his song 'Hoover Factory', Elvis Costello sang of the scrolls and inscriptions which decorate that art deco edifice on the Western Avenue. Designed by architects Wallis and Gilbert in 1932, it was later acquired by Tesco and converted into a supermarket.

HAMPTON

Birthplace of guitarist Brian May, 19.7.47 (Queen); guitarist Colin Earle (Mungo Jerry).

Future Yardbirds Jim McCarty and Paul Samwell-Smith first met at Hampton Grammar, where Brian May was also a pupil (gaining ten O levels and 4 A levels).

Home of Sixties beat group The Others, who often appeared at the Thames Hotel R&B club.

Teenage riot girls Skinned Teen became early Nineties cult faves.

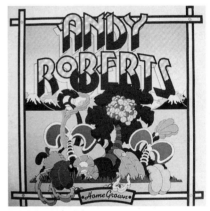

Andy Roberts' solo album

HARROW

Birthplace of Mike Vernon, 20.11.44 (producer); guitarist Andy Roberts (Liverpool Scene); Peter Andre, 27.2.73 (number one with Flava in September '96).

Former pupils of Harrow Art School include Charlie Watts (Rolling Stones), Malcolm McLaren, Marco Pirroni (Adam's chief Ant), The Models (punkers), Blancmange (electro poppers).

Former pupils of Harrow County Grammar School include Episode Six, who lost their impetus when two of them (Roger Glover and Ian Gillan) joined Deep Purple in '69, Kimberley Rew (guitarist/songwriter in Katrina & The Waves) and Jamie Stewart (bass player in The Cult).

Harrow public school frowned on the pursuit of popular music, but five pupils sought fame and fortune as The Band Of Angels. Singer Mike D'Abo found both when he replaced Paul Jones in Manfred Mann and guitarist John Gaydon was later manager of Roxy Music and ELP. Another Harrow pupil was Chris Blackwell, founder of Island Records.

Aspiring politician/rock'n'roll star Screaming Lord Sutch was a local lad, working as a plumber's mate before his dreams got the better of him. During the Seventies, he lived at the White Lodge in Watford Road.

Keith Moon went to night classes at Harrow Tech – studying transistors. He secured a position as drummer with local group The Beachcombers at an audition at the Conservative Hall in Lowlands Road.

The British Legion Hall in Northolt Road, South Harrow became an R&B venue during the mid-Sixties; Little Walter played there in October '64.

Local R&B group the Bo Street Runners won the *Ready Steady Go!* talent contest in '64; The Karibas were led by light-headed Don James; and Wainwright's Gentlemen featured Ian Gillan on vocals. After he left, they evolved into The Sweet.

Legendary Beetle

HAYES

Birthplace of disc jockey Chris Denning, 10.5.41; drummer Honey Lantree, 28.8.43 (Honeycombs); bass player Frank Allen, 14.12.43 (Searchers); Fifties rocker Larry Page (then known as The Teenage Rage – later manager of The Kinks and The Troggs); bass player Steve Priest, 23.2.50 (Sweet).

Rick Wakeman's first band, The Atlantic Blues, made their début at a pub in Hayes. His organ had been shaken to pieces in the van and he had to play the pub piano – at the other end of the room from the rest of the band.

Home of Rick Barrow, singer with Aloof.

HEATHROW AIRPORT

Weeping fans waved off the US bound Beatles in February '64; revolted travellers reeled as The Sex Pistols puked and swore in January '77.

Rick Wakeman surrounded by adoring keyboards

Rick Wakeman attended and was baptised at South Harrow Baptist Church, where he was also a Sunday School teacher.

During the mid-Seventies, the Tithe Farm in Eastcote Lane was part of the Pub Rock circuit, presenting the likes of Brinsley Schwarz and Graham Parker – but changing tastes reduced it to a disco.

Ritual were early Eighties goths; during the early Nineties, local bands included youthful grunge trio Bowlfish (sic) and crusties Children Of The Bong. In the mid-Nineties came ambient/techno phenomenon Bedouin Ascent.

You want trivia? Check this: the owner of the white Volkswagen LMW 281F, pictured on the sleeve of Abbey Road, belonged to Malcolm Tanner – then resident in North Harrow.

Ritchie Blackmore's first ever session as a guitarist, recorded while at work

Ritchie Blackmore worked as an aircraft radio mechanic in the early Sixties; a few years later, student Freddie Mercury worked in the catering department.

Lemmy's first bass was bought at a London Airport auction. He acquired it for £27.50.

HESTON

Birthplace of guitarist Jimmy Page, 9.1.44, at the Grove Nursing Home, 18 The Grove.

Ritchie Blackmore (Deep Purple) attended Heston Secondary – now Lampton Comprehensive.

Sometime home of singer Polly Brown (Pickettywitch).

HILLINGDON

Birthplace of Ron Wood, 1.6.47 (Rolling Stones); Steve Luscombe, 29.10.54 (Blancmange).

In the Seventies, disc jockey Dave Cash lived in Tudor Way.

HOUNSLOW

Birthplace of Ian Gillan, 19.8.45 (Deep Purple); Ian McLagan, 12.5.46 (Small Faces).

Housed above the A1 Car Showrooms in the High Street, opposite the bus station, was hot R&B club the Attic, which became the Ricky Tick in '66 – presenting the likes of Cream, Hendrix (November '66), Eric Burdon & The New Animals (November '66) and Pink Floyd (February '67).

The Strawbs with Sandy Denny whose deft hand at the chalk later featured on a Fairport Convention sleeve

During the late Sixties, Dave Cousins of The Strawbs ran an Arts Lab at the White Bear pub in Kingsley Road. His attempts to bring mixed-media events to the suburbs went unheeded by a hippie audience interested only in loud progressive rock. Strawbs guitarist Dave Lambert was previously in local band Fire, whose *Magic Shoemaker* album (ignored at the time) is now worth considerably more than 32/6d.

Local band Scissor Fits will be remembered for their' 78 single 'I Don't Want To Work For British Airway'. Actifed were early Eighties punks.

Depeche Mode's video of 'See You' was shot in McLary's Easi-Coin Launderette and Woolworth's, both in the High Street.

After five years of rehearsing in their rented Hounslow home, 189 Brabazon Road, The Bluetones (cited as Prince's favourite UK group) emerged in '95 with the Top Twenty album *Bluetonic*. For a time, Dodgy also lived there.

Local mid-Nineties hopefuls included Blowfly.

The Rifleman was a late Nineties indie gig.

Ex-Arts Lab founder, Keith Monroe, recorded a stereo demonstration disc in his Hounslow front room

ICKENHAM

Home of hot early Nineties indie band The Wilsons.

ISLEWORTH

Birthplace of Fifties coffee bar rocker Vince Taylor, 14.7.39 (the subject of a Golden Earring single and an inspiration to David Bowie); guitarist Fast Eddie Clarke, 5.10.50 (Motorhead, Fast Way).

In September '64, 18-year-old Freddie Mercury started at Isleworth Polytechnic.

KENTON

Kevin Rowland lived in Kenton as a teenager.

NORTHOLT

Home of rapper and television host Normski.

NORTHWOOD

A resident of Frome Court in Pinner Road, Elton John started his career as a pub pianist at Northwood Hills Hotel in '64.

Another local lad, Tim Blake released a couple of solo albums as well as playing with Gong and Hawkwind.

PERIVALE

Birthplace of Chris Thomas, 13.1.47 (producer); keyboard star Rick Wakeman, 18.5.49 (Strawbs, Yes); guitarist Richard Oakes, 1.10.76 (Suede).

PINNER

Birthplace of Elton John, 25.3.47, who was educated at Pinner County Grammar.

Simon LeBon attended West Lodge Infants and Primary School, and sang in the choir at Pinner Parish Church.

PONDERS END

Birthplace of Dave Peacock, 24.5.45 (Chas And). He went to Elmer Road School and actually recorded a track (on an early Chas & Dave album) called 'Ponders End Allotments Club'! How obscure can you get?

The Paranoids at the London Colney Mosquito Museum, 1980

(Mick Young)

RUISLIP

Local groups include The Paranoids (punks).

Roy Wood was educated at Ruislip Manor.

SHEPPERTON

In '77, The Who purchased a chunk of Shepperton Studios for rehearsal, storage, filming, etc.

SOUTHALL

Birthplace of bass player Nick Simper, 3.11.46 (Deep Purple); and jazz singer Cleo Laine, 28.10.27, who met her future husband, Johnny Dankworth after a gig at Southall British Legion Club in '51.

During the Fifties/Sixties, the town's main venue was the Dominion – now a Sikh temple.

Future manager Ken Pitt first saw Manfred Mann at the Hamborough Tavern in '63. The pub continued to present bands until a 4 Skins gig in July '81, when it was burned to the ground during race riots which erupted between local Asians and NF skinheads/pinheads.

Top progressive venue was the Farx Club at the Northcote Arms. Mott The Hoople played the first of several gigs there in December '69.

Operational base of punk band The Ruts, who found the '79 Top Ten with 'Babylon's Burning'. The group foundered after the heroin death of singer Malcolm Owen in July '80.

People Unite was a record label with offices at 45 Lea Road. Early releases were by Misty In Roots.

STAINES

The Town Hall was a popular gig in the Sixties.

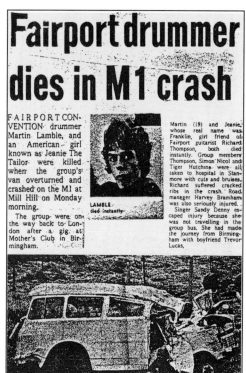

Fairport drummer dies in M1 crash

FAIRPORT CONVENTION drummer Martin Lamble, and an American girl known as Jeanie The Tailor were killed when the group's van overturned and crashed on the M1 at Mill Hill on Monday morning.

The group were on the way back to London after a gig at Mother's Club in Birmingham.

LAMBLE: died instantly

Martin (19) and Jeanie, whose real name was Franklin, girl friend of Fairport guitarist Richard Thompson, both died instantly. Group members Thompson, Simon Nicol and Tiger Hutchins were all taken to hospital in Stanmore with cuts and bruises. Richard suffered cracked ribs in the crash. Road manager Harvey Bramham was also seriously injured.

Singer Sandy Denny escaped injury because she was not travelling in the group bus. She had made the journey from Birmingham with boyfriend Trevor Lucas.

(Barnet Express)

The sad death of Martin Lamble

STANMORE

Fairport Convention were taken to the Royal National Orthopaedic Hospital after their van careened off the M1 in May '69. The others survived, but doctors were unable to save either drummer Martin Lamble or their friend Jeannie Franklyn, who made clothes for rock stars. Jack Bruce dedicated his first solo album to her memory – *Songs For A Tailor*.

SUDBURY

In '60, the first line-up of Screaming Lord Sutch & The Savages rehearsed in the back room of the Swan public house.

SUNBURY-ON-THAMES

In its eighth year (August '68), the National Jazz Blues & Rock Festival was held at Kempton Park racecourse. Arthur Brown was the star, but 74 fans were injured when a catwalk roof collapsed.

Noel Coward

TEDDINGTON

Birthplace of Noel Coward, 16.12.1899.

When he was discovered and turned into a star, Matt Monro was a bus driver on the number 27 route between Teddington and Highgate.

When Tony James and Mick Jones were forming their punk group London SS, they lived at opposite ends of that very route – a two and a half hour ride, just to rehearse and formulate plans.

TWICKENHAM

Birthplace of Dave King, 1929 (Top Five with 'Memories Are Made Of This' in '56); guitarist Vic Briggs, 14.2.45 (Animals) and Justine Frischman, 1968 (Elastica), who went to St. Pauls Comprehensive School – along with Senseless Things drummer Cass Browne.

The hotel on Eel Pie Island (approached by the footbridge at the end of Water Lane) contained a dance hall which was first used as a jazz club in '56. By the early Sixties, it had become one of the hottest R&B venues in the London area. The Rolling Stones played there 23 times over summer '63, and were followed by Jeff Beck, The Who and any other group that could wail into the night – including Pink Floyd, who played there several times in early '67, and Mott The Hoople, who played there

in October '70. Already beaten up, it gradually disintegrated and finally burned down in '71. Now covered in town houses.

It was (so the story goes) on Twickenham station, following an Eel Pie Island gig in January '64, that Rod Stewart was approached by Long John Baldry to join him in fronting The Hoochie Coochie Men.

In late '69, Genesis played their second ever gig at Eel Pie Island (then briefly known as Col Barefoot's Rock Garden) and their third at Twickenham Technical College in Egerton Road. They got paid five quid and fifty quid respectively.

Operational base of The Strawbs (originally a folk trio called the Strawberry Hill Boys), The Muleskinners (with future Small Face Ian McLagan), hot R&B combo The Downliners Sect, and No Sweat (who failed to make it despite a contract with local resident Pete Townshend's Eel Pie label).

Both *Hard Day's Night* and *Help* were filmed at Twickenham Studios, and additional scenes were shot in nearby Ailsa Avenue.

Teenager Ritchie Blackmore's first group had a residency at Vicki Burke's Dancing Studio in King Street. He left them to join another Twickenham group, Mike Dee & The Jaywalkers.

The Crown at 174 Richmond Road housed an epochal folk and blues club where the likes of The Levee Breakers, Bert Jansch and Davy Graham played.

Pete Townshend was a Twickenham resident for years, living by the riverbank opposite Eel Pie Island, where he had a home studio. His Eel Pie studio is now also by the river, close to Twickenham Bridge.

The Winning Post on the Great Chertsey Arterial Road was a hot progressive era venue.

Brian May's first band 1984 rehearsed at Chase Bridge Primary School before their début at St. Mary's Church Hall in October '64.

When he moved down from Liverpool in the early Seventies, Elvis Costello worked at the Midland Bank's Netherton branch.

Operational base for Nineties bands The Grateful Dads and The Senseless Things – who won a contract with Epic and took 'Easy To Smile' into the '92 Top Twenty.

UXBRIDGE

Denham was the birthplace of the great R&B pioneer Cyril Davies, 1932.

Local bands include The Lurkers ('76) from Ickenham. They plotted in the Coach & Horses pub.

In late '69, Genesis played one of their earliest gigs at Brunel College; in November '78, Joy Division played their second southern gig there. In the mid-Seventies, future Generation X punk Tony James was a student.

In March '82, Gary Numan was acquitted of carrying an offensive weapon – a baseball bat – at the Magistrates Court.

The Rolling Stones and friends

WEALDSTONE

One of the hottest R&B venues of the mid-Sixties was the Railway Hotel, adjacent to Harrow and Wealdstone station. It was here that The Who were accidentally discovered by future manager Kit Lambert, who just happened to be driving past one evening in late '64 and thought he'd investigate the long queue. The promoter was Pete Townshend's Ealing Art School pal Richard Barnes, who later wrote a book on The Who.

WEMBLEY

Keith Moon's childhood home was 224 Tokyngton Ave – until at the age of three, when the family moved to 134 Chaplin Road. He went to Alperton Secondary Modern School (where another pupil was pioneer R&B guitarist Bernie Watson), and joined the Sea Cadets in Linthorpe Road. Moon was still living in Chaplin Road when he married Kim Kerrigan and became a father.

Mari Wilson (Top Ten with 'Just What I Always Wanted' in '82) went to Preston Manor Grammar. Piano genius Nicky Hopkins went to the County Grammar. Maxine Nightingale (Top Ten with 'Right Back Where We Started From' in '75) was also a local lass.

Two of the London area's largest venues are next door to each other – the Arena (formerly the Empire Pool) and the outdoor Stadium.

The Arena has presented rock shows since the Fifties – usually multi-starred packages. The Beatles appeared there four times, always as one of many acts at the *NME*'s annual Poll-Winners' Concert. When the pop audience expanded, single acts were able to fill it amply – for example David Bowie (six nights in May '76). Most bizarre gig was when Rick Wakeman presented his ice spectacular. Recent stars have included The Manic Street Preachers and Catatonia (December '98), Sheryl Crowe and Robbie Williams (February '99).

The Stadium has resounded to Little Richard ('72... Malcolm McLaren was a programme seller), Elton John and

The Beach Boys (June '75), The Who (August '79), Live Aid (July '85), Wham's farewell concert (June '86), four nights of Genesis (June '87), three of Madonna (August '87), Nelson Mandela's 70th birthday tribute (June '88), seven nights of Michael Jackson (July '88), Bon Jovi (June '95) and many more, including Bruce Springsteen, Queen, U2 and The Rolling Stones. Mick Ronson's last appearance was at the Freddie Mercury Tribute Concert in April '92. Fifties star Ronnie Carroll never made the stage there, but in '49, as an Irish Schoolboy international, he scored directly from a corner kick in a 2-1 victory over England Schoolboys.

The Rediffusion Studios in Empire Way were used for the last series of *Ready Steady Go*!, and The Rolling Stones (with assistance from John & Yoko, Jethro Tull, Eric Clapton, The Who, Marianne Faithfull and others) filmed their *Rock & Roll Circus* there in December '68. It was finally screened in October '96.

The first customers at the new De Lane Lea studios, opened in September '81, were Queen, who cut the demo tape which eventually secured a recording contract.

WEST DRAYTON

Home base for Cliff Bennett & The Rebel Rousers and Ron Wood's R&B group, The Birds.

In the Nineties, the Angler's Retreat earned a reputation as a good indie venue.

WHITTON

During the late Seventies, Elvis Costello lived here and Yardbirds singer Keith Relf died here – of electrocution in May '76.

In '71, Madness saxplayer Lee Thompson broke into Whitton Hospital and made off with a bag containing 130 quid - resulting in a thirteen month sentence.

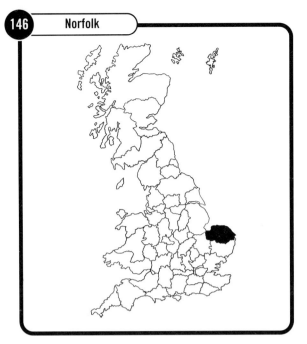

NORFOLK

Legendary John The Postman album

DISS
The notorious Singing Postman had a ditty about a Pretty Little Miss From Diss!

Early Seventies progressive band the Global Village Trucking Company were based here.

EAST DEREHAM
When pre-hit Pink Floyd played the Wellington Club April '67, uncomprehending turnip-head punters threw beer bottles at them. Jimi Hendrix appeared there in October'67 and apparently survived unscathed.

Some of Eighties Peel faves The Farmers Boys came from here; in the Nineties, The Badgers were being touted as the area's best ever band.

FELTWELL
Katrina & The Waves were based here. Two of the group's parents lived on the US air base.

GREAT YARMOUTH
Birthplace of trad jazz and skiffle pioneer Ken Colyer, 18.4.28.

The only local bands of note appear to have been Sixties beatsters The Sons Of Fred — remembered for their name rather than their music — and the rather more successful Peter Jay & The Jaywalkers, whose leader went on to run a multi-million pound entertainment empire embracing the Hippodrome Circus, the Royalty Theatre, Rosie O'Grady's night club and Wally Windmill's play centre.

The Billy Fury movie *I Gotta Horse* was largely shot in the area, while Billy was in summer season; and Madness shot their 'House Of Fun' video at Great Yarmouth Funfair.

The Beatles appeared at the ABC cinema in Regent Road twice in summer '63.

Tiffanys on Marine Parade was an Eighties gig.

In the Eighties, Tich Turner's Escalator were tipped to break out — but didn't.

Local indie bands Stare and Ivy began to gig nationally in the early Nineties.

HEMSBY
Pontin's Holiday Centre in Beach Road became a favourite venue for rock'n'roll weekends. Elvis Presley's sidekicks, Scotty Moore and DJ Fontana, played there in October '93. Other star guests have included Bill Haley's Comets and Gene Vincent's Blue Caps.

KINGS LYNN
Birthplace of drummer Roger Taylor, 26.7.49 (Queen), who attended Gaywood Primary.

Home base for Sixties beat group The Boz People — led by Boz Burrell, later of King Crimson and Bad Company. Other local bands include Government Issue (punks), The Nuclear Socketts (Eighties), Shine and Strike! (Nineties).

The Regis Rooms and the Corn Exchange have always been popular gigs. Hawkwind played the latter as the first date on their '72 Space Ritual tour – and returned to the same venue in September '98. The Levellers visited in December '98.

Atlantic Records exec Phil Carson (who alerted the company to Led Zeppelin and AC/DC) went to King Edward VIII Grammar before joining The Karl Denver Trio; Blow Monkeys' leader Dr. Robert spent his youth here.

Operational base of Throbbing Gristle offshoot Chris & Cosey ("the industrial Sonny & Cher") and late Nineties arty-indie band Magoo (the only Sassenach band signed to Glasgow's Chemical Underground label).

Awesome heavy guitar monster album shot in the grounds of the University of East Anglia

NORWICH
Birthplace of jazz singer Beryl Bryden, 11.5.26 (she played washboard on Lonnie Donegan's 'Rock Island Line'); influential Fifties rocker Tony Sheridan, 21.5.40, who lived and went to school at Thorpe St. Andrew.

Sheridan's erstwhile backing group, The Beatles, made their one and only visit to the town in May '63, when they played the Grosvenor Rooms in Prince of Wales Road.

There were scores of local groups during the Sixties, but none made it out of East Anglia... Mr. Toad, Kiss, The Moving Finger, The Versions, The Plastic Dreamboat, The News and The Breakaways (led by Mike Patto). Also Pete Miller, who cut a couple of ultra-collectable singles.

In November '86, Billy Bragg was arrested and charged with criminal damage at a CND demo at the Bawburgh military base.

Home base of Eighties faves Serious Drinking – famous for their indie albums *The Revolution Starts At Closing Time* and *They May Be Drinkers Robin, But They're Also Human Beings*. Also of The Bardots, Gee Mr. Tracey, The Disruptions and The Farmers Boys – all of whom recorded for local label Backs, operating from St. Mary's Plain.

St. Andrews Hall was on the circuit during the Seventies/Eighties: Dr. Feelgood played there in September

'78; The Cure in May '81.

It was while discussing the integrity of his band The Manic Street Preachers with DJ Steve Lamacq after coming offstage in Norwich, that guitarist Richey Edwards took out a razor blade and cut 4 REAL into his forearm.

Local lass Cathy Dennis reached the '91 Top Five with 'Touch Me All Night Long'.

Catherine Wheel made their début at the Arts Centre in September '90, and began their chart run a year later. Other early Nineties hopefuls included Basti, The Passing Clouds, Red Harvest, Fur, Magic Johnson, Oilseed Rape, Yoghurt Belly and The Spinning Jennys. In the mid-Nineties came The Halftime Oranges (football obsessed), Action Jacks (garage surf), The Lemongrowers, Goober Patrol, Waddle (grunge trio), Beth Orton (who had an *NME* Single of the Week in '96) and Fiel Garvie (who had an *MM* Single of the Week).

Passing through the University of East Anglia were The Higsons and half of Haircut 100. Robyn Hitchcock alluded to the former in his song 'Listening To The Higson's, which included the classic couplet "The Higsons come from Norwich, they eat a lot of porridge". Years later, Messiah, who came together at the University, watched their rave-friendly version of 'I Feel Love' sail into the '92 Top Twenty. Next university band was Navigator ('96)

In the Eighties, Cromwells in Edward Street was a popular

The Waterfront venue in Norwich

(Steve Forster)

venue; in the Nineties, the places to be were the Waterfront and Fat Pauley's. Based at the Arts Centre at 62 St. Benedicts Street, the Wilde Club has been going since '88 and is an ardent supporter of local acts and cool name bands. King Of The Slums was first visitor, followed by Oasis, Catatonia, Shed Seven, Lush and many more.

SNETTERTON
In his motor racing début on the circuit here, Andrew Ridgeley came 20th.

WEST RUNTON
The Pavilion was a popular venue, presenting everyone from Motorhead to The Cure to The Buzzcocks to Generation X.

NORTHAMPTONSHIRE

CORBY

Big Country's album *Steeltown* was dedicated to Corby.

Operational base of mid-Sixties group The Champagne, who recorded for Pye, and Jonathan King's proteges St. Cecilia, who are remembered only for the execrable 'Leap Up And Down (Wave Your Knickers In The Air)'.

Sometime home of Bill Drummond (Big in Japan, KLF), who attended the Grammar School in Oakley Road, and session drummer John Shearer, who moved to London to join Moon and subsequently played with Joan Armatrading and Mike Oldfield.

Joe Strummer of The Clash promised the people of Corby a Pink Cadillac – which was delivered, but never became roadworthy.

Local venues include the Festival Hall and the Earlstrees Club.

A '72 compilation album *Corby Catchment Area* sold 23 copies, mainly to family and friends of the featured acts. Late Seventies band Scene Stealer looked promising, but split after one album.

Popular Seventies venue the Nag's Head re-opened for gigs in the early Nineties.

Local early Nineties band Peggy's Boys (best described as thrash-folk) have apparently been banned from most local pubs – so they must be doing something right. Seen as rather more acceptable are Full Moon Scientist.

Sandy at home

BYFIELD

Home of Sandy Denny, singer with Fairport Convention – who used to rehearse in the village hall at nearby Aston Le Walls.

DEENE

Since the early Nineties, the annual Greenbelt Festival has been held at Deene Park.

The hallowed Fotheringay band logo

That album with The Kettering Song

FOTHERINGHAY

The Fairport Convention song 'Fotheringay' was written after Sandy Denny had visited the castle where Mary Queen Of Scots was beheaded in 1587. She never got the spelling right, not even when she left Fairport to form a group called Fotheringay.

HIGHAM FERRERS

Home of early Nineties indie band The Wishplants.

KETTERING

Birthplace of *6.5 Special* star Jim Dale, 15.8.35; and Jim King, 5.5.42, who lived in Hawthorn Road and led James King & The Farinas before moving to London with Family.

Sometime communal home of Dandelion group Principal Edwards Magic Theatre, who included 'The Kettering Song' on their '71 album *The Asmoto Running Band*.

Late Sixties psychedelic band The Surgeons mutated into early Seventies prog rock band Dodo Resurrection – whose album now fetches colossal money at collectors' fairs.

Watercress Harry's became a hot local gig in the early Nineties.

In the late Nineties, The Juneket were looking to infiltrate the London scene.

NORTHAMPTON

Birthplace of guitarist Harvey Hinsley (Hot Chocolate); singer Copper Marshall, 21.4.48 (Paper Dolls); guitarist Tony Poole, 28.7.50 (leader of Seventies band Starry Eyed And Laughing); keyboard player Richard Coles, 23.6.62 (Communards); disc jockey Jo Whiley, 1965 (Radio 1).

A local resident during the mid-Sixties, Ian Hunter lived in St. James' End and Alcombe Street. He had moved from Shrewsbury to play in local bands The Apex and The Shriekers. In '66, he moved to London to join Freddie 'Fingers' Lee's rock'n'roll band and three years later emerged as the star front man of Mott The Hoople.

The Fairport Convention song 'Close To The Wind' describes events leading up to the last public mass hanging in Britain.

The Sex Pistols played an early gig at Northamptonshire's Cricket Club in Wantage Road – where punk band 999 made their début in January '77.

Rockabilly revivalists The Jets scored a string of early Eighties hits. From St. James End, they regularly played the St. James Working Man's Club and drank at the Welcome in Grafton Street.

Operational base of mid-Eighties indie-cult The Jazz Butcher; sometime home of indie label star Ivo Watts-Russell, who started 4AD.

Led by Rolo McGinty, The Woodentops signed with Rough Trade and topped the indie charts with two late Eighties albums. Their local rivals were Where's Lisse?

In the early Eighties, various local musicians and art school bods from groups like The Submerged Tenth and The Craze channelled their energies into Bauhaus, who made waves nationally until leader Peter Murphy left to go solo and become a screen star. Offshoot group Love & Rockets made the global big time in summer '89, with US Top Three hit 'So Alive'. Another off-shoot Tones On Tail, languished in indie isolation.

Home of Nice singer/bass player Lee Jackson, Matthews Southern Comfort guitarist Mark Griffiths, Hollies singer Allan Clarke (in a nearby village), and Ram Jam Band bassplayer Dick Rabel, who opened the Music Market. Another chart star with local connections is Des O'Connor, who worked in Church's shoe factory until becoming a Butlins redcoat. (Des also played football for Northampton FC).

Local Sixties beatsters The Primitives (singles on Pye) boasted longer hair than The Pretty Things; the home-pressed début album by Seventies prog-rockers The Dark was said by *Record Collector* to be among Britain's rarest collectors' treasures, worth £1,500; in the Eighties, local indie faves included The Telltale Hearts and their offspring, The Head Skaters.

In the Nineties came Venus Flytrap, rapper MC Wildski, hip-hoppers Express and Sumosonic.

Nineties venues include the Roadmenders Club (local and national bands) and the Irish Centre.

OUNDLE

Singer/guitarist Nick Garvey (Ducks DeLuxe, The Motors) went to Oundle public school before going coast to coast. A later pupil was Iron Maiden's Bruce Dickinson, who is rumoured to have been expelled for urinating in a master's dinner. Surely this can't be true.

Drummer Ginger Baker (Graham Bond, Cream) lived at nearby Polebrook before moving to the States.

The Ship Inn presented interesting indie bands in the Nineties – including the local Hoover Dam, who attracted press acclaim on early London visits.

ROTHWELL

Childhood home of Jim Dale, who reached the '57 top three with 'Be My Girl'. He went to Northampton Grammar, but left at 15 to become an office boy.

RUSHDEN

Operational base of politicos Tribe Of Dan, who released their first album in '92.

SPRATTON

Operational base of early Eighties neo-mods The Retreads, whose '81 single 'Would You Listen, Girl' now changes hands for 40 quid or more.

WATFORD GAP

In the Sixties and Seventies, the Blue Boar service station on the M1 was a traditional pit-stop for one-nighter bands – but the food and ambience drew pointed criticism. Roy Harper was moved to record his observations on 'Watford Gap' – which was hastily removed from his album *Bullinamingvase* after EMI were threatened with legal action over such colourful descriptions as "grease" and "crap".

WELLINGBOROUGH

Birthplace of Bauhaus singer Peter Murphy. The group made its début at the Cromwell pub on New Year's Eve '78.

Also the birthplace of singer Thom Yorke, 7.10.68 (Radiohead).

WOLLASTON

John Peel did a regular Friday night gig at the Nags Head during the early Seventies, featuring up and coming groups like Wishbone Ash and Help Yourself.

NORTHUMBERLAND

BERWICK-UPON-TWEED
Birthplace of Susan Maughan, who wanted to be 'Bobby's Girl'.

BLYTH
Birthplace of Graham Bell (Skip Bifferty, Bell & Arc).

CRAMLINGTON
Between September '74 and July '76, Sting taught at St. Pauls, a Primary school.

Lindisfarne on tour, 1978

Lindisfarne the place   (Nikki Lloyd)

HOLY ISLE
Site of the first establishment of Celtic Christianity in England, this was formerly called Lindisfarne – a name which the Newcastle group resurrected.

WARK
Home of Kathryn Tickell, the country's leading player of the Northumbrian pipes.

NOTTINGHAMSHIRE

BLYTH
Home of the late James Hamilton (died summer '96), respected disc jockey and critic. His house reportedly contained over 100,000 records, which were auctioned off.

BURTON JOYCE
Sometime home of pioneering music journalist Richard Williams, son of a local vicar.

Operational base of Nineties indie band The Fat Tulips.

LONG EATON
Birthplace of singer Corinne Drewery, 21.9.59 (Swing Out Sister).

MANSFIELD
First big local group was Shane Fenton & The Fentones. The guy who later became Alvin Stardust was in fact the second Shane... the first one died.

Previously known as Ricky Storm & The Storm Cats, The Mansfields were mid- Sixties faves. Split up when drummer Ric Lee joined Ten Years After.

It was at the Granada in October '62 that Little Richard first introduced a bogus heart attack routine into his act... falling from the top of his piano as if dead.

On tour with Helen Shapiro, The Beatles played the Granada Cinema in West Gate in February 63 – and returned there with Chris Montez and Tommy Roe the following month.

Home of new wavers B-Movie, heavy metallurgists Limelight and punk band Riot Squad, who reached the indie Top Twenty with their articulate '83 offering 'I'm Ok, Fuck You'.

Nineties faves are mod trio The Hybirds (sic), who recorded for Heavenly and toured as support to Oasis, and Slaughterhouse Five, who seemed to fare better in the States.

NEWARK
Home of original Fentones guitarist Jack Wilcock – now more famous for his guitar tuition tapes.

Sometime home of former Monkee Mickey Dolenz, who purchased a nearby farm and was often seen shopping in town.

Alvin Lee

NOTTINGHAM
Birthplace of guitar maestro Alvin Lee, 19.12.44 (Ten Years After); saxplayer Elton Dean, 28.10.45 (Bluesology, Soft Machine), from whom Reg Dwight took half his name; Rick Kenton, 31.10.45 (Roxy Music); drummer Ian Paice, 29.6.48

(Deep Purple); actress Su Pollard, 7.11.49 (Top Three with 'Starting Together' in '86); singer Graham Russell, 1.6.50 (Air Supply); singer Rob Birch, 11.1.61 (Stereo MC); singer Stuart Staples, 12.11.65 (Tindersticks).

Lonnie Donegan made his variety début at the Empire Theatre in September '56.

Formed in '61, The Jaybirds were billed as "the biggest sounding trio in the country". After working as The Ivy League's backing group, they became Ten Years After in November '66, releasing a dozen hit albums and touring the States 28 times before their demise in March '74.

In a different league altogether were the town's other big success, Paper Lace – two of whom were born in Nottingham: Philip Wright, 9.4.48; and Chris Morris, 1.11.54. They appeared to disappear after three '74 hits.

Other local breakouts include Sons And Lovers and The Nerve (Sixties); Deep Joy and Which What (early Seventies prog rock); Plummet Airlines (made waves on mid-Seventies London pub circuit); Gaffa (picked to click in '77 – but didn't), Fatal Charm and Medium Medium (new wave); Pinski Zoo, One Million Fuzztone Guitars and The Asphalt Ribbons (Eighties indie); The Naturalites (reggae); Concrete Sox and Heresy (thrash); C Cat Trance (Eighties weird).

The Tindersticks in early cassette release produced by John Langford of The Mekons and The Three Johns (see Leeds)

Notts County's Meadow Lane ground was the setting for a rock festival in summer '69, featuring Marmalade and Van der Graaf Generator.

In February '72, Paul McCartney & Wings turned up unannounced at the university and asked if they could do a gig. They could and did... a low profile world début!

David Coverdale's Whitesnake were supposed to make their world début at the Sky Bird Club in February '78 but the stage was too small – so they blew it out and travelled on to Lincoln.

In November '77, a copy of The Sex Pistols album, *Never Mind The Bollocks*, displayed in the window of Virgin Records in King Street, caused offence to a policewoman. (How very heartwarming that anyone in the police force could be fazed by the word bollocks!) A subsequent court case found Virgin not guilty to obscenity charges.

Paul Smith, founder of the Blast First label, was once a city bus driver. Keith Selby, founder of the Black Magic label, also ran the top vinyl emporium Selectadisc Records (three different shops in Market Street) – where Tindersticks singer Stuart Staples once worked.

In the Sixties, the major venues were the Dungeon and the Boat House on Trentside, where Led Zeppelin played in March '71. Later on, the Ad Lib Club at 41 St. Mary's Gate became fashionable, but in the Eighties/Nineties, the primo gig was Rock City in Talbot Street, where (among many millions more) The Damned played in October '86, Oasis in August '94, The Saw Doctors in November '98. Opened in October '97, the Bomb at 45 Bridlesmith Gate became a primo clubbers venue; the Maze catered for up and coming indie bands; the Running Horse was more folk and blues orientated.

Bands/artistes emerging in the Nineties included soul singer Donovan Whycliffe, Lawnmower Deth, Fudgetunnel, Bomb Everything (who used to be called Bomb Disneyland until the some emissary from the late Walt's empire got funny), State Of Grace, The Screaming Souls (featuring the daughter of ex-England footballer Dave Watson on vocals!) and Asphalt Ribbons, who evolved into the internationally successful Tindersticks.

In the mid-Nineties came Tabitha Zu, Pitch Shifter, 3:6 Philly, DIY, Godflesh (speed metal band led by local legend Justin Broadrick), Bob Tilton (Peel faves), The Wood Thieves and Six By Seven.

RETFORD
The Porterhouse at 20 Carolgate became one of the most popular gigs on the circuit, presenting such up and comers as Def Leppard, The Meteors and The Damned.

WORKSOP
Birthplace of Bruce Dickinson, 7.8.58 (Iron Maiden).

Billy Fury made his variety début at Worksop Regal in March 59.

Is that it? Pretty boring for such a large town.

Hang on, all is forgiven: it was also the operational base for early Eighties new wavers Bikini Atoll and the unforgettable Kev And Paul Play Shite All Night.

The only local Nineties gig appeared to be the Frog and Nightgown.

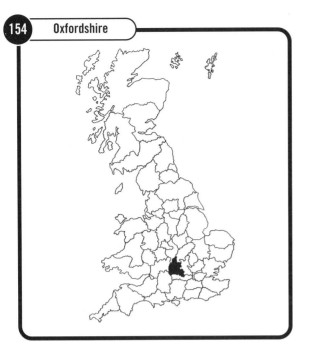

OXFORDSHIRE

Fairport Convention pause for a refresher at their Cropredy local

ABINGDON
Birthplace of Barron Anthony, 15.6.40 (Barron Knights); Carl Fysh, 25.1.63 (Brother Beyond); singer Tom Hingley, 9.7.65 (Inspiral Carpets).

Students at the exclusive Abingdon School in Park Road formed a band called On A Friday – a name later discarded in favour of Radiohead (after a track on the '86 Talking Heads album *True Stories*).

Unbelievable Truth broke out in the late Nineties – fronted by Andy Yorke, brother of Radiohead's Thom.

ASTON TIRROLD
During the late Sixties, Joe Cocker and Traffic occupied adjacent cottages on the Downs. The sleeve photos on the first two Traffic albums were shot here.

BANBURY
Birthplace of Gary Glitter, 8.5.40; techno guru Richie Hawtin, 1970 (Fuse, Plastikman), whose family emigrated to Ontario.

The back page of the *Daily Sketch* revealed how thugs known as the Swallow Gang attacked Sixties star Danny Storm for autographing local girls' knickers!

The Rolling Stones came to town to play the Winter Gardens in August '63.

Local early Eighties goth band Play Dead released a few singles and an album.

At the end of the Eighties, three Banbury Art College students and a friend formed Ride, who would sign with Creation and reach the Top Ten with Leave Them All Behind.

The Mill was a popular Nineties venue, presenting all the up and coming Oxford bands.

BARFORD ST. MICHAEL
Location of Wormwood Studios, made famous by Fairport and Jethro Tull.

BECKLEY
The Tribal Gathering at Otmoor Park in May '95 was Britain's biggest legal rave and a two-fingered salute to the Criminal Justice Act.

BICESTER
Deep Purple drummer Ian Paice grew up in Bicester.

Led by the newly arrived Fish, Marillion made their world début at the Red Lion pub in the Market Square in March '81.

CHINNOR
Birthplace of bass player Adam Clayton, 13.3.60 (U2).

CHIPPING NORTON

Owned and operated by producer Mike Vernon, the town's celebrated recording studio at 28-30 New Street has turned out hits for Level 42, Duran Duran, Howard Jones, The Proclaimers and scores more. Radiohead cut their '92 *Drill* EP there.

During the early Seventies, Keith Moon was co-owner of the Crown and Cushion public house in the High Street. Among his illustrious visitors were Elton John, Viv Stanshall and Ringo Starr.

CROPREDY

Sometime home of Fairport Conventionals Simon Nicol, Dave Swarbrick and Dave Pegg, who quaffed ale at The Brasenose – pictured on the sleeve of their album *Nine*. They played their "final" gig here on 4.8.79, and placed the village firmly on the folk-rock map with ever more stellar annual reunion concerts. The title track of their '88 album *Red And Gold* discusses the civil war battle which took place here in 1644.

DIDCOT

Pete Townshend and Karen Astley were Married at Didcot Register Office in May '68.

EPWELL

It was here that Van Morrison wrote many of the songs for his '79 album *Into The Music*. He got into pastoral mode by touring the area: Rolling Hills is his paean to the Cotswolds.

HENLEY-ON-THAMES

When rockers make it big, they look at houses in the Henley area. Among those who bought are George Harrison, Kenny Lynch, Tony Hicks (Hollies), Jon Lord (Deep Purple), Mick Ralphs (Bad Company), Joe Brown and Dave Edmunds.

Following local resident Dusty Springfieldís death in March 1999, fans lined the streets of Henley to pay their last respects as a glass-sided, horse drawn hearse carried her coffin to the funeral service at the Church of St Mary The Virgin.

LONG COMPTON

The Rollright Stones inspired a track on Traffic's '73 album *Shoot Out At The Fantasy Factory*. It was also the title of a piece on Mike Simmons' '98 ambient album *Compositions Of Stone*.

OXFORD

Birthplace of Legs Larry Smith, 18.1.44 (Bonzo Dog Band); singer Kip Trevor, 12.11.46 (Black Widow); Colin Fletcher, 27.10.54 (Troggs); Pennie Leyton, 1958 (Belle Stars); guitarists Ed O'Brien, 15.4.68, and Jonny Greenwood, 5.11.71, and bass player Colin Greenwood, 26.6.69 (all three of Radiohead); Mark Gardener, 6.12.69 – the same day as Altamont (Ride).

Despite its luxuriant literary heritage, the city of dreaming spires was a rock'n'roll dead zone. The biggest group appears to have been Mr Big, remembered for their '77 top five hit 'Romeo'. Six More Prophets were a mod band and The Half Human Band were weird.

In the Fifties, local lad Roy Young (from St. Ebbe's... his mother is thought to have worked at Joe's Cafe in Between Towns Road, Cowley) made a splash by covering Little Richard hits on *6.5 Special* while Mal Ryder from Wolvercote (leader of Mal Ryder & The Spirits) went to Italy to become a massive star.

Lonnie Donegan's smash hit 'Does Your Chewing Gum Lose Its Flavour On The Bedpost Overnight?' was recorded live at the New Theatre in George Street (later renamed the Apollo) in December '58.

Eric Clapton, then in R&B group The Roosters, played his first professional gig at the Carfax Assembly Rooms off Cornmarket in early '63. The Beatles also played there in February '63, supported by local group The Maddisons.

In June 64, The Rolling Stones prematurely completed a US tour and spent £1,500 on air fares to honour a longstanding booking at Magdalen College. Their fee... £400! Support group was again The Maddisons, who by this time had gone fully pro as The Falling Leaves.

The Forum was a jazz club cum R&B venue in the High Street in the early Sixties.

In March '64, at the zenith of their media popularity, The Beatles were persuaded to attend a charity dinner at Brasenose College – organised by future MP and author Jeffrey Archer! It was here that George Harrison examined the lavish fare and offered to trade his autograph for a jam butty!

David Bowie made his début as a mime artist in Lindsay Kemp's Pierrot In Turquoise at the New Theatre (Apollo) in December '67.

The Oxford Poly Gipsy Lane campus: students patiently await the formation of Radiohead

(R & M S, Oxford Brookes University)

The Eagles made their UK début at Oxford Polytechnic in Gypsy Lane, Headington, where the art school lecturers have included Humphrey Ocean, formerly in Ian Dury's group Kilburn & The High Roads, and Chris Dawsett, once in John's Children.

Most famous Oxford University student was Rhodes scholar Kris Kristofferson, who studied English at Merton and recorded for Top Rank as Kris Carson. He was also a light middleweight boxing blue in '59, but quit the sport on medical advice.

Other University students include Paul Jones, Paula Yates, June Tabor, Mike Ratledge (Soft Machine), Kit Lambert (manager of The Who), Simon Park (he of the Orchestra), Paul Gambaccini (author and disc jockey), Andrew Lloyd Webber, Jack Good (television producer), Johnny Rogan (rock author), Andrew Eldritch (Sisters Of Mercy).

Before she set her sights on Bob Geldof, Paula Yates went out with John Otway, who she met when he played the Oranges And Lemons pub in St. Clements Street. It was a brief affair... she stood him up on their second date. Who can blame her?

Mr Branson's manor

The Corn Dolly was a great Seventies/Eighties venue for up and coming bands like The Cure, who played there in December '78. Contemporary local acts included English Subtitles and Talulah Gosh.

At Oxford Crown Court in November '75, Bay City Roller Les McKeown was found guilty of assaulting two photographers and causing criminal damage after a gig at the New Theatre. He was fined £750 and sentenced to three months, suspended.

In tragic decline at 30, Bee Gee's brother Andy Gibb died at the John Radcliffe Hospital in March '88.

In the Nineties, it all started happening in Oxford as groups like Ride, The Candyskins (including two sons of actor Kenneth Cope), Radiohead and Swervedriver began to create a scene. Other early Nineties bands included The Jennifers, 2 Die 4, Death By Crimpers, The Purple Rhinos, Saturn V, Blueboy and Arthur Turner's Lovechild (a bizarre allusion to the former manager of Oxford United!). In the mid-Nineties came Supergrass (a Jennifers spin-off), who topped the '95 album chart with *I Should Coco*, the indie-ish Underbelly, beat-pop combo Thurman (Uma salivators) and The Nubiles.

The Jericho Tavern was a supportive venue – until it was closed and turned into a theme pub in '95. The Zodiac at 190 Cowley Road became a focal point, along with the Bullingdon Arms at 162 Cowley Road and the Point (formerly the Cape of Good Hope), where up and coming bands like Catatonia, Ultrasound and Space found a showcase.

In '97 (after Radiohead's album *The Bends* had been declared one of the finest in the history of rock), Oxford was proclaimed Radio One's Sound City and a slew of new bands began making waves – including The Full Monty, Dustball, Unbelievable Truth, Cody, The Bigger The God, Badge, Hurricane # 1, Beaker, Tumbleweed (including Charlie Coombes, younger brother of Gaz) and Animal House (led by ex-Ride singer Mark Gardener).

PYRTON
The video for Blur's '95 number one single Country House was shot at Pyrton Manor.

SHILLINGFORD
Birthplace of Bonzo Dog Band leader and noted eccentric Viv Stanshall, 21.3.43.

SHIPTON-ON-CHERWELL
In March 71, Virgin Records boss Richard Branson purchased the Manor House for £30,000 and turned it into a recording studio. His first signing, Mike Oldfield, spent a year there making *Tubular Bells*, which fortunately became a massive seller and the cornerstone of Branson's burgeoning Virgin empire. On 22.7.72, he married Kristen Tomassi at Shipton Parish Church.

THAME
UK residence of The Bee Gees, whose road crew are often to be seen quaffing in the local hostelries.

UFFINGTON
The White Horse, carved into the hillside off the A420 was the inspiration for the XTC album *English Settlement*.

UPPER HEYFORD
Thirty years before the jets took off for Libya, US Air Force serviceman Johnny Duncan was stationed here. He took advantage of the skiffle boom to reach the top three with 'Last Train To San Fernando' – but then swiftly disappeared.

WALLINGFORD
The Springs Hotel, a mock Tudor affair built in 1874, was the late Seventies home of Deep Purple singer Ian Gillan. It was he who installed the guitar-shaped swimming pool.

WATCHFIELD
The site of an August '75 free festival featuring 150 groups, including Hawkwind and The 101ers.

WHEATLEY
Operational base of Supergrass, who had found the *NME* rather more interesting than lessons at Wheatley Comprehensive. The Mystics are an extra-curricular spin-off.

WITNEY
Gentle Influence were late Sixties hopefuls.

(The Springs)

The Springs Hotel now has to explain Gillan's guitar-shaped pool to its guests

Hoffnung rocks Oxford

WOODSTOCK
Not the site of the famous festival (that was in New York State), but Barry Manilow did play at Blenheim Palace in '84. The gig was not a commercial success, by all accounts.

SHROPSHIRE

LUDLOW
Birthplace of sax player Dick Heckstall Smith, 26.9.34 (Graham Bond Organisation, Colosseum).

OSWESTRY
Birthplace of singer Ian Hunter, 3.6.39 (Mott The Hoople); drummer Alan Whitehead, 24.7.47 (Marmalade).

Carole Decker from pool attendant to T'Pau

(Quarry Swimming & Fitness Centre)

SHREWSBURY
Birthplace of drummer Simon Kirke, 28.7.49 (Bad Company).

In the Sixties, the Music Hall in the Square was the town's big venue. The Beatles played here in December '62 and April '63 – and managed to squeeze in a gig at the Granada Cinema in Castle Gates in February '63. Joe Brown played Wishee Washee in the Granada's Christmas '63 panto, Aladdin.

In the early Sixties, the appropriately named Outlaws (including Ritchie Blackmore and Chas Hodges) were in trouble with the local constabulary for opening the side door of their Dormobile and pelting pedestrians with bags of flour.

It was his adoration of local beauty queen Irene Wilde, whom he used to see in Barker Street bus station, that made teenager Ian Hunter (then a pupil at Priory Grammar School) determined to become a rock'n'roll star.

John Peel went to Shrewsbury School – as indeed did *Private Eye* founders Richard Ingrams and William Rushton, and James mainman Tim Booth.

Home of splendidly named new wave group Quality Fish and mid-Eighties Peel favourites The June Brides.

T'Pau singer Carol Decker did an art foundation course at college here, and in the summer holidays worked as a lifeguard, teaching toddlers to swim at Shrewsbury Baths.

TELFORD
The Oakengates Theatre is a happening late Nineties venue.
Surely something must have happened here!

WELLINGTON
In January '48, 13-year-old Brian Epstein started at Wrekin College – his ninth school!

Carol Decker moved here with her family at the age of five. Later she went to Wellington Girls' High School.

WESTON-UNDER-REDCASTLE
In March' 66, after watching Dave Vickers win a motorcycle scramble at Hawkstone Park, Roy Orbison broke his foot while taking a lap of honour. He continued his UK tour on crutches, remaining seated on stage.

SOMERSET

BATH

Birthplace of drummer Pete Salisbury, 24.9.71 (Verve).

In the early hours of Easter Sunday, 17.4.60, following a car crash on the outskirts of Chippenham, Eddie Cochran, Gene Vincent and Sharon Sheeley were taken to St. Martin's Hospital. Vincent had broken his collar bone and several ribs; Sheeley (Eddie's girlfriend) had a fractured pelvis; Cochran had multiple head injuries, from which he died that afternoon. His body was flown back to Los Angeles for burial, but later his fan club created a memorial garden in the hospital grounds.

The Beatles played at the Pavilion on North Parade in June '63; The Rolling Stones in November '63; Jimi Hendrix in February '67; Pink Floyd in April '67; Led Zeppelin in December '68 – they got £75; The Who (eight times between '65 and '70). Do bands of this calibre play in Bath these days?

After localised success as Graduate, Curt Smith and Roland Orzabal became Tears For Fears and put Bath on the map with a string of Top Ten hits. They first met at Beechen Cliff School.

Solsbury Hill

(Courtesy of the Bath Chronicle)

Bath University produced Naked Eyes (hot in the States in the mid-Eighties but soon forgotten here). Mark Kelly from Marillion was a student at the Academy of Art.

The Mirror and The Moquettes (both big locally in the mid-Sixties) and Interview (new wave) are among the few local acts to have made national ripples.

Local residents have included Peter Gabriel, Hugh Cornwell from The Stranglers and Van Morrison, who moved his administrative offices here in February '88. He was one of a number of hot acts to record at Wool Hall Studio at Castle Corner in nearby Beckington. Another was The Smiths, who cut *Strangeways Here We Come*.

Made world famous by Peter Gabriel on his début single, 'Solsbury Hill' is a local landmark rising between the villages of Batheaston and St. Catherine, to the north-west of town. Seven ley-lines pass through it – as would an A46 detour, if the Ministry of Transport had its way.

Before forming The Thompson Twins, Tom Bailey had a music workshop in Bath.

The celebrated Bath Festivals of the early Seventies were actually held in Somerset – at Shepton Mallet – except for the very first, which took place at City's football ground, Twerton Park in May '70. It featured Chicken Shack, Wishbone Ash and is memorable only as Peter Green's final gig with Fleetwood Mac.

Moles at 14 George Street acquired a reputation as the hottest late Eighties/early Nineties venue. James played a secret gig there in March '93.

In the Nineties, several local bands emerged – including Bigger Than God, The Warm Jets (an Eat spin-off) and The Propellorheads, who reached the '97 Top Ten with On Her Majesty's Secret Service.

CASTLE CARY
Yeovil band Blyth Power released an album titled *Guns On Castle Cary*.

FROME
Frenzy were a mid-Eighties rockabilly trio.

GLASTONBURY
One of the hippie era's great celebrations was the Glastonbury Fayre of June '71. The Pink Fairies, Al Stewart, Hawkwind (unveiling Stacia for the first time) and David Bowie were among the entertainers. It was £1 to get in – but you got free milk.

Nineties stars Reef formed here (initially as Naked) before removing to London and finding the '95 Top Twenty with Naked and Weird; Kula Shaker's Paul Winter-Hart was born here and was the drummer in Naked; Jurassic Shift stone-rockers Ozric Tentacles and their techno offshoot Eat Static lived here.

The Waterboys tried to catch the town's ambience on their '93 single, 'Glastonbury Song'.

(Karl Badger)

A young Karl Badger poses for the first ever Glastonbury Festival programme

GURNEY SLADE
This village gave its name to the rather strange '60's Anthony Newley television series. Its theme tune was a Top Ten hit for Max Harris.

KEYNSHAM
Through his incessant advertising on Radio Luxembourg, Horace Batchelor – inventor of "the Infradraw Method for the Football Pools" – gave this town legendary status. The Bonzo Dog Band later revived the name as the title of their fourth album.

MELLS
A large rambling farm housed a commune which included psychedelic group Magic Muscle and folksinger Keith Christmas.

MIDSOMER NORTON
Birthplace of Anita Harris, 3.6.44.

MINEHEAD
The rest of Status Quo first met Rick Parfitt at Butlins in summer '65. Rick was in The Highlights, a one boy/two girl trio. They shared dressing rooms with wrestlers who fixed their fights upfront.

PENSFORD
Birthplace of Mr Acker Bilk, 28.1.29. He broke out of the jazz clubs with the '60 hit 'Summer Set' – dedicated to his beloved county. It seems he could play clarinet better than he could spell.

PILTON
Worthy Farm became the June setting for the annual Glastonbury CND Festival, which always featured interesting acts. For example: New Order and Aswad in '81; Madness in '86; Elvis Costello in '87; Radiohead, Blur and Oasis in '94; Pulp in '96 (25th anniversary headliner); Bob Dylan in '98. In '84, Paddy Ashdown was a guest speaker; in '86, Billy Bragg's set was interrupted when the news came through that Maradona's hand of God goal had knocked England out of the World Cup; in '94, the pyramid stage burned down a week before the festival but was miraculously rebuilt by local craftsmen; in '98, the site became a mud bath. So what's new, asked punters.

PORTISHEAD
The coastal town made famous by the eponymous group, whose début album *Dummy* was a smash hit in '94.

SHEPTON MALLET
In June '69, only about 12,000 fans congregated at the

Keynsham, the album

curiously named Bath Festival, held here at the Bath and West Showground. Led Zeppelin headlined over The Nice, John Mayall, Taste, Ten Years After and Fleetwood Mac. Led Zep were also billtoppers a year later, over a glorious cast including Pink Floyd, Jefferson Airplane, The Byrds, The Moody Blues, Frank Zappa, Dr John, Santana, Country Joe and more. Over 150,000 turned up for that one.

In July '82, the same venue was the setting for the first WOMAD Festival – World of Music, Arts and Dance, underwritten by Peter Gabriel, who would continue to champion World Music and watch its gradual absorption into the rock mainstream.

STRATTON-ON-THE FOSSE
Echo & The Bunnymen drummer Pete de Freitas went to Downside Public School, where he played in Rigor Mortis & The Gravediggers.

STREET
Founded in '35 by Somerset cricketer Jack Meyer, Millfield Public School turned out a good line in disc jockeys, like Tony Blackburn and Pete Drummond, and sportsmen like Ian Botham, Gareth Edwards and Duncan Mayhew. Times change: recently the school has been the subject of lurid tabloid stories involving rape, booze and drugs.

Operational base for Nineties band The Tony Head Experience.

TAUNTON
Birthplace of violinist Darryl Way, 17.12.48 (Curved Air).

The Beatles played at the Gaumont Cinema twice – in February and September '63. Their manager, Brian Epstein had briefly attended Clayesmore public school.

Home of early Seventies Transatlantic label group Marsupilami.

WESTON-SUPER-MARE
Birthplace of Sixties thrush Valerie Mountain, 6.8.42; guitarist Ritchie Blackmore, 14.4.45 (Deep Purple, Rainbow); folkie, bluesman and *Folk Roots* editor Ian A Anderson, 26.7.47; guitarist Peter Gunn, 16.5.55 (Inmates).

Dezo Hoffmann's famous photos of The Beatles cavorting on the beach in Victorian bathing costumes were taken here in July '63, when they played six nights at the Odeon.

One of the few groups to make it out of town was rock'n'roll band Fumble; another was late Seventies Rak chartsters Racey. Local guitarist Graham Gregory (aka Kirby) worked with Stretch and Curved Air.

In '86, Vivian Stanshall entered Broadway Lodge in yet another doomed attempt to curb his reliance on pills and booze.

Home of classically trained session musician Anne Stephenson (Banshees, Marc Almond), formerly of The Ravishing Beauties.

YATTON
Home base for idiosyncratic early Seventies group Stackridge, who immortalised the town in 'Spaceships Over Yatton'. Members Andy Davis (born here on 10.8.49) and James Warren later formed The Korgis, internationally successful with 'Everybody's Got To Learn Sometime'.

YEOVIL
Birthplace of guitarist Jim Cregan, 9.3.46 (Cockney Rebel, Rod Stewart); Polly (PJ) Harvey, 9.10.69.

Mutter Slater's mum worked in Acorn Records, beaming happily whenever she sold an album by her son's group Stackridge.

Johnson Hall was a gig for name bands during the Sixties and Seventies.

Operational base of early Eighties anarchist trainspotters The Mob, whose leader later formed Blyth Power – named after a diesel loco scrapped in '75. Also of late Eighties group The Chesterfields, whose Ask Johnny Dee made the indie chart Top Five, and Nineties funsters The Family Cat, who cut minor hits on Dedicated. Paddy Ashdown's son played in local indie band The Becketts – who attracted press criticism for anti-Thatcher lyrics!

Polly Harvey studied at the Art College and played in local late Eighties band Automatic Dlamini. In the early Nineties, she championed Gutless. Other bands on the scene included techno duo Global Communications (and their alter-egos, Reload and Jedi Knights), indie hopefuls Basinger, Gear and Furnt (both spin-offs from The Chesterfields), The Psychonauts (electro) and Elliot Green. Supertramp lived at Southcombe Farm (somewhere in deepest Somerset, but not sure where) in late '73, writing *Crime Of The Century.*

Womad at Shepton Mallet

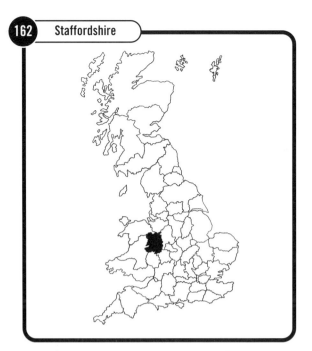

Julian Cope poses in Fazeley Saint Motors (Polsworth, near Tamworth) for his *Saint Julian* sleeve

STAFFORDSHIRE

BURSLEM
Birthplace of bass player Ian Kilminster, 24.12.45 – better known as Lemmy from Motorhead.

BURTON-UPON-TRENT
Birthplace of Joe Jackson, 11.8.55.

The happening punk gig was the Oasis Club, where The Sex Pistols played (later released as *Original Pistols Live*). Also popular was the 76 Club at 76 High Street. The Star & Garter seems to be a Nineties equivalent.

The Telescopes were late Eighties hopefuls.

CANNOCK
Birthplace of drummer Ric Lee, 20.10.45 (Ten Years After) and Robert Lloyd, whose bands include The Prefects, The Nightingales and The New Four Seasons.

The town's first star was Tanya Day, early Sixties chanteuse.

The Danilo Theatre presented The Rolling Stones in May '64.

Trapeze were formed locally in '68.

Hottest export of the late Eighties was Balaam & The Angel.

In December '92, Charlatans keyboard player Rob Collins was arrested for participating in the armed robbery of a local off-licence. He was subsequently sentenced to eight months in prison but, thanks to good behaviour, was back tickling the ivories after four. After his tragic car-accident death in July '96, local lad Tony Rodgers took his position in The Charlatans.

DARLASTON
Birthplace of John Fiddler, 25.9.47 (Medicine Head, British Lions).

HANLEY
The 1,600 capacity Victoria Hall in Albion Square was the start of the Kalin Twins/ Cliff Richard package tour of October '58. For the first time, Hank Marvin and Bruce Welch appeared as Cliff's sidemen. Forty years later, in November '98, Marvin would make a nostalgic detour to play the town's Theatre Royal.

The Beatles played at the Gaumont Cinema in Piccadilly twice in '63 – with the Helen Shapiro and

Roy Orbison package tours. The Stones played there in February '64.

The Place in Bryan Street was one of the first and most famous rhythm & blues clubs in Britain, presenting everyone from John Mayall to Derek & The Dominoes – and, in March '71, when they were absolutely huge, Led Zeppelin. "If it's going to happen, it'll happen at the Place first" said the posters.

In the late Nineties, the most popular jazz and blues venue was Satchmo's Lazy Bar in Glass Street.

LEEK

Hunter were tipped to become the new Cockney Rebel but were submerged by the New Wave.

The Swan is a late Nineties venue.

LICHFIELD

Local blues group The Broom Dusters split up in '67, when leader Jeremy Spencer helped form Fleetwood Mac.

The Victorian Parents released an album in the early Eighties; Madhalibut were early Nineties hopefuls; American TV Cops did a couple of mid-Nineties Peel sessions.

NEWCASTLE-UNDER-LYME

The town's most celebrated group was The Cyril Dagworth Players, featuring David (Isn't She Lovely?) Parton.

Nearby Madeley was the venue for the Hollywood Rock Festival of May '70 (so called because of adjacent thicket of holly trees), which featured Traffic, Colosseum, Quintessence and the UK début of The Grateful Dead.

One of Britain's first folk festivals was held at Keele University in '65. Former Keele students include Jem Finer of The Pogues.

Bridge Street Arts Centre is one of the best venues in the area.

ROCESTER

Birthplace of drummer Graeme Edge, 30.3.42 (Moody Blues).

RUGELEY

In June '89, en route from London to Liverpool, Bunnymen drummer Pete de Freitas was killed on the motorbike he'd ridden in the video for Julian Cope's 'China Doll'.

STAFFORD

Birthplace of Pete Haycock, 4.4.52 (founder of Climax Blues Band, the city's most famous group... he still lives here); Miranda Joyce, 26.7.62 (Belle Stars); Fran Healey, 1973 (Travis).

Bingley Hall was a major gig in the Seventies; The Who did two nights in October '75; Keith Richards crashed his car driving home from there in May '76; and Bowie filled it for three nights in June '78. Rush played there in July '79; Police in December '80. In September '81, it was the venue for the Futurama Festival headlined by Simple Minds. Bob Marley played his last UK concert there in July '80.

Medicine Head formed at the Art College, where John Fiddler and Peter Hope Evans were both students.

Home of Nineties techno-dance stars Altern 8 (Top Three with Activ 8 in '91) and rave faves Bizarre Inc (Top Five with 'Playing With Knives' in '91). An offshoot of the latter was operating by '98 – Psychedelia Smith!

The Regent Theatre, Piccadilly, formerly The Gaumont Cinema where the Beatles played in '63

STOKE-ON-TRENT

Birthplace of Mike Wilsh, 21.7.45 (Four Pennies); singer Sylvia Tatler (Silkie); Nick Garvey, 26.4.51 (Ducks Deluxe, Motors); Jem Finer, 20.7.55 (Pogues).

The Kings Hall in Glebe Street was the hot venue. The Beatles played here in January '63; the Stones in November '63.

First local group to make it out were The Marauders, who found their way to Tin Pan Alley and scored a minor hit with 'That's What I Want' in August' 63. Hipster Image were produced by Alan Price, but were destined to remain local faves – as were Cat's Eyes and Pye group Lance Harvey & The Five Pins.

The much more successful Sutherland Brothers were from the council estate in Blythe Bridge, and still live in the area. Their first group was New Generation, who reached the '68 Top Forty with Smokey Blues Away. Iain later ran a recording studio in Longton, while Gavin (who went to Moreside School and wrote Rod Stewart's hit 'Sailing') led local band The Rockets.

Any Trouble guitarist Chris Parks went to Stoke Poly; the rest of the group were either at college or school here too. Most of their early gigs were in the Potteries.

Kevin Godley (10cc) went to Stoke Art College.

Local punks Discharge attracted national notoriety. They first appeared on the Clay label, based at 26 Hope Street and run by local record shop owner Mike Stone.

Trying to crack the Nineties scene were Broken Bones, Venus Beads, Reverse, blues guitarist Pete Latham and Sure Is Pure – a spin-off from Candy Flip, who reached the '90 Top Three with 'Strawberry Fields Forever'.

Nineties venues included the Wheatsheaf (closed in July '98), Shelly's, the Void at 20 Glass Street, the 300 seater Riddles Music Bar at the Talbot Hotel in Church Street, and Brannigans.

TAMWORTH
Birthplace of guitarist Dave Clempson, 5.9.49. He made waves leading the local Bakerloo Blues Line, which split up when he joined Colosseum. He became even more famous in Humble Pie.

In February '63, The Beatles played at the Assembly Rooms in Corporation Street; the Stones played there in December '63.

The Julian Cope coat of arms for 1987

Former leader of The Teardrop Explodes, Julian Cope grew up here... his albums are peppered with local references. At school, he was in Can-influenced group Softgraundt; in '77, as a summer job, he worked at Alder's Paper Mill.

In the early Nineties, the Rathole established itself as a popular venue.

TUNSTALL
Family home of Robbie Williams.

UTTOXETER
Iain Sutherland was educated at Uttoxeter Grammar.

The Crayons and Yeah Jazz were late Eighties hopefuls.

SUFFOLK

the cranberries
Linger

Single sleeve shot in St. Mary's Church, Walpole

Sometime home of Christian James (Halo James), who flitted into the '89 Top Ten with Could Have Told You So.

Most interesting of Nineties groups was Jacob's Mouse – who later adopted the more positive name Machismo.

Vienna's was a venue hosting interesting Nineties up and comers.

The birth of an empire: Andys Records in Bury

BECCLES
Home of mid-Nineties drum'n'bass/remixers E-2 Rollers.

BURY St. EDMUNDS
Boo Hewerdine from The Bible used to work in the warehouse at Andy's Records. Another warehouse here is that of Music Sales, the UK's biggest sheet music publishers – with everything from The Beatles and Elton John to The Spice Girls and Oasis.

It was at Bury St. Edmunds Register Office in June '89 that Rolling Stone Bill Wyman (52) secretly married his teenage sweetheart Mandy Smith – a romantic companion since "she blew him away" at age 13. The happy couple moved into their £2.5 million starter home Gedding Hall.

CLARE
During the late Seventies, progressive rockers The Enid lived communally at Claret Hall farm.

HARLESTON
With early Nineties singles on the Wilde Club label, Hypnotize tried to put this village on the map.

IPSWICH

In March '58, Buddy Holly & The Crickets stayed at the White Horse Hotel in Tavern Street after playing three shows (in one day) at the Gaumont in St. Helen's Street. In January '60, the same venue saw the start of the Gene Vincent/Eddie Cochran package tour, and in May '63, The Beatles appeared there on a package show with Roy Orbison and Gerry & The Pacemakers. Ike & Tina Turner and The Rolling Stones visited in October '66; Jimi Hendrix played there in March '67, along with The Walker Brothers, Cat Stevens and Engelbert Humperdinck. The Gaumont was still the town's major showcase when The Cure visited in April '81.

Local Sixties groups included The Sullivan James Band (Parlophone), Nix Nomads (HMV) and The Beazers (Decca). They often filled the support slots at the Manor Ballroom.

Ipswich's Liz Horsman abandons domestic science for a career with Food Records

Brian Eno was a student at Ipswich Art School.

In the early Eighties, Nik Kershaw worked in the DHSS office while playing in semi-pro groups like Half Pint Hog and Fusion.

The Adicts were early Eighties punks; Condemned 84 were skinhead types; The Stupids were John Peel favourites; Extreme Noise Terror were KLF collaborators.

Bleach, Elmer Hassell and Big Ray were early Nineties hopefuls; in the mid-Nineties came techno whiz Kirk di Georgio (who records as As One), Photek (drum'n'bass), The Black Dog (techno) and Chocolate (led by Ed Shred, late of The Stupids). Local lad Dickon was half of Orlando – pioneers in the shortlived late Nineties Romo movement.

LOWESTOFT

The Rolling Stones played the Grand Hotel Ballroom in September '63 and returned to play the Pavilion four months later. In May '64, Little Richard played at the Royal Hotel.

In June '90, a 'bassplayer wanted' advert in Andy's Records attracted Dave Hawes to The Catherine Wheel, completing their line-up. They made their début three months later.

Home of ambient artist Cosmic Kommqando (who also DJs as Mike Dread), hard-rockers A, and drum'n'bass act PFM.

MILDENHALL

Birthplace of producer and musician Phil Thornalley, 5.1.60 (The Cure).

The American air base was a favourite venue for soulified R&B groups like Georgie Fame & The Blue Flames and Geno Washington's Ram Jam Band.

TATTINGSTONE

In January '67, a farmworker discovered two suitcases containing the naked torso and limbs of a 17-year-old Muswell Hill warehouse worker – a homosexual known to record producer Joe Meek. Seventeen days later, as police enquiries proceeded, Meek took his life. No-one was ever charged with what the press called "the suitcase murder".

U2's Achtung Baby Trabants: painted by the stars in Walpole

WOODBRIDGE

Birthplace of Brian Eno, 15.5.48 (Roxy Music, solo); Nick Lowe, 25.3.49 (Brinsley Schwarz, Rockpile, solo).

SURREY

(including boroughs in the Greater London area, but with Surrey postal addresses)

ADDLESTONE
During the mid-Sixties boom, the Dukes Head put on weekly folk nights attracting such guests as Julie Felix and Martin Carthy.

Home to Nashville Teens singers Ray Phillips and Art Sharp, both of whom went to the local St. Pauls School.

ALBURY
In September '73, Bad Company held their first rehearsals at Albury village hall, not far from Guildford.

ASHTEAD
Birthplace of Cream lyricist and bizarro beatster poet Pete Brown, 25.12.40.

From '61 to '70, Joe Strummer was a pupil at the fee-paying City of London Freeman's School in Ashtead Park.

The very working class City of London Freemen's School, an obvious place for Joe Strummer

CAMBERLEY
Birthplace of lyricist Richard Stilgoe, 28.3.43.

In late '66/'67, the Agincourt Ballroom was hot enough to attract and present such illustrious groups as Cream and The Pink Floyd.

Early Seventies home of Ritchie Blackmore (Deep Purple).

Graham Parker grew up in Deep Cut and called his first group The Deep Cut Three. Their big gig was Black Down Youth Club. Next hot local group was The Members, who fingered the area in their '79 hit 'The Sound Of The Suburbs'.

The Members write about their Camberley environment

R and J Stone, who scored a one-off hit with 'We Do It' in January 76, lived in Kroone Road.

Rick Wakeman took former page three model Nina Carter to be his wife at the United Reform Church in November 84.

The town's major export was Bros – late Eighties teen heart throbs who lived on the Heatherside estate and went to Collingwood County Secondary in Kingston Road. Their plans for world domination were hatched in various pubs, including the Wheatsheaf, the White Hart and the Kings Head. They were also said to frequent the Monday night disco at the Civic Hall and Pantiles night club on the London Road.

Splintered were early Nineties hopefuls.

Ridge Farm Studios, Dorking

(Lynette Southam)

CARSHALTON
Birthplace of singer Les Gray, 9.4.46 (Mud).

Cliff Richard lived at 47 Windborough Road from September '48 until October '49, when he attended Stanley Park Road Primary School. Because of his tan, acquired during his childhood in India (born Lucknow, 14.10.40), unpleasant schoolmates called him Nigger.

Operational base of Seventies chartbusters Mud and Eighties hopefuls The Cardiacs.

CATERHAM
Just prior to joining The Damned, Rat Scabies was appearing in the Yorkshire Theatre Company's production of *Puss In Boots.*

CHERTSEY
It was here, on the Thames, that former Bonzo Dog Band leader Vivian Stanshall lived on a houseboat... before it sank with all his possessions in '84.

In Spring '71, Keith Moon and his recently estranged wife Kim got back together to start anew at Tara House –

Keith avoids the Chertsey N.C.P.

Keith, in Rolls, dropped in

purchased for £65,000. The bizarre house – shaped like five pyramids – was the venue for a fabulous party to launch *Who's Next* in the summer of '71. The Golden Grove pub, located at the end of the drive, was Keith's local. During the next few years, he was regularly ambulanced to St. Peter's Hospital for resuscitation following excessive drug and alcohol abuse, and he once appeared at the local Magistrates Court charged with possessing a firearm without a licence. It was at Tara that he drove his Rolls Royce Silver Cloud into a pond. 10cc star Kevin Godley purchased the property from him in '74, but it has since been demolished.

The video for Ten Pole Tudor's Wunderbar was shot in Thorpe Park.

CHESSINGTON
On moving from Dublin to England, The Boomtown Rats took over a mansion said to have been a gift from Henry VIII to one of his mistresses.

The video for 'Give Me Your Heart Tonight' by Shakin' Stevens was filmed at Chessington Zoo.

CHIDDINGFOLD
It was here that The Stranglers lived while plotting to ride the punk boom to glory.

COBHAM
In June '70, Moody Blues singer Ray Thomas bought a palatial residence for £16,000! The Moody Blues subsequently based their Threshold label at 53/57 High Street.

CROYDON
Birthplace of Matthew Fisher, 7.3.46 (Procol Harum); Kirsty MacColl, 10.10.59 (sang with local punk group Drug Addix before going solo on Stiff); sisters Vernie, 17.5.71, and Easther Bennett, 11.12.72 (Eternal).

It was in Croydon in '52 that 16-year-old Christopher Craig shot policeman Sidney Miles: the subject of Elvis Costello's song 'Let Him Dangle'.

Eden Kane's first public appearance was at Croydon Youth Club in '59.

Operational base of Group X, remembered only for the title of their early Sixties single 'There Are Eight Million Cossack Melodies' and 'This Is One of Them'.

The Star Hotel at 296 London Road, Broad Green was part of the Crawdaddy R&B circuit in the Sixties.

In March '63, The Beatles/Tommy Roe/Chris Montez package show visited the ABC cinema in London Road.

The Greyhound pub in Park Lane was a major gig during the Seventies, when up-and-comers like David Bowie and Genesis played there. The Electric Light Orchestra made their début there in '72 and on their hit 'Saturday Gigs', Mott The Hoople (who first visited in December '69) imply that playing there was the turning point of their career. It changed with the times: The Buzzcocks played there in September '77.

Punk entrepreneur Malcolm McLaren and punk designer Jamie Reid both went to Croydon Art School, as did Kinks leader Ray Davies, blues producer Mike Vernon and Robin Scott (M of Pop Music fame). Ian Dury's first band, Kilburn & The High Roads, made their début there in December '71.

Late Seventies indie label Bonaparte Records operated from 101 George Street.

Fairfield Hall has long been a prestigious concert venue, noted for its excellent acoustics. The Beatles appeared three times, and by common consent The Who gave their finest ever performance of *Tommy* on the premises in September '69. "The sound in that place – oh, Croydon, I could bloody play there all night," said Townshend. Elton John was in the audience and noted in his diary that The Who were "excellent". It was here that Rat Scabies, employed as a porter, first met Captain Sensible, working as a toilet cleaner and practising guitar in the Royal Box. Both resolved to improve their situations and formulated plans to launch The Damned. The Captain later recorded his '82 chart topper Happy Talk at Matthew Fisher's studio in Croham Road.

The Quiet Five were Sixties questers whose singer Richard Barnes later enjoyed a modicum of solo success; Strength were

Loop (later Main) of Croydon

late Eighties hopefuls on Arista; Loop attracted press acclaim and Peel sessions in the late Eighties, when their album *Fade Out* topped the indie charts; the optimistically named Faith Over Reason were early Nineties hopefuls – as were The Loveblobs, The Ultras, Anna, Remi Vibesman (drum'n'bass), and Freeform (a techno guy, aka Simon Pike).

The Cartoon was a top venue through the Eighties and into the Nineties.

Bob Stanley and Pete Wiggs were Croydon lads – but had moved to Tufnell Park by the time their group St. Etienne began their long chart run with 'Nothing Can Stop Us' in '91. Also local was Alvin Gibbs, who played bass with the UK Subs and Iggy Pop.

Starting with Stay in October '93, pioneering swingbeat sisters Eternal set records as the only girl group to rack up over ten consecutive Top Twenty hits.

Captain Sensible had a track called 'Croydon' on his first solo album; The Brian Auguster Trinity cut a '67 B-side called 'Oh Baby, Won't You Come Back Home To Croydon Where Everybody Beedles And Bos'!

DORKING

Simon Napier Bell agreed to manage John's Children after seeing them play at a barbecue at Burford Bridge in summer '66.

Having dropped out of school, Genesis moved into a cottage in Dorking (owned by their roadie's parents) to write their first Charisma album *Trespass*.

In '76, 10cc converted an old cinema into their new studio, Strawberry South.

EAST HORSLEY

The Psychedelic Furs got started here – at Richard and Tim Butler's home.

Page 28—MELODY MAKER, February 28, 1970

Wednesday, 25 February	**Revolution**
Thursday, 26 February	**Blaises**
Friday, 27 February	**Brunel University, Uxbridge**
Saturday, 28 February	**Essex University, Colchester**
Sunday, 1 March	**Farx Club, Southall**
Monday, 2 March	**Mistrale Club, Beckenham**
Tuesday, 3 March	**Upstairs at Ronnie Scott's**

Marcus Bicknell
01-937 3793
No sole agency

Trespass period Genesis on tour

EAST MOLESEY
Birthplace of Kinks drummer Mick Avory, 15.2.44.

EGHAM
In June '77, when Jimmy Helms was forced to pull out of the Shoreditch College of Education's Valedictory Dance, an enterprising student nipped up the road to Elton John's house in Virginia Water and asked if the millionaire was up for the gig. Elton played his heart out. The fee: two bottles of wine!

The Congregation were early Nineties hopefuls; Supermodel released indie singles in the mid-Nineties.

Home of Billy Reeves, singer and guitarist with late Nineties faves Theaudience (sic).

Brookfield House

ELSTEAD
In the early Seventies, Stephen Stills (and his large entourage) lived here, at Brookfield House, a haunted mansion set in 23 acres – part of which inspired the song 'Johnny's Garden' (dedicated to his assiduous gardener). It had previously been owned by Ringo Starr, and before that ('64-68) by Peter Sellers and Britt Eckland. In September '98, it was on the market for £1.7 million.

After his expulsion from the Army in March '59, Terry Dene recuperated at St. Ebba's Hospital.

EPSOM
Birthplace of Petula Clark, 15.11.33; producer Glyn Johns, 15.2.42.

As a schoolboy, Jimmy Page lived in Miles Road.

Geoff McClelland and Chris Dawsett, founders of John's Children, met up at Epsom Art School. Richard Butler of The Psychedelic Furs was a later pupil.

Boy/Girl Soup were early Nineties hopefuls.

John's Children from Epsom

ESHER
In late '64, George Harrison paid £20,000 for Kinfauns, 16 Claremont Drive, a noble residence on the Claremont Park Estate, where he lived from February '65 until December' 69. It was here that he was busted for possession of cannabis in March '69.

Harrison married Pattie Boyd at the Leartherhead & Esher Register Office, on 21.1.66.

EWELL
Elvis Costello's pub-rock group Flip City played their last gig at North East Surrey College of Technology – supporting Climax Blues Band in December '75.

FARNHAM
Pink Floyd drummer Nick Mason was educated at Frensham Heights public school.

In the mid-Seventies, local synthesiser trio Zorch were tipped as "Britain's Tangerine Dream". It wasn't to be.

FRIMLEY
In September '98, the head teacher at Tomlinscote School sent girls home for "tottering around" in Spice Girls-style platform shoes. That Geri Halliwell's got a lot to answer for!

Charterhouse: hot house of pop insurrection

GODALMING
Pupils at Charterhouse public school sidelined academic pursuits to form Genesis in '67. Their first producer was another Charterhouse graduate, Jonathan King.

Splendidly named Charterhouse pupil Rivers Job (originally in school group The Anon with Mike Rutherford) went on to play bass in The Savoy Brown Blues Band.

Another Charterhouse chap was Fifties disc jockey, *Cool For Cats* compere and wrestling commentator Kent Walton.

Keith Tillman, sometime bass player in John Mayall's Bluesbreakers, ran a late Sixties blues club at the Angel Hotel.

GREAT BOOKHAM
Birthplace of Roger Waters, 9.9.44 (Pink Floyd).

GUILDFORD
Birthplace of Tony Blackburn, 29.1.43 (at Mt. Alvernia Nursing Home); Mike Rutherford, 2.10.50 (Genesis); saxophonist Iain Bellamy, 20.2.64 (Earthworks).

Local bands include The Stormsville Shakers, who evolved into Circus; Camel (Seventies progressive), The Stranglers (originally known as the Guildford Stranglers) and The Vapors (Eighties).

Rather less famous were myriad late Seventies hopefuls like House, The Famous Rondini Brothers, Poker and Head Waiter.

Local residents have included Jackie Lynton (Savoy Brown), Mel Collins (King Crimson), Philip Goodhand Tait (songwriter) and Ray Dorset (Mungo Jerry).

Eric Clapton, who lives nearby, often started or finished his UK tours at Guildford Civic Hall – primarily so that his granny could come and see him. His very first group, The Roosters, used to rehearse at the Wooden Bridge Hotel in '63 – during which year The Rolling Stones played seven gigs there.

The Beatles played at the Odeon in Epsom Road in June 63 – their only visit to the town.

Led Zeppelin made their world début at the University of Surrey on 15.10.68. The Stranglers, recording a special here for BBC2, left the stage after three numbers, castigating the audience as "a bunch of elitist cunts".

In '70, Free wrote 'All Right Now' in the Civic Hall dressing room; in '78, both The Sex Pistols and The Stranglers were banned from playing there.

The promotional video for Eurythmics' 'Sweet Dreams Are Made Of This' was shot in fields just outside the town.

Local Nineties bands included Beautiful People and Salt Tank.

In the Nineties, Stoke Park became the venue for an annual festival.

HERSHAM
Truculent local punk Jimmy Pursey put the last syllable of his town into Sham 69.

The funeral of pop manager and multi-millionaire Gordon Mills took place at St. Peters Church.

Early Cure

HORLEY
Birthplace of saxplayer Dick Morrissey, 9.5.40 (If, Morrissey Mullen); Lol Tolhurst, 3.2.59 (Cure) obviously a reincarnation of Buddy Holly; Matthieu Hartley, 4.2.60 (Cure), in nearby Smallfield.

Robert Smith, Lol Tolhurst, Simon Gallup and Matthieu Hartley (The Cure) all lived here at various times. Smith and Tolhurst attended St. Francis School; Gallup and Hartley went to Balcombe Road Comprehensive.

Gallup played in local bands Lockjaw, The Magazine Spies and Fool's Dance.

In the mid-Nineties came punk/hardcore band the All-New Accelerators.

KEW
The Boat House was a popular early Sixties gig, when groups like Cliff Bennett & The Rebel Rousers, Neil Christian & The Crusaders and Screaming Lord Sutch would pull the punters.

KINGSTON-UPON-THAMES

Birthplace of singer David Clayton Thomas, 13.9.41 (Blood Sweat & Tears); Richard Butler, 5.6.56 (Psychedelic Furs); drummer Rat Scabies, 30.7.57 (Damned).

Kingston Art School alumni include Sandy Denny, John Renbourn, Keith Relf and Eric Clapton. Angela Bowie, Jona Lewie (Stop The Cavalry), Richard James (The Aphex Twin) and Mike Paradinas (U-ziq) all studied at Kingston Poly.

In September '63, The Rolling Stones played an early gig at the Cellar Club, 22a High Street. Jimmy Reed played there in November '64.

Plans to form The Yardbirds (originally The Metropolis Blues Quartet) were hatched in the bar of the Railway Hotel, Norbiton.

Very early Yardbirds promo shot

(Kingston Daily Press)

Sandy Denny made her début at the Barge, a floating folk club moored at Townsend Wharf. It was a gig here that led directly to John Martyn getting signed up by Island.

Local band National Flag won a Marquee residency in '76 – but then vanished. The Outsiders, led by still-gigging Adrian Borland, were late Seventies punks who evolved into The Sound and released three acclaimed but non-selling albums.

The first UK offices of Beserkley Records (Jonathan Richman, The Rubinoos, etc) were at 97 Kingston Hill.

Ruptured Dog were mid-Nineties hopefuls.

LEATHERHEAD

Most celebrated local group were John's Children, whose manager (Simon Napier Bell) actually bought them a club... the Bluesette, a converted nissen hut in Bridge Street. Group members included Andy Ellison (later of Jet and Radio Stars) and Marc Bolan.

In January '78, Police cut their first album at Nigel Gray's Surrey Sound Studio at 70 Kingston Road. It cost £2,000 and made millions.

In early '69, Freddie Mercury sang with local band Sour Milk Sea (named after the Jackie Lomax single).

MITCHAM

The Game were Sixties schoolkids managed by Kenny Lynch. Rather more successful was another local bunch, Mud.

Mick Jones (The Clash) spent the first two years of his life at 20 Fair Green Court.

MORDEN

The Yardbirds made their first recordings at R.G.Jones Studio in February '64.

NEW ADDINGTON

Home of Sixties R&B group The Kingpins, whose singles were not highly collectable then but are now!

Reached vinyl on 'From Paddington to New Addington', a '78 single by punk band The Drug Addix (featuring Kirsty MacColl).

Kirsty Macoll makes a record

NEW MALDEN

Birthplace of John Martyn, 11.9.48 – though he was raised in Glasgow.

With royalties from Fleetwood Mac hits, Peter Green purchased a house in Coombe Gardens – which he named Albatross.

PURLEY

The Orchid Ballroom was a hot venue in the Sixties. The Jimi Hendrix Experience played there in February '67.

REDHILL

Birthplace of organist Roy Lines, 25.11.43 (original line-up of Status Quo).

The Cure played several formative gigs at Lakers Hotel during the last half of '78.

REIGATE

Manfred Mann singer Mike D'Abo was born at nearby Bletchworth, 1.3.44.

Home of Third Ear Band leader Glen Sweeney. His Fifties skiffle group, The Anacondas, had a residency at the Bridge House.

Childhood home of Norman Cook (The Housemartins, Fatboy Slim), who recently talked about his youth in a "suburban hellhole".

Norman dons a suit and becomes Freakpower

(Adrian Green)

RICHMOND

Birthplace of singer Keith Relf, 22.3.43 (Yardbirds).

During the late Fifties, the focal point for the area's large art school/beatnik contingent and later the Mod crowd was L'Auberge coffee bar, down from the Odeon.

It was during their Sunday residency (16 weeks) at the Crawdaddy Club, in the Station Hotel, that The Rolling Stones were discovered by future manager Andrew Oldham – in April '63. Shortly afterwards (in June), club owner Giorgio Gomelsky moved the Crawdaddy to the clubhouse of Richmond Athletic Club on the A316. The Yardbirds, T-Bones and Authentics were early favourites. (The Station Hotel was later revamped as the Bull And Bush.)

Jeff Beck and Brian Niles, two of The Nightshift at the 4th Jazz & Blues Festival, Richmond 1964

(Peter Moody Collection)

The first five annual National Jazz Blues & Rock Festivals (precursors to Reading Festival) were held at the Richmond Athletic Ground – from '61 to '65. The first two were all jazz; Cyril Davies and the Stones crept onto the third; ten R&B groups made the fourth; by '65 R&B held sway.

Eric Clapton came to join The Yardbirds in October '63, when they were rehearsing at the South Western Hotel (opposite the Station Hotel... now Drummonds).

In September '72, Ron Wood paid a reputed £140,000 for The Wick on Richmond Hill – previously owned by film star John Mills. Pete Townshend bought it from him in the Nineties.

Home base for Eighties innovators The Lemon Kittens.

Future Kula Shaker members Crispian Mills and Alonza Becan met at college here, ran psychedelic rock club the Mantra Shack, and gigged around in prototype band The Kays.

RIPLEY

Eric Clapton was born (30.3.45) and raised at 1 The Green. He went to Ripley Primary and St. Bedes Secondary Modern and still lives nearby.

SHALFORD

In the early Eighties, Phil Collins lived at the Croft on Shalford Common.

SHAMLEY GREEN

Richard Branson spent his earliest years at his parents' cottage, Easteds. Later, the family moved to Tanyard Farm in the same village.

Chris Dreja of The Yardbirds

(Kingston Daily Press)

SURBITON

Birthplace of Chris Dreja, 11.11.46, who later attended the art school annexe of Hollyfield Road Secondary Modern... where he met fellow guitar enthusiast Top Topham. They would form the core of The Yardbirds. Also the birthplace of Lynn Ripley, 15.7.47 – better known as Sixties chart star Twinkle.

Petula Clark went to St. Bernard's School.

The Toby Jug at 1 Hook Rise, Tolworth was a prestige gig during the Sixties and early Seventies. Captain Beefheart played there in '68 and Bowie started his *Ziggy Stardust* tour there in February '72. For a while, John Lennon's father Fred was a barman.

The idiosyncratic Cardiacs attracted a cult following in the late Eighties.

SUTTON

Birthplace of Clark Datchler, 27.3.64 (Johnny Hates Jazz).

Jimmy Page attended Sutton art school in late '62/early '63.

Roulettes guitarist Peter Thorp and jazz-rock saxplayer Dick Morrisey were educated at Sutton High School.

Some of The Rolling Stones' earliest gigs were those they promoted themselves at the Red Lion pub. Between November '62 and April '63, they played here nine times.

THAMES DITTON

10 Kings Drive was the operational base of late Seventies indie label Cocteau Records.

THORNTON HEATH

Birthplace of Paul Simonon, 15.12.55 (Clash), at 1 Beulah Crescent.

TOLWORTH

The Toby Jug was a hot circuit gig in the Sixties. Led Zeppelin played there in April '69.

May Blitz perform a tribute to the women of Virginia Waters on their debut album

VIRGINIA WATER

Elton John, Gary Numan, Five Star and bandleader Ted Heath are among pop stars to have purchased mansions in the locality. On the first Tyrannosaurus

Rex album, Marc Bolan sang of a 'Chateau In Virginia Waters'.

Holloway Sanitorium was the setting for two chart topping videos... 'Goody Two Shoes' by Adam & The Ants and 'Total Eclipse Of The Heart' by Bonnie Tyler.

WALLINGTON

Birthplace of guitarist Jeff Beck, 24.6.44.

Wallington Public Hall in Stafford Road housed the Kazoo Club, a Sixties venue whose resident group was Peter Frampton & The Herd. The Stones played there in April '64.

Operational base of pioneer New Wave group The Banned, who reached the '77 Top Forty with Little Girl – originally issued on their indie label Can't Eat, based at 64 Link Lane.

The Banned: Wallington's flaming groovies

WALTON-ON-THAMES

Birthplace of Gary Taylor, 28.11.47 (Herd).

George and Pattie Harrison found themselves in the Magistrates Court in March '69, charged with possession of cannabis; each was fined £250 after pleading guilty to this heinous crime.

Disc jockey Mike Read grew up here and played with local late-Sixties group Just Plain Smith – who left behind a collectable single.

WARLINGHAM

When not away at school, Joe Strummer spent his childhood at the family home – 15 Court Farm Road.

WEYBRIDGE

Home base for the Nashville Teens – heroes of 'Tobacco Road', whose punitive recording contract gave them less than one penny per record sold!

Two of the Beatles lived on the St. George's Hill Estate. In July 64, John Lennon paid twenty grand for Kenwood, where he and Cynthia lived until their divorce in November '68. (Earlier that year, however, John had slipped in with Yoko to record the *Two Virgins* album in his home studio). In July '65, Ringo paid 37 grand for Sunny Heights, where he and Maureen lived until moving to Elstead in November '68. Other residents on this exclusive estate have included Cliff Richard, Tom Jones, Gordon Mills (Tom's manager), and Mike Read... while Gilbert O'Sullivan lived in nearby Byfleet.

In summer '67, John Lennon and Kenny Everett wandered around Weybridge golf course stoned out of their gourds on LSD.

Masterswitch were new wavers remembered for their '78 single 'Action Replay'.

WINDLESHAM
Birthplace of Wham! Founder Andrew Ridgeley, 26.1.63.

WOKING
Birthplace of songwriter Les Reed, 24.7.35 (hits for Engelbert, etc); singer Art Sharp, 26.5.41 (Nashville Teens); rocker and author Ian Whitcomb, 10.7.41 (who hit the US Top Ten with 'You Turn Me On' in '65); producer Gus Dudgeon, 30.9.42; organist Dave Greenslade, 18.1.43; Mark Wynter, 29.1.43; Billie Davis, 22.12.45 (Sixties poppet and Jet Harris escort); Rick Parfitt, 12.10.48 (Status Quo... in Church Street); Dana Gillespie, 30.3.49; Peter Gabriel, 13.2.50; Bruce Foxton, 1.9.55, Paul Buckler, 6.12.55, and Paul Weller, 25.5.58 (all of whom formed The Jam).

Local band Unicorn released a couple of David Gilmour produced albums in the Seventies.

The Jam all attended Sheerwater Comprehensive in Albert Drive – later renamed Bishop David Brown School. Weller attended Maybury Primary (as seen in

Anything The Beatles do Paul can do better

he video for his '92 solo single 'Uh Huh Oh Yeh') and lived at 8 Stanley Road (later a solo album title), where the group used to rehearse. When Stanley Road faced redevelopment, the Wellers moved to 44 Balmoral Drive. Buckler went to Goldsworth Primary and lived in Church Street. Foxton went to Sheerwater Junior and lived on the Maybury estate. Strategies were discussed at the Princess of Wales and the Wheatsheaf; formative gigs were at Sheerwater Youth Club and the Working Men's Club in Walton Road. In the mid-Seventies, they refined their style as resident band at Michael's night club in Goldsworth Road.

Emerging in the late Seventies, Squire were a rather less successful nouveau-mod band.

Badfinger star Pete Ham hanged himself at his Woking home in April '75.

The earliest rock venue was the Atlanta Ballroom in Commercial Road, where the Rolling Stones played in August 63.

SUSSEX, EAST

BEXHILL
Bob Marley & The Wailers made their UK début at the De La Warr Pavilion in July '72.

BODIAM
Adam & The Ants filmed their Ant Rap video at Bodiam Castle.

Bodium Castle

(Nikki Lloyd)

BRIGHTON
Birthplace of keyboard player Dave Greenfield, 29.3.49 (Stranglers); drummer Steve Ferrone, 25.4.50 (Average White Band, Eric Clapton).

1956 saw the first local skiffle groups – The James Boys and The Checkers – followed by the first wave of rock'n'roll groups: Bobby Sansom & The Giants, Ray DuVal & The Downbeats, Gene Coburn & The Chimes, Count Downe & The Zeros.

Sixties groups included The Motion, The Untamed and The Web.

A profusion of venues/meeting places included the Whiskey A Go Go coffee bar in Queens Square, the Starlight Rooms under the now demolished Montpelier Hotel in Montpelier Road, the Box disco above the Wimpy Bar in Western Road, the California and Zodiac coffee bars in West Street, Tiffanies coffee bar opposite the Kemp Town Odeon, the Mallaca in Duke Street, Jimmy's in Steine Street, and the Zodiac in St. James Street.

The Hippodrome in Middle Street (going since the Forties) presented The Beatles (three times, starting in June '63) and Rolling Stones before becoming a television studio and then a bingo and social club. Sixties package shows also visited the Essoldo Cinema in North Street, and the Top Rank opened in '65.

In May '64, mods and rockers had some of their bloodiest skirmishes on the seafront. Mods used to go to the Florida Rooms (adjoining the Aquarium), which housed the Cadillac Club. They would pick up girls and throw them in the sea! Pilled up, they would swagger through the all-nighters, before zooming back to London on their Vespas. In '64 The Who played the Florida Room nine times, occasionally as The High Numbers, and The Hippodrome twice. Postcards of the early Who kitted out as Mods are still on sale on Brighton pier.

The Dome at 29 New Road was a hot Sixties venue. In May '65, Britain's one and only National Festival Of Song was held there. Kenny Lynch won, Lulu came second, and the event lost £1,500. Since then, everyone from Kim Wilde (October '82) to Del Amitri (November '98) have played there – and Van Morrison's '98 live album *Doberman* was recorded there.

In the early Sixties, Brighton beach was a favourite destination for London's coffee bar cowboys, beatniks and CND devotees... including the likes of Long John Baldry, Rod Stewart and Wally Whyton. Twenty five years later, that same strand provided the setting for the amorous interlude recounted in Marillion's 'Three Boats Down From The Candy' – the Candy being the only one with its name painted on the side.

In the early Eighties, Brighton beach also provided a stage for Pookiesnackenburger, a bunch of local buskers who soon graduated to Covent Garden piazza and a Stiff recording contract.

It was while tinkling the ivories in a Brighton seafront bar called Harrison's that local bank clerk Keith Emerson was spotted by a representative of R&B group Gary Farr & The T Bones, who persuaded him to jack in his job and join them in their quest for fame. The group never found it, but Emerson did– a few years later when he started The Nice and, later, ELP.

The T-Bones were managed by Gary's brother Rikki, who also operated the Perfumed Garden club at the Florida Rooms. He later mounted the Isle of Wight festivals.

In '74, the Eurovision Song Contest was held at the Dome... Abba won with 'Waterloo'.

Despite its size and status, Brighton has produced few bands of national repute. The Piranhas looked set to establish themselves in new wave terms but ultimately succeeded only with novelty revivals of Tom Hark and Zambesi. The Amazor-blades, The Depressions, and The Lambrettas cut a few records... but what of The Parrots, Spoons, Krakatoa, Lodestone, Beggars Death, Joby & The Hooligans, The Chefs, Wrist Action, Nicky & The Dots, No Exit, The Vandells, and The Dodgems?

Punk pioneers Vi Subversa and her Poison Girls made it to London; Bone Orchard, The Chefs, The Pop Guns and The Mobiles made it to the Eighties indie charts.

Bing Crosby played his last gig at the Brighton Centre in Kings Road, as did The Jam in December '82. Bruce Springsteen, The Who and other major league acts also played this 5,000 seater.

Other local venues include the Poly, the Sussex Sports Centre in Queens Square, the Hotel Metropole, the university, the Zap Club, Jenkinsons and the Top Rank in Kings West, the New Regent in West Street, the Buccaneer

in Madeira Drive, and the Alhambra at 24 Kings Road – a great seafront pub/punk rock gig, now demolished.

The punk scene revolved around the Resource Centre in North Road, a shabby converted church hall. The Stranglers (including local lad Dave Greenfield) used to rehearse here.

Sherry's Disco in West Street presented Culture Club before revamping as the Pink Coconut.

Several bands got started at the university of Sussex at Brighton, but few turned pro... late Sixties blues group Jellybread did, and so did Affinity (early Seventies jazz rock), but the hottest success was Billy Idol – former philosophy student (it says here). Clash drummer Rob Harper studied here – as did Saxon drummer Nigel Glockler, who was intending to become a vet but "couldn't grasp the essential Latin".

Jellybread keyboard player Pete Wingfield became versatile singer, session man and producer.

The Darts were originally students from the Poly, as was Harvey Goldsmith, whose first promotion was Deep Purple and Jellybread at the college's Cockroft Hall in '69.

Attrix Records was based at 3 Sydney Street in the late Seventies, with a roster including The Piranhas, The Dodgems and The Chefs.

Future Creation boss Alan McGee moved here from East Kilbride. One of his acts would be Brighton band Pacific.

Local resident Anne Nightingale worked on the *Brighton Argus* before graduating to Radio One. Her husband made a single for Stiff; her son Alex works for Primal Scream, who moved down to Brighton in the early Nineties.

Transvision Vamp singer Wendy James is a local lass too.

Peter & The Test Tube Babies were early Eighties oi!-punk specialists, famous for such acquired-taste albums and cassettes as *The Mating Sounds of South American Frogs*, *Pissed And Proud* and *Rotting In The Fart Sack*.

The Zap Club under the seafront arches was a happening late Eighties venue; the Wayne Foundation was a happening band – as were the Frazier Chorus, who seemed set to break out, but releases on 4AD and Virgin attracted only a cult following. Other late Eighties hopefuls included Blow Up, 14 Iced Bears and Whirl.

In the Nineties came Huggy Bear (some local), Brighter, The Coffin Nails, Spitfire, Eusebio, Goat, Earwig (and spin-off Insides), Chuck, Arthur, Espiritu, These Animal Men, Dog Hunch, Pan, Hal, Blubber, First Down, Vibrasonic, I'm Being Good, Republica vocalist Saffron, new goths Elephant and trip-hopper REQ.

In '94, The Levellers converted a four storey factory complex (originally making clocks) into the Metway – their rehearsing, recording, merchandising and administrative base.

Operational base for dance producer Christian Vogel, and the Skint label.

CROWBOROUGH

Luxford House was a country house owned by Charisma boss Tony Stratton Smith, once occupied by Lord Beaverbrook, the newspaper magnate. It was here that Genesis wrote and rehearsed their *Nursery Cryme* album, and that guitarist Bert Jansch recorded tracks for *L A Turnaround* with producer Mike Nesmith.

EAST HOATHLEY

Birthplace of keyboard player Tony Banks, 27.3.50 (Genesis).

The swimming pool at Cotchford Farm

EASTBOURNE

Birthplace of Leapy Lee, 2.7.42; Peter 'Spider' Stacey, 14.12.58 (Pogues).

It was in Eastbourne that Tony Stratton Smith first saw Genesis, soon to become the flagship of his Charisma label.

Ultravox shot their video for 'Reap The Wild Wind' at nearby Beachy Head; Kevin Coyne celebrated Eastbourne Ladies on his album Marjory Razorblade.

Led Zeppelin manager Peter Grant retired to Eastbourne after the Zeps called it a day following John Bonham's death. By all accounts this former pirate of the rock seas became a pillar of the local community, and was even asked to become a magistrate. He declined.

Operational base for The Mobiles, whose 'Drowning In Berlin' went Top Ten in '82.

ETCHINGHAM

Local residents Ashley Hutchings and Shirley Collins formed The Etchingham Steam Band in '74 – precursor to The Albion Band.

FRANT

Brian Epstein was briefly a boarder at Beaconsfield Public School.

HALLAND

In September '67, Rolling Stone Charlie Watts bought Peckham's, a 13th century farmhouse with a 40-acre spread. His previous residence had been The Old Brewery House at Southover.

HARTFIELD

In the early hours of 3.7.69, the unconscious body of former Rolling Stone Brian Jones was recovered from the swimming pool of his country residence, Cotchford Farm – once owned by *Winnie The Pooh* author A.A.Milne. He was dead by the time medical assistance arrived.

Luxford House

HASTINGS

Birthplace of folksinger Shirley Collins, 5.7.35 (worked with Davy Graham, Ashley Hutchings and sister Dolly); singer Suggs, 13.1.61 (Madness); singer/songwriter John Wesley Harding.

The Rolling Stones appeared at the Pier Ballroom in January '64, The Jimi Hendrix Experience in October '67 (supported by The Orange Seaweed!).

The video for David Bowie's '80 chart topper 'Ashes To Ashes' was shot here with extras recruited from Blitz in Covent Garden.

The Teenbeats and The Hollywood Killers were local late Seventies bands.

Sometime home of John and Beverly Martyn.

HAYWARDS HEATH
Birthplace of Brett Anderson, 27.9.67, and Matt Osman, 9.10.67, who would play in local groups and go off to university before forming the hottest band of '92, Suede.

HEATHFIELD
Birthplace of maverick guitarist Fred Frith, 17.2.49 (Henry Cow); sometime home of the equally maverick Ron Geesin.

In February '67, Brian Epstein laid out £25,000 for an idyllic country retreat, Kingsley Hall in the outlying village of Warbleton.

HELLINGLY
The funeral of Led Zeppelin manager Peter Grant was held here in December '95. He died from a heart attack in the back of a car taking him to his home in Eastbourne.

HOVE
Ringo Starr and Maureen Cox had their honeymoon in Hove.

LEWES
Drummer Pete Thomas (Elvis Costello's Attractions) attended Lewes Grammar School and played in local group Grobs.

NEWHAVEN
Birthplace of drummer Nigel Glockler, 24.1.53 (Saxon); Eric Goulden, 18.5.54 (better known as Stiff recording artiste Wreckless Eric).

PLUMPTON
In its ninth and tenth years, the National Jazz Blues & Rock Festival was held at Plumpton Racecourse. In August '69, The Nice were accompanied by a 40 piece orchestra, and the landlord of the Sun on Plumpton Green

complained to the press that punters had stolen every glass in the place. Though it began as a jazz festival, practically all trace of jazz had been phased out by '70.

In '72, Jimmy Page bought the 18th century manor house, set in 50 acres. One of the few times he played locally was in September '77 when he and Ron Wood jammed with Arms And Legs (led by the unknown Joe Jackson) at the Half Moon pub.

The Half Moon, Plumpton

RYE
Southern residence of Paul McCartney, where he owns a farm.

SEAFORD
A youthful Richard Branson spent a year studying at Cliff View House.

Sometime home of punk star Jordan – real name, Pamela Rooke.

UPPER DICKER
In '71, under the pseudonym of Springwater, Phil Cordell recorded 'I Will Return' in a local barn for a couple of hundred quid – and watched it zoom into the Top Five.

WADHURST
Jeff Beck made tabloid headline news in August '89 when a jilted lover complained that the 46-year-old rock star had stolen his 25-year-old girlfriend and installed her at his million pound mansion, River Hall near Wadhurst.

SUSSEX, WEST

BOGNOR REGIS
Birthplace of Shadows rhythm guitarist Bruce Welch, 2.11.41.

Noth London group Russ Sainty & The Nu Notes went pro when they took a summer residency at Butlins in July '60.

David Bowie and Elton John first met at Bognor's Shoreline Club in June '66. Elton was in Bluesology, backing Long John Baldry, and support group was David Bowie & The Buzz.

Elaine Paige's father was an estate agent in Bognor.

Staa Marx carried local hopes for new wave recognition.

BURGESS HILL
Hometown of brothers Al, Hugh and Hank Barker of mid-Nineties band Animals That Swim – soon to be London based.

Keith and Mick have their day in court

CHICHESTER
In June 67, Mick Jagger and Keith Richards found themselves in the dock at West Sussex Quarter Sessions defending drugs charges (see West Wittering). They were found guilty but jail sentences were quashed after widespread indignation.

Brussels Spaceship were Nineties hopefuls – but were pushing their luck with a name like that.

When the nearby Goodwood Motor Circuit was reopened in September '98, Annett Mason crashed her husband's £250,000 Maserati during a test lap, fracturing her collar bone and cutting her head. Said husband is car enthusiast Nick Mason, drummer with Pink Floyd.

CRAWLEY
Robert Smith, Lol Tolhurst and Michael Dempsey all went to Notre Dame Middle School and St. Wilfred's Comprehensive, where they formed The Cure – originally known as Malice, then Easy Cure. They had their first rehearsal at St. Edwards Church Hall in January '76, made their début in nearby Worth Abbey (as Malice) in December '76, and played their second gig at St. Wilfred's later the same month. As Easy Cure, they played formative gigs at The Rocket.

Porl Thompson (Malice, Easy Cure) went to Thomas Bennett Comprehensive.

Before The Cure, the hottest band in town was Brett Marvin & The Thunderbolts, who did a nifty name change to Terry Dactyl & The Dinosaurs and went Top Three in '72 with 'Seaside Shuffle'. Idiosyncratic frontman Jona Lewie went solo and scored a perennial hit with 'Stop The Cavalry'.

The Starlight Club was a popular Seventies venue.

In '80, local postman Frank Bell cut a single 'I'm a Cult Hero' with The Cure.

Local nineties bands include The Spectrum Zero (indie/guitar) and Fast Freddie's Fingertips (soul combo led by the fastest bricklayer in Sussex!). Techno buffs include Peel favourite Luke Slater and Matt Cogger, who records as Neuropolitique.

EAST GRINSTEAD
Birthplace of Robyn Hitchcock, 3.3.52 (Soft Boys, Egyptians, R.E.M. mate).

Cutting Crew leader Nick Van Eede went to Imberhorne School, having been born in the Ashdown Forest on 14.6.58.

Richard and Fred Fairbrass – two thirds of Right Said Fred – spent their teenage years at the family home in Furzefield Road.

FULKING
Nothing happened here – I just like the name. Captain Sensible occasionally drinks in a pub here, so he tells me.

HORSHAM
Birthplace of Bob Stanley, 25.12.64 (St. Etienne, whose December '93 single was called 'I Was Born On Christmas Day'!)

Home of the aptly named Beat Merchants, after whom author Alan Clayson titled his definitive examination of Sixties groups. They often played at St. Leonards Hall – as did The Rolling Stones, in August '63.

Home of mid-Nineties techno maverick Dave Clarke.

LITTLEHAMPTON
Operational base of late Nineties Christian rockers Delirious.

PATCHING
Widely regarded as the most shambolic rock festival of all time, Phun City was held at Ecclesden Common in July '70. In their UK début, MC5 topped the bill over the cream of British underground bands.

SELSEY BILL
Paul Weller wrote 'Eton Rifles' while on holiday in his parents' caravan. Madness namecheck the place on 'Driving In My Car'.

SHOREHAM-BY-SEA
Birthplace of Leo Sayer, 21.5.48.

In the early Sixties, Rod Stewart was among a bunch of beatniks who used a derelict barge, moored on the estuary, as a refuge... much to the consternation of the local establishment, always anxious to oust them.

In March '76, local singer/songwriter Chris White had a Top Forty hit with 'Spanish Wine'.

WEST WITTERING
Rejecting the notion that an Englishman's home is his castle, 15 police officers burst into Redlands, the

Redlands before the fire   (David E. Lolley)

elegant, thatched, moated, timbered Tudor country home of Keith Richards, in February '67. They arrested the owner and his guest Mick Jagger, and bundled them off to face charges relating to drug possession and use. A few years later, in July '73, Redlands was badly damaged by fire.

Local group The Mars Bars were late Eighties hopefuls.

WORTHING
The Mexican Hat Club was the place to be in the Sixties, when The Otis Men were the hottest local band.

Operational base of Steamhammer, whose Martin Quittenton played on Rod Stewart albums and co-wrote 'Maggie May' and 'You Wear It Well'.

Several London pub-rock bands recorded in Pebble Beach Studios at 12 South Farm Road.

During their first UK tour, R.E.M. played at the Carioca (April '84).

TYNE AND WEAR

BLAYDON

I seem to remember that one of Eric Burdon's relatives wrote 'Blaydon Races'.

CULLERCOATS

Chas Chandler, Animals bassist and manager of Hendrix and Slade, was laid to rest here in July '96.

DUNSTON

Birthplace of singer Brian Johnson, 5.10.47 (Geordie, AC/DC).

GATESHEAD

Birthplace of Animals drummer John Steel, 4.2.41.

Local trio Prelude reached the '74 chart with their acapella version of Neil Young's 'After The Goldrush'.

Dubstar began a hit run with Stars in summer '95.

GOSFORTH

Birthplace of Neil Tennant, 10.7.54 (Pet Shop Boys).

Alan Hull (Lindisfarne) was a nurse at St. Nicholas Psychiatric Hospital.

Mark and David Knopfler both went to Gosforth Grammar. The Dire Straits song 'Down To The Waterline' is about the Tyne.

Sting's band Last Exit had a '76 residency at the Gosforth Hotel.

JARROW

Birthplace of singer John Miles, 23.4.49 (mid-Seventies hits), whose Sixties band The Urge was based in nearby Hebburn.

'Jarrow Song' was a Top Ten hit for Alan Price in '74.

The Shadows rare E.P. called simply "Tony"

NEWCASTLE-UPON-TYNE

Birthplace of Hank Marvin, Britain's most influential guitarist ever, 28.10.41. He lived at 138 Stanhope Street, and was educated at Todds Nook School, Snow Street School and Rutherford Grammar – where he met Bruce Welch. The pair of them united in The Railroaders Skiffle Group, before moving to London to seek fame and fortune in April '58.

Also the birthplace of Chas Chandler, 18.12.38, and Eric Burdon, 4.5.41 (both of The Animals); Lee Jackson, 8.1.43 (Nice); singer Alan Hull, 20.2.45 (Lindisfarne – who also went to Rutherford Grammar); drummer Paul Thompson, 13.5.51 (Roxy Music).

As a schoolboy, Bruce Welch lived in a flat above Nazam's Fish and Chip Shop at 126 Elswick Road.

The Newcastle Empire hosted a string of rock'n'roll stars, from Charlie Gracie on up. Guitarist Bert Weedon made his variety début there in '59... at age 38!

The Beatles first visited to play the Majestic Ballroom in Westgate Road in January '63. The Odeon was a major package tour venue: The Rolling Stones, Bo Diddley and The Everly Brothers played there in October '63.

Meanwhile, the stage of the City Hall in Northumberland Street has seen everyone from Buddy Holly (March '58) to The Beatles (five times) to Bad Company, who made their début there in March '74. It was here also that Andy Summers skilfully impersonated the indisposed Mike Oldfield for a performance of *Tubular Bells* in autumn '75. Ironically, the support group was Sting's Last Exit.

Buddy Holly & The Crickets stayed at the Royal Turks Head Hotel.

Students passing through Newcastle University have included Bryan Ferry and John Porter (they formed

Geordie legend John Porter upstaged somewhat by Roxy Music's Eno

soul/R&B group the Gas Board here and were later reunited in Roxy Music), Wilko Johnson (Dr. Feelgood), and jazz trumpeters Ian Carr and John Walters (the latter went south with The Alan Price Set, became a television presenter and jovial chatterbox).

Lee Jackson went to St. Mary's Technical School – the very place that Stewart Copeland first saw Sting, playing with Last Exit in December '76.

A vibrant club/pub scene has always thrown up interesting groups: The Animals put Newcastle on the international map in '64, while The Von Dykes (with Lee Jackson, later in The Nice), Toby Twirl, Shorty & Them, Gin House and The Juneco Partners (with producer Bob Sargeant) found only localised success. The Gamblers (originally seen as Animals rivals) became Billy Fury's backing group after The Tornados. The Chosen Few contained Alan Hull (later of Lindisfarne), Mickey Gallagher

and John Turnbull (both later in Ian Dury's Blockheads); they had residencies at the long-gone Manhole and Key clubs. Popular in the late Sixties were Skip Bifferty, led by Graham Bell.

The weird and wonderful Skip Bifferty (which one's Skip?)

The most famous Sixties venue was the Club A Go Go in Percy Street. Home of The Animals, it presented every group from The Yardbirds to Hendrix. No alcohol was served in the Young Set room, but they had booze and gambling until 3am in the Jazz Lounge, where The Animals would play for up to five hours a night. That and sister club the Downbeat were owned and operated by Mike Jeffreys – later manager of The Animals and Hendrix. After a local gig, Fleetwood Mac went to the A Go Go to unwind but incurred the wrath of some local hardnuts who duffed them up for innocently engaging in conversation with their women. They commemorated the evening on 'Somebody's Gonna Get Their Head Kicked In Tonight' – and vowed never to return to Newcastle.

In the early Seventies came Geordie, who made national waves. Their singer Brian Johnson was reduced to doing vacuum cleaner ads when AC/DC revitalised him.

Later in the Seventies came a whole raft of new bands... The Young Bucks, Penetration, The Carpettes, Neon, and Last Exit – led by Sting.

The early Eighties saw the arrival of Punishment Of Luxury (arty farty progressive), Blind Fury, Darkness & Jive, Avenger, Raven (all metal), Wavis O'Shave, Arthur 2-Stroke, Erogenous Zones, and The Noise Toys. Later in the decade came Pop Dick & Harry, The Skywalkers, The Blues Burglars, The R&B Rockers, The Bats, and The Tribe Of Toffs, who reached the '89 Top Twenty with their novel 'John Kettley Is A Weather Man'.

Punishment Of Luxury: gagged by the critics

We looked out for Bob Smeaton & The Loud Guitars, Ian McCallum, The Dead Flowers, Soviet France, And All Because The Lady Loves, and Dum Dum Score, but none seemed to venture in this direction.

Late Eighties happening venues included the Bridge Hotel in Castle Square (home of the Jumping Jive Club); the Mayfair in Newgate Street (where Mott played in August '70); the Playhouse Theatre in the Haymarket; the Cornerhouse in Heaton Road (pub); the Jewish Mother in Leazes Lane (blues/R&B pub); the Broken Doll in Blenheim Street (pub with good R&B); the Poly in Sandyford Road; the Riverside at 57 Melbourne Street (club and studio complex)... and loads more; the whole city appeared to be jumping!

Owned by AC/DC man Brian Johnson, Lynx Studio was the town's hottest. Producer Dave Brewis was also in The Kane Gang (who made their début at local Tiffany's in December '83), early stars of the Kitchenware label, which operated from St. Thomas Street Workshops. Their first signing was the local Hurrah! in '82.

Many songs have been written about the locality. Lindisfarne's *Fog On The Tyne* was the biggest selling album of '72. The Nice recorded an album inspired by the Five Bridges spanning the Tyne.

In January '88, the Bucks Fizz tour bus crossed onto the wrong side of the Great North Road and crashed headlong into a lorry. Singer Mike Nolan was badly hurt.

Two numbers into an Oasis gig at the Riverside Club in August '94, some goon jumped onstage and hit Noel Gallagher, cutting his face. There's one in every crowd.

Local label Slampt issued the first single by Kenickie.

Local early Nineties acts included Hug, Puppy Fat, Planet Swerve, Feral (from Ryton), The Crisis Children, Lavender Faction, Duke, Those Nice People From Straightsville, Clockwork Dogs, Elementz Of Noise (drum'n'bass), Spraydog, and The Lighthouse Family, who became national stars with 'Lifted' in '95.

NORTH SHIELDS

Birthplace of guitarist Hilton Valentine, 22.5.43 (Animals... he lived at 56 Church Street); bass player Rod Clements, 17.11.47, and drummer Ray Laidlaw, 28.5.48 (both Lindisfarne).

A good current venue is the Wolsington House.

SOUTH SHIELDS

In May '57, Hank Marvin's Crescent City Group won the North East Skiffle competition, held at the Pier Pavilion.

In the mid-Sixties, The Urge (led by John Miles) and The Gas Board (led by Bryan Ferry) both played the Boys Brigade Hall and St. Hilda's Youth Club – as did top local faves The Shades Of Blue.

Jimi Hendrix came to town in February '67 to play the New Cellar Club – and Muhammad Ali came to town to get married at the Mosque. The whole town turned out to watch him riding down King Street in an open-topped double decker bus.

Doubling at Club Latino in Crossgate and Tito's in Stockton, every night for a week over New Year '68, Elton John played his last gigs with Long John Baldry & Bluesology. As soon as he got home, he quit the band to work for Dick James Music as a songwriter. "Who knows, I might write a hit one day," he figured.

Gerry Monroe, who went Top Five with the excruciating 'Sally' in 70, lived at 17a Mortimer Road – and that has got to be the most trivial of rock trivia sniff-snaff!

Beckett (led by Terry Wilson Slessor) were Seventies hopefuls, but their records made little headway. Marginally more successful were George Harrison proteges Splinter, whose '74 hit 'Costafine Town' was said to have been about South Shields.

The Angelic Upstarts grew up on the Brockley Whinns estate. Their stage set resembled a dungeon and gigs were terrifying. Early vinyl appeared on the shortlived Angelic Upstarts label – based at 411 South Palmerston Street.

Hometown of 'Ginger', leader of The Quireboys and The Wild Hearts, and Chris McCormac, leader of 3 Colours Red.

The Customs House is a very civilised late Nineties venue.

New Rising are late Nineties hopefuls.

SUNDERLAND

Birthplace of guitarist George Bellamy, 8.10.41 (Tornados); guitarist Mick Grabham, 22.1.48 (Procol Harum); guitarist Dave Stewart 9.9.52 (Tourists, Eurythmics).

Tommy Steele made his variety début at the Empire Theatre in the High Street in November '56; his bother Colin Hicks and Marty Wilde made theirs at the same venue in November '57. The Beatles played there twice, in February and November 63 – and in May 63, they fitted in a gig at the Rink Ballroom in Park Lane.

In December '63, a package show at the Odeon Cinema

The Five Bridges Suite by The Nice

(Virgin Records)

in Holmside featured Duane Eddy, Gene Vincent, The Shirelles, Mickie Most and Carter Lewis & The Southerners – featuring teenager Jimmy Page on guitar.

The Locarno was a top venue in the Seventies. Mott The Hoople played there in March '71.

Bryan Ferry's first group, The Banshees were based here. (Avid fan Siouxsie adopted the name!)

Cirkus were early Seventies prog-rockers; Highway released an album in '74; Battleaxe were early Eighties heavy metal heroes; The Toy Dolls reached the '84 Top Five with 'Nellie The Elephant' and later celebrated Sunderland FC's chairman on 'Tom Cowie's Car'; local punks Red London missed the charts with 'Sten Guns In Sunderland' but Red Alert reached the '82 indie Top Ten with 'Take No Prisoners'.

Toni Halliday recorded a solo album before forming early Nineties Peel faves/chart busters Curve; Leatherface were early Nineties grunge rockers; China Drum were early Nineties punks who moved out to Ovington; Rain and AOS 3 broke into the mid-Nineties college circuit.

The three females in hot Nineties band Kenickie (all born '78) met as 12 year olds at St. Anthony's Catholic school and later hung out in Mowberry Park together. Inevitably, they formed a band, named after John Travolta's sidekick in *Grease*. They débuted at The Broken Doll public house in late '95 and released their first single the following year.

Profundo Ross emerged as mid-Nineties punks; Hooton 3 Car were Peel faves.

If you can believe your eyes and ears dept: Saltburn resident Craig Rutherford won a '98 heat of the television show *Stars In Their Eyes* impersonating Denny Doherty of The Mamas And Papas.

TYNEMOUTH

Birthplace of guitarist Simon Cowe, 1.4.48 (Lindisfarne); guitarist Andy Taylor, 16.2.61 (Duran Duran); Johny Brown (singer with The Band Of Holy Joy).

Val McKenna cut several singles in the Sixties but was unable to find a hit.

Later founders of Lindisfarne, Rod Clements and Si Cowe met at King's School. Another pupil was Bob Sergeant – soon to join local R&B band The Juneco Partners, later to produce many hits.

Sting lived on the Marden Farm estate and was married to actress Frances Tomelty at St. Oswins Roman Catholic Church, Front Street, in May '76.

WALKER

On the B-side of their first single, The Animals covered an American hit by Timmy Shaw, 'Gonna Send You Back To Georgia'. They recorded it as 'Gonna Send You Back To Walker' – a Newcastle suburb!

WALLSEND

Birthplace of harmonica player Ray Jackson, 12.12.48 (Lindisfarne); Gordon Sumner, better known as Sting, 2.10.51 (Police).

Ray Jackson's pre-Lindisfarne band was the locally popular Autumn States.

Sting lived in Gerald Street and then in a flat above his father's dairy business in Station Road. He was educated at St. Cuthberts Grammar in Benwell Hill.

The town's oldest pub was also the best venue – the Ship In The Hole.

Dave Wood converted an old theatre at 71 High Street East into a recording studio – which was later the operational base of his indie label Neat Records – which introduced The Tygers Of Pan Tang, Venom, Blitzkreig and White Spirit.

WASHINGTON

Birthplace of Roxy Music leader Bryan Ferry, 26.9.45.

Home of late Eighties cult band Martin Stephenson & The Daintees.

WHITLEY BAY

The Rolling Stones played the Club A Go Go here November '63.

In the late Sixties, Alan Hull (later leader of Lindisfarne) ran the Folk Arts Club in the café at the Rex Hotel.

The Dire Straits song 'Tunnel Of Love' was inspired by fond memories of Spanish City, a seaside funfair.

The Tygers Of Pan Tang were late Seventies heavy metal grinders; guitarist John Sykes became a star in Thin Lizzy and Whitesnake.

In December '84, as 'Last Christmas' rose up the chart, Wham! kicked off their world tour at the town's primo venue, the Ice Rink. The Happy Mondays played there in November '90.

WARWICKSHIRE

LEAMINGTON SPA

Birthplace of bass player Arthur Grant, 14.5.50 (Edgar Broughton Band).

Hazel O'Connor went to Leamington Spa art college.

In the mid-Eighties, local band Mummy Calls were signed by Geffen, given a huge deal, but split after only one single.

Other local groups include Peppermint Rainbow (early Seventies), School Meals, The Shapes and The Defendents (all late Seventies), and The Joyce McKinney Experience (late Eighties).

Operational base of early Nineties techno star Banco de Gaia.

LONG MARSTON

Setting for the annual (July) Phoenix Festival. Headliners include Billy Bragg ('93), The Wonder Stuff and Beautiful South ('94), Suede ('95), The Manics and Neil Young ('96). It was to be The Prodigy and New Order in '98, but the festival was cancelled. Not a good year for gigs.

NUNEATON

Birthplace of Peter Becker (Eyeless In Gaza).

When The Rolling Stones played the Co-op Hall in November '63, a contingent of fans threw cream buns at them – covering Charlie Watts, who was not amused!

In '71, The Fresh Maggots recorded a non-selling/now collectable album for RCA.

The 77 Club was a punk/new wave venue.

Justin Welch went to George Elliot Comprehensive but sidelined academia to play drums with Elastica.

RUGBY

Birthplace of Pete Kember and Jason Pierce, both on 18.11.65 (founders of Spacemen Three).

Clifton Hall, owned by madcap rock manager Reg Calvert, became an early Sixties teen paradise/ commune for his stable of would-be stars – including Buddy Britten, Mike West, Tracey Martin, The Fortunes and Gullivers Travels. A bemused Jerry Lee Lewis accepted an invitation to stay overnight.

Local groups include The Mighty Avengers, who cut Jagger/Richard songs produced by Andrew Oldham; Pinkerton's Assorted Colours, who flickered through the charts in '66; and The Flying Machine (what was left of The Pinkertons), who scored one

Nikki Sudden sets light to his Harbury home for his band's debut album sleeve

big US hit. In '75, Jigsaw – comprising ex-members of the above bands – scored a US Top Three hit with 'Sky High'.

Operational base of late Eighties indie faves, Spacemen 3, whose singer Sonic Boom (aka Pete Kember) was once a pupil at the public school. Spectrum and Spiritualized were early Nineties spin-off bands.

Genesis P Orridge (Throbbing Gristle, Psychic TV) is said to have once worked as a cleaner at the

The Flying Machine of Rugby

Royal Showground; Guy Chadwick (House of Love) was once a dustman for Rugby Council .

SHIPSTON-ON-STOUR

During the Seventies, Kenny Everett lived at Old Red Lion House in Cherington – formerly owned by the actor Hugh Griffith.

STRATFORD-UPON-AVON

Birthplace of drummer Simon Gilbert, 15.5.65 (Suede) – and his cousin, keyboard player Neil Codling, 5.12.73 (also Suede).

Screaming Lord Sutch represented the National Teenage Party in a '63 by-election – the first of many vain attempts to become a Member Of Parliament. He drew a ton of publicity but only 209 votes.

TANWORTH-IN-ARDEN

Singer songwriter Nick Drake lived here with his family.

WARWICK

Birthplace of brothers Edgar, 24.10.47, and Steve Broughton, 20.5.50 – founders of hot late Sixties underground/progressive group The Edgar Broughton Band.

Operational base of The Hangover Blues Band – fronted by rabid Gene Vincent fan Sam Powell.

WATER ORTON

Operational base of Eighties indie favourites Felt, who cut the great indie chart topper 'Primitive Painters'.

WEST MIDLANDS

ASTON

Birthplace of guitarist Tony Iommi, 19.2.48; drummer Bill Ward, 5.5.48; singer Ozzy Osbourne, 3.12.48; bassplayer Geezer Butler, 17.7.49 – all of whom formed Black Sabbath in '69. Ozzy lived at 14 Lodge Road, Bill grew up in Grosvenor Road and Tony's mother had a sweet shop in Park Lane. They rehearsed at Aston Community Centre.

Also the birthplace of guitarist Trevor Burton, 9.3.49 (Move).

BRMB's radio studio in Aston Road North was formerly ATV's Alpha Television Studio. *Thank Your Lucky Stars* was broadcast from here during the Sixties.

The Elbow Room in the High Street opened in February '68, presenting such groups as Sam Gopal's Dream and Fairport Convention.

BILSTON

Birthplace of drummer Don Powell, 10.9.46 (Slade). He went to Villiers Road Primary, and then Etheridge Secondary Modern.

Slade regarded the Trumpet in the High Street as their local pub.

The Robin Hood 2 is a cool late Nineties venue.

BIRMINGHAM

Birthplace of bass player John Rostill, 16.6.42 (Shadows); songwriters/singers John Carter, 20.10.42, and Ken Lewis, 3.12.42 (Ivy League); keyboard player Mike Pinder, 12.12.42 (Moody Blues); singer Carl Wayne, 18.8.44 (Move); drummer Bev Bevan, 24.11.44 (Move); drummer Nick Mason, 27.1.45 (Pink Floyd); guitarist Roy Wood,

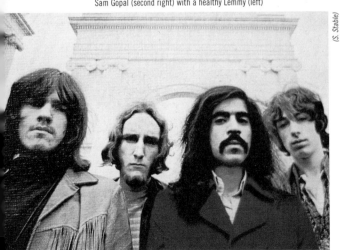

Sam Gopal (second right) with a healthy Lemmy (left)

(S. Stable)

Nick Mason

(Kate Koumi)

8.11.46 (Move); drummer Mike Kellie, 24.3.47 (Spooky Tooth); bass player Dave Pegg, November 47 (Fairport Convention); guitarist Jeff Lynne, 30.12.47 (Idle Race, Move, ELO); bassist Clint Warwick, 25.6.49 (Moody Blues); Steve Winwood, 12.5.48 (Spencer Davis Group, Traffic); Carl Palmer, 20.3.51 (Atomic Rooster, ELP); Andy Cox, 25.1.56, Dave Wakeling, 19.2.57, and Ranking Roger, 21.2.61 (all of The Beat); John Taylor, 2.6.60, and Nick Rhodes, 8.6.62 (both Duran Duran); Roland Gift, 28.5.62 (Fine Young Cannibals); Michael Ball, 27.6.62.

Lol Creme (10cc) and Dave Swarbrick (Fairport) both went to Birmingham College of Art.

Local hero Steve Gibbons has been leading bands since the late Fifties. First Brum group to record was Jimmy Powell & The Dimensions ('62) and the first to hit the Top Ten was The Applejacks with 'Tell Me When' (March 64).

The Idle Race

Among the millions of bands to get going in the Sixties were Big Bertha, The Fortunes, Raymond Froggatt, The Idle Race, The King Bees, Judas Priest, Gerry Levene & The Avengers, Locomotive, The Rockin' Berries, Mike Sheridan & The Nightriders, The Uglys, Carl Wayne & The Vikings, Pat Wayne & The Beachcombers, The Meddy Evils, etc etc etc. Far too many to mention.

Most popular Sixties acts were The Spencer Davis Group, who had a residency at the Golden Eagle (obliterated for a car park); The Moody Blues, who used to hang around Jack Woodroffe's music shop hoping an agent would come in and offer them a gig; and The Move, who got together at the Cedar Club in Constitution Hill — one of the city's primo haunts.

After gigs, many groups would meet at the Alex Fleur de Lys mobile pie stall at the end of Hill Street, opposite the Albany Hotel and just along from the Crown pub where Denny Laine & The Diplomats were resident. The Move formed after initial discussions over pie and chips.

In the Seventies came E.L.O. ('71), Wizzard ('72), City Boy, Suburban Studs, Magnum ('77), The Beat, Dexy's Midnight Runners, Duran Duran ('78), The Au Pairs, The Prefects ('79), and more.

The Maisonettes on Heartache Avenue, Birmingham

In the Eighties came UB40 ('80), The Bureau, Nikki Sudden, Orphan, The Maisonettes, Fashion ('82), Terry & Gerry, Red Shoes ('83), Felt, Swans Way ('84), Jaki Graham ('85), Great Outdoors, The Boatyman, Fuzzbox, Scarlet Fantastic ('86), Hollywood Beyond (87), The Hudson Giants, Dogs D'Amour, Dandelion ('88), and more.

In the Nineties followed a new wave of bands: And Why Not? (who found chart success on Island), Electribe 101 (who charted on Mercury before mutating into The Original Rockers), Cerebral Fix, Korova Milk Bar (*Clockwork Orange* fans), Doodlebug, L-Kage, Delicious Monster, Sweet Jesus, Terminal Power Company, Monkey Messiah, Asia Blue (who charted briefly with their début single), Higher Intelligence Agency, Weird's War, The Kittenbirds, Broadcast, Dissident Prophet, Novak, and big beat frontrunners Bentley Rhythm Ace (led by Richard March, ex Pop Will Eat Itself), who reached the '97 Top Twenty.

Post-Dexy's offshoot The Bureau with Mick Merton (Merton Parkas) (left)

Venues come and go. At different times the Odeon in New Street and the Town Hall were happening – but the National Exhibition Centre spelt the demise of most large halls. In the Sixties, it was essential to play the Ma Regan circuit – run by the venerable woman herself.

Prime Sixties blues venue was Henry's Blueshouse, upstairs (now full of heating ducts) at the Crown Hotel in Station Street, which resounded to such shakers as Rory Gallagher and Jethro Tull. Booker/organiser was *Brum Beat* publisher Jim Simpson, who initially set it up as a showcase for the Bakerloo Blues Line and later became manager of Black Sabbath, who played devastating early gigs there. Jim now manages King Pleasure & The Biscuit Boys and continues to release albums on his Big Bear label.

The Railway pub on Curzon Street was hot in the Seventies, when Steve Gibbons was one of the few singers keeping the local scene alive... but it became a Mexican restaurant.

Barbarella's in Cumberland Street (now buried under some convention centre site) was the groovy club throughout the Seventies, when its cheesy red lighting and sticky carpeting even inspired an album track by The Photos. Duran Duran did their earliest gigs there. When it closed down, the new romantic set moved on to the Underworld, the Cedar Club and Hawkins Wine Bar before settling at the Rum Runner (which had been going since the Sixties). Housed under Don Berrow's betting shop in Broad Street, it became world famous as Duran Duran's home base and as such remains a shrine for fans, despite having been bulldozed and redeveloped. Simon LeBon's début with the group was at the Hosteria, a wine bar in Hurst Street.

Rebecca's in Lower Severn Street was a popular new wave venue: the famous Police line-up of Sting/Copeland/Summers made their début there in August '77. Dexy's Midnight Runners played there when they were still Lucy & The Lovers.

The oldest recording studio in Birmingham is Zella, housed in a rented church hall in Ampton Road. Everyone from The Move to The Maisonettes worked there. Probably more famous is UB40's studio, the Abattoir (a converted slaughter house) at 92 Fazeley Street, on the canal. Rich Bitch, at 505 Bristol Road, Selly Oak was also hot, with the likes of Fuzzbox and Ruby Turner recording there.

The Vindaloo label, run by Rob Lloyd (Prefects, Nightingales) from an address in Balsall Heath, gave Fuzzbox their first release.

Before he zapped into view with Sigue Sigue Sputnik, Martin Degville had a clothes stall in the Oasis Street Market. It was known as Degville's Dispensary and Boy George was an occasional sales assistant.

ELO

ELO recorded Birmingham Blues; Mott The Hoople cut Birmingham (contrasting Brum with its Alabama namesake).

Rolf Harris reckons the turning point to hip Glastonbury-style acceptance came with a gig at Birmingham University in early '93, not long after 'Stairway To Heaven' had charted. The same venue saw the last ever performance by Joy Division, in May '80.

Hot late Nineties rave venues include the Pulse in Hurst Street and the Church in Broad Street.

BLOXWICH
Ambrose Slade used to play Mossley Youth Club and Noddy Holder used to quaff ale at the Three Men In A Boat in Stephenson Avenue on the Beechdale estate.

BRIERLEY HILL
Screaming Lord Sutch wiped his nose on the brand new stage curtains at the Town Hall, causing the caretaker to throw a dramatic wobbler.

Brierley Hill Youth Club was a regular venue for The 'N Betweens (later Slade).

The Robin Hood Inn is a happening Nineties venue.

CASTLE BROMWICH
Birthplace of Roger Taylor, 26.4.60 (Duran Duran).

The Bel Air Club was a Sixties venue.

COVENTRY
Birthplace of disc jockey Brian Matthew, 17.10.28 (*Saturday Club*); early Sixties stars Vince Hill, 16.4.37, and Frank Ifield, 30.11.37; singer Hazel O'Connor, 16.5.55 (at 136 Wyken Ave, Wyken – educated at Foxhill Comprehensive); singer Terry Hall, 19.3.59 (Specials, Colour Field); singer Julianne Regan, 30.6.62 (All About Eve); Clint Mansell, 7.11.62 (Pop Will Eat Itself).

In November '62, The Beatles made their Midlands début at the Matrix Hall – supported by The Mark Allen

Group and Lee Teri – all for 5/6d. The Fab Four returned to play the Coventry Theatre in Hales Street twice – in February and November '63.

In May '64, the headmaster of Woodlands Comprehensive suspended eleven boys for sporting Rolling Stones hairstyles. He reinstated them when they compromised with neater Beatles' styles.

The first record shops in town were Jill Hanson's at 8 Market Way, and the Record Centre in Smithford Way.

The town's first breakout group was The Sorrows, who hit with 'Take A Heart' in '65. Five years later, lead singer Don Fardon reached the Top Three with 'Indian Reservation'. In the mid-Seventies, Fardon was the landlord of the Alhambra pub, just behind Sainsbury's.

Less successful Sixties groups included The Sovereigns, Rufus' Rebels, The Sabres, The Toreadors, and The Peeps (obviously a Lady Godiva allusion).

Pre-The Peeps: The Penny Peeps

The Locarno was a popular Sixties/Seventies venue. Pink Floyd played there in February '72.

In June '68, John Lennon and Yoko Ono planted two acorns outside Coventry Cathedral.

October' 72 saw two Coventry chart-toppers. Lieutenant Pigeon (who also recorded as Stavely Makepeace) cut 'Mouldy Old Dough' in the front room of Robert Woodward's house; Chuck Berry's biggest (and arguably worst) hit, 'My Ding A Ling', was recorded live at Tiffany's in Smithford Way during the Lanchester Arts Festival of '72. Lieutenant Pigeon faded quickly from view, but not before immortalising their local shopping centre on 'Gosford Green Rag'.

Indian Summer (progressive) and Dando Shaft (folk) both made albums in the Seventies.

Coventry was the home of the neo-ska 2-Tone sound which swept Britain soon after its inception in February '79. Originators were The Specials ('77) and Selecter ('79). Fast behind were The Swinging Cats ('79). Fun Boy Three and Roddy Radiation & The Tearjerkers were both Specials' descendents, and Terry Hall's Colour Field was third generation.

As a local talent showcase, the General Wolfe on Foleshill Road was a focal point on the scene. The Dog & Trumpet (next to HMV!) was another good place to see bands.

Horizon Studios in Warwick Road was the home of the 2-Tone sound, while Paul Sampson ran Cabin Studios on London Road.

All but forgotten Coventry groups include The Flys, God's Toys and The Criminal Class.

Before Birdland were The Zo-Mos

More memorable Eighties breakers were King (hits!), The Primitives (hits!), The Giraffes, The Pink Umbrellas, Birdland (hits!) and After Tonight (who were produced by ex-Special Lynval Golding).

In the Nineties came The Ludicrous Lollipops, Family Gotown, Adorable, Billy Sagoo, The Chrome Daisies, and The Relatives.

Among pupils at Coventry Drama school were Paul King (King) and Loz Netto (Sniff & The Tears).

Pupils at Coventry Art School included Specials organiser Jerry Dammers.

Before becoming lead singer in Selecter, Essex-born Pauline Black was studying biochemistry at Lanchester Poly. She also worked in the radiography unit at Coventry Hospital.

As lead singer in The Reluctant Stereotypes, Paul King played his first gig at the Climax, a pub in the Arcade in January '80. After a run of mid-Eighties hits as King, he became a face on MTV and Sky.

Peter & Gordon's Lady Godiva was their last hit; The Specials' '81 number one 'Ghost Town' was a sad commentary on the city's decline.

The city's most successful music biz man is Pete Waterman, a mad Tamla Motown fan who ran the Soul Hole record shop and was a disc jockey at Tiffany's. Riased in a council house, he left school at 14 – and went on to produce over 160 hits – starting with his own 'Goodbye-ee' (recorded under the name of 14-18) and 'Alright Baby' by

Coventry group Stevenson's Rocket (who were erroneously tipped as the next Bay City Rollers).

The Warwick Arts Centre is a comfortable late Nineties venue presenting international names.

DIGBETH

A popular venue since the Sixties, the Barrel Organ is still going. The Civic Hall in Milk Street presented bigger acts.

Ozzy Osbourne worked in a slaughter house here, killing "a minimum of 250 cattle a day".

The Sanctuary in the High Street is a favourite late Nineties rave venue.

Steel Pulse

DUDLEY

Birthplace of Lennie Henry, 29.8.58, who went to the Bluecoat School.

In February '66, 16-year-old Jenny Wren cut a single for Columbia: 'Chasing My Dream All Over Town'.

JBs in King Street has been described as the best rock club in the Midlands. Robert Plant has used it for press gigs and video shoots. Some of the audience are reputed to have stood on the same spot for 15 years or more! Fleetwood Mac and Black Sabbath played there in the Dark Ages; The Stone Roses in March '89, The Exploited in October '98.

Local group The Montanas were poised for national breakthrough in the Sixties... but it wasn't to be. The Maisonettes enjoyed brief success with their '82 Top Tenner 'Heartbreak Avenue'.

When he joined Led Zeppelin, John Bonham was living at 27 Butterfield Court, Eves Hill.

Graduate Records, based at 1 Union Street, released singles by Eazie Ryder, The Venigmas, The Chefs, The Last Gang, The Circles, and Mean Street Dealers before zooming into the top five with UB40's 'King'/'Food For Thought' in March '80.

Local Nineties bands include Ember Days.

The Robin Hood is a cool late Nineties venue.

EDGBASTON

In the Sixties, the Cecilia coffee bar at Five Ways, just around the corner from Ladywood police station, was a meeting place for impressionable teenagers, arty types, layabouts and potential pop stars. Steve Gibbons & The Dominettes often played there; Roy Wood and Jeff Lynne talked about their favourite records.

The Cheetahs were Sixties beatsters managed by the legendary Ma Regan, from her house at 31 Woodbourne Road.

Toyah Wilcox was educated at the Church of England College for Girls.

Steve Gibbons lived in Yew Tree Road – as did graphic artist and disc jockey Mike Horseman, in whose house The Beat are said to have formed, UB40 are said to have conjured up their name, and Boy George is said to have stayed.

One of the strangest gigs Black Sabbath ever played was a convent in Edgbaston.

Specialist blues and jazz label Big Bear Records started at 190 Monument Road.

ERDINGTON

Bill Ward (Black Sabbath) formed his first band, The Rest, at Slade Road School.

Mothers Club was one of the most famous progressive/underground venues in Britain. Led Zeppelin played there in March '69, Pink Floyd in January '69, Mott The Hoople in January '70.

The Pandora achieved only local notoriety.

HANDSWORTH

Local residents Steel Pulse called their '78 début album *Handsworth Revolution*.

Ozzy Osbourne lived here with other members of his first group The Music Machine.

Also local were The Equators, The Beat and Fine Young Cannibals.

The Beat's record label Go Feet had offices at 116 Hamstead Road.

Home of BBC Radio One presenter and recording star, Apache Indian, who stormed the Nineties charts.

The Plaza Ballroom was a popular Sixties venue... part of the Ma Regan circuit. The Rolling Stones played here in August and September '63 – doubling each time at the Plaza in Old Mill.

KINGS HEATH

Birthplace of Toyah Wilcox, 18.5.58.

UB40 played their first gig at the Hare And Hounds in February '79 and recorded their first album in a makeshift studio in Bob Lamb's house at 68

Toyah pops the questions

Cambridge Street. Duran Duran also cut their first demos there. Lamb then moved to a custom built studio in Highbury Road, where the likes of Slade, Ruby Turner and Stephen (Tin Tin) Duffy have recorded albums.

The Ritz Ballroom was the local gig during the Sixties — another Ma Regan venue.

Bob Lamb's studio made famous by Stephen Duffy and partners

KINGSTANDING
Steve and Muff Winwood spent much of their spare time listening to records in Matty's record shop (now Rumbelow's) in Hawthorn Road.

Local group The Debonaires released Hoochie Coochie Man.

KINGSWINFORD
Birthplace of bass player Alex Griffin, 29.8.71 (Ned's Atomic Dustbin) and the late Rob Jones (Wonder Stuff).

KINVER
During the Seventies, Roy Wood lived at Gothersley Hall in nearby Stourton.

LONGBRIDGE
During their March '58 UK visit, Buddy Holly & The Crickets were given a tour of the Austin/BMC factory. Buddy was interested in purchasing an Austin Healey and was quoted $2,303 plus $138 shipping charges to Texas.

MOSELEY
Birthplace of bass player Ace Kefford, 10.12.46 (Move).

The Fortunes started at Moseley Grammar School, as did Denny Laine & The Diplomats. Other pupils included Bev Bevan (ELO) and Jasper Carrot.

Roy Wood and Jeff Lynne went to Moseley Art College.

The Move's album sleeve: a product of Moseley Art School

The Au Pairs were based in Moseley, as were Dangerous Girls, Fashion, and The Noseflutes.

Blues singer Ruby Turner made her début at the Fighting Cocks pub, backed by two guitarists.

The Jug of Ale became a cool venue in the Nineties, presenting up and comers like Ocean Colour Scene — album chartbusters in '96 with *Moseley Shoals*.

Local Nineties bands include Pram and Urban South.

NECHELLS
1982 chart toppers Musical Youth all went to Duddeston Manor School.

OLD HILL
The Plaza in Halesowen Road was part of Ma Regan's circuit. The Beatles played there in January '63; the Stones in August and September '63.

PERRY BARR
Ozzy Osbourne went to Birchfield Secondary Modern.

Joan Armatrading attended Canterbury Cross Secondary Modern (later the Broadway School).

QUARRY BANK
Birthplace of singer Jonn Penney, 17.9.68, and bass player Matt Cheslin, 28.11.70 (both of Ned's Atomic Dustbin).

SEDGLEY
Birthplace of keyboard player Rob Collins, 23.3.63 (Charlatans); guitarist Gareth Pring (aka Rat), 8.11.70, and drummer Dan Wharton, 28.7.72 (both of Ned's Atomic Dustbin).

SELLY OAK
Operational base of Nineties indie band Dan Dare's Dog.

SHARD END
Jeff Lynne attended Alderlea Secondary Modern. He and Roy Wood plotted the formation of The Electric Light Orchestra at the Pack Horse – where Musical Youth later made their début.

SMALL HEATH
Operational base of Carter Lewis & The Southerners, which evolved into The Ivy League, The Flowerpot Men, and First Class.

The Ivy League (back girls!)

SOLIHULL
Birthplace of bassplayer Steve Bingham, 4.4.49 (Foundations, Slim Chance); Nina Carter, (Blonde On Blonde – and later Mrs Rick Wakeman).

The Applejacks were hot in '64 – 'Tell Me When' was their big hit. Unusually, they had a girl bassplayer – called Megan Davies. In September '64, she married guitarist Gerry Freeman at St. Alphege Church – after which they scuttled down to Wilton Hall in Bletchley, where they had a gig that night.

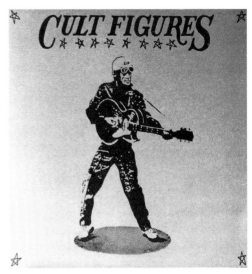

Sensational Solihull Swell Maps spin off single 'Zip Nolan'

Before moving to Sheffield and forming The Human League, Phil Oakey was at school here – as was Spizz, who fronted Spizz 77, Spizz Oil, Spizz Energi, Athletico Spizz and various other Spizz orientated outfits. Spizz Energi topped the '80 indie chart with 'Where's Captain Kirk?' Some of Swell Maps were from here too.

The NEC (National Exhibition Centre) is at Bickerhill. Rory Gallagher was the first rock act to play here, followed by Rod Stewart and hundreds more. Now one of the country's major venues. Wonder Stuff star Miles Hunt (whose uncle Bill was in Wizzard) worked there as a litter picker before making it as a guitar picker.

When she fronted The Lazers, Carol Decker sang outside the entrance to the NEC – promoting the *Brum Beat* album. Locals smiled when she vowed to headline there some day. She did, of course, with T'Pau.

Hottest local group of the late Eighties – The Fanatics.

Ocean Colour Scene broke out in the early Nineties, progressing slowly until '96 Top Tenner 'You've Got It Bad'.

SPARKHILL
Bev Bevan's mother used to run a record store in Stratford Road – Heavy Head Records.

STETCHFORD
When she first arrived in Britain from St. Kitts, Joan Armatrading lived with her family in a single room at 22 Coralie Street in Brookfields.

STOURBRIDGE
Hottest mid-Sixties band was Sounds Of Blue, with Christine Perfect and Stan Webb.

Most top Sixties bands played at the Town Hall, where the stage was so close to the audience that undoing the singer's trousers became a local ritual.

Diamond Head were big on the Eighties heavy metal scene.

The Belfry Hotel was a major circuit gig in the Seventies when everyone from Bowie to Mott The Hoople played there.

Members of Wild And Wondering and From Eden redistributed themselves to form late Eighties national breakouts Pop Will Eat Itself (Top Ten with 'Get The Girl! Kill The Baddies!' in '93) and The Wonder Stuff (top five with 'The Size Of A Cow' in '91).

After support spots on Wonder Stuff tours, Ned's Atomic Dustbin (the name was *Goon Show* inspired) formed their own Furtive label (based in Oldbury), then signed with Sony and went top five with the album *God Fodder* in '91. Disbanded in '96; splinter groups Groundswell and Floyd are locally based.

Also emerging in the Nineties were Fret Blanket and Joyland.

TIVIDALE

Home of ace Nineties psyche-pop quartet Laxton's Superb – named not only after the apple but also the working title for The Beatles' *Revolver* track 'I Want To Tell You'.

SUTTON COLDFIELD

Birthplace of singer Rob Halford, 25.8.51 (Judas Priest).

In February '63, The Beatles made their only visit – to play at St. Peter's Church Hall in Maney Hill Road.

In early '66, The Move made their début at the Belfry, a prime venue of the national circuit in the Sixties but now a world famous Ryder Cup golf course. Mott The Hoople played there in March '72.

The Mellotron was developed and produced at 328 Aldridge Street in Streetly. The first models went on sale at the end of '63 and production continued here until '86. Among the many bands to benefit from this unique instrument were The Beatles, The Moody Blues, Pink Floyd, Genesis, King Crimson, The Beach Boys and Led Zeppelin.

WALSALL

Birthplace of singer/guitarist Noddy Holder, 15.6.46 (Slade). He lived in New Hall Street and went to Blue Coats Infants, followed by T.P.Riley Comprehensive. Noddy presented a Harp Beat rock plaque to the Mayor to commemorate Slade's first gig, at the Town Hall in April '66.

Also the birthplace of drum'n'bass pioneer Goldie, 1966.

Judas Priest singer Rob Halford grew up in Lichfield Street.

The Moody Blues played their earliest gigs in an upstairs room at the Stork Hotel – then an R&B club, later a Berni Inn.

The Big Boss Men were local Sixties R&B hopefuls.

In August '68, Jimmy Page travelled to West Midlands College of Higher Education in Gorway Road to check out a singer for his new group... Robert Plant, then leading local hopefuls Hobstweedle. He got the job! At the time,

Birthplace of Robert Plant

Plant was living at 21a Bloxwich Road... and a local agent had just told him that he "would never make it as a professional singer as long as he'd got a hole in his arse".

Paul Fenech, guitarist with The Meteors, caused an affray and was caught with an offensive weapon at a Walsall gig in late '85. He got sent down for nine months.

The Junction is a cool Nineties venue.

WARLEY

Christine McVie's father lived in Lightwoods Hill, Bearwood – and gave violin lessons.

The Kings Head in Bearwood was a popular Sixties gig.

WEDNESBURY

Home of *Thank Your Lucky Stars* panelist Janice Nichols who made "I'll give it five" a Sixties cliche.

Slade drummer Don Powell went to Wednesbury Technical College.

The Youth Centre in Woden Road North was known locally as "the Teen Pan Alley of the Midlands" – and no wonder! Among the groups they put on were Shane Fenton & The Fentones (who were paid £80), The Merseybeats (£50), The Paramounts (£55), The Merseybeats (£50), The Outlaws (£50), Mike Berry & The Innocents (£85), Denny Laine & The Diplomats (£110), Herman's Hermits (£20). Support groups like Danny Cannon & The Ramrods, Mel Fender & The Spartans, and Rikki Topaz & The Diamonds got £10 – more than they'd have got at the Marquee!

Robert Plant logo inspired by a Wolverhampton Wanderer

WEST BROMWICH
Birthplace of Robert Plant, 20.8.48. He moved to Walsall when he was 16, but on joining Led Zeppelin, gave his address as 46 Trinity Road, West Bromwich.

The Beatles played at the Adelphi Ballroom in New Street in November '62 – doubling at the Baths in Smethwick.

Spencer Davis first encountered Steve and Muff Winwood at the Golden Lion pub. The Adelphi was another Sixties haunt.

Paul Lockey, a teacher at Charlemont Junior School, was in The Band Of Joy with Robert Plant and John Bonham during the late Sixties.

The Sea Urchins got going in the early Nineties; local rapper Darren Deere was an apprentice at West Brom FC; the youthful Credit To The Nation, led by Mattie Hanson, broke out with a string of mid-Nineties hits.

WILLENHALL
In their early days as The 'N Betweens, Slade regularly played St. Giles Church Youth Club.

Locally based Makin' Time were a hip mid-Eighties mod and soul band who cut two albums but were stranded when Stiff records went tits up. They mutated into The Gift Horses, two of whom moved north and formed The Charlatans.

WINSON GREEN
Birthplace of singer Wendy Wu, 29.11.59 (Photos).

Ozzy Osbourne was incarcerated in Winson Green prison for six weeks, for non-payment of fines.

WOLVERHAMPTON
Birthplace of guitarist Brian Pendleton, 13.4.44 (Pretty Things); folkie Bill Caddick, 27.6.44 (Home Service); bass player Jim Lea, 14.6.49 (Slade); singer Kevin Rowland, 17.8.53 (Dexy's Midnight Runners); John Hyatt (Three Johns); Tjinder Singh, 12.2.68 (Cornershop).

At Christmas 55, Jimmy Young was starring in panto – *Robinson Crusoe* at the Grand Theatre.

Slade guitarist Dave Hill went to Warstones Primary, Springdale Infants, and Highfields Secondary Modern.

Before they became Slade, The N'Betweens played local pubs the Connaught, the Woolpack and the Ship And Rainbow. Jim Lea had actually been born in a pub, the Melbourne Arms (long since demolished). Noddy Holder joined the group after long negotiations in Beatty's coffee bar in the High Street.

Finders Keepers were another local group. Things were looking good when Scott Walker produced them... but they split when Glenn Hughes and Mel Galley went off to form Trapeze. There were also The Californians, The Wolves (Pye) and Zuider Zee (CBS).

Local singer John Ford hoped to do an Engelbert by changing his name to Eli Bonaparte – but the ruse was not successful.

The Victims were the town's first punk group; The Circles were late Seventies nouveau mods; Weapon Of Peace were at the forefront of the early Eighties UK reggae scene.

Wolverhampton Poly in Wulfruna Street has put on gigs since the Sixties. Motorhead made their local début in the refectory, on a stage made of dining tables taped together, and when Sonny Terry & Brownie McGhee played, Sonny was so inebriated he had to be carried on stage.

Local lads done proud

The Catacombs in Temple Street was a popular venue, as was the Lafayette Club in Thornley Street. The Pistols and The Pretenders played there, and local group Magnum were always called when groups pulled out. There wasn't a glass or neon tube left in the place after The Angelic Upstarts took on some local fascist thugs. Police were called and were not amused to find a pig's head with a copper's helmet on it... an Upstarts' stage prop. It closed down and became a casino. Some of the stories I've heard about the place would make your pubic hair curl.

The Keys To The Highway was a blues club which opened at the Queens Head, but moved to the Ship And Rainbow. Everyone from Champion Jack Dupree to Robert Plant has sung there.

Another perennial meeting place was the Milano coffee bar in Darlington Street.

Hottest late Eighties group was The Mighty Lemon Drops, who started in spring '85 and made their début in the upstairs room of the Opposite Lock. Others included Neon Hearts, The Wild Flowers, Arcana, Dogs D'Amour, and The Sandkings – led by Jas Mann, who under his next *nomme de guerre* Babylon Zoo would top the '96 charts with TV-ad promoted 'Spaceman'.

In January '90, when their former label FM Revolver re-promoted an old single against their wishes, The Stones Roses visited their offices at 152 Goldthorn Hill, Penn and vented their spleen, causing over £20,000 worth of damage. They pleaded guilty and were fined £3000 each.

Robert Plant and Bev Bevan remain staunch Wolves fans, despite all their ups and downs.

In their early days, Oasis played Wulfrun Hall twice – in November and December '93. For smaller bands, the Varsity Tavern proved an ideal Nineties gig.

Tjinder Singh (Cornershop) grew up here, in the Sikh community. Also local were twins Jackie and Pauline Cuff (who charted with Nineties group Soho); the Anglo-Asian dance act Intermix, drum'n'bass guru Goldie (a '95 Top Tenner with his début album Timeless), and indie combo The Slingbacks.

YARDLEY

Birthplace of bass player Overend Watts, 13.5.47 (Mott The Hoople);

Denny Laine (Move, Wings) and Dave Pegg (Fairport) went to Yardley Grammar; Ace Kefford (Move) went to Yardley Wood Secondary Modern.

The Twitch Club and the Swan public house were the places to go during the mid- Sixties beat boom. Pink Floyd played the latter in July '67.

The Trumpet (Bilston)

Shuffle, of The Beat, on an Erdington street corner

(M. Halasa)

WILTSHIRE

BOX

Previously known for Brunel's 1830s railway tunnel linking it to Corsham (at two miles, the longest to date), the village of Box is now famous as the location of Peter Gabriel's Real World Studio. After it opened, much modification was needed to eliminate vibration from express trains.

(Hypnosis)

Peter Gabriel drives out to Box

BRADFORD-ON-AVON

Sometime home of Mike Edwards and Simon Matthews (Jesus Jones).

CALNE

Nineties home of Julian Cope and Rustic Rod's Mail Order, run by Rod Goodway (ex Magic Muscle, Bevis Frond).

CHIPPENHAM

In the first minutes of Sunday 17.4.60, the Ford Consul taking Gene Vincent, Eddie Cochran and his girlfriend Sharon Sheeley from Bristol to Heathrow spun out of control and crashed into a concrete lamp post on the A4 at Rowden Hill, on the outskirts of town. (This was before the construction of the M4 motorway). All three were rushed to hospital in Bath. The driver, George Martin from Hartcliffe in Bristol, and road manager Patrick Thompkins emerged unhurt

Future pop star Dave Dee was the policeman entrusted to look after Cochran's possessions, including his guitar, until arrangements were made to ship them back to California.

Gold-diggers was a major Seventies/Eighties venue.

Home of Spiritualized keyboard player Kate Radley and singer/guitarist Jason Pierce — her boyfriend until The Verve's Richard Ashcroft won her affection.

EAST KNOYLE

Not only the birthplace of Christopher Wren, 20.10.1632, but also the location of Hays House Residential and Nursing Home, where both Phil Lynott and his father-in-law Leslie Crowther sought to uncomplicate their lives.

ENFORD

Birthplace of Trevor Davies, 27.11.44, and Ian Amey, 15.5.44 — better known as Dave Dee's pals Dozy and Tich.

GREAT DUNFORD

Sting married longtime lover Trudi Styler locally and settled into a £2 million starter home in this tranquil village.

LITTLE SOMERFORD
In '90, Van Morrison purchased a country retreat here.

MARLBOROUGH
Singer songwriter Nick Drake was a pupil at Marlborough School.

In November '90, Rolling Stone Ronnie Wood was on the M4 waving traffic away from his broken down car when some twat struck him and broke both his legs.

MELKSHAM
After more than a decade in oblivion, 28-year-old Paul Gadd made one last dramatic bid for recognition – relaunching himself as the sequinned, spangled Gary Glitter. As such he made his début at the Assembley Hall in July '72.

Badgeman are a Nineties indie band.

NORTH WRAXALL
After his hits, Curt Smith from Tears For Fears purchased a 16th century pad here.

SALISBURY
Birthplace of singer and actor Brian Protheroe (reached '74 Top Thirty with 'Pinball'). Also of David (Dee) Harman, 17.12.43, John Dymond, 10.7.44 and Michael Wilson, 4.3.44, who with a couple of mates from Enford formed the city's most famous group – Dave Dee, Dozy, Beaky, Mick and Tich. They reached their commercial peak with chart topping 'Legend Of Xanadu' in '68, but soon went off the boil. Once a police cadet, Dave Dee became a record company executive while his cohorts kept at it. Mick Wilson was subsequently a driving instructor in town.

Rather less successful was The Purge, whose solitary '65 single went nowhere.

Kerry Minnear of Gentle Giant also came from round here – as did progressive band Pussy, who realised they

Fetching sleeve to the Pussy Plays album

wouldn't get far with a name like that and changed their name to Jerusalem. Ironically, Pussy's album is now worth a fortune on the collectors market.

In January 71, Uriah Heep called their second album *Salisbury*.

Late Eighties metal group Tokyo Blade emerged from the ashes of several predecessors, including White Diamond, Genghis Khan and Shogun – but by '90 had split into two factions: Mr Ice and Jagged Edge. Late Eighties indie band Bubblegum Splash reached the indie charts before evolving into Jane From Occupied Europe. Mad Cow Disease were Nineties hopefuls.

Buddy Holly & The Crickets played at the Gaumont in March '58 and stayed at the Old George Hotel. The Gaumont became a regular package tour venue – everyone from The Everly Brothers to Walker Brothers played there.

The Beatles played the City Hall in Fisherton Street in June '63. Later on, Cream, David Bowie, Pink Floyd, Led Zeppelin, Toyah Wilcox, Big Country and everybody else played there

The Alexandra Dance Rooms in New Street was a cool venue in the late Sixties, when a weekly blues night presented John Mayall, Chicken Shack, Fleetwood Mac and other circuit bands.

The Technical College in Southampton Road was a good late Seventies venue. Dimwit local bikers disrupted an Adam & The Ants gig, resulting in the nearest the city has seen to a riot. The Grange Hotel in St. Marks Avenue presented current cutting edge bands like The TV Personalities and Crass – but then went cabaret as Concordes Nightclub. The Arts Centre in Bedwin Street was a good late Eighties venue, putting on Napalm Death, The Fuzztones and even Michelle Shocked.

Thin Lizzy leader Phil Lynott died at the city's General Infirmary in January '86. Aged 36, he was suffering from pneumonia, heart failure, kidney malfunction and severe liver deterioration. The last song he wrote was called 'I'm Still Alive'.

SHERSTON
In late '80, when he was living in London, Marvin Gaye would seek tranquility at the country home of Lady Edith Foxwell.

STONEHENGE
Scene of myriad summer solstice festivals in the Seventies – usually involving Hawkwind and usually thwarted by the police.

SWINDON
Birthplace of Rick Davies, 22.7.44 (Supertramp); Justin Hayward, 14.10.46 (saviour of The Moody Blues/victor in

Stonehenge used on an album of early '60's doo wop!

The War Of The Worlds); drummer Terry Chambers, 18.7.55, and bass player Colin Moulding, 17.8.55 (XTC); Billie, 22.9.82.

After paying dues in such bands as The Helium Kidz, Breeze, Dice and Star Park, the aforementioned Chambers and Moulding united with friends Andy Partridge and Barry Andrews to form XTC, who rode the new wave to a Virgin contract and subdued global acclaim. Moulding went to Headlands School, Andrews to Park Comprehensive – after which both secured day jobs as dustmen.

XTC gained much local exposure as their manager also owned the town's grooviest night club, The Affair. Andrews later jumped ship and formed Restaurant For Dogs, then Shriekback.

Other local bands include The Stadium Dogs, led by Jonathan Perkins.

Gilbert O'Sullivan and Rick Davies went to Swindon Art College and played together in Supertramp forerunner Rick's Blues.

The currently cool venues are the Brunel Rooms in Havelock Square and the Footplate & Firkin – but in the Sixties, the place to be was McIlroys Ballroom in Havelock Square. The Beatles played there in July '62, the Stones several times in '63/'64, Mott The Hoople in October '70.

In November '90, following his M4 accident (see Marlborough), Ronnie Wood spent several days at the Princess Margaret Hospital.

Techno duo Meat Beat Manifesto originated locally, but removed to London for a chart flicker and abundant studio work – leaving Eva Luna to describe themselves as "the town's best band since XTC". Countering that boast are Brit-poppers Cinnamon Smith.

Billie (Piper) was a pupil at Brookfields Primary in the late Eighties; a decade later she was topping the charts with her début single 'Because We Want To'.

TROWBRIDGE

Birthplace of Bob Day, 21.2.42 (half of The Allisons, our '61 Eurovision representatives).

The Psychic Pig was a top indie gig.

Sometime home of prog-rockers Ozric Tentacles and their techno offshoot Eat Static.

WARMINSTER

The Marquis of Bath's country seat, Longleat House, is now famous for lions – but in August '64, The Rolling Stones gave an open air concert there. 25,000 fans paid 2/6d each and the Stones got £1,000. The usual hysterical, squashed girls were stretchered away; the police were not amused: "We could easily have some dead on our hands if things go on as they are."

Enfield group Hocus Pocus changed their name to UFO after reading about the unexplained unidentified flying objects seen hovering over Warminster in the Sixties – when Cradle Hill and Cley Hill would be dotted with spotters.

The A-Heads were local early Eighties anarcho-punks.

Swindon's Meat-Beat Manifesto

WORCESTERSHIRE

BROMSGROVE
Dire Straits bass player John Illsley was educated at Bromsgrove School.

CASTLEMORTON
On spring Bank Holiday '92, some 25,000 teenagers unexpectedly descended on the village for Britain's biggest illegal rave to date.

EVESHAM
Birthplace of keyboard player Poli Palmer, 25.5.43 (Family); drummer Jim Capaldi, 24.8.44 (Traffic); guitar player Luther Grosvenor, 23.12.49 (Spooky Tooth).

In September '63, Jet Harris and his girlfriend Billie Davis were injured when his chauffeur driven car crashed into a bus. He never reached the charts again.

Local groups include punk band Satan's Rats (collectable singles); early Eighties new wavers The Photos, led by Wendy Wu (they recorded a tribute to Barbarella's in Birmingham); and The Dancing Did (ecologically inclined folk-rockers best known for the song 'Squashed Things On The Road').

Steve Eagles (ex Photos) was the mastermind behind Nineties band Bang Bang Machine.

GREAT MALVERN
Local groups include The Tights (new wave) and Stephen Tin-Tin Duffy's Lilac Time.

Birthplace of the Cherry Red label.

In '93, local band Blessed Ethel beat 50 contestants to win the Manchester In The City award for best newcomer. Rivals on the local scene included Hipkiss.

Poli Palmer (second right) an Evesham Family man

And also The Trees pose beside Inkberrow Manor

INKBERROW

The Fiction label signed local band And Also The Trees in the early Eighties.

KEMPSEY

During his Led Zeppelin days, Robert Plant's only extra-curricular work was producing (and singing backing vocals on) a single by Brummie group Dansette Damage at the Old Smithy Studio in Post Office Lane. The single, 'NME'/'The Only Sound', is now changing hands for £80 and rising.

KIDDERMINSTER

Birthplace of organist Roger LaVern, 11.11.38 (Tornados).

Led by Stan Webb and Christine (McVie) Perfect, Chicken Shack were one of the most successful blues-boom bands of the late Sixties. Jess Roden's band Bronco comprised mainly local guys. Big Front Yard were Seventies hopefuls.

In the Seventies, Robert Plant lived at Jennings Farm, Blakes Hall, near Wolverley.

John Bonham's funeral took place near his home at Rushock in October '80.

Operational base of the Big Town Playboys, techno guru Ewan Pearson (who records as Villa America), indie band Stop The World.

REDDITCH

Birthplace of brothers Alan, 18.5.40, and Dave Sealey, 20.2.46, who formed music hall/folk act Cosmotheka in '71; drummer John Bonham, 31.5.48 (Led Zeppelin).

The Cravats were the local punk group, who vinylised the town on Precinct; their offshoot The Very Things were Peel faves.

Dreamgrinder carried on the tradition in the Nineties.

Local lads Nigel Clarke and Matthew Priest moved to Hounslow, where they formed Nineties chartbusters Dodgy.

STOURPORT

Birthplace of singer Ray Thomas, 29.12.42 (Moody Blues).

Singer/songwriter Clifford T Ward was a local lad. His group Cliff Ward & The Cruisers were mid-Sixties Midlands favourites.

Home of Rouen, highly touted pop-rockers who mysteriously and sadly nose-dived after massive radio play for their indie single.

TENBURY WELLS

For reasons that have never been explained, The Beatles appeared at the Riverside Dancing Club at the Bridge Hotel in Teme Street in April 63 – the week 'From Me To You' rocketed into the charts.

WEST HAGLEY

Led Zeppelin star John Bonham lived at Blagdon, 3 Newfield Road.

WORCESTER

Birthplace of Dave Mason, 10.5.46. His first group was the locally renowned Hellions, but he made his name in Traffic.

Singer Jess Roden led The Shakedown Sound before moving to London to join The Alan Bown Set. Other local Sixties outfits were The CMJ Group and The Cherokees. In the late Seventies came punk group The Samples.

In March '58, Buddy Holly & The Crickets played the Gaumont at 21 Foregate Street. Buddy met a local female fan, with whom he had a sexual liaison. Obviously treating it rather more seriously than he did, she would subsequently send him a series of letters.

The Beatles appeared at the Gaumont twice, in June and September '63; Jimi Hendrix played there in April '67; Mary Hopkin started her first tour there in March '69.

Fabulous were Nineties punk revivalists; Tribute To Nothing were precocious teenagers; Another Fine Mess were Laurel and Hardy fans.

Late Nineties home of techno giant Mike Paradinas (aka Jake Slazenger), who records as u-ziq.

Huntingdon Hall is a cool late Nineties venue.

The Huntingdon Hall

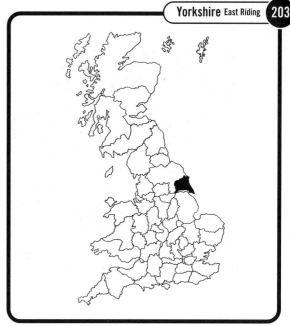

YORKSHIRE
EAST RIDING

BEVERLEY
The only venues for local bands appear to be Nellie's pub (the White Horse) and the Regal night club at the old cinema. Meanwhile, bigger international stars appear at the Picture Playhouse in the Market Place (formerly the Corn Exchange).

BRIDLINGTON
Birthplace of Bob Wallis, 3.6.34 (leader of popular trad-era band the Storyville Jazz Men); guitarist Graham Jones, 8.7.61 (Haircut 100).

The Rolling Stones came to town to play at the Spa Royal Hotel in May '64. It was still a hot venue in July '71, when Mott The Hoople played there.

Radio 270, last to join the pirate fleet in June '66, broadcast from a converted Dutch lugger moored three miles off the coast. It shut down in August '67, after it had relocated to a mooring off Scarborough.

Sometime home of Mississippi-born singer Ted Hawkins.

In November '95, The Stone Roses chose the Spa Pavilion for their first big gig in five years.

DRIFFIELD
Kudos was a local early Eighties band.

It was at Slaughterhouse Studio that Terrorvision cut the demos which aroused industry interest – and that The Happy Mondays recorded *Bummed*.

HORNSEA
Home of new wavers Indians in Moscow.

HULL (Kingston-Upon-Hull)
Birthplace of Fifties swooners Ronnie Hilton, 26.1.26, and David Whitfield, 2.2.26; Shan of The Kaye Sisters,

15.8.38; singer songwriter Philip Goodhand Tait, 3.1.45; Trevor Bolder, 9.6.50 (Spiders From Mars, Uriah Heep); Henry Priestman, 21.6.55 (Christians); Ted Key, 1.7.60, and Hugh Whittaker, 18.5.61 (both Housemartins); Dave Hemingway, 20.9.60, and David Rotheray, 9.2.61 (both Beautiful South).

In 1952, David Whitfield was operating a cement mixer on a building site in Hull. The following year, he topped the charts with 'Answer Me', and in '54 he was the third UK artist (after Vera Lynn and Eddie Calvert) to win a gold disc (for 'Cara Mia').

Also the birthplace of guitarist Mick Ronson, 26.5.46, who left Maybury High School at 15 with no qualifications. In the late Sixties, he lived in a flat in

Mick Ronson: after Hull, pre-Mars

Alva Avenue. Between stints as a council grass cutter, he played in various local groups — but only won acclaim after he and a couple of mates, Trevor Bolder and Woody Woodmansey, moved south to become David Bowie's Spiders From Mars. Woody, who took his surname from a local village, went on to drum with The Screen Idols; Bolder went with Uriah Heep. Ronson died in April '93 and is buried here.

John Cambridge, who played in David Bowie's Hype and Junior's Eyes, returned to Hull and in the mid-Nineties was landlord of the Foresters Arms.

Buddy Holly & The Crickets played at the Regal cinema in March '58 and stayed at the White Horse Hotel in Jameson Street. The Beatles appeared twice at the Top Rank Majestic Ballroom in Witham (October '62 and February '63) and twice at the ABC cinema in Ferensway (November '63 and October '64). The Rolling Stones came to town in October '63, when they played the Majestic.

The Countrymen were an early Sixties folk trio, whose one hit 'I Know Where I'm Going' was not prophetic.

The Silkie got together at Hull University in summer '63 and won the patronage of The Beatles, who wrote and played on their only hit, 'You've Got To Hide Your Love Away'. Other University alumni include John Pilgrim (Vipers Skiffle Group), Everything But The Girl (Tracey Thorn and Ben Watt, who met there), poet and Scaffolder Roger McGough.

Chirpy Yorkshire Cockney: Wreckless Eric

Stiff recording star Wreckless Eric was educated at Hull College of Art, where he also led Addis & The Flip Tops. For part of this period, his residence was a length of sewage pipe which he furnished from local rubbish tips. Brad from The Specials was a fellow student.

Singer/songwriter Michael Chapman was a local schoolteacher (who immortalised the Polar Bear pub in Springbank on 'Polar Bear Fandango'); Lene Lovich grew

up here (having been born in Detroit); Steeleye Span bass player Rick Kemp worked in Hammonds department store (later Debenhams); Snips Parsons went to college here and played in Nothineverappens before joining Sharks; bass player John Bentley moved south to join Squeeze.

Local punk band Dead Fingers Talk (produced by Mick Ronson) made national waves in the late Seventies; The Luddites made a single or two in the early Eighties; Red Guitars topped the '84 indie singles chart with Marimba Jive.

Def Leppard made their first recordings at Fairview Studios in Great Gutter Lane, Willerby, in November '78.

Self-styled "fourth best band in Hull", The Housemartins made their début at the Hull University bar in October '84. Hugh Whittaker and Ted Key met at Sir Henry Cooper Senior High in Orchard Park; Stan Cullimore (at the Uni) lived at 70 Grafton Street; all drank at the Grafton pub. Stan and Paul Heaton busked in the Whitefriargate pedestrian precinct while refining their act. Paul has been known to take ale at the Mainbrace.

After The Housemartins split in '88, the most successful splinter group was The Beautiful South, who played a jubilant homecoming gig at the City Hall in November '90. Meanwhile, Norman Cook moved back to his hometown Brighton (to emerge as Fatboy Slim) and Hugh Whitaker found himself sewing mailbags after being sentenced to six years for assault in May '93.

Also on the late Eighties scene were The Mighty Strike, Pink Noise, The Brontes and Planet Wilson (who evolved from Red Guitars).

Best late Eighties local venue was the Adelphi Club at 89 De Grey Street. Tiffany's in Ferensway and the Wellington Club at 105 Beverly Road also presented name bands.

Although born in Birmingham, Roland Gift grew up in Hull and sang in local groups Blue Kitchen and Acrylic Victims before going back to Brum to make it big with those superfine Fine Young Cannibals.

Local early Nineties bands included Kingmaker ("a cross between The Pixies and Cream"!), Peel faves Hustlers' Convention, Fog, Looking For Adam, Spacemaid, The Joeys. Female trio Scarlet formed here but moved to London for '95 chart success with 'Independent Love Song'.

In the mid-Nineties came Secret Of Life (who cut an *NME* single of the week), Fila Brazilia (dance), and indie hopefuls Salako.

In '98, Paul Heaton and Dave Rotheray of The Beautiful South opened a cycle store in Savile Court — Blazing Saddles!

WITHERNSEA
Birthplace of trad-jazz trumpeter Kenny Baker, 1.3.21.

YORKSHIRE
NORTH

BLAKEY
Home of jazz-rock trio Back Door, who broke out in '72.

FILEY
In summer '59, pre-fame Joe Brown played a season at Butlins Holiday Camp as guitarist with Clay Nicholls & The Blue Flames. A year later, the resident group was Billy Gray & The Stormers, whose bass player was Chas Hodges, later half of Chas & Dave.

HARROGATE
Birthplace of violinist Mik Kaminski, 2.9.51 (ELO).

Local Sixties R&B group The Beat Preachers included subsequent disc jockey and record producer Stuart Colman.

The Beatles played at the Royal Hall in Ripon Road in March '63.

Promoted by Bob Harris and Rick Wakeman, the foolishly named Seventies band Wally were designed to invite derogatory comments. One of their album was named after the town's Valley Gardens.

Late Eighties heavy metal hopefuls were Acid Reign.

KIRKLEVINGTON
During the Sixties, the Country Club presented every group ever invented, including The Jimi Hendrix Experience in January '67 and Mott The Hoople in March '70. Lindisfarne were paid £30 when they played there in October '70. Later known as Martha's Vineyard.

MARSKE
Birthplace of Peter Bradley, 12.9.74 (Subcircus).

MIDDLESBROUGH
Birthplace of drummer Pete York, 15.8.42 (Spencer Davis Group); singer Paul Rodgers, 17.12.49 (Free/Bad Company); singer Chris Rea, 4.3.51; singer Claire Hammill, 1955; bassist Pete Trewavas, 15.1.59 (Marillion)... not to mention East Enders star Wendy Richard, who allowed Mike Sarne to seduce her on his '62 chart topper 'Come Outside'.

Rocker Terry Dene made his variety début at the Empire in June '57.

In June '63, The Beatles played the Astoria Ballroom in Wilson Street; in July '63, The Rolling Stones played their first northern gig at the town's Alcove Club (not, Bill Wyman insists, at the Outlook Club as some locals assert).

A hot mid-Sixties R&B group was The Roadrunners, who moved to London in '67. Their line-up included Paul Rodgers (later in Free), Mick Moody (later in Whitesnake) and Bruce Thomas (later in Elvis Costello's Attractions).

Best record shop in town was Alan Fearnley Records at 224 Linthorpe Road.

Martin Fry made his public début with Vice Versa at primo new wave club the Rock Garden at 208 Newport Road. Joy Division played an early gig there (when they were still called Warsaw) in October '77.

Late Seventies punks Basczax made the indie chart.

Several of Chris Rea's songs contain local references: 'Steel River' is the Tees, and Stainsby Girls School is in the suburb of Acklam.

Local Nineties hopefuls included Spit The Pips, Shrug and Golden Starlet.

ontana **The Spencer Davis Group / The Second Album**

Pete York sits this one out

REDCAR

Birthplace of drummer Pete York, 15.8.42 (Spencer Davis Group).

The Coatham Bowl in Majuba Street was and is a popular venue.

Redcar Jazz Club at the Coatham Arms went R&B with John Lee Hooker in May '65. By '67, it was presenting Pink Floyd, Robert Plant & The Band Of Joy, and Procol Harum. The Ike & Tina Turner Revue blew the place apart in August '68, Black Sabbath in May '70.

Local Sixties favourites included The Real McCoy, The Skyliners, The Denmen, Rivers Invitation and The Government – featuring singer David Coverdale, whose day job was in local menswear shop Gentry.

The Losers won the *Melody Maker* Folk/Rock contest in '78 – but lived up to their name by disbanding soon afterwards.

One of the earliest gigs Terrorvision played was at the Sandpiper in June '89, when they were still called The Spoilt Bratz.

Tyrrel Corporation broke out with a string of Nineties club hits, starting with 'The Bottle' in March '92.

RICHMOND

Screaming Lord Sutch fought the Richmond by-election in February '89. He polled 167 votes... even less than he mustered in his first attempt 26 years earlier!

RIPON

The video for OMITD's hit 'Joan Of Arc' was shot at Fountains Abbey.

SALTBURN-BY-THE-SEA

Birthplace of heavy metal titan David Coverdale, 22.9.49 (Deep Purple, Whitesnake). His first group was called Denver Mule.

SCARBOROUGH

First local group to record was The Incas, who cut 'One Night Stand'.

Robert Palmer went to the Boys High School, then the Art College, where he formed The Mandrakes. After a long apprenticeship with The Alan Bown Set, Dada and Vinegar Joe, he made it as a solo star.

Between June '66 and August '67, the pirate station Radio 270 broadcast from a converted Dutch lugger moored three miles off Scarborough.

On a gig here in '72, Lonnie Donegan met plumber's daughter/autograph hunter Sharon (then 14, but pretending to be 17), who would later (in '79) become his third wife.

The 2,000 seater Futurist Theatre on the South Bay provided a stage for The Beatles in December '63 and again in August '64. The Stones played there in August '65. Later on, the Penthouse at 35 St. Nicholas Street and the Candlelight were two nationally famous hippie, underground era clubs. Everyone from Family to Hendrix to T.Rex to Colosseum played at one or the other.

Local new-wavers The Jags had a '79 Top Twenty hit with 'Back Of My Hand' – and the northern-soulish Friday Club had one of the last releases on 2 Tone.

In April '80, the appearance of several neo-mod bands and the film *Quadrophenia* sparked off a brief mod revival, complete with beach hooliganism. Scarborough took the main impact, with 217 arrests.

Michael Chapman still brilliant today, a Fully Qualified Survivor

On his '70 album *Fully Qualified Survivor*, Michael Chapman recorded 'Postcards From Scarborough'.

Home of ebullient Little Richard and Jerry Lee Lewis biographer Chas White, better known as Dr. Rock.

After supporting Aerosmith on tour, local Polydor signing The Little Angels hit the charts – reaching number one in '93, with their album *Jam*.

The Corner Café is a cool late Nineties venue.

SELBY

Coffee bar rocker Keith Kelly (hits in '60) went to Selby Art College before moving to York to start his career as guitarist/singer in The John Barry Seven.

Sometime home of Bill Nelson.

Pink Floyd were headliners at the Selby Arts Festival in July '69.

SKIPTON

Birthplace of guitarist Charlie Whitney, 24.6.44 (Family).

Hometown of former *Melody Maker* writer, Who archivist and current Omnibus Press editor Chris Charlesworth, who played guitar in local bands The Pandas and Sandra & The Montanas (from nearby Cross Hills).

In the Sixties, the town's most popular venue was the Clifford Hall in the Black Horse Hotel, where gigs invariably ended in bloody fights. Contrary to rumour, The Silver Beetles never played there.

Top band in the Sixties was The Black Sheep, who played soul and R&B and gigged around the villages of the Yorkshire Dales in an old hearse. 'Cag' Thompson is fondly remembered as a local bop promoter and DJ.

WHITBY

Birthplace of Arthur Brown, 24.12.44.

Marillion guitarist Steve Rothery grew up here, having been born in West Melton on 25.11.59. (Where the hell is West Melton?)

YORK

Birthplace of Katy Jane Gartside, 8.7.68 (Daisy Chainsaw).

Also the birthplace of John Barry, 3.11.33, who was educated at St. Peter's School. After a rock'n'roll apprenticeship in the Fifties, leading The John Barry Seven, he wrote film scores – most famously the James Bond theme. He also contributed to Cockney rhyming slang with his *Juke Box Jury* theme, 'Hit And Miss'. His father owned two cinemas in town – the Clifton and the Rialto in Fishergate (later a bingo hall), where The John Barry Seven made their professional début, supporting touring US star Mitchell Torok in spring '57.

The Beatles appeared at the Rialto four times in '63; The Stones made it there in February '64.

In the Sixties, Dustin Gee used to work at Armstrong Patents (engineering) and led Gerry B & the Rockerfellers – one of York's most popular groups.

In '66, local group The Shots changed their name to The Smoke and released the classic single 'My Friend Jack (Eats Sugarlumps)'. The Roll Movement remained semi-pro.

John Leyton spent nine months in repertory at the Theatre Royal, where he was spotted by Robert Stigwood and turned into a pop star.

Vicky Aspinall (The Raincoats) studied at York University.

Echo & The Bunnymen, Sisters Of Mercy, Spear Of Destiny, The Chameleons headlined the first York Rock Festival, at the Racecourse in September '84.

The Mood scored three minor national hits in '82; the most popular late Eighties band was Zoot & The Roots. Cult skinhead band Brick Supply performed the original version of the '96 Dubstar hit 'Not So Manic Now'.

The Red Rhino label, operating from 9 Gillygate, started with The Odds and The Dead Beats. They had moved to Coach House in Fetter Lane by the time they released Pulp's first single, 'My Lighthouse'.

Nineties bands include Shed Seven (who began a long hit string with 'Dolphin' in June '94), St. Christopher, God's Little Monkeys, Dirty Monkey, The Crossing, The Butter Mountain Boys.

Pre-O.B.E., John Barry composed advertising jingles

On the mid-Nineties techno/ambient front, Beaumont Hannant and Germ both made waves.

After leaving the Manchester-based Stone Roses, guitarist John Squire went to York to recruit musicians for his next band, The Seahorses (an anagram of 'he hates Roses' and also the name of a York pub whose sign fell on his head!). Chris Helme had sung and played guitar in local band Chutzpah but was spotted busking outside Woolworths; bassist Stuart Fletcher was in R&B group The Blue Flies; drummer Andy Watts (soon to leave) was in Fred Carter's Milk Round.

(David Calderley)

The book on which Jarvis based his career

YORKSHIRE SOUTH

BARNSLEY
Birthplace of folkie Dave Burland, 12.7.41.

Home of Sixties Pye group First Gear, heavy metal band Saxon, and gothic marauders Danse Society.

Formed in '77 from the ashes of Son Of A Bitch, Saxon made their début at Denbeigh Dale Youth Club.

Sometime home of Lance Fortune (Top Five with 'Be Mine' in '60), who was said to be operating a mobile shop here during the Eighties.

CONISBROUGH
Birthplace of balladeer Tony Christie, 25.4.44.

DONCASTER
Birthplace of Dewey Bunnell, 19.1.52 (the English member of America); Steve Hogarth, who replaced Fish as the singer in Marillion.

Having renounced rock'n'roll for religion five years earlier, Little Richard made his UK début in October '62, singing gospel to a puzzled audience at the Gaumont. Anxious promoter Don Arden convinced him to revert to manic rock'n'roll for the rest of the tour.

Doncaster Baths in St. James Street was a big gig in the early Sixties, presenting groups like Shane Fenton & The Fentones, Johnny Kidd & The Pirates, The Beatles (February '63) and The Rolling Stones (December '63). The Fab Four had first played Doncaster in August '62, at the Co-op Ballroom in St. Sepulchre Gate.

In the Gaumont's star-studded Christmas '64 panto *Once Upon A Fairytale*, Marty Wilde played Prince William, his wife Joyce was Princess Maria, Lulu was Witch Hazel and Heinz was Captain of the Palace Guard.

To beat local bans, imposed in '77, The Sex Pistols appeared at the Outlook Club as the Spots (Sex Pistols On Tour Secretly). Sheffield band Vice Versa made their début at the Outlook, supporting Wire.

Late Seventies progressive/heavy metal groups Bitter Suite and Ponders End battled for national recognition. Their lead guitarist John Parr eventually found it in '85 when St. Elmo's Fire zipped up charts around the world.

Early Eighties groups included Harlow, B-Troop, Richard & The Taxman, The Diks, and The Shy Tots – all of whom played at the town's primo venue, Rotters Club in Silver Street.

Vinyl home of The Darling Buds, Treebound Story and Screaming Trees was the independent label Native Records, based at 36 Beckett Road.

Local Nineties bands included rap duo Club St. Louis (who evolved into Honky and cut an *NME* Single of the Week in '93), Rare Bare Mary (renowned for disrobing on stage), the grunge trio Boneyard (who signed with Kitchenware) and punk rock'n' roll trio Groop Dogdrill.

MEXBOROUGH

Birthplace of Graham Oliver, 6.7.52 (Saxon).

Sometime home of Alan Brown, leader of mid-Eighties Peel favourites Big Flame.

ROTHERHAM

Birthplace of comedian Dougie Brown, 7.8.40, who for twelve years played in rock group The Imps (their commercial peak was an appearance on *6.5 Special*); Steve Dawson, 24.2.52 (Saxon); Maggie deMonde (Swans Way, Scarlet Fantastic).

Local venues have included the Travellers Rest in Main Street, the Florence Nightingale in Moorgate, Elliots in the Westgate Centre, the Ball Inn at Bramley, the Sub Club in Main Street, and the Madhouse in Nelson Street.

The Windmill Club at Rotheram Football Club had punk nights with the likes of 999, Generation X and The Doctors Of Madness.

Future Comsat Angels Steve Fellows and Mick Glaisher were schoolfriends in Rotheram.

Perversely named local group Phil Murray & The Boys From Bury put the town on the indie map with 'Rainy Night In Rotherham'. Don Valley & The Rotherhides were a popular club act.

Rotherham Arts Centre today

(Rotherham Museum & Arts)

Pulp made their world début at the Arts Centre in July '80. Only Jarvis Cocker would survive to the current group.

Hottest local late Eighties/early Nineties indie band was Screaming Trees, who scored a couple of minor hits; hottest commercial success was Jive Bunny & The Mastermixers, who celebrated '89 with three number ones.

In the mid-Nineties came V, whose singer sported a fetching Rotherham United bobble hat on stage.

SHEFFIELD

Birthplace of jazz guitarist Derek Bailey, 29.1.32; Sixties star Dave Berry, 6.2.41 (in the mining village of Beighton, where the first line-up of his Cruisers originated); singer Joe Cocker, 20.5.44; guitarist Chris Spedding, 17.6.44; singer Paul Carrack, 22.4.51 (Ace, Squeeze, Mike & The Mechanics); guitarist Michael Vaughan, 27.7.50 (leader of Paper Lace); drummer Pete Gill, 9.6.51 (Saxon, Motorhead); drummer Pete Thomas, 9.8.54 (Elvis Costello's Attractions); singer Joe Elliott, 1.8.59 (Def Leppard); Pulp frontman Jarvis Cocker, 19.9.63 (at Intake); Gloria Robakowski (studio singer for Rick Astley and ABC; soloist as Romana).

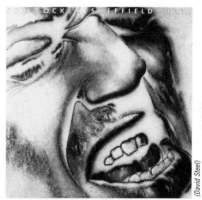

Mr Sheffield steel Joe Cocker

(David Steel)

In December '58, teen singer Laurie London made his pantomime début in *Babes In The Wood* at Sheffield Empire – along with Edna Savage, who had recently married Terry Dene.

Dave Berry was the first local star; he went to Woodhouse Secondary School and now lives in Dronfield. The star of his late Sixties Cruisers was guitarist Frank White, the first guy in England with a twin necked guitar. He held a long Eighties residency at the Pheasant Inn on Sheffield Lane Top. White used to live in Bilton Road, Dornall and was the first Englishman to record for the Californian Fantasy label.

Next up was Joe Cocker, who lived in Tasker Road, Crookes, and led several locally popular groups before moving to London to make it. With him went loyal henchman Chris Stainton (who lived in Woodseats) and keyboard player Tommy Eyre (who became Wham's musical director). Cocker worked for the East Midlands Gas Board (as indeed did Mark White from ABC) and at the wholesale newsagents near the station.

Other Sixties groups included Shape, The Sheffields (no hits)... but that was about it for ten lean years! In the Seventies, The Shape Of The Rain cut an album; High Tide (some of whom were local) cut two.

University students include Geoff Downes (Buggles, Asia), Jamie West-Oram (The Doll, The Fixx), Martin Fry (ABC), Bridget St. John (singer/songwriter), Ian Ball (Gomez) and Jason Gomez (inspiration for band's name!).

First of the experimental synth bands was Cabaret Voltaire, who were years ahead of their time and débuted in May '75. On their heels came The Human League, who cut their first vinyl utterings in a 2-track studio on Devonshire Lane in January '78. This studio was later owned by producer Steve Singleton, founder of ABC.

The late Seventies New Wave swell also inspired Artery, Clock DVA, The Comsat Angels, I'm So Hollow, Musical Januaryeens, 2.3, The Flying Alphonso Brothers, Stunt Kites, Vendino Pact, and They Must Be Russians – who celebrated their city on 'Doom And Decay The Sheffield Way'!

Vice Versa emerged after long rehearsals in a Bowood

Dr Who cast-off: National Centre for Popular Music

(Mark Harvey)

Road cellar and moved to London and the big-time as ABC. Martin Fry joined after going to interview them for his fanzine *Modern Drugs*. (He and Steve Singleton first met at the Batchelors food factory).

Clock DVA, I'm So Hollow, Stunt Kites and Vice Versa all made their début on Neutron Records, launched by Steve Singleton and Mark White from Vice Versa.

The Limit Club on West Street was the cool place to be at the zenith of late Seventies activity. The Human League, The Cabs, Siouxsie, Simple Minds and U2 all played there.

Also popular was the George IV on Infirmary Road.

The Eighties threw up Hula, The Mau Maus, Treebound Story (with Frank White's nephew Richard Hawley on guitar), The Sharp Cuts (who made New Faces!), The Toy Shop, Funky Worm, Vision, In The Nursery, Chakk and two members of Living In A Box. Pulp would claim the world record for Longest Gestation Period, having formed in '80 and taken a leisurely course to their chart début 13 years later. Their singer (and only constant element) Jarvis Cocker – no relation to Joe – attracted local press in '86 when, acting the goat, he fell from a window ledge and fractured his wrist, ankle and pelvis. He spent several weeks in hospital and several months in a wheel chair.

In the Sixties, the city's most illustrious venues were the Esquire Club at the Leadmill, 9 Leadmill Road (a pillar rose from the stage to hold up the roof). Resident R&B/soul groups were Vance Arnold (Joe Cocker) & The Avengers and The Scott William Combo; Club 60 on Shalesmoor – a Cavern style place in the cellar of an old pub; and the Mojo Club at Pitsmore – run by then unknown/soon world famous nightclub operator Peter Stringfellow. The Small Faces made their provincial début here in July '65.

A Sheffield lad, Stringfellow's first venture was the Black Cat Club at St. Aiden's Church Hall on City Road. From there he moved to the Blue Moon (another vestry hall in The Wicker), and then started the Mojo which became one of the most famous provincial clubs of the R&B era.

Later council funded, the Leadmill was converted to a rock venue/arts centre and presented the likes of Fairground Attraction, Tom Tom Club, Texas and local hopefuls Pulp, who played their second ever gig there in August '80. Oasis played there in November '93.

Other local venues have included the Uni, the Poly in Pond Street, the Groovy Fishtank (held at Take Two in Staniforth Road), the Black Swan (otherwise known as the Mucky Duck and, for a while, the Compleat Angler), the Top Rank in Arundel Gate, the Rockingham Arms in Wentworth, the Royal and the Broadfield pub, which has presented every local group from Def Leppard to the Human League. Not to mention Penny's Disco (which served fresh fruit), the Bee Hive and the Hallamshire on West Street (a favourite Jarvis Cocker hangout), Café Piccolo's, the Crucible Theatre's cafe and bar, and the Fiesta Club in Arundelgate – which once put on The Jackson 5!

The Limit Club in West Street and the Marples in Fitzallan Square were key turn of the Eighties venues, as were the Lyceum Theatre and the Penthouse.

It was at futurist night club/disco the Crazy Daizy in the High Street that Phil Oakey spotted two gyrating schoolgirls (Suzanne Sulley and Joanne Catherall) and invited them to "come and tour the States as dancers with The Human League" – which of course they did.

Until it was replaced during alterations in '84, the stage of the City Hall was notorious for its slope. A lighting gantry toppled over and almost crushed Marillion during an early Eighties concert.

In August '69, Deep Purple played at the University, supported by Middlesbrough band The Government, led by David Coverdale. Jon Lord was so impressed that he took Coverdale's phone number... four years later, he became Deep Purple's singer.

The Clash made their world début at the Black Swan supporting The Sex Pistols in August '76. ABC made their world début at the Psalter Lane Art College.

The biggest band ever to come out of Sheffield were Def Leppard, who made their début at Westfield School in July '78. They also used to play at Dial House Working Mens Club, and the Wapentake Bar (where they indulged in under-age drinking).

Local musicians Ray Stewart (The Mainliners) and John Fleet (The Cruisers/Joe Cocker) became radio personalities on Radio Hallam and BBC Sheffield respectively.

The city has been immortalised on such waxings as 'Sheffield Steel' by Joe Cocker, 'West Street' by The Naughtiest Girl Was A Monitor, and' Sheffield Sex City' by Pulp.

Phil Oakey and Martyn Ware (Heaven 17) met at Myers Grove School; Oakey marked time as a porter at the Children's Hospital on Western Bank and moved to Ecclesall during his hits heyday.

Bruce Dickinson (Iron Maiden) and Paul Heaton (Housemartins) went to King Edwards School in Glossop Road, where Jilted John was once head boy! Steve Singleton (ABC) and Joe Elliot (Def Leppard) both attended Hunters Bar Middle School where they formed a band together.

Tom Bailey was a teacher at Brook Comprehensive before hotfooting it back to Chesterfield to start The Thompson Twins.

Hometown of Ivor Biggun, who hit the '78 Top Thirty with 'Winker's Song (Misprint)' – banned by the BBC, for whom he later worked with Esther Rantzen on *That's Life* under the name of Doc Cox.

The Human League and The Comsat Angels (later called The Head Hunters) had studios in the Red Tape complex. Western Works was the home of Cabaret Voltaire. Chakk ploughed money into Fon Studios at 3 Brown Street, where Pulp recorded their album *Separations*.

Bruce Springsteen filled United's Bramall Lane football ground in July '88; Tony Christie ran a night club at Wednesday's ground, Hillsborough.

Sheffield based producer Robert Gordon has cut hits with Pop Will Eat Itself, Krush, Treebound Story, and Yazz – at Fon Studios. The Fon label is based at Sheldon Row in The Wicker.

A-ha did their first demos at Vibrasound Studios, the Wicker.

In February '63, a promising group called The Beatles were one of many to play the Azena Ballroom in Whites Lane, Gleadless... now a supermarket.

A disconsolate Elton John spent Christmas week '67 playing with Long John Baldry & Bluesology to chicken-in-the-basket noshers at the 1,000 seater Cavendish Club in Bank Street. "Is this where my future lies?" he mused. Within a fortnight, he'd left the band and was planning his solo career.

After a long gestation, Pulp finally broke through in '94 with the Mercury Prize nominated album *His 'N' Hers*.

Gomez were "discovered" in the Record Collector store in Broomhill, when guitarist Ian Ball took in a tape for proprietor Barry Everard and ex-Comsats mainman Steve Fellows to hear. From there, it was a magic carpet ride to stardom.

Red Tape Studios (as above) hosted the now legendary Gomez showcase of October '97, when 26 labels fought to sign them. Madonna's A&R men had flown into Manchester and taken a cab over the Snake Pass – but were unsuccessful in their bid.

Current venues include the Boardwalk Club, the Embassy, the Foundry & Firkin, Sheffield Arena and the Don Valley Stadium. Club Generation (formerly the Music Factory) at 33 London Road and the Republic at 112 Arundel Street are paradise for late Nineties clubbers; The Chemical Brothers and Mr C headlined the opening of rave club NY Sushi at the Unit, Milton Street, in September '98.

Bramall Lane: The Boss plays to a low turnout

(Chorley Handford. Premier Image)

Local early Nineties acts include The Sons, Higher Ground, Blammo!, The Seaside, The Dylans (formerly 1,000 Violins), Ephraim, Various Vegetables (a trio with an aggregate age less than that of their champion John Peel), Roadhouse, The Lovebirds, Newspeak, This Machine Kills, Heights Of Abraham (a Chakk offshoot), Rhythm Invention, Blameless, Baby Bird (led by former Telford resident Steve Jones), Manna and Speedy.

The techno-dance label Warp Records is based at 1 Brown Street. Employees formed their own dance act RAC.

In spring '98, a trio of local DJs/remixers dubbed themselves The All-Seeing Eye to reach the Top Twenty with a revival of 'The Beat Goes On' – which became a tribute to composer Sonny (& Cher) Bono, who was killed while they were recording it.

In '98, Pulp drummer Nick Banks bought the Wellington public house. Will it be selling Banks Bitter?

The National Centre for Popular Music, housed in a £15 million custom-designed building at Paternoster Row and Charles Street, opened in March '99.

THURCROFT
Birthplace of Paul Quinn, 26.12.51 (Saxon), who was educated at Holgate Grammar School.

THURNSCOE
Birthplace of early Sixties songstress Carol Deene, 3.8.44. She lived in Garden Street and was married at St. Helens Church.

YORKSHIRE
WEST

Matthew's Northern Comfort: Ian Matthews

ARMLEY

Operational base of both Chumbawamba and skunk-rockers Bedlam A-Go-Go.

BATLEY

Birthplace of Robert Palmer, 19.1.49, who went professional with The Alan Bown Set in '68 and finally cracked the Top Ten with 'Addicted To Love' eighteen years later.

During the Sixties, Batley Variety Club was mocked by the rock establishment as the acme of the chicken-in-the-basket cabaret circuit.

BINGLEY

Operational base of The Skeletal Family, who topped 84 indie charts with their album *Burning Oil*.

BRADFORD

Birthplace of Mike Sagar, 27.9.40 (early rock'n'roller); Kiki Dee, 6.3.47; Susan Fassbender (Twilight Cafe); Brendan Croker, 15.8.53 (Notting Hillbillies); not to mention David Hockney and Denis Healey.

The Beatles opened their first national tour at the Gaumont in New Victoria Street in February '63. Helen Shapiro was top of the bill. The fabs returned to the Gaumont in December '63 (when they were seen but barely heard by the editor of this book!) and October '64.

In October '64, Charlie Watts secretly married longtime girlfriend Shirley at the Register Office.

In the mid-Sixties, Ian Matthews (Fairport Convention and Matthews Southern Comfort) was an apprentice at Bradford City FC.

Students at St. Bede's Grammar (and living next door to Alice) formed Kindness, who changed their name to Smokie for a run of Seventies hits. Less successful were prog-rockers Igginbottom's Wrench (featuring later respected jazz-rock guitarist Allan Holdsworth) and the city's first punk outfit The Luddites.

Eighties groups include the Radio 5, New Model Army (hit big in '85, wearing clogs made in Hebden Bridge), Southern Death Cult (fronted by Ian Astbury who lived in Forrest Road and later led The Cult to stardom), Getting The Fear (SDC descendants), Baby Tuckoo (heavy metal), Joolz (punk poet), Steven 'Seething' Wells (poet and journalist, who was once rude about me – but I'll let him off), Psycho Surgeons, Excalibur, Somebody's Brother (R&B). Zodiac Mindwarp and Little Brother also hail from Bradford.

Early Nineties thrashers included Slammer and Peel favourites Carcass — noted for such titles as 'Disgrace To The Corpse Of Sid' and 'Crepitating Bowel Erosion'.

Poet John Hegley and Strangler Jean Jacques Burnel went to Bradford University; Mark Yates and Leigh Marklow (Terrorvision) met as students at the Art College. The last piece of the Terrorvision jigsaw fell into place when Yates met singer Tony Wright at the Wheatsheaf public house. After much determination, they reached the '96 Top Five with 'Perseverance'.

All the local groups used to rehearse in the Flexible Response, a studio in Church Lane.

When Liverpool punk band Big In Japan played at the Royal Standard, the promoter told them he "wouldn't be letting any Pakis in". The band were so incensed that Bill Drummond pissed in the teapot they'd just emptied... and got caught by said promoter. He took them to court but lost the case because of his racist remarks! Joy Division played an early gig at the Royal Standard in September '78.

The power of poetry. Linton Kwesi Johnson's George Lindo documented the case of an innocent Jamaican factory worker who was fitted up and found guilty by an all white jury. His conviction was reversed on appeal and he got £25,000 compensation.

Gomez guitarist/bassist Paul Blackburn studied pharmacy at the university.

In '95, the progressive city Art Gallery at Cartwright Hall, Lister Park presented Sound & Fury, an exhibition of the art and imagery of Heavy Metal (including some rather fine family trees!), which subsequently toured the country.

Also emerging in the Nineties were The Poppy Factory (jangly), Loud (heavy), The Unique 3 and Fun-da-mental (rap), Tasmin Archer, who gave up her factory job when she topped the '92 chart with 'Sleeping Satellite' 0, Surge, Monorail (nouveau mods) and Rootsman (reggae).

Perversely, the band called Bradford, who released a single called 'Liverpool', were actually from Blackburn.

BRAMLEY
Birthplace of singer David Gedge, 23.4.60 (The Wedding Present).

BRIGHOUSE
PJ Proby worked as a farm labourer somewhere in the locality.

In November '77, The Brighouse & Rastrick Brass Band reached the top three with 'Floral Dance'.

Jane Harrison, the classical singer who won *Opportunity Knocks* in '88, was born here.

Though Embrace have their studio in nearby Huddersfield, group founders the McNamara brothers grew up here.

DEWSBURY
Operational base of Impaler, who released their first album in '92. Prior to them, only The Psykik Volts reached vinyl.

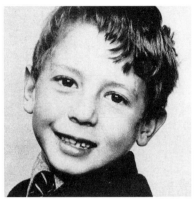
(Richard Norris)

Butch Yorkshire lad, Marc Almond, at school in Guiseley

GUISELEY
Marc Almond was educated at Aerborough Grammar.

HALIFAX
Birthplace of *6.5 Special* star Don Lang.

Home of peroxide-blond Sixties beat group The Quare Fellas — too literary for their own good, by the sound of it — who were managed by Shirley Crabtree, better known as wrestler Big Daddy!

Setting for the Krumlin Festival of August '70, which had all-star line-up including Fairport Convention, Elton John, The Move and many more. Gales ripped the place to shreds on Saturday night, and Sunday had to be cancelled.

Local lass Catherine Howe cut a couple of albums in the Seventies; The Spurs were just about the only late Eighties band; Elevation followed in the early Nineties.

Before she moved to Newcastle to join Dubstar, Sarah Blackwood lived in Elworth Avenue.

HEBDEN BRIDGE
Operational base of mid-Eighties John Peel Show regulars Bogshed.

A local clog-maker claimed that New Model Army fans had saved his business from going bust. (Shades of The Beatles, erstwhile saviours of the corduroy industry).

Home of Eliot Rashman, where he and Mick Hucknall hatched plans for Simply Red in early '83.

Indie band The Last Peach emerged in the Nineties, cutting acclaimed singles.

Hebden Bridge was one of many towns listed in the Justified Ancients of Mu Mu's '91 Top Tenner 'It's Grim Up North'.

KLF graffiti on the M1 northbound, Watford, covering previous scrawl by The Tea Set

(Tenzing Scott-Brown)

HOLMFIRTH

Birthplace of Roy Castle, 31.8.32.

Described by estate agents as *Last Of The Summer Wine* country — not surprisingly, since it is filmed here — Holmfirth is the sometime home of Jenny Haan (Babe Ruth) and Alan Davey (Hawkwind).

HONLEY

Birthplace of singer Biff Byford, 15.1.52 (Saxon), who was raised here and in Skelmanthorpe. He fronted Coast, then Son Of A Bitch, which mutated into Saxon.

HUDDERSFIELD

Birthplace of keyboard player Billy Currie, 1.4.52 (Ultravox); drummer Dave Stead, 15.10.62 (Housemartins); guitarist Tim Bricheno, 6.7.63, and bass player Andy Cousin, 28.6.63 (both of All About Eve).

The Beatles played the ABC cinema in Market Street in November 63 — and The Sex Pistols played their last ever UK gig at Ivanhoe's Club on Christmas Day '77.

Local Sixties beatsters Sammy King & The Voltairs recorded for HMV — unsuccessfully.

Billy Currie studied at Huddersfield Poly; bass player John McCoy (Gillan and other heavy outfits too numerous to list!) studied at Huddersfield Hairdressing College.

Local late Seventies groups included Jab Jab; in the Eighties came The Instigators (noisy), Roberta Junk (poppy), Arrin (folky), The Killermeters (parkas and scooters), Rhabstallion (heavy metal), Hotline (house-funk) and The Stinging Jellyfish (defy description!); the Nineties saw the arrival of The Suncharms, The Headmen, The Frogs Of War and Kava Kava.

Dance Act Shiva hit the '95 Top 40 with 'Work It Out' — but tragically, singer Louise Dean was killed by a drunk driver a week later.

ILKLEY

The Jimi Hendrix Experience were due to play the Gyro Club at the Troutbeck Hotel in February '67, but the police refused to allow the gig to proceed because of over-crowding.

Communal base for '98 Mercury Prizewinners Gomez.

KEIGHLEY

Nikkers Club at 59 Cavendish Street featured new wave and punk bands (like Generation X) in the late Seventies.

Home town of drummer Shutty Shuttleworth and guitarist Leigh Marklow (founders of Terrorvision), who became friends at Greenhead Grammar School.

LEEDS

Birthplace of Fifties thrush Marion Ryan, 4.2.33 (worked as an assistant in a drapery store); singer/songwriter Michael Chapman, 24.1.41; Jeff Christie, 1946 (number one with 'Yellow River' in 1970); guitarist Lek Leckenby, 14.5.46 (Herman's Hermits); twins Paul and Barry Ryan, 24.10.48 (sons of Marion); singer Stevie Wright, 20.12.48 (Easybeats); Spice Girl Melanie Brown, 29.5.75 (aka Mel B, Scary Spice); Sean Conlon, 20.5.81 (5ive).

Muddy Waters made his UK début here in October '58.

Jimmy Savile was manager of the Spinning Disc, one of the first Mecca discotheques.

Sixties groups included The Cherokees (Top 40 with Seven Daffodils), Jan Dukes De Gray, Root and Jenny Jackson, The Accent, The Cresters and The Bedrocks.

Hottest Sixties venue was the Three Coins in Albion Walks. Their All Nighters presented the likes of John Lee Hooker, Carl Perkins and the city's own Blue Sounds.

Frankie Vaughan was a student teacher at the College of Art. Jake Thackray was educated by Jesuits at St. Michael's College and then taught in Leeds for six years. Barry Cryer studied English at the university — and then went on to record Purple People Eater!

Jon King and Andy Gill both studied art at Leeds University, but were more interesting in starting up The Gang Of Four, who played their first gig at Leeds Corn Exchange in May '77.

(Jolyon Burnham)

The Gang Of Four celebrate their home town hall

Other Leeds University students include drummer Bill Bruford (Yes, King Crimson), Fad Gadget, Andy Kershaw (disc jockey/radio journalist), Ted Key (Housemartins), The Three Johns (all of them), Tom Gray (Gomez) and English student Mark Knopfler, who in July '95 returned to collect an honorary doctorate. As a cub reporter on the *Yorkshire Evening Post*, he had borrowed 18/3d from the coffee machine – which he was asked to stump up. You know what they say about Yorkshiremen.

Brendan Croker was a stage designer at Leeds Playhouse.

Buzzcocks and Magazine founder Howard Devoto went to Leeds Grammar School.

Soft Cell (who met there) made their début at a Leeds Polytechnic party in '78. Scritti Politti (who formed at the art college) also made their début in '78.

The Queens Hall in Sovereign Street was the setting for Futurama, the annual sci-fi rock festivals. Playing the first, in September '79 were the unlikely bedfellows Joy Division, PIL, The Fall, Echo & The Bunnymen and Hawkwind. The Cult headlined Futurama in September '83.

Late Seventies/early Eighties bands included The Delta 5, Girls At Our Best, Icon, The Xpellaires, The Mekons, Music For Pleasure, and Sisters Of Mercy – who made it to the national stage after years of toil.

The Beatles played both the Odeon Cinema and the Queen's Hall in June '63; Queen started their first major tour at the Town Hall in November '73, supporting Mott The Hoople.

The Warehouse at 19 Somers Street was a popular early Eighties gig – Marc Almond was sometime disc jockey. ABC made their first foray out of Sheffield to play there in '80; Frankie Goes To Hollywood made their first foray out of Liverpool to play there in July' 82. Also on the circuit were Brannigans in Call Lane and the Fforde Green Hotel in Roundhay Road, Harehills – where local heavy metal band Praying Mantis made their début in June '81.

Late Eighties faves were The Wedding Present who got going in '85; graduated from their own Reception label to RCA in '89; and in '92, logged an astonishing twelve Top Thirty hits in one year. Also breaking out during the Eighties were Age Of Chance, Ghost Dance, Brendan Croker & The Five O'Clock Shadows, Surfing Dave & The Absent Legends, The Hollow Men, Abrasive Wheels and The Parachute Men. The March Violets and the marvellously idiosyncratic Red Lorry Yellow Lorry were Peel and Kershaw favourites.

In September '89, punk poet Joolz was fined £100 for using offensive words during a recital outside the Town Hall.

In '90, disc jockeys Tim Garbutt and Jez Willis teamed up to form Utah Saints; Cud scored hits on A&M.

Chumbawamba were a Leeds-based underground collective who started gigging in '83 but only became a household name after the anthemic 'Tubthumpin'' topped the charts in '97 and Danbert Nobacon doused John Prescott at the '98 Brit Awards dinner. They were banned from the university for ten years after a Bust Fund benefit at the Riley-Smith Hall in October '86 turned into a riot and heavy handed police made 34 arrests.

Leeds Live albums:
who cribbed who?

The Who, The Macc Lads and John Martyn have all released albums called *Live At Leeds*. The Who's famous live album was recorded at the Uni on Valentine's Night, '70.

A maelstrom of early Nineties activity saw the emergence of The Pale Saints, The Edsel Auctioneer, Fluff, Headtime, Greenhouse, Violet Hour, Bloo, LFO (Low Frequency Oscillation), Cassandra Complex, A Secret Life, Ringo's High, Tsetse Fly, La Costa Rasa and Zoopsie.

In the mid-Nineties came Black Star Liner (reggae); The Glamorous Hooligan (techno); Polaris, Chest and Baby Harp Seal (indie); Lazerboy (post-rock); Spacehog (grungers, bigger in the States); Fuzzbird (late Nineties Peel faves).

Varieties is a cool late Nineties venue.

NETHERTHONG

Nico lived here for several years before her death in Ibiza in July '88. Although she was buried in Germany, a special memorial service was held here.

NORMANTON

Local groups include the new wave Donkeys, who excited a little national interest.

OSSETT

Home of Black Lace, bare-faced perpetrators of 'Agadoo'.

Front cover to *Best Wishes* by Ultrasound in Wakefield outside a hostile HMV branch!

OTLEY

Birthplace of bass player Craig Adams, 4.4.62 (Cult).

In April '58, rock'n'roller Wee Willie Harris was fined five quid by Otley magistrates for using a car with inefficient brakes.

Sometime home of Wedding Present mainman David Gedge.

SHIPLEY

Local tongues were wagging in summer '68 when Paul McCartney arrived at the Town Hall to record The Black Dyke Mills Band for the Apple label.

SOUTH ELMSALL

Birthplace of guitarist John McLaughlin, 4.1.42 (Blue Flames, Mahavishnu Orchestra).

Minsthorpe High School acquired a reputation for putting on name bands – like The Wedding Present, The Wonder Stuff and The Lemonheads.

TODMORDEN

Birthplace of keyboard wizard Keith Emerson, 1.11.44 (Nice, ELP); saxplayer John Helliwell, 15.2.45 (Supertramp).

Also the birthplace of orchestra leader Geoff Love, who recorded hits as Manuel & His Music Of The Mountains.

Victoria Mansion were early Nineties hopefuls; Langfield Crane's '90 début album won a modicum of critical acclaim.

WAKEFIELD

Birthplace of former local government officer Bill Nelson, 18.12.48, who led Global Village, Be-Bop Deluxe and Red Noise while establishing his solo identity. His earliest recordings were made right here in town at Holyground Studio. Northern Dream was a private recording available only from Gloria's Record Bar.

In February '63, just as they were taking off, The Beatles played the Regal Cinema in Kirkgate.

Child broke out with teenybop hits in the late Seventies. During the Eighties, Stranger Than Fiction, Fiat Lux and Vardis made ripples. Strangeways attracted press attention; they played at the Unity Hall and the Technical College but couldn't progress.

Theakston's Brewery sponsored rock events at Nostel Priory in the early Eighties. Jethro Tull appeared here in August '82, giving a leg-up to unknown bottom of the bill Marillion.

In August '90, The Spoilt Bratz appeared under their new name Terrorvision for the first time at the Players Snooker Club – to an audience of less than 20.

Guitarists Richard Green and Tiny Wood met at Wakefield District College in '90. A year later, they moved to Newcastle to join Sleepy People before going to London to form Ultrasound – one of the few indie acts to break big in '98.

Wild Planet and Chopper were early Nineties hopefuls – but the town's biggest star was Jane McDonald, a cruise ship entertainer made famous by a BBC TV series. Her July '98 début album topped the charts.

WETHERBY

In 93, local indie band Boyracer won a contract with Sarah Records.

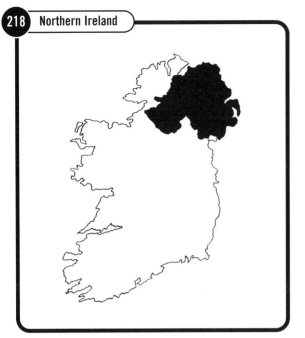

NORTHERN IRELAND

ANTRIM

BALLYMENA

The Flamingo Ballroom was where the action was. The Gentry were Sixties residents; The Rolling Stones played there in July '64; Pink Floyd in September '67.

Operational base of respected showband The Freshmen – Ireland's answer to The Beach Boys.

Local lad David McWilliams was expelled from Ballymena Technical School for drinking wine! Later, he almost had a UK hit with 'The Days Of Pearly Spencer', which was furiously hyped in *NME* and played to death on Radio Caroline.

Belfast gypsies Them find a bombed out location

BELFAST

Van Morrison was born at 125 Hyndford Street on 31.8.45. He went to Elmgrove Primary School in Beersbridge Road and Orangefield Secondary but left to clean windows (recalled on the '82 album *Beautiful Vision*) and join The Monarchs, a showband. In various early Sixties ensembles, he played the Willowfield Cinema in Woodstock Road, the Strand Cinema in Holywood Road, the Brookborough Hall in Sandown Road, the Harriers Hall in Hyndford Street.

In early '64, he became the singer with Them, who made their début (April '64) and played their earliest gigs at the Maritime Hotel, a mission for seamen in College Square North. One of Van's most repeated quotes asserts that Them "lived and died as a group on the stage at the Maritime" – though they emerged as one of the hottest groups on the UK R&B scene. This period is chronicled in their track 'The Story Of Them'. Van's later songs are peppered with local references... to Cyprus Avenue, Sandy Row, Orangefield, Hyndford Street, etc.

In late '78, Morrison played a triumphant gig at the Whitla Hall at Queens College – his first Belfast concert for over a decade.

Also the birthplace of crooner Ronnie Carroll, 18.8.34; singer-songwriter David McWilliams, 4.7.45; guitarist Eric Bell, 3.9.47 (Thin Lizzy); singer Ernie Graham, 14.6.46 (Eire Apparent, Clancey); guitarist Gary Moore, 4.4.52 (Thin Lizzy, solo).

In '57, establishment opposition to rock'n'roll resulted in Bill Haley playing to a half empty Hippodrome Theatre. His film *Don't Knock The Rock* was banned in the city as "a bad influence on the young".

In July '64, the streets were lined with union jack wavers when The Rolling Stones came to town, but their concert at the Ulster Hall turned to pandemonium and was terminated after 12 minutes. A stage invasion by hysterical girls resulted in 25 hospital cases, with six detained. Fighting broke out between police and fans, 3,000 of whom had crammed into the 1,200 fire-limit hall. No such scenes greeted Led Zeppelin when they played there in March '71.

Sixties groups included The Mad Lads (R&B), The Belfast Gypsies (Them descendants), and The Wheels. Not to mention The Bats, who hitch-hiked to London in September '64 to locate producer Mickie Most and audition for him. He signed them but they were not destined to follow his other acts – The Animals, The Nashville Teens and Herman Hermits – into the charts.

Most famous Sixties club gig was the Spanish Rooms, as mentioned in the autobiographical song 'Story Of Them'…"made the scene at the Spanish Rooms on the Falls". Other popular Sixties haunts were Sammy Hustons and Clarkes, among many others. The Maritime Hotel became Club Rado and bands like the Interns, The Wheels and Taste all had residencies there.

The Beatles played in Northern Ireland only twice – both times in Belfast: at the Ritz Cinema in Fisherwick Place in November '63 and at the King's Hall in November '64. Bob Dylan made his first visit in May '66, when he played the ABC Theatre.

Queens University graduate Phil Coulter became a famous producer (Bay City Rollers, Slik, Billy Connolly) and a prolific songwriter, penning Eurovision entries 'Puppet On A String' and 'Congratulations'.

Fruupp made many excursions over the Irish Sea during the early Seventies progressive rock era.

The Starjets sing about 10 years of "the Troubles"

Formed in '77, Stiff Little Fingers were the hottest punk/new wave band.

Other late Seventies/Eighties acts included Protex, Rudi, Ruefrex, The Defects, The Starjets, Big Self, Friction Groove (one of them, anyway), Sweet Savage, Victim (who moved to Manchester), The Outcasts, Xdreamysts, Mama's Boys, Jake Burns & The Big Wheel, and singer/songwriter Andy White.

Most influential local indie label was Good Vibrations, formed by Terry Hooley and operating from 102 Great Victoria Street. The Derry based Undertones got their start on it in '78.

Songs about the city include 'Belfast Child' by Simple Minds, 'Belfast Boy' by Don Fardon, 'Belfast' by Boney M, 'Belfast' by Energy Orchard, 'Belfast' by Orbital, 'Belfast' by Barnbrack, 'Michael Caine' by Madness, plus any number by local writers.

In the Eighties, hopes were pinned on The Adventures (Starjets descendents), Energy Orchard, Brian Kennedy, Four Idle Hands, Jackie Quinn and Peel faves Therapy?

In the Nineties came Colenso Parade, Chimera, LMS and Tunic.

CARRICKFERGUS

The title of a folk ballad which several rock singers have found attractive – notably Bryan Ferry (on *The Bride Stripped Bare*) and Van Morrison (with The Chieftains). Van had played the Town Hall as early as '61, with show band The Monarchs.

GIANT'S CAUSEWAY

Some of the 37,000 hexagonal basalt columns are pictured on the sleeve of Led Zeppelin's '73 album *The Houses Of The Holy* – but you were probably too busy examining the naked teenage nymphets to notice.

(A. Powell/Hypnosis)

PORTRUSH

Kelly's in Bushmills Road is the focus of late Nineties club activity.

ARMAGH

PORTADOWN

Operational base for psychedelic group The People, who became Eire Apparent. Managed by future Stiff boss Dave Robinson and produced by Jimi Hendrix, they looked like happening. Guitarist Henry McCullough later joined Joe

Cocker; singer Ernie Graham went solo; drummer Davy Lutton was in T Rex; bassist Chris Stewart was later in Poco.

In 94, local band Joyrider toured supporting Therapy?, whose Andy Cairns produced their first single.

COUNTY DOWN

DOWNPATRICK
Birthplace of Ian Mitchell, 22.8.58 (Bay City Rollers).

Backwater were operating locally in the mid-Nineties – as were Ash, who achieved international popularity after breaking into the UK Top Twenty with their August '95 hit Girl From Mars.

NEWRY
In the greatest tragedy in Irish music, three of The Miami Showband were killed and the others injured when a bomb, planted in their van, exploded at a road block on the A1 between Bainbridge and Newry.

Operational base of The 4 of Us, who released several singles in the early Nineties.

WARRENPOINT
Birthplace of Clodagh Rodgers, 5.3.49.

FERMANAGH

ENNISKILLEN
Neil Hannon moved here at age 11, and subsequently formed The Divine Comedy, with whom he would enjoy wide success.

DERRY

COLERAINE
Local mid-Nineties bands included The Catchers.

LIMAVADY
In July '87, Richard Branson and Per Lindstrand's hot-air balloon touched down here after their heroic Atlantic crossing – only to rise up again and end up in the sea.

LONDONDERRY/DERRY
Birthplace of producer/songwriter Phil Coulter, February '42 (Them, Twinkle); Dana, 30.8.52 (she left Thornhill Convent of Mercy to top the '70 chart with 'All Kinds Of Everything'; in '97 revealed ambition to become President of Ireland, having been pursuing Christian ministry in Alabama for many years); singer Feargal Sharkey, 13.8.58 (Undertones); Divine Comedy leader Neil Hannon, 7.11.70 (whose father was rector of Christ Church, and who lived at the Rectory, 80 Northland Road).

Home of imaginative late Seventies garage rockers The Undertones and (when they split in '83) their descendants: Feargal Sharkey and That Petrol Emotion. Bass player Mickey Bradley later became a successful local radio DJ; drummer Billy Doherty now runs a recording/rehearsal studio; guitarist John O'Neill formed Nineties trip-hoppers Rare.

The Moondogs were early Eighties indie-poppers.

Local lad Jimmy McShane scored an '85 Top Three hit with 'Tarzan Boy' – under the name of Baltimora.

Home of Peter Cunnah, who got nowhere in local late Eighties indie band The Stunning, but (with session man assistance) broke huge as D:Ream. His '94 chart topper 'Things Can Only Get Better' was adopted as the Labour Party's victory anthem.

Local Nineties bands included Schtum, whose '94 début single won unanimous praise, and Cuckoo.

TYRONE

OMAGH
Birthplace of Jimmy Kennedy, 1902, who wrote many Tin Pan Alley hits, including the lyrics for The Platters' US chart-topper 'My Prayer'.

The terrible bombing in August 98 inspired *Across the Bridge of Hope*, a fund-raising album featuring U2, Van Morrison, The Corrs, Enya and other stars.

STRABANE
Birthplace of Paul Brady, 6.5.47, who emerged as a potent singer/songwriter after an apprenticeship in The Johnstons.

Operational base of Ireland's very first showband, Clipper Carlton – formed in 1949.

Dominic Behan in easy-listening sing-a-long stab at the charts

EASTER WEEK AND AFTER Songs of the I.R.A.

DOMINIC BEHAN

topic

EIRE

This is supposed to be a gazetteer of Great Britain - but a brief word about Eire. (For a much fuller picture, read Irish Rock by Mark J. Prendergast or have a chat with Johnny Rogan.).I've arranged it alphabetically by town, rather than county.

(John Carder Bush)

Neither virgin or prune: Gavin Friday, man about Dublin

ARKLOW Wicklow
Van Morrison sang about the 'Streets Of Arklow' on his '74 album *Veedon Fleece*.

BALLYBRICKEN Limerick
Birthplace of singer Dolores O'Riordan, 6.9.71 (Cranberries).

BALLYSHANNON Donegal
Birthplace of guitarist Rory Gallagher, 2.3.48.

BIRR Offaly
Home of mid-Nineties solo artist Mundy.

BLESSINGTON Wicklow
In '91, Celt rockers the Prayer Boat signed with RCA to record the album *Oceanic Feeling*.

CLONAKILTY Cork
Former Jimi Hendrix Experience bassist Noel Redding moved here in the Seventies, forming The Clonakilty Cowboys.

CORK
The Rolling Stones played the Savoy Theatre in January '65; The Smiths in May '84.

One of Ireland's most popular showbands, The Dixies had a residency at the Arcadia Ballroom during the Sixties.

Rory Gallagher formed his blues trio Taste here in summer '66. They became the first group from southern Ireland to reach UK album chart, in February '70.

Microdisney were idiosyncratic late Seventies new wavers.

Grimmo (left) ex-Zerra One, joins Cathal Coughlan in The Fatima Mansions

(Andy Earl)

The local Fatima Mansions (perversely named after tenements in Dublin) reached the Top Ten with '(Everything I Do) I Do It For You' in '92 – in which year The Sultans Of Ping began their considerable chart run. Both bands relocated to London – as did The Frank And Walters (named after two local eccentrics of their acquaintance), who began to attract recognition with Happy Busman.

The Cranberries played seminal early gigs at O'Henry's Club.

In the mid-Nineties, The Emperor Of Ice Cream began gigging in Britain; later in the decade, the Young Offenders began to attract attention.

COROFIN Clare
Sharon Shannon grew up in nearby Ruan.

The Cranberries of Limerick pose in south Dublin where *The Commitments* was filmed

(Andy Earl)

DUBLIN
Birthplace of Fifties balladeer Michael Holliday, 26.11.28; Ronnie Drew, 18.9.35 (Dubliners); Paddy Maloney, 1.8.38 (chief Chieftain); Barney MacKenna, 16.12.39 (Dubliners); Christy Moore, 7.5.45; premier showband singer Dickie Rock, 1946 (in Cabra); Terry Woods, 4.12.47 (Pogues); Bob Geldof, 5.10.54 – in Dun Laoghaire (Boomtown Rats); Mary Black, 22.5.55; Siobhan Stewart, 10.9.58 (Bananarama, Shakespears Sister); Sinead O'Connor, 8.12.66 (at Cascia Nursing Home, 13 Pembroke Street); Mikey Graham, 15.8.72, Keith Duffy, 1.10.74, Stephen Gateley, 17.3.76, Shane Lynch, 3.7.76, Ronan Keating, 3.3.77 (all five of whom came together as Boyzone).

Some observers contend that Irish rock began with Bluesville, an early Sixties R&B outfit started at Dublin University by true blue Englishman Ian Whitcomb. He went off to America to become a solo star (with hit 'You Turn Me On') while the rest of the group evolved into the pioneers of the London pub rock scene, Bees Make Honey.

The Dubliners formed in O'Donaghue's bar in Merrion Row in '62, and were soon recording for Transatlantic; The Chieftains formed in the late Fifties and cut their first album for the Claddagh label in '64.

Early venues included the Number Five Club and the Caroline Club, operating in a converted cinema in the south coastal region of the city. The Rolling Stones played the Adelphi Theatre in January' 65.

Mike Carr, composer of Shadows hits 'Man Of Mystery' and 'Kon Tiki', was raised in Russell Street – a few doors down from Brendan Behan.

Most successful mid-Sixties chart act was The Bachelors, who reached number one with 'Diane' in '64. All three were born in Dublin.

When his mid-Sixties R&B band Them split up, Van Morrison lived in Dublin... at the flat of Dave Robinson – later roadie for Jimi Hendrix and the boss of Stiff Records.

The other Skid Row got there first!

(Roger Armstrong)

Most important Sixties group was Skid Row, led by Brush Shiels (born Dublin, 1952) and containing at various times Phil Lynott (born in English West Midlands, 20.8.49, but raised in Dublin) and Gary Moore (born in Belfast).

Lynott left to form Orphanage with Brian Downey (they'd both gone to CBS Crumlin and Clogher Road Technical School), which became Thin Lizzy with the arrival of Belfast born Eric Bell. In January '73, they became the first band from Eire to crack the UK singles chart – with 'Whiskey In The Jar'. (Unless you count the folksy Dubliners, with 'Seven Drunken Nights').

Skid Row had already reached the UK album chart, briefly in October '70.

Strabane-born Paul Brady was at the University of Dublin when he joined The Johnstons in '67; Chris de Burgh was a Trinity graduate.

Folk rock group Dr Strangely Strange (soon to record for Island) formed in a house on Mount Street in '69, around the time that the local Tir Na Nog were signing to Chrysalis.

Horslips introduced Celtic rock in the early Seventies.

The Boomtown Rats changed their name from The Nightlife Thugs during the interval of their début gig, on

Tir Na Nog

U2's powerful 'Sunday Bloody Sunday' could refer to the shooting of thirteen civilians in January 72... or, as some suggest, it could be about an incident in 1920 when English soldiers gunned down several people at a football match in Croke Park – which, incidentally, was the venue for U2's biggest ever Dublin concert, in June '85.

In the Eighties came Blue In Heaven, Princess Tiny Meat, A House (notorious for their late Eighties indie hit 'Kick Me Again Jesus'), Cactus World News (whose bassist was Eamonn Andrews' son), The Stars Of Heaven, An Emotional Fish, The Fat Lady Sings, Light A Big Fire, Paul Cleary, Hot House Flowers (Top Three in '88 with album *People*), half of My Bloody Valentine (who moved to London to sign with Creation) and Ton Ton Macoute (fronted by the unknown Sinead O'Connor).

Emerging in the Nineties were The Power of Dreams (two minor hits on Polydor), The Pale (a minor hit with 'Dogs With No Tails' in '92), The Forget Me Nots, The Harvest Ministers, The Frames (a tribute band, obviously), The Whipping Boy, Candy Apple Red, Brilliant Trees, The Honey Thieves, Into Paradise (whose album *Churchtown* was a clue to their provenance), Scary Eire, Pet Lamb, Engine Alley, Blink, Wormhole, Puppy Lovebomb, Sack (who won a Best Irish Music Video award in '94), The Sound Crowd Orchestra (techno), Bawl (indiepop), Pelvis and Chicks (who broke out as support to Ash on their '98 European tour).

Halloween '75, at Bolton Street College of Technology – where Johnnie Moylett, Gerry Cott and Pete Briquette had been studying architecture. Bob Geldof was living in a flat in Clyde Road, and Gary Roberts was at Trinity College. 'Rat Tra'p was said to have been written about the city's Five Lamp area.

The city's most popular Seventies rock club was Moran's, in the basement of Moran's Hotel.

In February '79, Dark Space was Dublin's first punk festival, held at the Project Arts Theatre. Bands included U2, Protex, Rudi, The Attrix, Virgin Prunes, The Vipers and Ireland's first reggae outfit, Zebra.

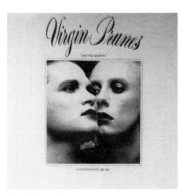

More Irish easy listening

Dublin mods The Josephs

(Adrian Green)

The Virgin Prunes made international progress on Rough Trade; The Radiators From Space (whose singer Steve Rapid came up with the name U2) signed with Chiswick; and U2 went with Island – hitting the UK chart with their album *Boy* in August '81 and going on to become one of the biggest bands in rock history. They formed at Mount Temple School, where all were students. Adam Clayton and the Edge were from England, but Bono (born 10.5.60 at Rotunda Hospital, and subsequently resident at 20 Cedarwood Avenue, Ballymun) and Larry Mullen (born 31.10.61) were Dubliners.

The Royal Dublin Society Hall was the venue for the '81 Eurovision Song Contest – won by Bucks Fizz with 'Making Your Mind Up'. Dublin resident Johnny Logan (born in Melbourne, Australia) won the Eurovision Song Contest in '80 ('What's Another Year') and '87 ('Hold Me Now') – and wrote Linda Martin's '92 winner 'Why Me?'

Meanwhile, tax exiles like Spandau Ballet and Howard Jones, and Tory haters like Elvis Costello, spent time relaxing in Dublin's fair city.

The Cranberries recorded their '93 number one album *Everybody Else Is Doing It, So Why Can't We* at Windmill Lane Studio. Made famous by U2, the studio was covered in more than a decade's worth of fan graffiti – prompting a December '98 council decision to sandblast and paint away the offending scrawl – which had extended way beyond the studio walls and up the road. After negotiation, it was allowed to remain "as a shrine to U2".

In '94, dance routine group Boyzone were brought together Monkees-style by a newspaper advertisement and were soon international teenybop heroes. A revival of The Osmonds 20-year-old hit 'Love Me For A Reason' provided their breakthrough. A female version, B*witched, went Top Three with all their '98 singles.

In the mid-Nineties, Carole King was said to be living in Castle Bar.

In the late Nineties, the happening place was Lily's Bordello in Grafton Street.

DUNDALK Louth
From here emerged The Corrs, who topped late Nineties album charts and headlined stadium gigs internationally.

Home also of Eurovision Song Contest star Dawn Martin and late Nineties singer-violinist Pat Treacy (who hails from the townland of Hackballscross).

GALWAY
Origin of seminal folk-rock group Sweeney's Men (including Andy Irvine, Johnny Moynihan, Terry Woods), who got together in summer '66.

On their tour of Eire in late '84, The Smiths played at Leisureland.

Home of singer/songwriter Mary Coughlan, who broke through with her '85 album *Tired And Emotional*.

Local early Nineties bands include Toasted Heretic.
The coolest late Nineties venue is the Roisin Dubh in Dominick Street.

GWEEDORE Donegal
All five members of Clannad (formed in '70, and Top Five with 'Harry's Game' in '82) were from this tiny village. Enya – born 17.5.61 – left them to go solo and topped the '88 chart with 'Orinoco Flow'. Two of her uncles were Clannad founders.

HOWTH Dublin
In Tua Nua formed here in '82. Violinist Steve Wickham later joined The Waterboys.

KILKENNY
Local Nineties bands include My Little Funhouse and Kerbdog.

KINCASSLAGH Donegal
Birthplace of Daniel O'Donnell, 12.12.61, who became the biggest Country & Irish star ever. His albums were so successful that in '91, an excuse was found (too MOR) to exclude them from the UK country chart, which he had dominated.

LETTERKENNY Donegal
In November '84, The Smiths played the Leisure Centre.

LIMERICK
Birthplace of Terry Wogan, 3.8.38; guitarist Noel Hogan, 25.12.71, and bass player Mike Hogan, 29.4.73 (The Cranberries).

Progressive/underground group Granny's Intentions formed here. They were signed by Deram but made marginal headway in UK – as did Eugene Wallace.

And £150 buys you their first E.P.

Local early Nineties bands include They Do It With Mirrors and The Cranberries, who made their début at Ruby's, a local basement club, and were soon topping the UK chart with their '93 début album *Everybody Else Is Doing It, So Why Can't We?*

In the late Nineties came nu-rockers The Driven.

(Rex Features)

The Boss takes on Dublin

LISMORE Waterford
Birthplace of Patrick Campbell Lyons, 1943 (instigator of flower power champions Nirvana).

MULLINGER West Meath
Birthplace of Joe Dolan, 16.10.43, who reached the '69 UK Top Three with 'Make Me An Island'.

NEWBRIDGE Kildare
Home of Christy Moore and Donal Lunny, who played together in Planxty and Moving Hearts.
   Thin Lizzy made their début here in April '70.

PARTEEN Clare
Birthplace of drummer Feargal Lawler, 4.3.71 (Cranberries).

ROOSKY Roscommon
Birthplace of ballroom builder and Taoiseach Albert Reynolds, November '35.

SLANE Meath
In Tua Nua signed with Island the same week they supported Bob Dylan at Slane Castle in summer '84. The venue subsequently presented concerts by the world's biggest acts, including R.E.M. (June '85), Oasis (July '95), The Manic Street Preachers (August '98).

TIPPERARY
Born in Kent, Shane McGowan grew up here – but moved to London in time to form punk band The Nips and the wild folk-rocking Pogues.

TUAM Galway
In autumn '68, Marianne Faithfull, pregnant with Mick Jagger's child, sought the peace of a country house here – one of several she stayed in during this turbulent period.
   Operational base of The Saw Doctors, whose first ('89)

single was 'N 17' – the road out of town. Having gone professional to tour with The Waterboys, they called their début album *If This Is Rock And Roll, I Want My Old Job Back*. Their second album was *All The Way From Tuam*. Their single 'I Useta Love Her' is one of the biggest sellers in Irish history.

WATERFORD
Birthplace of Val Doonican, 3.2.29 (he attended De La Salle College, Waterpark and made his professional début in the '48 summer season at Courtown Harbour); singer Brendan Bowyer, 12.10.38 (Royal Showband, Big 8); omnipresent Seventies chart artist Gilbert O'Sullivan, 1.12.46.
   The Olympia Ballroom was the hottest venue in the area, presenting everyone from The Tremeloes to Creedence Clearwater Revival. It was also home base for The Royal Showband – the most popular of all such outfits during the Sixties, when their version of 'The Hucklebuck' became one of the best selling records in Irish history. Their singer Brendan Bowyer was acclaimed as Eire's Elvis.
   Sinead O'Connor quit boarding school here and fled to Dublin to enrol at the College of Music and emerge as a fine singer.
   Karan Casey was a student at the Regional Technical College before becoming lead singer in Solas and ultimately moving to Queens, New York.

WEXFORD
Born in Buenos Aires, 15.10.47, Chris de Burgh moved here when his family bought a dilapidated castle for conversion to a restaurant and hotel in '60. He later attended Dublin University before being discovered at a London party.
   Birthplace of Pierce Turner, late Eighties breaker on the Beggars Banquet label.

WICKLOW
Birthplace of Sonny Condell, 1.7.49 (leader of Horslips).
   The sleeve of their album *Kip Of The Serenes* shows Dr Strangely Strange on the banks of the River Dargle.

SCOTLAND, EAST CENTRAL

Angus, Clackmannanshire, Dundee City,
City of Edinburgh, Falkirk, Fife, East & West Lothian,
Midlothian, Perth & Kinross,

ALLOA Clackmannanshire
Following their celebrated audition for Larry Parnes, The Silver Beetles started their Scottish tour – backing Johnny Gentle – at the Town Hall.

AUCHTERMUCHTY Fife
The Proclaimers grew up here, going from bedroom group to touring with The Housemartins, who had heard their demo tape.

BATHGATE West Lothian
Home of Sixties beat group The Golden Crusaders – signed to a punitive EMI contract after a two day audition which drew almost every unsigned group in Scotland.

In the late Eighties came Goodbye Mr Mackenzie, with a run of minor hits and the Top Thirty album *Good Deeds And Dirty Rags*.

BLAIRGOWRIE Perth & Kinross
Home of Hurricane #1 singer Alex lowe, who was previously a boxer of local renown.

COUPAR ANGUS Perth & Kinross
In '93, the début album by Long Fin Killie attracted critical acclaim.

SCOTLAND

COWDENBEATH Fife
Big Country leader Stuart Adamson was educated at Beath High School.

CROSSGATES Fife
Manchester born Stuart Adamson moved here at six months. His first group, Tattoo, made its début at Crossgates Miners Welfare Institute.

DALKEITH Midlothian
Fish (Marillion) was raised and educated here.
Operational base of punk band The Threats.

DUNBAR East Lothian
Birthplace of bass player Jimmy Bain (Rainbow, Dio, etc).

The original location of the pirate station Radio Scotland was three miles off the coast near Dunbar. It broadcast from the former Irish lightship Comet (built on the Clyde in 1904)

Goodbye Mr Mackenzie: Shirley Manson gets wed

from January to May '66, when it sailed to a new mooring in the Firth of Clyde. Stuart Henry was its most famous disc jockey.

On their first foray north of the border, Marillion played at the Goldenstones Hotel.

DUNDEE City

Birthplace of Roger Ball, 4.6.44, and Robbie McIntosh, 6.5.50 (both in The Average White Band, where they were also known as The Dundee Horns); Billy Mackenzie, 27.3.57 (Associates); Ricky Ross, 22.12.57 (Deacon Blue).

Goodbye Mr Mackenzie: much missed Associate

Tommy Steele almost gave up touring when fans put him in hospital after all but wrenching his arm from its socket when he played Caird Hall in City Square in May '58. It became an important package tour venue in the Sixties/Seventies. The Beatles played there in October' 63 and October '64; Led Zeppelin in November' 71 and January '73 (which was the first gig Big Country's Stuart Adamson ever attended)..

The Bay City Rollers played their first major gig at the J M Ballroom in spring '70.

The Poor Souls recorded for Decca in the Sixties; The Sleaz Boys were big locally in the early Seventies; The Head Boys made some national headway in the late Seventies; Rokotto and Ignatz were late Seventies funk outfits; The Associates never equalled their '82 début hit 'Party Fears Two'.

Dundee based promoter/agent Andy Lothian also ran his own label ALP, with releases by Alan Gorrie's group The Vikings, The Poor Souls (as above) and Red Hawkes.

Scotland's first punk indie label was N-R-G, operating from 17 Union Place.

Home also of new wavers The Scrotum Poles (who weren't going far with a name like that), Bread Poultice & The Running Sores (ditto!) and The Visitors. Former Jozef K singer Paul Quinn went solo and duetted with stars but faded fast. Before starting The Associates, Billy Mackenzie had a clothes shop called the Crypt.

Most successful late Eighties groups were Virgin signing, Danny Wilson (Top Three with 'Mary's Prayer') and CBS signing, Deacon Blue (Top Ten with 'Real Gone Kid').

A hive of mid-Nineties activity saw the emergence of acclaimed guitar bands Honeyrider, Broccoli and Spare Snare.

DUNFERMLINE Fife

Birthplace of Barbara Dickson, 27.9.47, who attended Woodmills Secondary School.

The town's first major export were Seventies mainstream rockers Nazareth, who evolved from local club group The Shadettes.

Nazareth's Manny Charlton was originally in Sixties group The Mark Five, who walked from Dunfermline to London to demand a record deal! They got one... on Fontana. Was it worth it, one wonders?

Richard Jobson as chief Skid

Also the birthplace of Richard Jobson, 6.10.60 – instigator of punk band The Skids, who played their first gig at the Belleville Hotel in August '77. Their first vinyl appearance was on No Bad Records, operating from Queen Anne Street. After four years, guitarist Stuart Adamson left to form Big Country with Dunfermline pal Bruce Watson.

Hometown of Rezillos singer Fay Fife (Sheelagh Hynde) – now a successful actress.

EDINBURGH City of

Birthplace of Stu Sutcliffe, 23.6.40 (Silver Beetles/Beatles); Mike Heron, 12.12.42 (Incredible String Band); Ian Anderson, 10.8.47 (Jethro Tull); Neil Murray, 27.8.50 (Whitesnake, Black Sabbath); David Paton, 29.10.51, and William Lyall, 26.3.53 (both Pilot); Derek Longmuir, 19.3.52, Alan Longmuir, 20.6.53, Eric Faulkner, 21.10.54, Les McKeown, 12.11.55, and Stuart Wood, 25.2.57 (all Bay City Rollers); Paul Buchanan, 16.4.56 (Blue Nile); Mike Barson, 21.4.58 (Madness); Fish, 25.4.58

Art school hopefuls The Rezillos

(Pete Barrett)

(Marillion... at the Simpson Maternity Hospital – same place as the Rollers!); Shirley Manson, 1966 (Garbage); Finley Quaye, 25.3.74.

First local to tap the teenage market was *6.5 Special* star Jackie Dennis – more memorable for his kilt than his '58 smash 'La Dee Dah'.

The Beatles played only twice in Edinburgh – both times at the ABC Cinema (April '64 and October '64).

No local early Sixties groups made it nationally although The Boston Dexters, The Moonrakers, The Athenians and Hipple People tried. In the later Sixties, The Buzz, Boots, Brainchild, East-West and Plastic Meringue were contenders, but only Writing On The Wall (heavy/underground/ progressive) acquired any sort of national reputation.

Bert Jansch was a landscape gardener here before taking the Soho folk world by storm in '64.

The Gamp was a beat-boom venue; the Place featured folk and blues – including a televised concert by Joan Baez. In the underground era, the Place became Middle Earth North and presented the likes of Wishbone Ash and Moby Grape.

On their way home to Glasgow in March '65, The Blues Council were involved in a car crash which killed James Griffin and Frazer Calder. Guitarist Les Harvey survived to join Stone The Crows.

In '69, Gallagher and Lyle (from Largs) moved to London to join McGuinness Flint and write their Top Three hit 'When I'm Dead And Gone'.

After an apprenticeship at the Top Storey Club, The Bay City Rollers broke nationally in the mid-Seventies, provoking the most hysterical fan worship since The Beatles, and racking up ten Top Ten hits. Their manager, Tam Paton, previously led the resident orchestra at the city's Palais de Danse.

Pilot were also hot in the mid-Seventies singles chart, reaching number one with 'January'.

The Rezillos formed at the art college in '76, and became the vanguard of the city's punk/new wave. After them came

Boots For Dancing, TV 21, Another Pretty Face, Matt Vinyl & The Decorators, The Valves, The Scars, The Switch, Metropak, The Flowers, Avo 8, Josef K, Paul Haig, The Fire Engines, The Delmontes, Strawberry Switchblade and more. The Questions were one of a handful of acts signed to Paul Weller's Respond label in the mid-Eighties. Tiffany's Ballroom on St. Stephens Street, Clouds at 3 West Tolcross, the Playhouse at 20 Greenside Place and the Astoria in Abbey Mount were happening late Seventies venues.

In the late Eighties, emerged The Indian Givers, The Chimes, The Shop Assistants, Jesse Garon & The Desperadoes, The Dog Faced Hermans, The Wendys, The Apples and Botany 5.

The egg of Ege Bamyasi

In the Nineties came The Joyriders, Ege Bamyasi (named after the '72 Can album), Finitribe (minor hits), Riverhead, Forkeye, Nectarine Number 9 (an offshoot of Win), The Kaisers, Freshly Squeezed and Idlewild (whose '98 release 'Everyone Says You're Fragile' was an *NME* single of the week).

One of Scotland's first independent labels was Zoom, run by the owner of Bruce's Records, Bruce Findlay. His first release was by The Valves, his second by PVC 2 (aka Slik), his tenth by Simple Minds from Glasgow. He operated from 45 Shandwick Place.

Even more influential was Fast Product, an indie label based at 3 East Norton Place, Abbeyhill. Shrewd owner Bob Last snapped up The Mekons, 2.3, The Human League, The Gang of Four... all Yorkshire based, oddly.

The Bay City Rollers were local heroes. Les McKeown and the Longmuir brothers were born at the Simpson Memorial Maternity Hospital. Stuart Wood was born at Chalmers Hospital and Eric Faulkner at the Royal Infirmary. McKeown went to Forresters High School, Woody to St. Augustines Secondary, the Longmuirs to Tynecastle Secondary, and Eric to Liberton Secondary. While various members struggle on in cabaret bands, Derek Longmuir became an SRN in the Cardiac Unit of Edinburgh Infirmary.

Abbeyhill resident Mike Scott left Another Pretty Face to start the Waterboys.

In the late Seventies, Fish was singing with Not Quite Red Fox, who rehearsed at the Carlton Theatre in the Royal Mile. One of his subsequent Marillion hits was 'Heart Of Lothian' – inspired by the heart-shaped symbol embedded in the cobblestones nearby.

The Proclaimers were born here but raised in Fife. They're now back, looking out over Leith from time to time.

The 900-capacity Traverse Theatre in Cambridge Street has kept pace with the times and in the late Nineties was an occasional rave venue.

Most successful export of the Nineties was Shirley Manson, who sang with Goodbye Mr McKenzie (made the '86 indie Top Ten with 'The Rattler') and their offshoot Angelfish before getting a passport and moving to Wisconsin to join Garbage.

FALKIRK Falkirk
Later the owner of several record stores, Bruce Findlay started here – operating the only import service in Scotland.

Childhood home of Robin Guthrie (see below).

Hubba Bubba were popular on the mid-Nineties techno/dance circuit.

In the late Nineties came Peel favourites Arab Strap – one of the most idiosyncratic groups on the scene.

GLENEAGLES Perth & Kinross
Oasis were launched at a Sony press party here in March '94. Their set was recorded – and 'I Am The Walru's was extracted for use as the B-side of 'Cigarettes And Alcohol'.

GLENROTHES Fife
Birthplace of Jackie Leven, leader of late Seventies challengers Doll By Doll.

This new town was the inspiration for The Skids song 'Sweet Suburbia'.

The Rothes Arms was part of Fife's late Seventies punk/heavy metal circuit; Rothes Halls is the cool late Nineties venue.

Local band The Thursdays were part of the Fast Records set-up in the late Seventies.

GOGAR City of Edinburgh
Bay City Rollers' manager Tam Paton controlled his empire from his home Little Kellerstain, where in December '81 he was arrested and sentenced for committing indecent acts and screening such dubious films as *Tina With The Big Tits*.

GRANGEMOUTH Falkirk
Birthplace of Elizabeth Fraser, 29.8.58, and Robin Guthrie, 4.1.62, (The Cocteau Twins).

HADDINGTON East Lothian
Birthplace of Bruce Robert Howard, 2.5.61 (later known as Dr. Robert of The Blow Monkeys).

Home of post-Marillion Fish when he returned to his homeland.

KIRKCALDY Fife
Birthplace of Craig Logan, 22.4.69 (Bros).

In October '63, with 'She Loves You' at number one, The Beatles played two houses at the Carlton Theatre in Sinclairtown.

The happening late Nineties venue is the Adam Smith Theatre.

KIRRIEMUIR Angus
Birthplace of songer Bon Scott, 9.7.46 (AC/DC).

LIVINGSTON West Lothian
The Skroteez were early Eighties punks.

Home of Pet Shop Boys protégé (David) Cicero, who made the '92 Top Twenty with 'Love Is Everywhere'.

Sometime home of Silverfish singer Lesley Rankine.

MONTROSE Angus
Birthplace of Molly Duncan, 24.8.45 (Average White Band).

PENICUIK Midlothian
Home of The Jury, who turned into Writing On The Wall.

PERTH Perth & Kinross
Birthplace of Eve Graham, 19.4.43 (New Seekers); Alan Gorrie, 19.7.46 (Average White Band).

Home of Fiction Factory (hot in '84) and Aspidistra (early Nineties hopefuls).

The Ingle Neuk was a mid-Sixties mod/soul club but is now a car repairs shop.

PITTENWEEM Fife
Birthplace of Ian Stewart, founder of The Rolling Stones who manager Andrew Oldham persuaded to become their roadie instead.

PRESTOPANS East Lothian
Bay City Rollers' manager Tam Paton worked in the family potato business based here. The Rollers were also employed here in various capacities... until 'Keep On Dancing' took off.

STENHOUSEMUIR Falkirk
Operational base of mid-Nineties hopefuls Cage.

ABERDEENSHIRE

Andy Cameron betrays his roots

ABERDEEN
Birthplace of folk pioneer Ian Campbell, 10.6.33 (Ian Campbell Folk Group, sire of UB40); Len Tuckey, 15.12.47 (guitarist with/ex husband of Suzi Quatro); drummer Stuart Tosh, 26.9.51 (Pilot, 10cc); Annie Lennox, 25.12.54 (Tourists, Eurythmics); Jimmy The Hoover, 31.8.58 ('83 chartmaker and teen mag pin-up).

In January '63, shortly before Beatlemania swept the land, The Beatles played at the Beach Ballroom. Led Zeppelin played the Music Hall in January '73.

Other primo venues were the Capitol at 431 Union Street, Ruffles at 13 Diamond Street, and the University Students Union in Broad Street.

NORTHERN SCOTLAND

Aberdeenshire, Highland, Moray, Orkney Islands, Shetland Islands, Western Isles

Home of neo-progressive Pallas, Eighties indie politicos The Shamen, funk-dancers APB, and Creation hopefuls The Jasmine Minks.

Annie Lennox went to the High School for Girls; local guitarist Dave Flett joined Manfred Mann's Earth Band.

In September '79, after an argument in a local record shop, only hours before a gig, two of Siouxsie's Banshees (Kenny Morris and John McKay) walked out. After a few days rehearsals, she picked up the tour with Budgie on drums and Robert Smith (from support band The Cure) on guitar.

Local mid-Nineties hopefuls included Loveless (APB offshoot) and Coast; in the late Nineties came hot indie frontrunners Geneva.

The Lemon Tree is the cool late Nineties venue.

Acid Doodles on Ben Nevis

BRAEMAR
Birthplace of Gordon Waller, 4.6.45 (Peter and Gordon).

FRASERBURGH
In May '60, Johnny Gentle & The Silver Beetles played Dalrymple Hall in Seaforth Street.

PETERHEAD
The last gig on the May '60 Johnny Gentle/Silver Beetles Scottish tour was at the Resue Hall in Prince Street.
Birthplace of Iain, 17.11.48, (at Ellon) and Gavin Sutherland, 6.10.51 (Sutherland Brothers & Quiver).

HIGHLAND

ALNESS
Local punks The Tools recorded for the Aberdeen based Oily label.

AULTGUISH INN
During the blizzards of January '78, Glasgow group The Subs (who recorded for Stiff) saved the lives of a Huddersfield couple whose car had become buried in a snow drift on the A835. They were so resigned to their fate that they were writing out their will. Subs bass player Derek Forbes was later in Simple Minds.

BEN NEVIS
In 1819, Keats climbed Britain's highest peak and wrote a sonnet at the summit. In '67, Cream climbed the mountain while tripping on acid. Photographs taken that day adorn the sleeve of *Disraeli Gears*.

DINGWALL
In January '63, a week before the release of 'Please Please Me', The Beatles played at the Town Hall.

GLENCOE
Underrated group Glencoe (containing two of Ian Dury's future Blockheads) took their name from the site of the 1692 massacre of the Macdonalds by the Campbells – also the setting for Robert Louis Stevenson's *Kidnapped*. (Just thought I'd slip in an educational note here.)

GOLSPIE
In July '69, John Lennon was involved in a car crash after visiting his aunt in Durness. His wounds required 17 stitches at the Lawson Memorial Hospital.

INVERNESS
In May '60, The Silver Beetles played at the Northern Meeting Ballroom in Church Street, backing Johnny Gentle.
Jethro Tull singer Ian Anderson was also owner of the Strathaird Salmon Processing factory, which opened in Inverness in '82.
The Cateran were local late Eighties hopefuls who split in '91. (The Edinburgh based Joyriders were an offshoot).
Hometown of techno-dance boffin Neil Landstrumm, who moved to Edinburgh to find an audience.
The Eden Court Theatre is a happening Nineties venue.

LOCH NESS
In '70, Jimmy Page bought Aleister Crowley's old residence Boleskine, on the south side of the Loch near Foyers.
Alex Harvey made an album for K-Tel called *Alex Harvey Presents The Loch Ness Monster*.

NAIRN
The Beatles (as The Silver Beetles) played the Regal Ballroom in Leopold Street, backing Fontana recording star Johnny Gentle in May '60.
Birthplace of guitarist Robin McDonald, 18.7.43 (Billy J Kramer & The Dakotas).

SKYE
Gaelic rockers Run Rig were formed here and began gigging in and around the islands. Later based in Edinburgh.
Roger Whittaker and Des O'Connor unexpectedly found themselves in the '86 indie charts with 'The Skye Boat Song' – released on the former's Trembo label.

THURSO
Birthplace of guitarist Martin Carr, 29.11.68 (Boo Radleys).
Home of new wavers Radio City.

WICK
It was here, on a café juke box that The Alex Harvey Soul Band first heard 'Shout' by The Isley Brothers!

MORAY

BUCKIE
Home of Sixties group Johnny & The Copy Cats, who became My Dear Watson after the failure of their one and only single.

CRAIGELLACHIE

Zoot Money & His Big Roll Band played a mid-Sixties gig at the Town Hall. Why? It's miles from anywhere!

ELGIN

Birthplace of Harry Robinson (Lord Rockingham's XI); Mark Gillespie, 28.11.66 (Big Fun).

Base for Albert Bonicci, one of Scotland's biggest agents. He and Andy Lothian had exclusive rights to Brian Epstein's stable.

The Two Red Shoes Club on Lossie Wynd hosted groups like Cream and Pink Floyd (July '67) during the Sixties. Their most famous booking was The Beatles in January '63.

FORRES

Johnny Gentle and the Silver Beetles strutted their stuff at the Town Hall in May 60.

KEITH

St. Thomas' Hall in Chapel Street was the prestigious venue for the fourth gig on the Johnny Gentle/Silver Beetles tour of May '60. The Beatles were due to return to Keith in January '63 (to play the Longmore Hall in Church Road), but the date was cancelled due to horrendous weather.

SPEYMOUTH

In digs where his landlady would allow him only one bath a week, Derek Dick would make the most of it – lying submerged for at least two hours. "What are you... a fucking fish?" asked his mate. The name stuck. From then on, he was Fish – and as such sang with Marillion. (Saved him the embarrassment of revealing his real name).

ORKNEYS & SHETLANDS

LERWICK

Birthplace of traditional fiddler Aly Bain, 15.5.46; Ian Bairnson, 3.8.53 (Pilot); bass player Charlie Sinclair (Kilburn & The High Roads).

Home of singer Astrid Williamson (Goya Dress).

WESTERN ISLES (OUTER HEBRIDES)

Pop stars are thin on the ground... venues even thinner. The late Alex Harvey used to regale journalists with stories of how in his youth he would tour the remote Scottish islands as Eddie Cochran, performing a set composed entirely of Cochran songs, and the audience thought he was the real thing.

In the late Sixties, Cream star Jack Bruce bought Sandray, a 400 acre island at the bottom end of the Outer Hebrides.

Punk group Noise Annoys hail from here.

SCOTLAND, SOUTH

Borders, Dumfries & Galloway

ANNAN Dumfries & Galloway
Usual start of Scottish tours by acts from Larry Parnes' stable. It was here that the Big Three backed Duffy Power for the first time, in May '60.

DUMFRIES Dumfries & Galloway
Birthplace of jazz trumpeter and author Ian Carr, 21.4.33.

The Stagecoach Hotel was a Seventies venue presenting everyone from Frankie Miller to The Pirates to Toyah.

EYEMOUTH Borders
In February '63, shocked town councillors demanded a written apology after Screaming Lord Sutch appeared on stage with a lavatory seat around his neck.

GALASHIELS Borders
Nearby village of Gattonside was home of bass player Neil Murray (Whitesnake, Black Sabbath).

The main Sixties gig was the Volunteer Hall, which presented The Who, The Zombies and other chart acts.

Local group Blewitt used to play at the Golden Lion in the early Eighties. Their singer was Fish, later of Marillion.

Jessie Rae, he of the Viking helmet and broadsword, lived on a farm at nearby St. Boswells.

Local mid-Nineties bands included The Pralines; in the late Nineties came self-styled "indie weirdos" Dawn Of The Replicants, who had two *NME* Singles of the Week in '97.

HAWICK Borders
Operational base of the Duncan McKinnon Agency – one of the biggest bookers of the Sixties. Handled all the Larry Parnes' acts and scheduled The Beatles first foray over the border.

Birthplace of mid-Eighties Celtic-dub-swinger Champion Doug Veitch, a Peel and Kershaw fave.

LOCKERBIE Dumfries & Galloway
Among the passengers aboard the Pan-Am jumbo which crashed on the town in December '88 was former Cockney Rebel bass player Paul Jeffreys.

NEWTON STEWART Dumfries & Galloway
Birthplace of Bill Drummond, leader of Liverpool punk group Big In Japan, the chart topping Timelords and The KLF.

The Foundations played here once – and that was like the event of the century.

Self-pressed debut from Galashiels Weirdos

SCOTLAND, WEST CENTRAL

Argyll & Bute, Ayrshire, Dunbartonshire, City of Glasgow, Inverclyde, Lanarkshire, Renfrewshire and Stirling.

AIRDRIE North Lanarkshire
Birthplace of singer Dean Ford, 31.5.47 (Marmalade); organist Hugh McKenna, 28.11.49 (SAHB).

AYR South Ayrshire
Birthplace of Mike Scott, 14.12.58 (Waterboys).

Brian Poole & The Tremeloes were resident group at Butlin's Holiday Camp during summer '61.

Robert Plant's Band Of Joy made their world début at Ayr Ice Rink. The other hot venue was the Pavilion on the Esplanade.

The Dead End Kids were a local group who flitted into the '77 Top Ten with a revival of 'Have I The Right?'

BELLSHILL North Lanarkshire
Birthplace of Sheena Easton, 27.4.59; Norman Blake, 20.10.65, and Francis MacDonald, 21.11.70 (both Teenage Fanclub). When MacDonald left (later to join The Pastels), he was replaced by another Bellshill native Brendan O'Hare, 16.1.70.

BISHOPBRIGGS East Dunbartonshire
Birthplace of bass player Jack Bruce, 14.5.43 (Cream).

BLANTYRE South Lanarkshire
Home of mid-Nineties up and comers The Gyres.

BRIDGE OF ALLAN Stirling
Birthplace of Alan Rankine (Associates).

In January '63, the comparatively unknown Beatles played at the Museum Hall in Henderson Street.

BRIDGE OF ORCHY Argyll & Bute
Setting for the video of Nick Heyward's first solo hit, 'Whistle Down The Wind'.

CAMBUSLANG South Lanarkshire
Midge Ure was born at 24 Park Street on 10.10.53. His first school was Cambuslang Primary.

CLYDEBANK West Dunbartonshire
Home of punk group Adultery.

Wet Wet Wet were all pupils at Clydebank High School. They would go mega with 'Wishing I Was Lucky' in April '87 and nova with 'Love Is All Around' in May 94 – by which time, they were sponsors of Clydebank FC.

DALMELLINGTON East Ayrshire
Les McKeown's first public appearance was with Threshold at Dalmellington Town Hall.

DUMBARTON West Dunbartonshire
Birthplace of David Byrne, 14.5.52 (moved to the New World at two and later started Talking Heads); guitarist Jimmy McCulloch (Thunderclap Newman, Wings... at 13, he was lead guitarist in local group One In A Million, who played at the Ally Pally 14 Hour Dream).

EAST KILBRIDE South Lanarkshire
Birthplace of William, 28.10.58, and Jim Reid, 29.12.61 (founders of The Jesus & Mary Chain); Roddy Frame, 29.1.64 (Aztec Camera).

Other local groups include The Stilettos, The Exploited (who moved to Edinburgh), The Sinister Turkeys, Meat

Whiplash and The Jesus & Mary Chain – who scored the first of a long string of hits in '85. See See Rider seemed set to break out in the early Nineties; God's Boyfriend were late Nineties hopefuls. Geneva vocalist Andrew Montgomery was a local lad.

While waiting for Slik to click, Midge Ure was an apprentice at the National Engineering Laboratory.

GLASGOW, City of

Birthplace of Ivor Cutler, 15.1.23; Lonnie Donegan, 29.4.31; Karl Denver, 16.12.34; Alex Harvey, 5.2.35 (SAHB); Mike Patto, 22.9.42 (Boxer); Billy Connolly, 24.11.42; Bert Jansch, 3.11.43 (ace guitarist); Robin Williamson, 24.11.43 (Incredible String Band); Maggie Bell, 12.1.45 (Stone The Crows); Al Stewart, 5.9.45; Donovan, 10.5.46 (in Maryhill); Junior Campbell, 31.5.47 (Marmalade); John Martyn, 28.6.48; Mark Knopfler, 12.8.49 (Dire Straits); Hamish Stuart, 8.10.49 (Average White Band); Dougie Thompson, 24.3.51 (Supertramp); Jim Diamond, 28.9.51; Malcolm Young, 6.1.53, and Angus Young, 31.3.59 (both AC/DC); Brian Robertson, 12.9.56 (Thin Lizzy, Motorhead); Edwyn Collins, 23.8.59 (Orange Juice); Eddi Reader, 28.8.59 (Fairground Attraction); Jimmy Somerville, 22.6.61 (Communards); Clare Grogan, March '62 (Altered Images); Owen Paul, 1.5.62 (one hit wonder); Iain Harvie, 19.5.62, and Justin Currie, 11.12.64 (both Del Amitri); Bobby Gillespie, 22.6.64 (Primal Scream); also hundreds more we don't have room for!

Glasgow rock began with Scotland's answer to Tommy Steele, Alex Harvey who was born in a tenement building at 49 Govan Road (now a children's playground) and who played skiffle and rock'n'roll before forming The Big Soul Band in '60. A decade later, he combined with progressive rock group Tear Gas to form SAHB, The Sensational Alex Harvey Band, who made their début at Clouds in June '72. He died in February '81, a day short of his 46th birthday.

First Glaswegian to crack the national teen market was skiffle queen Nancy Whiskey in '57; first beat group to break nationally was Lulu & The Luvvers in May '64.

Other mid-sixties groups included the much loved Poets, The Pathfinders, The Beatstalkers, The House Of Lords, The Stoics, Studio Six, and Dean Ford & The Gaylords – who enjoyed many hits after changing their name to Marmalade in '67.

Package tours would invariably take in the Odeon in Renfield Street – visited by The Beatles five times. They also played the Concert Hall in Argyle Street (in October '63).

The most popular Sixties gig was the Barrowland Ballroom in Gallowgate, which closed down after the infamous Bible John murders, but re-opened to become a major venue. The Rolling Stones played there in January '64; R.E.M. in October '85; Simply Red in February '89; The

Seahorses in December '97; Cypress Hill in December '98; millions more.

The progressive/underground era brought Tear Gas, Stone The Crows, The Dream Police, White Trash, Blue and The Incredible String Band, who set the folk world on its head in '67.

In the early Seventies came Middle Of The Road ('Chirpy Chirpy Cheep Cheep'!), Frankie Miller, The Average White Band, String Driven Thing, and Slik – led by Midge Ure.

A prime venue was Greens Playhouse in Renfield Street, which was purchased by Frank Lynch (manager of Billy Connolly and Slik) and turned into Clouds Disco and Glasgow Apollo. In '72, Noddy Holder was cautioned for using obscene language onstage at Green's!

Another was the Electric Garden in Sauchiehall Street (later known as Shuffles and the Mayfair).

There was no pub circuit as such (they weren't allowed to charge entrance fees) but the Burns Howff on Sauchiehall Street became a popular venue.

The Maryland Club in Scott Street presented the likes of Skid Row and The Groundhogs.

Punk and the new wave saw the arrival of The Zones (ex Slik), The Subs, Simple Minds, Positive Noise, Orange Juice, The Cuban Heels and the Post Card label – run by Alan Horn from 185 West Princes Street.

Satellite City was a club named after the Bowie song and later the subject of its own song by Orange Juice. Simple Minds made their début here. Tiffany's in Sauchiehall Street was also hot in the Seventies.

In the Eighties came Berlin Blondes, Altered Images (hailed nationally as the best new band of '81), H2O, The Alleged, Restricted Code, The Bluebells, Strawberry Switchblade, Hipsway, The Primevals, Lloyd Cole & The Commotions, James King & The Lone Wolves, and Cuban Heels.

Love and Money, Hue and Cry, Golden Dawn, The Vaselines, The Soup Dragons, The Beat Poets, His Latest Flame, The BMX Bandits, Tantara Blade, The Pastels, Biff Bang Pow (local connections), The River Detectives (from Ravenscraig) and The Right Stuff were hopeful in the late Eighties – some with justification.

Alex Harvey lived in the Govan, went to Camden Street Junior and Strathbungo Secondary.

Progressive band Gentle Giant has its roots in the Gorbals, where the Shulman brothers, Ray and Phil, were born.

SAHB guitarist Zal Cleminson went to Penilee Secondary.

Former pupils of Eastwood High School include Brian Robertson (Thin Lizzy); Midge Ure went to Rutherglen Academy; Billy McIsaac went to Stow College.

Jim Kerr, Charlie Burchill and Brian McGhee all met at Hollyrood Roman Catholic School in '72 and formed Johnny

& The Self Abusers in '77, making their début at the Mars Bar Club in a side street off St. Enoch's Square. In '78, they became Simple Minds.

Clare Grogan went to Notre Dame Convent.

No-one appears to have gone to the School of Art in Renfrew Street, a stunning building designed by Charles Rennie McIntosh – acknowledged by Midge Ure in his song 'The Gift'.

Lloyd Cole & The Commotions got together in Tennents Bar on the corner of Byres Road and Highburgh Road, near the university.

Altered Images made their début at the Countdown pub in August '79.

The instigators of AC/DC were Glaswegian: the Young brothers emigrated to Australia with their family in '63.

In the Eighties, Justin Currie (born here on 11.12.64) was a barman at night club Furry Murry's, while getting Del Amitri together with Iain Harvie (b 19.5.62). Also emerging in the Eighties was Blue Nile, formed by three students at the university. Local electronics firm Linn sponsored them, funded them, even created a label for them. Renowned for the speed with which they throw out albums: a five year gap between the first and second; another seven years before the third.

Texas broke out with '89 Top Ten hit 'I Don't Want A Lover', then coasted until late Nineties renaissance.

Eddi Reader lived at 7 Anthony Street, Anderston, and attended St. Patrick's Church. In '67, she moved to Arden and went to Bellarmine Secondary School. Later, she would move to London and become famous as the singer in Fairground Attraction.

Early Nineties bands include Teenage Fanclub (string of hits on Creation), Almighty (hits on Polydor and Chrysalis), Gun (hits on A&M), Summerhill (Kershaw faves), Slide, The Vaselines (who became Captain America, then Eugenius after frontman Eugene Kelly), The Wild River Apples, Spirea X (Gourock based Primal Scream offshoot), Perspex Whiteout, The Orchids, Superstar, Murmur, One Dove, Fenn, Thrum, 18 Wheeler (formed at the University and soon nationally prominent), Shriek, Telstar Ponies (from the ashes of the Soup Dragons and BMX Bandits) and The Supernaturals (who charted with 'Lazy Lover' in '96).

In the mid-late Nineties came Moondial, The Delgados, Urusei Yatsura, The Bells Of Monica, Howie B, Bis (the first unsigned band to play *Top Of The Pops*), The Secret Goldfish, Future Pilot Aka (yet another Soup Dragons spin-off – so much family tree potential!), Travis, Gilded Lil, and Superstar – whose '98 album Palm Tree was universally acclaimed.

On 31.5.93, Creation Records boss Alan McGee was perspicacious enough to note that Oasis could probably make him several million quid. "They thought I was mad when I offered them a deal there and then," he says. Oasis

had travelled up with another Manchester band Sister Lovers to play King Tut's Wah Wah Hut – sharing the bill with Creations bands Boyfriend and 18 Wheeler. McGee was there by chance.

The Tunnel at 84 Mitchell Street is paradise for late Nineties clubbers; the Cottier Theatre favours more cerebral musicians.

GOUROCK Inverclyde
Operational base of mid-Nineties band Adventures in Stereo – formed by Jim Beattie (ex Primal Scream and Spirea X).

GREENOCK Inverclyde
Birthplace of John McGeoch, 28.5.55 (Magazine, PiL).

The Shakin' Pyramids were early Eighties skiffle revivalists.

HAMILTON South Lanarkshire
Birthplace of singer Brian Connolly, 5.10.49 (Sweet).

In May '64, The Rolling Stones came to town to play the Chantinghall Hotel.

Strathclyde Park is the setting for the annual T in the Park festival, sponsored by Tennent's lager. It started in '94, with Blur, Oasis and The Manic Street Preachers; Radiohead were acclaimed in '96; Robbie Williams, The Prodigy, Ash and Portishead were among the stars in '98.

HELENSBURGH Argyll & Bute
Birthplace of Kenny Hyslop, 14.2.51 (Slik, The Skids, Simple Minds). He lived in William Street and went to the Hermitage School.

Also the birthplace of Neil Mitchell, 8.6.65 (Wet Wet Wet... the rest of whom were born in Glasgow).

HOUSTON Renfrewshire
Birthplace of guitarist Miller Anderson, 12.4.45, who moved down to London with Karl Stuart & The Profile and later joined The Keef Hartley Band.

IRVINE North Ayrshire
Operational base of early Nineties hopefuls The Trash Can Sinatras (featuring Eddi Reader's brother).

LARGS North Ayrshire
Home of singer/songwriting duo Benny Gallagher and Graham Lyle.

James Galt released a few singles in the Sixties.

LENNOXTOWN East Dunbartonshire
The grandly named Lennox Castle maternity hospital saw the births of Onnie McIntyre, 29.5.45 (Average White Band); Lulu, 3.11.48; Jim McGinlay, 9.3.49 (Slik).

LOCH LOMOND West Dunbartonshire

In May '79, The Boomtown Rats and The Buzzcocks headlined the Loch Lomond Rock Festival, held at Cameron Bear Park in Alexandria.

MOTHERWELL North Lanarkshire

Birthplace of the Morris brothers – Des, Jim and Mark – who formed Balaam & The Angel, but relocated to Staffordshire as a more convenient base for their national assault. Also of Gerard Love, 31.8.67 (Teenage Fanclub).

Home of 12-year-old Neil Reid, whose excruciating 'Mother Of Mine' went Top Three in '72.

Midge Ure attended Motherwell Technical College.

MULL OF KINTYRE Argyll & Bute

Paul McCartney's rural retreat. He purchased his 183 acre farm, High Park near Machrihanish, in June '66 and bought a further 400 acres in January '71. His eponymous anthem topped the charts for nine weeks in '77 and was the first single to sell more than two million copies in the United Kingdom.

Wings and Mull of Kintyre

PAISLEY Renfrewshire

Birthplace of Gerry Rafferty, 16.4.47. He and Joe Egan played in local groups The Censors, Fifth Column and The Mavericks, and were later reunited in Stealers Wheel. Their album *Ferguslie Park* took its name from the notorious council scheme in Paisley, where once only

"problem" families were housed. (Nothing to do with Prince's record label!).

Also the birthplace of John Byrne, 6.1.40 (wrote television series *Tutti Frutti*, designed sleeves); Ian McMillan, 16.10.47 (Poets, Blue); Chris Glen, 6.11.50 (SAHB).

Stealers Wheel at Ferguslie Park

Chris Glen went to Paisley Academy.

Home of new wavers The Mental Errors, who felt at home in the Bungalow Bar – the town's major punk era venue.

Home of Creation singer Momus, whose track The Bishonen begins "I was born in the town of Paisley in early 1960".

Close Lobsters and The Stretch-Heads were both early Nineties Peel faves.

PORT GLASGOW Inverclyde

Home of Robert Rental and Thomas Leer – pioneers of early Eighties electro minimalism.

PRESTWICK South Ayrshire

It was at Prestwick Airport, on the evening of Wednesday March 2, '60, that Elvis Presley made his one and only visit to Britain. For the previous 17 months, US 53310761 Presley had been completing his national service in Germany. When the DC 7, in which he was flying home, stopped to refuel at Prestwick, the 25-year-old star spent an hour talking to fans, signing autographs, shaking hands and posing for photographs. Despite persistent rumours that he was considering a concert tour, Elvis never again set foot on British soil.

The author flanked by Elvis Presley's late '50's sidemen D.J. Fontana (left) and Scotty Moore (right) at Prestwick Airport where The King walked briefly in March 1960

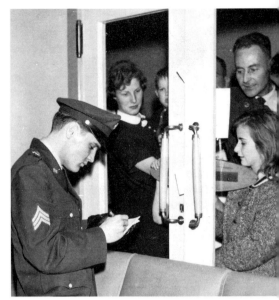

Elvis in transit at Prestwick   (The Herald & Evening Times)

In October '75, when The Who found themselves fogbound at the airport, Keith Moon (severely intoxicated as usual) appropriated a wheelchair and terrorised passengers with a toy gun. He was imprisoned and fined £30 at Ayr Sheriff's'Court the next morning.

ROTHESAY, ISLE OF BUTE Argyll & Bute
Birthplace of Billy McIsaac, 12.7.49 (Slik, Zones). He was born at Victoria Cottage Hospital, lived in Rothesay High Street and went to Rothesay Academy.

RUTHERGLEN South Lanarkshire
Birthplace of Hugh Nicholson, 30.7.49 (Poets, Blue).
Midge Ure (Ultravox) and brothers Dougie (Supertramp) and Ali (US solo success) Thompson all went to Rutherglen Academy.

SHOTTS North Lanarkshire
Mid-Nineties band Octopus (who charted with 'Your Smile' in June '96) includes the son of great train robber Bruce Reynolds.

STEVENSTON North Ayrshire
Birthplace of Ron Geesin, 17.12.43.

STIRLING Stirling
Birthplace of singer Glen Mason, 16.9.30, who scored minor '56 hits with Glendora and Green Door.
Riots followed Queen's gig at the University in March '74. Two of their road crew were attacked and two punters were stabbed.
In '93, Dr Alex Paterson of the Orb was voted honorary President of the University!

TROON South Ayrshire
Final location of the pirate ship Radio Scotland was three miles off Troon. Closed down in March '67.

WISHAW North Lanarkshire
Home of Sixties beatsters The Hi-Fis and '76 power-poppers The Jolt. Not to mention my dad.

WALES

There must be some little corgi jobsworth whose role is to keep changing the names of counties so that maps and gazetteers keep going out of date. So please forgive me if I arrange Wales in my own sweet way.

NORTH WALES

including Isle of Anglesey, Gwynedd, Conwy, Denbighshire, Flintshire and Wrexham

ANELOG Gwynedd
Mike Simmons' ambient album *From Anelog To Bardsey* reflects the peace and serenity of the Lleyn Peninsula.

ANGLESEY Isle of
The sleeve of Roxy Music's album *Siren*, featuring Jerry Hall in the ironic title role, was shot on the coast of Anglesey.

As a schoolboy, John Peel used to spend summer holidays at the Red House in Rhosneigr. Strangely, he also did his National Service in Anglesey. In March '60, he and his Army pals drove in convoy to see Gene Vincent and Eddie Cochran at the Liverpool Empire.

Two of The Super Furry Animals – Dafydd Ieuan and Cian Ciaran – are from Anglesey and are doing rather better than the island's previous (Sixties) pop duo Anan.

BANGOR Gwynedd
The Beatles, Mick Jagger and Marianne Faithfull were among those seeking spiritual guidance at the Maharishi's transcendental meditation centre in August '67.

Local lass Tammy Jones reached the '75 Top Five with 'Let Me Try Again' – her only hit.

The video for The Skids' single' Iona' was shot here... wrong coast, wrong country, but close.

Super Furry Animals founder Gruff Rhys is from Bethesda, just down the A5.

Guitarist Dominic Chad studied Russian and French at Bangor University, working at the Fat Cat public house to supplement his grant. He sidelined further study to become bar manager of the newly opened Fat Cat in Chester, where plans for Mansun were hatched.

'Day Trip To Bangor' was a Top Three hit for Fiddler's Dram in '80. Didn't we have a lovely time?

BETHESDA Gwynedd
Birthplace of singer/guitarist Gruf Rhys (Super Furry Animals).

BETWS-Y-COED Conwy
Late Nineties band Melys have issued singles and done Peel Show sessions.

BUCKLEY Flintshire
The Buzzcocks (November '77), Terrorvision (February '93) and Oasis (August '94) are among the many popular acts to have appeared at the Tivoli. It was here in November '96 that The Seahorses made their low key début.

FLINT Flintshire
Mansun guitarist-vocalist Paul Draper attended Sir Richard Gwynn High School.

LLANDUDNO Conwy
In August '63, The Beatles played twelve sets (two shows a night for six nights) to holiday makers at the Odeon Cinema.

MOLD Flintshire
Birthplace of keyboard player Chick Churchill, 2.1.49 (Ten Years After).

In January '63, The Beatles appeared at the Assembly Hall in the High Street.

The Prisoner: shot at Portmeirion, north Wales, the cult UK T.V. series influenced many a band with its striking theme by Ron Grainger

(Bam Caruso Records)

PORTMEIRION Gwynedd
Setting for the cult television series *The Prisoner*, and also the video for 'See Those Eyes' by Altered Images.

Written to reflect the enchantment of the village, as a celebration of one man's dream, *Portmeirion* was a '96 ambient album by Mike Simmons.

PRESTATYN Denbighshire
Birthplace of Neil Aspinall, 13.10.42 (Beatles roadie – now boss of their Apple empire); Karl Wallinger, 19.10.57 (Waterboys, World Party); and Mike Peters, 25.2.59 (Alarm).

The Royal Lido on Central Beach was a popular venue in the late Fifties/early Sixties, when Liverpool bands would descend – including The Beatles, in November '62, and the Stones in August '63.

PWLLHELI Gwynedd
It was at Butlins Holiday Camp in July '59 that 16-year-old Georgie Fame was discovered by Rory Blackwell, who persuaded him to move to London where he would find fame and fortune as a member of his Blackjacks. Within weeks, he was broke... but then fate played its hand.

It was at Butlins also that Paul McCartney made his public début, singing 'Long Tall Sally' while on holiday with his family – and Johnny Gentle (with whom The Silver Beetles would tour) won a talent contest which encouraged him to go to London and work his way into the Larry Parnes stable.

RHYL Denbighshire
Home of the effervescent Alarm (previously known as Seventeen), who moved to London in September '81 and soon charted with '68 Guns'. After ten years of hits, frontman Mike Peters went on to solo success.

Sometime home of *Melody Maker* journalist Chris Roberts, who later fronted Catwalk.

The Regent Dansette was a ballroom in the High Street. It was here that The Beatles made their first appearance in Wales, in July '62. A year later, they returned to play two nights at the Ritz Ballroom on the Promenade.

WREXHAM
Birthplace of drummer Steve Upton, 24.5.46 (Wishbone Ash); guitarist Andy Scott, 30.7.49 (Sweet), who went to Grove Park Grammar School.

In the early Nineties a spate of bands caused ripples, including dance act K-Klass and indie band Goodnight Said Florence. Crazy Little Sister were doing well until their drummer was forced to spend some time with his auntie in Poughkeepsie.

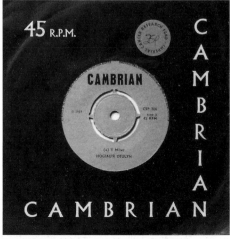

The Holy Grail for Manics fans: their first single, 1983

MID WALES

including Ceredigion and Powys

ABERYSTWYTH Ceredigion

Led Zeppelin's strangest concert took place at the King's Hall on 16.1.73. Unused to rock mania, the audience sat quietly throughout, offering only polite applause after each number. The Rolling Stones had also played a comparatively tranquil gig there, in September '63.

Catatonia played an early gig at the University in November '93.

Former member of the expanded Incredible String Band (who played at Woodstock in '69), Rose Simpson became Mayoress of Aberystwyth in '93.

Mid-Nineties indie band The Crocketts formed at the University; Murry The Hump were late Nineties hopefuls.

BRECON Powys

Birthplace of Roger Glover, 30.11.45 (Deep Purple); Peter Hope Evans, 28.9.47 (Medicine Head).

Bron-y-Aur, now owned by Robert Plant

Early Welsh Crusty E.P.

BRON-YR-AUR Ceredigion

Robert Plant and Jimmy Page rented a cottage on the River Dovey in May '70, to write and rehearse material for Led Zeppelin's third album – which contains the celebratory track 'Bron-y-Aur Stomp'.

CARDIGAN Ceredigion

Birthplace of David Glasper, 4.11.65 (Breathe).

MACHYNLLETH Powys

In the mid-Seventies, Robert Plant owned a sheep farm in the Llyfnant Valley.

WELSHPOOL Powys

Birthplace of Duster Bennett, 23.9.46 (popular late Sixties one-man blues band).

YSTRADGYNLAIS Powys

Birthplace of Steve Alexander, 20.11.62 (Brother Beyond).

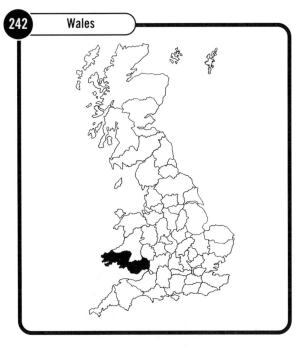

SOUTH WALES

including Pembrokeshire, Carmarthenshire, Swansea, Neath Port Talbot, Newport, Bridgend, Rhondda Cynon Taff, Vale of Glamorgan, Merthyr Tydfil, Blaenau Gwent, Caerphilly, Cardiff, Torfaen, Newport and Monmouthshire

ABERDARE Rhondda Cynon Taff
From nearby Cwmaman, The Tragic Love Company changed their name to The Stereophonics for a gig at the Coliseum in July '96 – and, in the contemporaneous South Wales A&R rush, were the first act signed by Richard Branson's V2 label. In summer '98, jealous Aberdare thugs beat up drummer Stuart Cable, necessitating 40 stitches.

ABERGAVENNY Monmouthshire
Title of a '68 Marty Wilde single which failed to reach the charts.

The Town Hall in Cross Street presented The Beatles in June '63. Unavoidably detained in London (appearing on *Juke Box Jury*), John Lennon caused a stir when he arrived in a helicopter, which landed in the Penypound football field.

Having crashed his BMW near Rockfields Studios in July '96, Charlatans keyboard player Rob Collins was taken to Abergavenny Hospital where he was pronounced dead.

BARRY Vale of Glamorgan
Sometime home of guitarist Bryn Merrick (Damned). He and Roman Jugg (see below) played in local early Eighties band The Missing Men.

BLACKWOOD Caerphilly
This former mining town is home to The Manic Street Preachers, who were friends through Primary school, Junior school and Oakdale Comprehensive and went on to become one of the biggest bands in the history of music. Their career path was planned in Dorothy's Café.

Hoping to follow in their footsteps were mid-Nineties bands Phoenix Trunk and Ether.

Roman Jugg   (Phil Smee)

CAERPHILLY
Home of splendidly named Roman Jugg, keyboard player in The Damned.

Scritti Politti's Green went to the Boys' Grammar School.

CARDIFF

Birthplace of Shirley Bassey, 8.1.37; Maureen Evans, 23.3.40 (early Sixties hits); singer Ramon Phillips, 23.8.41 (Nashville Teens); Gene Latter (R&B/soul singer); Dave Edmunds, 15.4.44; bass player Burke Sheeley, 10.4.47, and guitarist Tony Bourge, 23.11.48 (who formed Budgie); Shakin' Stevens, 4.3.48 (in Ely); Blue Weaver, 3.3.49, and Denis Bryon, 14.4.49 (both Amen Corner); Green Gartside, 22.6.56 (Scritti Politti); Cerys Matthews, 11.4.69 (Catatonia); Andy Bell, 11.8.70 (Ride).

It was at the Capitol Cinema that two of The Kinks, drummer Mick Avory and guitarist Dave Davies, had an onstage fight during their opening number, 'Beautiful Delilah'. Avory fled the building after cutting Davies' head with a cymbal. He was stitched up at Cardiff Royal Infirmary.

The Beatles played the Capitol Theatre in Dock Street three times; Bob Dylan played there in May '66.

First local rock band to take off was Amen Corner, with Gin House Blues in '67; Gene Latter celebrated his home town on the '69 single 'Tiger Bay'; local lad Tony Etoria had a '77 Top Thirty hit with 'I Can Prove It'.

After an apprenticeship in The Raiders, Dave Edmunds scored hits with the locally based Love Sculpture before going solo with '70 chart topper 'I Hear You Knocking'.

Budgie made national headway as an early Seventies heavy rock trio; Sassafras were prog-rock; Lone Star were mid-Seventies heavy metal; Red Beans & Rice were late Seventies pub rockers who moved to London for better gig accessibility.

New wavers included the Young Marble Giants, Demented Are Go and Addiction.

Local lad Ian Thomas was the only human drummer on George Michael's album *Faith*.

Late Eighties faves included Papa's New Faith, The Waterfront, Skin Games, Tiger Tailz, The Third Uncles, and Cefl Pren (Welsh language rockers... their name means Trojan Horse, roughly).

Manics' guitarist Richey Edwards maintained a flat in Cardiff Bay until his disappearance.

The chart-topping Catatonia came together after Mark Roberts saw Cerys Matthews busking outside Debenhams in '93. Progress was fairly slow until Mulder and Scully made them overnight stars, five years later.

The Super Furry Animals celebrate Howard Marks

(Andy Saunders)

The members of Super Furry Animals were in five different Welsh speaking bands and knew each other by sight. The other three gravitated to Cardiff to join local lads Guto Pryce and Huw Banford, and in early '96 – a year after getting together – they were signed up by Creation and found themselves in the charts with 'Hometown Unicorn'.

A floating stage in Scott Harbour was the setting for the Big Noise festival in May '97, when Paul Weller headlined. The event was held to celebrate the hundredth anniversary of Marconi's successful attempt to transmit radio waves across water – from Lavernock (Vale of Glamorgan) to Flat Holm Island in the Bristol Channel.

Local bands emerging in the Nineties include Kicking The Image, Jack-knife Disciples and Gouge.

CARMARTHEN

Home base of Sixties groups The Vikings, The Blackjacks and Brothers Grimm.

CRYNANT Neath

Birthplace of organist Verden Allen, 26.5.44 (Mott The Hoople), who went to Neath Technical College.

CWMNRAN Torfaen

Hometown of drummer Henry Spinetti (Eric Clapton, Joan Armatrading).

The Mirrors were a local late-Seventies band.

DERI Caerphilly
Birthplace of singer Julian Cope, 21.10.57 (Teardrop Explodes).

A Welshman in New York: John Cale in 1963

GARNANT Carmarthenshire
Birthplace of bass player/singer/writer/producer John Cale, 5.12.40 (Velvet Underground and beyond). He went to Amman Valley Grammar School. At the time of *The Academy In Peril*, he called his publishing company Garnant Music — and both Garnant and Ammanford are mentioned in 'Ship Of Fools'.

LLANELLI Carmarthenshire
Birthplace of guitarist Deke Leonard, 18.12.44 (Man).

Beat groups included Lucifer & The Corncrackers, The Casanovas, Elvin Leroy & The Meteorites, The Spartans, The Cavaliers, The Dream and Plum Crazy.

The Glen Ballroom was on the national circuit in the Sixties/Seventies. Mott The Hoople played there several times.

Home town of Catatonia drummer Aled Richards.

MAERDY Carmarthenshire
In late '78, local painter and decorator Kingsley Pugh changed his name by deed poll... to Mick Jagger!

MERTHYR TYDFIL
Birthplace of Fifties singer Malcolm Vaughan, 22.3.29 (at Troedyrhiw); guitarist Mickey Jones, 7.6.46 (Man).

Tom Jones was spotted by future manager Gordon Mills at the Top Hat Club. Then known as Tommy Scott, he was fronting The Senators.

Home of The Bystanders, who became an international Seventies cult band as Man.

Home of Chris Sullivan, leader of early Eighties clothes-horse band Blue Rondo A La Turk.

Local mid-Nineties bands include The Pocket Devils.

The Eyes of Blue of Neath

NEATH
The Mustangs and The Smokestacks mutated into the 'Eyes Of Blue', who were *Melody Maker's* tip for stardom in '66. It wasn't to be. They mutated into Pete Brown's backing group Piblokto. Other Sixties groups included The King Bees, Quicksand (album on Dawn) and Liquid Umbrella.

NEWPORT
Birthplace of Steve Strange, 28.5.59, who left town with The Sex Pistols, became a roadie for Generation X, and launched the New Romantics movement.

Police made their world début at the 600-capacity Stowaway Club at 40 Stow Hill in March '77, supporting New York punk star Cherry Vanilla. The Cure played early gigs at the Village (February '79) and The Stowaway (May '79).

Local groups included The Vultures, an R&B group including Joe Strummer (then known as Woody Mellor), who lived here during '73/4; Good Habit, who evolved into Racing Cars and reached the '77 Top Twenty with 'They Shoot Horses Don't They?' Also Fifties revivalists Crazy Cavan & The Rhythm Rockers, The Beetroots (reggae), plus some of Amen Corner and their direct descendants Judas Jump. Spring made an album in '71 — ignored at the time; now rare and valuable.

Home of late Eighties breakers The Senators — and The Darling Buds, who come from Caerleon and played all their early gigs at TJ's Disco in Clarence Place. The same venue incubated The Abs, The Blood Brothers — and mid-Nineties breakouts The 60 Ft Dolls, who made their début there in '93.

The 60ft Dolls

(Adrian Green)

Other local Nineties bands include The Cowboy Killers, Novocaine, Dub War, Suck and Crush.

Local lass Donna Matthews moved to London to become guitarist in Elastica.

When he lived in the area (at Penallt), Robert Plant played squash at the Newport Centre.

Van Morrison persuaded the landlord of the Kings Head to start a blues club in '88 – and Morrison attended a Johnny Mars gig. When he was invited on stage, he left hurriedly never to be seen again!

Shades of Abbey Road: after the town's coat of arms appeared on the sleeve of The Stone Roses' '94 single 'Love Spreads', anything bearing the crest was pilfered by fans.

PENARTH Vale of Glamorgan

Man's first live album was recorded at the Padgett Rooms.

Home of new wave group The Electric Shavers.

PONTARDAWE Neath Port Talbot

Birthplace of Mary Hopkin, 3.5.50, whose earliest musical training was in the choir at Pontardawe Congregational Tabernacle.

PONTYPOOL Torfaen

Syd Barrett played his last gig with Pink Floyd at the ICI Fibres Club in February '68.

PONTYPRIDD Rhondda Cynon Taff

Sometime home of Nick Burton, member of Westworld.

Local punk band The Tax Exiles found many of their '77 gigs full after The Sex Pistols played "secret" gigs under that name.

PORTHCAWL Bridgend

Home of identical twins Jay and Mike Aston, who formed Gene Loves Jezebel and moved to London for mid-Eighties chart tickles.

Smile are mid-Nineties hopefuls.

RAGLAN Monmouthshire

Much of Robert Plant's solo dream sequence in *The Song Remains The Same* was shot at Raglan Castle, between Abergavenny and Monmouth.

RHYMNEY Caerphilly

Coal miner Idris Davies, a friend of Dylan Thomas, went to night school and became a scoolteacher in London. Pete Seeger came across his poem 'The Bells Of Rhymney' and set it to music. The Byrds recorded it on their first album; there are also versions by Judy Collins and Cher.

ROCKFIELD Monmouthshire

Converted from pig farming barns, Rockfield Studio was the brainchild of the Ward brothers, Charles and Kingsley. Investor Dave Edmunds cut his first big hit 'I Hear You Knocking' in '70 – since when everyone from Queen to Del Shannon to The Boo Radleys have recorded there. Read about The Teardrop Explodes' hilarious adventures there in Julian Cope's unputdownable autobiography *Head-On*.

JULIAN COPE
HEAD-ON
Memories of the Liverpool Punk-scene and the story of The Teardrop Explodes; 1976-82

Taff-born Julian Cope recorded outside the village 'Saint Julian'

SKEWEN Neath Port Talbot

Birthplace of Bonnie Tyler, 8.6.53.

The Ritz was the local gig in the late Sixties/early Seventies.

No chapter on Wales would be complete without reference to ex-Goon and God-bothering Meatloaf influence: The acid heavy guitar rock of Harold Secombe

SWANSEA

Birthplace of Harry Secombe, 8.9.21 (Fifties chart stars The Goons); R&B group leader Spencer Davis, 17.7.41; Pete Ham, 27.4.47, and Mike Gibbins, 12.3.49 (both of Badfinger); Terry Williams, 11.1.48 (Man).

Early local groups included The Fleetwoods, The Jets, Smokeless Zone, The Comancheros, and The Iveys (named after Ivey Place), who moved to Liverpool and found Apple patronage and global fame as Badfinger.

Former Man guitarist Clive John immortalised the place in his '75 album track 'Swansea Town'. The Neutrons were a Man spin-off.

Thank You were popular locally in the Seventies; teenager Maldwyn Pope did several Peel sessions in the mid-Seventies, but failed to take off; Icons of Filth were early Eighties punks.

Les Harvey, guitarist with Stone The Crows, was electrocuted on stage at Swansea University in May '72.

The Who filled Swansea Town's football ground in June '76. Little Feat and The Sensational Alex Harvey Band supported.

Though usually stoned and invariably late with course work, introverted Manic Street Preachers guitarist Richey Edwards gained a degree in history and politics at Swansea University in Singleton Park.

Nineties bands include Zone, The Pooh Sticks (led by Hue, son of Man/Rockpile drummer Terry Williams), The Sweetest Ache, Helen Love (acclaimed for their '94 single Joey Ramoney) and Lovesick.

TONYPANDY Rhondda Cynon Taff

Gordon Mills lived here and worked as a bus conductor. He ended up managing Tom Jones and Engelbert Humperdinck.

TREFFOREST Rhondda Cynon Taff

Home of Thomas Woodward, better known as Tom Jones. He was born on 7.6.40, at 57 Kingsland Terrace, subsequently lived at 44 Laura Street and attended Trefforest Secondary Modern. At 16, he married and moved to 3 Cliff Terrace – and in '57, when he was working in a local glove factory, he made his professional début at the Non-Political Club in Wood Road, strumming his guitar and singing six songs (including 'Wabash Cannonball', 'Blue Suede Shoes' and 'Sixteen Tons'). He was paid one pound. He subsequently fronted a string of groups and was often billed as "The Twisting Vocalist From Pontypridd". Schools were closed and the streets were crowded when he returned to Wood Road in April '91 to present a Harp Beat rock plaque to the club where he started.

YNYSDDU Caerphilly

Birthplace of one hit wonder Ricky Valance.

YSTRAD Rhondda Cynon Taff

Birthplace of Andy Fairweather Low, 2.8.48 (Amen Corner).